Psyche

From the painting by Alfred de Curzon in the Luxembourg Gallery, Paris

THE FIVE-FOOT SHELF OF BOOKS
"THE HARVARD CLASSICS"
EDITED BY CHARLES W ELIOT LL D

ENGLISH POETRY

IN THREE VOLUMES
VOLUME II

FROM COLLINS TO FITZGERALD

WITH INTRODUCTIONS AND NOTES

VOLUME 41

P F COLLIER & SON
NEW YORK

Designed, Printed, and Bound at
The Collier Press, New York

CONTENTS

WILLIAM COLLINS

[*1720-1759*]

294

FIDELE

TO fair Fidele's grassy tomb
  Soft maids and village hinds shall bring
Each opening sweet of earliest bloom,
  And rifle all the breathing Spring.

No wailing ghost shall dare appear
  To vex with shrieks this quiet grove;
But shepherds lads assemble here,
  And melting virgins own their love.

No wither'd witch shall here be seen,
  No goblins lead their nightly crew;
The female fays shall haunt the green,
  And dress thy grave with pearly dew.

The redbreast oft at evening hours
  Shall kindly lend his little aid,
With hoary moss, and gather'd flowers,
  To deck the ground where thou art laid.

When howling winds, and beating rain,
  In tempests shake thy sylvan cell;
Or 'midst the chase, on every plain,
  The tender thought on thee shall dwell;

Each lonely scene shall thee restore,
  For thee the tear be duly shed;
Beloved, till life can charm no more;
  And mourn'd, till Pity's self be dead.

295

Ode Written in MDCCXLVI

How sleep the Brave, who sink to rest
By all their Country's wishes blest!
When Spring, with dewy fingers cold,
Returns to deck their hallow'd mould,
She there shall dress a sweeter sod
Than Fancy's feet have ever trod.

By fairy hands their knell is rung,
By forms unseen their dirge is sung:
There Honour comes, a pilgrim gray,
To bless the turf that wraps their clay;
And Freedom shall awhile repair
To dwell a weeping hermit there!

296

The Passions

An Ode for Music

When Music, heavenly maid, was young,
While yet in early Greece she sung,
The Passions oft, to hear her shell,
Throng'd around her magic cell
Exulting, trembling, raging, fainting,
Possest beyond the Muse's painting,
By turns they felt the glowing mind
Disturb'd, delighted, raised, refined:
'Till once, 'tis said, when all were fired,
Fill'd with fury, rapt, inspired,
From the supporting myrtles round
They snatch'd her instruments of sound,
And, as they oft had heard apart
Sweet lessons of her forceful art,
Each, for Madness ruled the hour,
Would prove his own expressive power.

First Fear his hand, its skill to try,
  Amid the chords bewilder'd laid,
And back recoil'd, he knew not why,
  E'en at the sound himself had made.

Next Anger rush'd, his eyes on fire,
  In lightnings own'd his secret stings;
In one rude clash he struck the lyre
  And swept with hurried hand the strings.

With woeful measures wan Despair,
  Low sullen sounds, his grief beguiled;
A solemn, strange, and mingled air,
  'Twas sad by fits, by starts 'twas wild.

But thou, O Hope, with eyes so fair,
  What was thy delighted measure?
Still it whisper'd promised pleasure
  And bade the lovely scenes at distance hail!
Still would her touch the strain prolong:
  And from the rocks, the woods, the vale
She call'd on Echo still through all the song;
  And, where her sweetest theme she chose,
  A soft responsive voice was heard at every close;
And Hope enchanted smiled, and waved her golden hair;—

And longer had she sung:—but with a frown
    Revenge impatient rose:
He threw his blood-stain'd sword in thunder down;
    And with a withering look
  The war-denouncing trumpet took
And blew a blast so loud and dread,
Were ne'er prophetic sounds so full of woe!
    And ever and anon he beat
    The doubling drum with furious heat;
And, though sometimes, each dreary pause between,
    Dejected Pity at his side
    Her soul-subduing voice applied,
  Yet still he kept his wild unalter'd mien,
While each strain'd ball of sight seem'd bursting from his head.

Thy numbers, Jealousy, to nought were fix'd:
  Sad proof of thy distressful state!
Of differing themes the veering song was mix'd;
  And now it courted Love, now raving call'd on Hate.

With eyes up-raised, as one inspired,
Pale Melancholy sat retired;
And from her wild sequester'd seat,
In notes by distance made more sweet,
Pour'd through the mellow horn her pensive soul:
    And dashing soft from rocks around
    Bubbling runnels join'd the sound;
Through glades and glooms the mingled measure stole,
  Or, o'er some haunted stream, with fond delay,
    Round an holy calm diffusing,
    Love of peace, and lonely musing,
  In hollow murmurs died away.

But O! how alter'd was its sprightlier tone
When Cheerfulness, a nymph of healthiest hue,
  Her bow across her shoulder flung,
  Her buskins gemm'd with morning dew,
Blew an inspiring air, that dale and thicket rung,
  The hunter's call to Faun and Dryad known!
The oak-crown'd Sisters and their chaste-eyed Queen,
  Satyrs and Sylvan Boys, were seen
  Peeping from forth their alleys green:
Brown Exercise rejoiced to hear;
  And Sport leapt up, and seized his beechen spear.

Last came Joy's ecstatic trial:
He, with viny crown advancing,
  First to the lively pipe his hand addrest:
But soon he saw the brisk awakening viol
  Whose sweet entrancing voice he loved the best:
They would have thought who heard the strain
    They saw, in Tempe's vale, her native maids
    Amidst the festal-sounding shades
To some unwearied minstrel dancing;
While, as his flying fingers kiss'd the strings,

Love framed with Mirth a gay fantastic round:
Loose were her tresses seen, her zone unbound;
And he, amidst his frolic play,
As if he would the charming air repay,
Shook thousand odours from his dewy wings.

O Music! sphere-descended maid,
Friend of Pleasure, Wisdom's aid!
Why, goddess, why, to us denied,
Lay'st thou thy ancient lyre aside?
As in that loved Athenian bower
You learn'd an all-commanding power,
Thy mimic soul, O nymph endear'd!
Can well recall what then it heard.
Where is thy native simple heart
Devote to Virtue, Fancy, Art?
Arise, as in that elder time,
Warm, energic, chaste, sublime!
Thy wonders, in that god-like age,
Fill thy recording Sister's page;—
'Tis said, and I believe the tale,
Thy humblest reed could more prevail
Had more of strength, diviner rage,
Than all which charms this laggard age,
E'en all at once together found
Cecilia's mingled world of sound:—
O bid our vain endeavours cease:
Revive the just designs of Greece:
Return in all thy simple state!
Confirm the tales her sons relate!

297

To Evening

If aught of oaten stop or pastoral song
May hope, chaste Eve, to soothe thy modest ear
Like thy own solemn springs,
Thy springs, and dying gales;

O Nymph reserved,—while now the bright-hair'd sun
Sits in yon western tent, whose cloudy skirts,
With brede ethereal wove,
O'erhang his wavy bed,

Now air is hush'd, save where the weak-eyed bat
With short shrill shriek flits by on leathern wing,
Or where the beetle winds
His small but sullen horn,

As oft he rises midst the twilight path,
Against the pilgrim borne in heedless hum,—
Now teach me, maid composed,
To breathe some soften'd strain

Whose numbers, stealing through thy darkening vale,
May not unseemly with its stillness suit;
As, musing slow I hail
Thy genial loved return.

For when thy folding-star arising shows
His paly circlet, at his warning-lamp
The fragrant Hours, and Elves
Who slept in buds the day,

And many a Nymph who wreathes her brows with sedge
And sheds the freshening dew, and, lovelier still,
The pensive Pleasures sweet,
Prepare thy shadowy car.

Then let me rove some wild and heathy scene;
Or find some ruin midst its dreary dells,
Whose walls more awful nod
By thy religious gleams.

Or, if chill blustering winds or driving rain
Prevent my willing feet, be mine the hut
That, from the mountain's side,
Views wilds and swelling floods,

And hamlets brown, and dim-discover'd spires;
And hears their simple bell; and marks o'er all
    Thy dewy fingers draw
    The gradual dusky veil.

While Spring shall pour his showers, as oft he wont,
And bathe thy breathing tresses, meekest Eve!
    While Summer loves to sport
    Beneath thy lingering light;

While sallow Autumn fills thy lap with leaves;
Or Winter, yelling through the troublous air,
    Affrights thy shrinking train
    And rudely rends thy robes;

So long, regardful of thy quiet rule,
Shall Fancy, Friendship, Science, smiling Peace,
    Thy gentlest influence own,
    And love thy favourite name!

GEORGE SEWELL

[*d. 1726*]

298 THE DYING MAN IN HIS GARDEN

WHY, Damon, with the forward day
Dost thou thy little spot survey,
From tree to tree, with doubtful cheer,
Pursue the progress of the year,
What winds arise, what rains descend,
When thou before that year shalt end?

What do thy noontide walks avail,
To clear the leaf, and pick the snail,
Then wantonly to death decree
An insect usefuller than thee?
Thou and the worm are brother-kind,
As low, as earthy, and as blind.

Vain wretch! canst thou expect to see
The downy peach make court to thee?
Or that thy sense shall ever meet
The bean-flower's deep-embosom'd sweet
Exhaling with an evening blast?
Thy evenings then will all be past!

Thy narrow pride, thy fancied green
(For vanity's in little seen)
All must be left when Death appears,
In spite of wishes, groans, and tears;
Nor one of all thy plants that grow
But Rosemary will with thee go.

ALISON RUTHERFORD COCKBURN

[*1712-1794*]

299 The Flowers of the Forest[1]

I've seen the smiling
Of Fortune beguiling;
I've felt all its favours, and found its decay;
Sweet was its blessing,
Kind its caressing;
But now it is fled—fled far away.

I've seen the forest
Adorned the foremost,
With flowers of the fairest, most pleasant and gay;
Sae bonnie was their blooming!
Their scent the air perfuming!
But now they are withered and a' wede away.

I've seen the morning
With gold the hills adorning,
And loud tempest storming before the mid-day.
I've seen Tweed's silver streams,
Shining in the sunny beams
Grow drumly and dark as he rowed on his way.

[1] "The flowers of the Forest" in this and the following song are the men of Ettrick Forest in Selkirkshire who fell at the battle of Flodden.

Oh, fickle Fortune!
Why this cruel sporting?
Oh, why still perplex us, poor sons of a day?
Nae mair your smiles can cheer me,
Nae mair your frowns can fear me;
For the flowers of the forest are a' wede away.

JANE ELLIOT

[*1727-1805*]

300 Lament for Flodden

I've heard them lilting[1] at our ewe-milking,
Lasses a' lilting before dawn o' day;
But now they are moaning on ilka green loaning[2]—
For the flowers of the forest are a' wede[3] away.

At bughts,[4] in the morning, nae blythe lads are scorning,
Lasses are lonely and dowie[5] and wae;
Nae daffin',[6] nae gabbin',[7] but sighing and sabbing,
Ilk ane lifts her leglin[8] and hies her away.

In har'st,[9] at the shearing, nae youths now are jeering,
Bandsters[10] are lyart,[11] and runkled,[12] and gray;
At fair or at preaching, nae wooing, nae fleeching[13]—
The Flowers of the Forest are a' wede away.

At e'en, in the gloaming, nae younkers are roaming
'Bout stacks wi' the lasses at bogle to play;
But ilk ane sits drearie, lamenting her dearie—
The Flowers of the Forest are weded away.

Dool and wae for the order, sent our lads to the Border!
The English, for ance, by guile wan the day;
The Flowers of the Forest, that fought aye the foremost,
The prime of our land, are cauld in the clay.

[1] Singing. [2] Lane. [3] Withered. [4] Pens, folds. [5] Doleful. [6] Toying. [7] Jeering. [8] Milking-stool. [9] Harvest. [10] Makers of strawbands for the sheaves. [11] Withered. [12] Wrinkled. [13] Flattering.

We'll hear nae mair lilting at the ewe-milking;
   Women and bairns are heartless and wae;
Sighing and moaning on ilka green loaning—
   The Flowers of the Forest are a' wede away.

CHRISTOPHER SMART

[*1722-1770*]

301

A Song to David

O thou, that sitt'st upon a throne,
With harp of high, majestic tone,
   To praise the King of kings:
And voice of heaven, ascending, swell,
Which, while its deeper notes excel,
   Clear as a clarion rings:

To bless each valley, grove, and coast,
And charm the cherubs to the post
   Of gratitude in throngs;
To keep the days on Zion's Mount,
And send the year to his account,
   With dances and with songs:

O servant of God's holiest charge,
The minister of praise at large,
   Which thou mayst now receive;
From thy blest mansion hail and hear,
From topmost eminence appear
   To this the wreath I weave.

Great, valiant, pious, good, and clean,
Sublime, contemplative, serene,
   Strong, constant, pleasant, wise!
Bright effluence of exceeding grace;
Best man! the swiftness and the race,
   The peril and the prize!

Great—from the lustre of his crown,
From Samuel's horn, and God's renown,
Which is the people's voice;
For all the host, from rear to van,
Applauded and embraced the man—
The man of God's own choice.

Valiant—the word, and up he rose;
The fight—he triumphed o'er the foes
Whom God's just laws abhor;
And, armed in gallant faith, he took
Against the boaster, from the brook,
The weapons of the war.

Pious—magnificent and grand,
'Twas he the famous temple plann'd,
(The seraph in his soul:)
Foremost to give the Lord his dues,
Foremost to bless the welcome news,
And foremost to condole.

Good—from Jehudah's genuine vein,
From God's best nature, good in grain,
His aspect and his heart:
To pity, to forgive, to save,
Witness En-gedi's conscious cave,
And Shimei's blunted dart.

Clean—if perpetual prayer be pure,
And love, which could itself inure
To fasting and to fear—
Clean in his gestures, hands, and feet,
To smite the lyre, the dance complete,
To play the sword and spear.

Sublime—invention ever young,
Of vast conception, towering tongue,
To God the eternal theme;
Notes from yon exaltations caught,
Unrivalled royalty of thought,
O'er meaner strains supreme.

Contemplative—on God to fix
His musings, and above the six
  The Sabbath-day he blessed;
'Twas then his thoughts self-conquest pruned,
And heavenly melancholy tuned,
  To bless and bear the rest.

Serene—to sow the seeds of peace,
Remembering, when he watched the fleece,
  How sweetly Kidron purled—
To further knowledge, silence vice,
And plant perpetual paradise,
  When God had calmed the world.

Strong—in the Lord, who could defy
Satan, and all his powers that lie
  In sempiternal night;
And hell, and horror, and despair
Were as the lion and the bear
  To his undaunted might.

Constant—in love to God, the Truth,
Age, manhood, infancy, and youth:
  To Jonathan his friend
Constant, beyond the verge of death;
And Ziba, and Mephibosheth,
  His endless fame attend.

Pleasant—and various as the year;
Man, soul, and angel without peer,
  Priest, champion, sage, and boy;
In armour or in ephod clad,
His pomp, his piety was glad;
  Majestic was his joy.

Wise—in recovery from his fall,
Whence rose his eminence o'er all,
  Of all the most reviled;
The light of Israel in his ways,
Wise are his precepts, prayer, and praise,
  And counsel to his child.

His muse, bright angel of his verse,
Gives balm for all the thorns that pierce,
  For all the pangs that rage;
Blest light, still gaining on the gloom,
The more than Michal of his bloom,
  The Abishag of his age.

He sang of God—the mighty source
Of all things—the stupendous force
  On which all strength depends;
From Whose right arm, beneath Whose eyes,
All period, power, and enterprise
  Commences, reigns, and ends.

Angels—their ministry and meed,
Which to and fro with blessings speed,
  Or with their citterns wait;
Where Michael, with his millions, bows,
Where dwells the seraph and his spouse,
  The cherub and her mate.

Of man—the semblance and effect
Of God and love—the saint elect
  For infinite applause—
To rule the land, and briny broad,
To be laborious in his laud,
  And heroes in his cause.

The world—the clustering spheres He made,
The glorious light, the soothing shade,
  Dale, champaign, grove, and hill;
The multitudinous abyss,
Where Secrecy remains in bliss,
  And Wisdom hides her skill.

Trees, plants, and flowers—of virtuous root;
Gem yielding blossom, yielding fruit,
  Choice gums and precious balm;
Bless ye the nosegay in the vale,
And with the sweetness of the gale
  Enrich the thankful psalm.

Of fowl—even every beak and wing
Which cheer the winter, hail the spring,
  That live in peace or prey;
They that make music, or that mock,
The quail, the brave domestic cock.
  The raven, swan, and jay.

Of fishes—every size and shape,
Which nature frames of light escape,
  Devouring man to shun:
The shells are in the wealthy deep,
The shoals upon the surface leap,
  And love the glancing sun.

Of beasts—the beaver plods his task;
While the sleek tigers roll and bask,
  Nor yet the shades arouse;
Her cave the mining coney scoops;
Where o'er the mead the mountain stoops,
  The kids exult and browse.

Of gems—their virtue and their price,
Which, hid in earth from man's device,
  Their darts of lustre sheath;
The jasper of the master's stamp,
The topaz blazing like a lamp,
  Among the mines beneath.

Blest was the tenderness he felt,
When to his graceful harp he knelt,
  And did for audience call;
When Satan with his hand he quelled,
And in serene suspense he held
  The frantic throes of Saul.

His furious foes no more maligned
As he such melody divined,
  And sense and soul detained;
Now striking strong, now soothing soft,
He sent the godly sounds aloft,
  Or in delight refrained.

When up to heaven his thoughts he piled,
From fervent lips fair Michal smiled,
As blush to blush she stood;
And chose herself the queen, and gave
Her utmost from her heart—'so brave,
And plays his hymns so good.'

The pillars of the Lord are seven,
Which stand from earth to topmost heaven;
His Wisdom drew the plan;
His Word accomplished the design,
From brightest gem to deepest mine,
From CHRIST enthroned to Man.

Alpha, the cause of causes, first
In station, fountain, whence the burst
Of light and blaze of day;
Whence bold attempt, and brave advance.
Have motion, life, and ordinance,
And heaven itself its stay.

Gamma supports the glorious arch
On which angelic legions march,
And is with sapphires paved;
Thence the fleet clouds are sent adrift,
And thence the painted folds that lift
The crimson veil, are waved.

Eta with living sculpture breathes,
With verdant carvings, flowery wreathes,
Of never-wasting bloom;
In strong relief his goodly base
All instruments of labour grace,
The trowel, spade, and loom.

Next *Theta* stands to the supreme—
Who formed in number, sign, and scheme,
The illustrious lights that are;
And one addressed his saffron robe,
And one, clad in a silver globe,
Held rule with every star.

Iota's tuned to choral hymns
Of those that fly, while he that swims
  In thankful safety lurks;
And foot, and chapiter, and niche,
The various histories enrich
  Of God's recorded works.

Sigma presents the social droves
With him that solitary roves,
  And man of all the chief;
Fair on whose face, and stately frame,
Did God impress His hallowed name,
  For ocular belief.

Omega! greatest and the best,
Stands sacred to the day of rest,
  For gratitude and thought;
Which blessed the world upon his pole,
And gave the universe his goal,
  And closed the infernal draught.

O David, scholar of the Lord!
Such is thy science, whence reward,
  And infinite degree;
O strength, O sweetness, lasting ripe!
God's harp thy symbol, and thy type
  The lion and the bee!

There is but One who ne'er rebelled,
But One by passion unimpelled,
  By pleasures unenticed;
He from himself hath semblance sent,
Grand object of his own content,
  And saw the God in Christ.

Tell them, I AM, Jehovah said
To Moses; while earth heard in dread,
  And, smitten to the heart,
At once above, beneath, around,
All Nature, without voice or sound,
  Replied, 'O Lord, THOU ART.'

Thou art—to give and to confirm,
For each his talent and his term;
All flesh thy bounties share:
Thou shalt not call thy brother fool:
The porches of the Christian school
Are meekness, peace, and prayer.

Open and naked of offence,
Man's made of mercy, soul, and sense:
God armed the snail and wilk;
Be good to him that pulls thy plough;
Due food and care, due rest allow
For her that yields thee milk.

Rise up before the hoary head,
And God's benign commandment dread,
Which says thou shalt not die:
'Not as I will, but as Thou wilt,'
Prayed He, whose conscience knew no guilt;
With Whose blessed pattern vie.

Use all thy passions! love is thine,
And joy and jealousy divine;
Thine hope's eternal fort,
And care thy leisure to disturb,
With fear concupiscence to curb,
And rapture to transport.

Act simply, as occasion asks;
Put mellow wine in seasoned casks;
Till not with ass and bull:
Remember thy baptismal bond;
Keep thy commixtures foul and fond,
Nor work thy flax with wool.

Distribute; pay the Lord His tithe,
And make the widow's heart-strings blithe;
Resort with those that weep:
As you from all and each expect,
For all and each thy love direct,
And render as you reap.

The slander and its bearer spurn,
And propagating praise sojourn
  To make thy welcome last;
Turn from old Adam to the New:
By hope futurity pursue:
  Look upwards to the past.

Control thine eye, salute success,
Honour the wiser, happier bless,
  And for their neighbour feel;
Grutch not of mammon and his leaven,
Work emulation up to heaven
  By knowledge and by zeal.

O David, highest in the list
Of worthies, on God's ways insist,
  The genuine word repeat!
Vain are the documents of men,
And vain the flourish of the pen
  That keeps the fool's conceit.

Praise above all—for praise prevails;
Heap up the measure, load the scales,
  And good to goodness add:
The generous soul her Saviour aids,
But peevish obloquy degrades;
  The Lord is great and glad.

For Adoration all the ranks
Of Angels yield eternal thanks,
  And David in the midst:
With God's good poor, which, last and least
In man's esteem, Thou to Thy feast,
  O Blessed Bridegroom, bidst.

For Adoration seasons change,
And order, truth, and beauty range,
  Adjust, attract, and fill:
The grass the polyanthus checks;
And polished porphyry reflects,
  By the descending rill.

Rich almonds colour to the prime
For Adoration; tendrils climb,
  And fruit-trees pledge their gems;
And Ivis, with her gorgeous vest,
Builds for her eggs her cunning nest,
  And bell-flowers bow their stems.

With vinous syrup cedars spout;
From rocks pure honey gushing out,
  For Adoration springs:
All scenes of painting crowd the map
Of nature; to the mermaid's pap
  The scalèd infant clings.

The spotted ounce and playsome cubs
Run rustling 'mong the flowering shrubs.
  And lizards feed the moss;
For Adoration beasts embark,
While waves upholding halcyon's ark
  No longer roar and toss.

While Israel sits beneath his fig,
With coral root and amber sprig
  The weaned adventurer sports;
Where to the palm the jasmine cleaves,
For Adoration 'mong the leaves
  The gale his peace reports.

Increasing days their reign exalt,
Nor in the pink and mottled vault
  The opposing spirits tilt;
And by the coasting reader spied,
The silverlings and crusions glide
  For Adoration gilt.

For Adoration ripening canes,
And cocoa's purest milk detains
  The western pilgrim's staff;
Where rain in clasping boughs enclosed,
And vines with oranges disposed,
  Embower the social laugh.

Now labour his reward receives,
For Adoration counts his sheaves,
To peace, her bounteous prince;
The nect'rine his strong tint imbibes,
And apples of ten thousand tribes,
And quick peculiar quince.

The wealthy crops of whitening rice
'Mongst thyine woods and groves of spice,
For Adoration grow;
And, marshalled in the fencèd land,
The peaches and pomegranates stand,
Where wild carnations blow.

The laurels with the winter strive;
The crocus burnishes alive
Upon the snow-clad earth;
For Adoration myrtles stay
To keep the garden from dismay,
And bless the sight from dearth.

The pheasant shows his pompous neck;
And ermine, jealous of a speck,
With fear eludes offence:
The sable, with his glossy pride,
For Adoration is described,
Where frosts the waves condense.

The cheerful holly, pensive yew,
And holy thorn, their trim renew;
The squirrel hoards his nuts;
All creatures batten o'er their stores,
And careful nature all her doors
For Adoration shuts.

For Adoration, David's Psalms,
Lift up the heart to deeds of alms;
And he, who kneels and chants,
Prevails his passions to control,
Finds meat and medicine to the soul,
Which for translation pants.

For Adoration, beyond match,
The scholar bullfinch aims to catch
  The soft flute's ivory touch:
And, careless, on the hazel spray
The daring redbreast keeps at bay
  The damsel's greedy clutch.

For Adoration, in the skies,
The Lord's philosopher espies
  The dog, the ram, and rose;
The planets' ring, Orion's sword;
Nor is his greatness less adored
  In the vile worm that glows.

For Adoration, on the strings
The western breezes work their wings,
  The captive ear to soothe—
Hark! 'tis a voice—how still, and small—
That makes the cataracts to fall,
  Or bids the sea be smooth!

For Adoration, incense comes
From bezoar, and Arabian gums,
  And from the civet's fur:
But as for prayer, or e'er it faints,
Far better is the breath of saints
  Than galbanum or myrrh.

For Adoration, from the down
Of damsons to the anana's crown,
  God sends to tempt the taste;
And while the luscious zest invites
The sense, that in the scene delights,
  Commands desire be chaste.

For Adoration, all the paths
Of grace are open, all the baths
  Of purity refresh;
And all the rays of glory beam
To deck the man of God's esteem
  Who triumphs o'er the flesh.

For Adoration, in the dome
Of CHRIST, the sparrows find a home;
And on his olives perch:
The swallow also dwells with thee
O Man of GOD'S humility,
Within his Saviour's Church.

Sweet is the dew that falls betimes,
And drops upon the leafy limes;
Sweet, Hermon's fragrant air:
Sweet is the lily's silver bell,
And sweet the wakeful tapers' smell
That watch for early prayer.

Sweet the young nurse, with love intense,
Which smiles o'er sleeping innocence;
Sweet when the lost arrive:
Sweet the musician's ardour beats,
While his vague mind's in quest of sweets
The choicest flowers to hive.

Sweeter, in all the strains of love,
The language of thy turtle-dove,
Paired to thy swelling chord;
Sweeter, with every grace endued,
The glory of thy gratitude.
Respired unto the Lord.

Strong is the horse upon his speed;
Strong in pursuit the rapid glede,
Which makes at once his game:
Strong the tall ostrich on the ground;
Strong through the turbulent profound
Shoots Xiphias to his aim.

Strong is the lion—like a coal
His eyeball—like a bastion's mole
His chest against the foes:
Strong the gier-eagle on his sail,
Strong against tide the enormous whale
Emerges as he goes.

But stronger still in earth and air,
And in the sea, the man of prayer,
And far beneath the tide:
And in the seat to faith assigned,
Where ask is have, where seek is find,
Where knock is open wide.

Beauteous the fleet before the gale;
Beauteous the multitudes in mail,
Ranked arms, and crested heads;
Beauteous the garden's umbrage mild
Walk, water, meditated wild,
And all the bloomy beds.

Beauteous the moon full on the lawn;
And beauteous when the veil's withdrawn,
The virgin to her spouse:
Beauteous the temple, decked and filled,
When to the heaven of heavens they build
Their heart-directed vows.

Beauteous, yea beauteous more than these,
The Shepherd King upon his knees,
For his momentous trust;
With wish of infinite conceit,
For man, beast, mute, the small and great,
And prostrate dust to dust.

Precious the bounteous widow's mite;
And precious, for extreme delight,
The largess from the churl:
Precious the ruby's blushing blaze,
And alba's blest imperial rays,
And pure cerulean pearl.

Precious the penitential tear;
And precious is the sigh sincere;
Acceptable to God:
And precious are the winning flowers,
In gladsome Israel's feast of bowers,
Bound on the hallowed sod.

More precious that diviner part
Of David, even the Lord's own heart
  Great, beautiful, and new;
In all things where it was intent,
In all extremes, in each event,
  Proof—answering true to true.

Glorious the sun in mid career;
Glorious the assembled fires appear;
  Glorious the comet's train:
Glorious the trumpet and alarm;
Glorious the Almighty's stretched-out arm;
  Glorious the enraptured main:

Glorious the northern lights a-stream;
Glorious the song, when God's the theme;
  Glorious the thunder's roar:
Glorious Hosannah from the den;
Glorious the catholic Amen;
  Glorious the martyr's gore:

Glorious,—more glorious,—is the crown
Of Him that brought salvation down,
  By meekness called Thy Son;
Thou that stupendous truth believed;—
And now the matchless deed's achieved,
  Determined, Dared, and Done.

ANONYMOUS

302

Willy Drowned in Yarrow

Down in yon garden sweet and gay
  Where bonnie grows the lily,
I heard a fair maid sighing say,
  'My wish be wi' sweet Willie!

'Willie's rare, and Willie's fair,
  And Willie's wondrous bonny;

And Willie hecht[1] to marry me
  Gin e'er he married ony.

'O gentle wind, that bloweth south,
  From where my Love repaireth,
Convey a kiss frae his dear mouth
  And tell me how he fareth!

'O tell sweet Willie to come doun
  And hear the mavis singing,
And see the birds on ilka bush
  And leaves around them hinging.

'The lav'rock[2] there, wi' her white breast
  And gentle throat sae narrow;
There's sport eneuch for gentlemen
  On Leader haughs[3] and Yarrow.

'O Leader haughs are wide and braid
  And Yarrow haughs are bonny;
There Willie hecht to marry me
  If e'er he married ony.

'But Willie's gone, whom I thought on,
  And does not hear me weeping;
Draws many a tear frae true love's e'e
  When other maids are sleeping.

'Yestreen I made my bed fu' braid,
  The night I'll mak' it narrow,
For a' the live-lang winter night
  I lie twined o' my marrow.[4]

'O came ye by yon water-side?
  Pou'd you the rose or lily?
Or came you by yon meadow green,
  Or saw you my sweet Willie?'

[1] Promised. [2] Lark. [3] Meadows by a river.
[4] Separated from my mate.

She sought him up, she sought him down,
She sought him braid and narrow;
Syne, in the cleaving of a craig,
She found him drown'd in Yarrow!

JOHN LOGAN

[*1748-1788*]

303 THE BRAES OF YARROW

THY braes were bonny, Yarrow stream,
When first on them I met my lover;
Thy braes how dreary, Yarrow stream,
When now thy waves his body cover!
For ever now, O Yarrow stream!
Thou art to me a stream of sorrow;
For never on thy banks shall I
Behold my Love, the flower of Yarrow.

He promised me a milk-white steed
To bear me to his father's bowers;
He promised me a little page
To squire me to his father's towers;
He promised me a wedding-ring,—
The wedding-day was fix'd to-morrow;—
Now he is wedded to his grave,
Alas, his watery grave, in Yarrow!

Sweet were his words when last we met;
My passion I as freely told him;
Clasp'd in his arms, I little thought
That I should never more behold him!
Scarce was he gone, I saw his ghost;
It vanish'd with a shriek of sorrow;
Thrice did the water-wraith ascend,
And gave a doleful groan thro' Yarrow.

His mother from the window look'd
With all the longing of a mother;

His little sister weeping walk'd
The green-wood path to meet her brother;
They sought him east, they sought him west,
They sought him all the forest thorough;
They only saw the cloud of night,
They only heard the roar of Yarrow.

No longer from thy window look—
Thou hast no son, thou tender mother!
No longer walk, thou lovely maid;
Alas, thou hast no more a brother!
No longer seek him east or west
And search no more the forest thorough;
For, wandering in the night so dark,
He fell a lifeless corpse in Yarrow.

The tear shall never leave my cheek,
No other youth shall be my marrow—
I'll seek thy body in the stream,
And then with thee I'll sleep in Yarrow.
—The tear did never leave her cheek,
No other youth became her marrow;
She found his body in the stream,
And now with him she sleeps in Yarrow.

HENRY FIELDING

[*1707-1754*]

304

A Hunting Song

The dusky night rides down the sky,
  And ushers in the morn;
The hounds all join in glorious cry,
  The huntsman winds his horn,
    And a-hunting we will go.

The wife around her husband throws
  Her arms, and begs his stay;

'My dear, it rains, and hails, and snows,
You will not hunt to-day?'
But a-hunting we will go.

'A brushing fox in yonder wood
Secure to find we seek:
For why? I carried, sound and good,
A cartload there last week,
And a-hunting we will go.'
Away he goes, he flies the rout,
Their steeds all spur and switch,
Some are thrown in, and some thrown out,
And some thrown in the ditch;
But a-hunting we will go.

At length his strength to faintness worn,
Poor Reynard ceases flight;
Then, hungry, homeward we return,
To feast away the night.
Then a-drinking we will go.

CHARLES DIBDIN

[*1745-1814*]

305 Tom Bowling

Here, a sheer hulk, lies poor Tom Bowling,
The darling of our crew;
No more he'll hear the tempest howling,
For Death has broached him to.
His form was of the manliest beauty,
His heart was kind and soft;
Faithful below he did his duty,
And now he's gone aloft.

Tom never from his word departed,
His virtues were so rare;
His friends were many and true-hearted,
His Poll was kind and fair:

And then he'd sing so blithe and jolly,
Ah, many's the time and oft!
But mirth is turned to melancholy,
For Tom is gone aloft.

Yet shall poor Tom find pleasant weather,
When He, who all commands,
Shall give, to call Life's crew together,
The word to 'pipe all hands.'
Thus Death, who kings and tars dispatches,
In vain Tom's life has doffed;
For though his body's under hatches,
His soul is gone aloft.

SAMUEL JOHNSON

[*1709-1784*]

306 On the Death of Dr. Robert Levet

Condemn'd to Hope's delusive mine,
As on we toil from day to day,
By sudden blasts or slow decline
Our social comforts drop away.

Well tried through many a varying year,
See Levet to the grave descend,
Officious, innocent, sincere,
Of every friendless name the friend.

Yet still he fills affection's eye,
Obscurely wise and coarsely kind;
Nor, letter'd arrogance, deny
Thy praise to merit unrefined.

When fainting nature called for aid,
And hovering death prepared the blow,
His vigorous remedy display'd
The power of art without the show.

In misery's darkest cavern known,
  His useful care was ever nigh,
Where hopeless anguish pour'd his groan,
  And lonely want retired to die.

No summons mock'd by chill delay,
  No petty gain disdain'd by pride;
The modest wants of every day
  The toil of every day supplied.

His virtues walked their narrow round,
  Nor made a pause, nor left a void;
And sure the eternal Master found
  The single talent well employ'd.

The busy day, the peaceful night,
  Unfelt, uncounted, glided by;
His frame was firm—his powers were bright,
  Though now his eightieth year was nigh.

Then with no fiery throbbing pain,
  No cold gradations of decay,
Death broke at once the vital chain,
  And freed his soul the nearest way.

307

A Satire

Long-expected one-and-twenty,
  Ling'ring year, at length is flown;
Pride and pleasure, pomp and plenty,
  Great (Sir John), are now your own.

Loosen'd from the minor's tether,
  Free to mortgage or to sell,
Wild as wind, and light as feather,
  Bid the sons of thrift farewell.

Call the Betseys, Kates, and Jennies,
  All the names that banish care;
Lavish of your grandsire's guineas,
  Show the spirits of an heir.

All that prey on vice and folly,
  Joy to see their quarry fly;
There the gamester, light and jolly,
  There the lender, grave and sly.

Wealth, my lad, was made to wander,
  Let it wander as it will;
Call the jockey, call the pander,
  Bid them come and take their fill.

When the bonny blade carouses,
  Pockets full, and spirits high—
What are acres? What are houses?
  Only dirt, or wet or dry.

Should the guardian, friend, or mother,
  Tell the woes of wilful waste,
Scorn their counsel, scorn their pother,—
  You can hang or drown at last!

OLIVER GOLDSMITH

[*1728-1774*]

308 When Lovely Woman Stoops

When lovely woman stoops to folly
  And finds too late that men betray,—
What charm can soothe her melancholy,
  What art can wash her guilt away?

The only art her guilt to cover,
  To hide her shame from every eye,
To give repentance to her lover
  And wring his bosom, is—to die.

309 Retaliation

Of old, when Scarron his companions invited,
Each guest brought his dish, and the feast was united.
If our landlord supplies us with beef and with fish,

Let each guest bring himself, and he brings the best dish:
Our Dean shall be venison, just fresh from the plains,
Our Burke shall be tongue, with the garnish of brains,
Our Will shall be wild fowl, of excellent flavour,
And Dick with his pepper, shall heighten the savour:
Our Cumberland's sweetbread its place shall obtain,
And Douglas is pudding substantial and plain:
Our Garrick's a salad; for in him we see
Oil, vinegar, sugar, and saltness agree:
To make out the dinner full certain I am,
That Ridge is anchovy, and Reynolds is lamb:
That Hickey's a capon, and by the same rule,
Magnanimous Goldsmith a gooseberry fool.
At a dinner so various, at such a repast,
Who'd not be a glutton, and stick to the last?
Here, waiter, more wine, let me sit while I'm able,
Till all my companions sink under the table;
Then, with chaos and blunders encircling my head,
Let me ponder, and tell what I think of the dead.
  Here lies the good Dean, reunited to earth,
Who mixed reason with pleasure, and wisdom with mirth:
If he had any faults, he has left us in doubt,
At least, in six weeks I could not find them out;
Yet some have declared, and it can't be denied 'em,
That sly-boots was cursedly cunning to hide 'em.
  Here lies our good Edmund, whose genius was such,
We scarcely can praise it, or blame it too much;
Who, born for the universe, narrow'd his mind,
And to party gave up what was meant for mankind:
Tho' fraught with all learning, yet straining his throat
To persuade Tommy Townshend to lend him a vote;
Who, too deep for his hearers, still went on refining,
And thought of convincing, while they thought of dining;
Though equal to all things, for all things unfit;
Too nice for a statesman, too proud for a wit;
For a patriot too cool; for a drudge disobedient;
And too fond of the *right* to pursue the *expedient*.
In short, 'twas his fate, unemploy'd, or in place, sir,
To eat mutton cold, and cut blocks with a razor.
  Here lies honest William, whose heart was a mint,

While the owner ne'er knew half the good that was in't;
The pupil of impulse, it forced him along,
His conduct still right, with his argument wrong;
Still aiming at honour, yet fearing to roam,
The coachman was tipsy, the chariot drove home;
Would you ask for his merits? alas! he had none;
What was good was spontaneous, his faults were his own.
  Here lies honest Richard whose fate I must sigh at;
Alas! that such frolic should now be so quiet!
What spirits were his! what wit and what whim!
Now breaking a jest, and now breaking a limb!
Now wrangling and grumbling to keep up the ball!
Now teasing and vexing, yet laughing at all!
In short, so provoking a devil was Dick,
That we wish'd him full ten times a day at Old Nick;
But, missing his mirth and agreeable vein,
As often we wish'd to have Dick back again.
  Here Cumberland lies, having acted his parts,
The Terence of England, the mender of hearts;
A flattering painter, who made it his care
To draw men as they ought to be, not as they are.
His gallants are all faultless, his women divine,
And comedy wonders at being so fine:
Like a tragedy queen he has dizen'd her out,
Or rather like tragedy giving a rout.
His fools have their follies so lost in a crowd
Of virtues and feelings that folly grows proud;
And coxcombs, alike in their failings alone,
Adopting his portraits, are pleased with their own.
Say, where has our poet this malady caught?
Or wherefore his characters thus without fault?
Say, was it that, vainly directing his view
To find out men's virtues, and finding them few,
Quite sick of pursuing each troublesome elf,
He grew lazy at last, and drew from himself?
  Here Douglas retires from his toils to relax,
The scourge of impostors, the terror of quacks:
Come, all ye quack bards, and ye quacking divines,
Come, and dance on the spot where your tyrant reclines:
When satire and censure encircled his throne,

I fear'd for your safety, I fear'd for my own;
But now he is gone, and we want a detector,
Our Dodds shall be pious, our Kendricks shall lecture;
Macpherson write bombast, and call it a style;
Our Townshend make speeches, and I shall compile;
New Lauders and Bowers the Tweed shall cross over,
No countryman living their tricks to discover;
Detection her taper shall quench to a spark,
And Scotchman meet Scotchman, and cheat in the dark.
Here lies David Garrick, describe him who can,
An abridgment of all that was pleasant in man:
As an actor, confess'd without rival to shine;
As a wit, if not first, in the very first line:
Yet, with talents like these, and an excellent heart,
The man had his failings—a dupe to his art.
Like an ill-judging beauty, his colours he spread,
And beplaster'd with rouge his own natural red.
On the stage he was natural, simple, affecting;
'Twas only that when he was off he was acting.
With no reason on earth to go out of his way,
He turn'd and he varied full ten times a day:
Though secure of our hearts, yet confoundedly sick
If they were not his own by finessing and trick:
He cast off his friends, as a huntsman his pack,
For he knew when he pleased he could whistle them back.
Of praise a mere glutton, he swallow'd what came,
And the puff of a dunce he mistook it for fame;
Till his relish grown callous, almost to disease,
Who pepper'd the highest was surest to please.
But let us be candid, and speak out our mind,
If dunces applauded, he paid them in kind.
Ye Kendricks, ye Kellys, and Woodfalls so grave,
What a commerce was yours while you got and you gave!
How did Grub-street re-echo the shouts that you raised,
While he was be-Roscius'd, and you were be-praised!
But peace to his spirit, wherever it flies,
To act as an angel and mix with the skies:
Those poets, who owe their best fame to his skill,
Shall still be his flatterers, go where he will;
Old Shakespeare receive him with praise and with love,

And Beaumonts and Bens be his Kellys above.
Here Hickey reclines, a most blunt pleasant creature,
And slander itself must allow him good nature;
He cherish'd his friend, and he relish'd a bumper;
Yet one fault he had, and that was a thumper.
Perhaps you may ask if the man was a miser?
I answer, no, no, for he always was wiser:
Too courteous perhaps, or obligingly flat?
His very worse foe can't accuse him of that:
Perhaps he confided in men as they go,
And so was too foolishly honest? Ah no!
Then what was his failing? come, tell it, and burn ye,—
He was, could he help it? a special attorney.
Here Reynolds is laid, and, to tell you my mind,
He has not left a wiser or better behind.
His pencil was striking, resistless, and grand;
His manners were gentle, complying, and bland;
Still born to improve us in every part,
His pencil our faces, his manners our heart:
To coxcombs averse, yet most civilly steering,
When they judged without skill he was still hard of hearing;
When they talk of their Raphaels, Correggios, and stuff,
He shifted his trumpet, and only took snuff.

310 The Deserted Village

Sweet Auburn! loveliest village of the plain,
Where health and plenty cheer'd the labouring swain,
Where smiling Spring its earliest visit paid,
And parting Summer's lingering blooms delay'd;
Dear lovely bowers of innocence and ease,
Seats of my youth, when every sport could please:
How often have I loiter'd o'er thy green,
Where humble happiness endear'd each scene!
How often have I paused on every charm,
The shelter'd cot, the cultivated farm,
The never-failing brook, the busy mill,
The decent church that topp'd the neighbouring hill;
The hawthorn bush, with seats beneath the shade,

For talking age and whispering lovers made!
How often have I bless'd the coming day,
When toil, remitting, lent its turn to play,
And all the village train, from labour free,
Led up their sports beneath the spreading tree!
While many a pastime circled in the shade,
The young contending as the old survey'd;
And many a gambol frolick'd o'er the ground,
And sleights of art and feats of strength went round;
And still, as each repeated pleasure tired,
Succeeding sports the mirthful band inspired—
The dancing pair that simply sought renown,
By holding out to tire each other down;
The swain mistrustless of his smutted face,
While secret laughter titter'd round the place;
The bashful virgin's side-long looks of love;
The matron's glance, that would those looks reprove.
These were thy charms, sweet village! sports like these,
With sweet succession, taught e'en toil to please;
These round thy bowers their cheerful influence shed;
These were thy charms—but all these charms are fled.

Sweet smiling village, loveliest of the lawn,
Thy sports are fled, and all thy charms withdrawn;
Amidst thy bowers the tyrant's hand is seen,
And Desolation saddens all thy green:
One only master grasps the whole domain,
And half a tillage stints thy smiling plain.
No more thy glassy brook reflects the day,
But, choked with sedges, works its weedy way;
Along thy glades, a solitary guest,
The hollow-sounding bittern guards its nest;
Amidst thy desert walks the lapwing flies,
And tires their echoes with unvaried cries:
Sunk are thy bowers in shapeless ruin all,
And the long grass o'ertops the mouldering wall;
And, trembling, shrinking from the spoiler's hand,
Far, far away thy children leave the land.

Ill fares the land, to hastening ills a prey,
Where wealth accumulates, and men decay.
Princes and lords may flourish, or may fade;

A breath can make them, as a breath has made:
But a bold peasantry, their country's pride,
When once destroy'd, can never be supplied.
  A time there was, ere England's griefs began,
When every rood of ground maintain'd its man;
For him light Labour spread her wholesome store,
Just gave what life required, but gave no more:
His best companions, Innocence and Health;
And his best riches, ignorance of wealth.
  But times are alter'd; Trade's unfeeling train
Usurp the land, and dispossess the swain;
Along the lawn, where scatter'd hamlets rose,
Unwieldy wealth and cumbrous pomp repose;
And every want to luxury allied,
And every pang that folly pays to pride.
Those gentle hours that plenty bade to bloom,
Those calm desires that ask'd but little room,
Those healthful sports that graced the peaceful scene,
Lived in each look, and brighten'd all the green—
These, far departing, seek a kinder shore,
And rural mirth and manners are no more.
  Sweet Auburn! parent of the blissful hour,
Thy glades forlorn confess the tyrant's power.
Here, as I take my solitary rounds,
Amidst thy tangling walks and ruin'd grounds,
And, many a year elapsed, return to view
Where once the cottage stood, the hawthorn grew—
Remembrance wakes with all her busy train,
Swells at my breast, and turns the past to pain.
  In all my wanderings through this world of care,
In all my griefs—and God has given my share—
I still had hopes, my latest hours to crown,
Amidst these humble bowers to lay me down;
To husband out life's taper at the close,
And keep the flame from wasting, by repose:
I still had hopes, for pride attends us still,
Amidst the swains to show my book-learn'd skill,
Around my fire an evening group to draw,
And tell of all I felt, and all I saw;
And, as a hare, whom hounds and horns pursue,

Pants to the place from whence at first she flew,
I still had hopes, my long vexations past,
Here to return—and die at home at last.
  O blest retirement, friend to life's decline,
Retreat from care, that never must be mine,
How blest is he who crowns, in shades like these,
A youth of labour with an age of ease;
Who quits a world where strong temptations try,
And, since 'tis hard to combat, learns to fly!
For him no wretches, born to work and weep,
Explore the mine, or tempt the dangerous deep;
No surly porter stands, in guilty state,
To spurn imploring famine from the gate;
But on he moves to meet his latter end,
Angels around befriending virtue's friend;
Sinks to the grave with unperceived decay,
While resignation gently slopes the way;
And, all his prospects brightening to the last,
His heaven commences ere the world be past!
  Sweet was the sound, when oft, at evening's close,
Up yonder hill the village murmur rose.
There, as I pass'd with careless steps and slow,
The mingled notes came soften'd from below;
The swain responsive as the milk-maid sung,
The sober herd that low'd to meet their young,
The noisy geese that gabbled o'er the pool,
The playful children just let loose from school;
The watch-dog's voice that bay'd the whispering wind,
And the loud laugh that spoke the vacant mind;—
These all in sweet confusion sought the shade,
And fill'd each pause the nightingale had made.
But now the sounds of population fail,
No cheerful murmurs fluctuate in the gale,
No busy steps the grass-grown footway tread
But all the bloomy flush of life is fled—
All but yon widow'd, solitary thing,
That feebly bends beside the plashy spring;
She, wretched matron,—forced, in age, for bread,
To strip the brook with mantling cresses spread,
To pick her wintry faggot from the thorn,

To seek her nightly shed, and weep till morn,—
She only left of all the harmless train,
The sad historian of the pensive plain.
  Near yonder copse, where once the garden smiled,
And still where many a garden-flower grows wild,
There, where a few torn shrubs the place disclose,
The village preacher's modest mansion rose.
A man he was to all the country dear,
And passing rich with forty pounds a year.
Remote from towns he ran his godly race,
Nor e'er had changed, nor wish'd to change, his place;
Unskilful he to fawn, or seek for power
By doctrines fashion'd to the varying hour;
Far other aims his heart had learn'd to prize,
More bent to raise the wretched than to rise.
His house was known to all the vagrant train;
He chid their wanderings, but relieved their pain;
The long-remember'd beggar was his guest,
Whose beard descending swept his aged breast;
The ruin'd spendthrift, now no longer proud,
Claim'd kindred there, and had his claims allow'd;
The broken soldier, kindly bid to stay,
Sat by his fire, and talk'd the night away;—
Wept o'er his wounds, or, tales of sorrow done,
Shoulder'd his crutch, and show'd how fields were won.
Pleased with his guests, the good man learn'd to glow,
And quite forgot their vices in their woe;
Careless their merits or their faults to scan,
His pity gave ere charity began.
  Thus to relieve the wretched was his pride,
And even his failings lean'd to virtue's side;
But in his duty prompt at every call,
He watch'd and wept, he pray'd and felt for all:
And, as a bird each fond endearment tries,
To tempt its new-fledged offspring to the skies,
He tried each art, reproved each dull delay,
Allured to brighter worlds, and led the way.
  Beside the bed where parting life was laid,
And sorrow, guilt, and pain, by turns dismay'd,
The reverend champion stood. At his control,

Despair and anguish fled the struggling soul;
Comfort came down the trembling wretch to raise,
And his last faltering accents whisper'd praise.
  At church, with meek and unaffected grace,
His looks adorn'd the venerable place;
Truth from his lips prevail'd with double sway,
And fools, who came to scoff, remain'd to pray.
The service past, around the pious man
With steady zeal, each honest rustic ran;
E'en children follow'd, with endearing wile,
And pluck'd his gown, to share the good man's smile;
His ready smile a parent's warmth express'd;
Their welfare pleased him, and their cares distress'd;
To them his heart, his love, his griefs were given
But all his serious thoughts had rest in heaven.
As some tall cliff that lifts its awful form,
Swells from the vale, and midway leaves the storm,
Though round its breast the rolling clouds are spread,
Eternal sunshine settles on its head.
  Beside yon straggling fence that skirts the way,
With blossom'd furze unprofitably gay,
There, in his noisy mansion, skill'd to rule,
The village master taught his little school.
A man severe he was, and stern to view;
I knew him well, and every truant knew:
Well had the boding tremblers learn'd to trace
The day's disasters in his morning face;
Full well they laugh'd with counterfeited glee
At all his jokes, for many a joke had he;
Full well the busy whisper, circling round,
Convey'd the dismal tidings when he frown'd.
Yet he was kind, or if severe in aught,
The love he bore to learning was in fault.
The village all declared how much he knew;
'Twas certain he could write, and cipher too;
Lands he could measure, terms and tides presage,
And even the story ran that he could gauge.
In arguing, too, the parson own'd his skill,
For even though vanquish'd, he could argue still;
While words of learned length and thundering sound

Amazed the gazing rustics ranged around;
And still they gazed, and still the wonder grew,
That one small head could carry all he knew.
But past is all his fame;—the very spot
Where many a time he triumph'd, is forgot.
  Near yonder thorn, that lifts its head on high,
Where once the sign-post caught the passing eye,
Now lies that house where nut-brown draughts inspired,
Where grey-beard mirth and smiling toil retired,
Where village statesmen talk'd with looks profound,
And news much older than their ale went round.
Imagination fondly stoops to trace
The parlour splendours of that festive place;
The whitewash'd wall, the nicely-sanded floor,
The varnish'd clock that click'd behind the door,
The chest, contrived a double debt to pay,
A bed by night, a chest of drawers by day,
The pictures placed for ornament and use,
The twelve good rules, the royal game of goose,
The hearth, except when winter chill'd the day,
With aspen boughs, and flowers, and fennel, gay;—
While broken tea-cups, wisely kept for show,
Ranged o'er the chimney, glisten'd in a row.
  Vain transitory splendours; could not all
Reprieve the tottering mansion from its fall?
Obscure it sinks, nor shall it more impart
An hour's importance to the poor man's heart.
Thither no more the peasant shall repair,
To sweet oblivion of his daily care;
No more the farmer's news, the barber's tale,
No more the woodman's ballad shall prevail;
No more the smith his dusky brow shall clear,
Relax his ponderous strength, and lean to hear;
The host himself no longer shall be found
Careful to see the mantling bliss go round;
Nor the coy maid, half willing to be prest,
Shall kiss the cup to pass it to the rest.
  Yes! let the rich deride, the proud disdain,
These simple blessings of the lowly train;
To me more dear, congenial to my heart,

One native charm, than all the gloss of art.
Spontaneous joys, where nature has its play,
The soul adopts, and owns their first-born sway;
Lightly they frolic o'er the vacant mind,
Unenvied, unmolested, unconfined:
But the long pomp, the midnight masquerade,
With all the freaks of wanton wealth array'd,
In these, ere triflers half their wish obtain,
The toiling pleasure sickens into pain;
And, even while Fashion's brightest arts decoy,
The heart distrusting asks, if this be joy?
  Ye friends to truth, ye statesmen, who survey
The rich man's joys increase, the poor's decay,
'Tis yours to judge how wide the limits stand
Between a splendid and a happy land.
Proud swells the tide with loads of freighted ore,
And shouting Folly hails them from her shore;
Hoards, even beyond the miser's wish, abound,
And rich men flock from all the world around.
Yet count our gains. This wealth is but a name
That leaves our useful products still the same.
Not so the loss. The man of wealth and pride
Takes up a space that many poor supplied;
Space for his lake, his park's extended bounds,
Space for his horses, equipage, and hounds;
The robe that wraps his limbs in silken sloth,
Has robb'd the neighbouring fields of half their growth;
His seat, where solitary sports are seen,
Indignant spurns the cottage from the green;
Around the world each needful product flies,
For all the luxuries the world supplies;
While thus the land, adorn'd for pleasure all,
In barren splendour feebly waits the fall.
  As some fair female, unadorn'd and plain,
Secure to please while youth confirms her reign,
Slights every borrow'd charm that dress supplies,
Nor shares with art the triumph of her eyes;
But when those charms are past, for charms are frail,
When time advances, and when lovers fail,
She then shines forth, solicitous to bless,

In all the glaring impotence of dress;
Thus fares the land by luxury betray'd;
In nature's simplest charms at first array'd;—
But verging to decline, its splendours rise,
Its vistas strike, its palaces surprise;
While, scourged by famine, from the smiling land
The mournful peasant leads his humble band;
And while he sinks, without one arm to save,
The country blooms—a garden and a grave!
  Where, then, ah! where shall poverty reside,
To 'scape the pressure of contiguous pride?
If to some common's fenceless limits stray'd,
He drives his flock to pick the scanty blade,
Those fenceless fields the sons of wealth divide,
And even the bare-worn common is denied.
  If to the city sped—what waits him there?
To see profusion that he must not share;
To see ten thousand baneful arts combined
To pamper luxury and thin mankind;
To see each joy the sons of pleasure know,
Extorted from his fellow-creature's woe:
Here while the courtier glitters in brocade,
There the pale artist plies the sickly trade;
Here while the proud their long-drawn pomp display,
There the black gibbet glooms beside the way:
The dome where Pleasure holds her midnight reign,
Here, richly deck'd, admits the gorgeous train;
Tumultuous grandeur crowds the blazing square,
The rattling chariots clash, the torches glare.
Sure scenes like these no troubles e'er annoy!
Sure these denote one universal joy!—
Are these thy serious thoughts?—ah, turn thine eyes
Where the poor houseless shivering female lies:
She once, perhaps, in village plenty bless'd,
Has wept at tales of innocence distress'd;
Her modest looks the cottage might adorn,
Sweet as the primrose peeps beneath the thorn:
Now lost to all, her friends, her virtue, fled,
Near her betrayer's door she lays her head,
And, pinch'd with cold, and shrinking from the shower,

With heavy heart deplores that luckless hour,
When idly first, ambitious of the town,
She left her wheel, and robes of country brown.
  Do thine, sweet Auburn, thine, the loveliest train,
Do thy fair tribes participate her pain?
E'en now, perhaps, by cold and hunger led,
At proud men's doors they ask a little bread!
  Ah, no. To distant climes, a dreary scene,
Where half the convex world intrudes between,
Through torrid tracts with fainting steps they go,
Where wild Altama murmurs to their woe.
Far different there from all that charm'd before,
The various terrors of that horrid shore;
Those blazing suns that dart a downward ray,
And fiercely shed intolerable day;
Those matted woods where birds forget to sing,
But silent bats in drowsy clusters cling;
Those poisonous fields, with rank luxuriance crown'd,
Where the dark scorpion gathers death around;
Where at each step the stranger fears to wake
The rattling terrors of the vengeful snake;
Where crouching tigers wait their hapless prey,
And savage men more murderous still than they:
While oft in whirls the mad tornado flies,
Mingling the ravaged landscape with the skies.
Far different these from every former scene,
The cooling brook, the grassy-vested green,
The breezy covert of the warbling grove,
That only shelter'd thefts of harmless love.
  Good Heaven! what sorrows gloom'd that parting day,
That call'd them from their native walks away;
When the poor exiles, every pleasure past,
Hung round their bowers, and fondly looked their last,
And took a long farewell, and wish'd in vain,
For seats like these beyond the western main;
And shuddering still to face the distant deep,
Return'd and wept, and still return'd to weep!
The good old sire the first prepared to go
To new-found worlds, and wept for others' woe;
But for himself, in conscious virtue brave,

He only wish'd for worlds beyond the grave.
His lovely daughter, lovelier in her tears,
The fond companion of his helpless years,
Silent went next, neglectful of her charms,
And left a lover's for a father's arms.
With louder plaints the mother spoke her woes,
And bless'd the cot where every pleasure rose,
And kiss'd her thoughtless babes with many a tear,
And clasp'd them close, in sorrow doubly dear;
Whilst her fond husband strove to lend relief
In all the silent manliness of grief.
O Luxury, thou cursed by Heaven's decree,
How ill exchanged are things like these for thee!
How do thy potions, with insidious joy,
Diffuse their pleasures only to destroy!
Kingdoms by thee to sickly greatness grown,
Boast of a florid vigour not their own;
At every draught more large and large they grow,
A bloated mass of rank unwieldy woe;
Till sapp'd their strength, and every part unsound,
Down, down they sink, and spread a ruin round.
E'en now the devastation is begun,
And half the business of destruction done;
E'en now, methinks, as pondering here I stand,
I see the rural Virtues leave the land.
Down where yon anchoring vessel spreads the sail
That idly waiting flaps with every gale,
Downward they move, a melancholy band,
Pass from the shore, and darken all the strand;
Contented Toil, and hospitable Care,
And kind connubial Tenderness are there;
And Piety with wishes placed above,
And steady Loyalty, and faithful Love.
And thou, sweet Poetry, thou loveliest maid
Still first to fly where sensual joys invade!
Unfit, in these degenerate times of shame,
To catch the heart, or strike for honest fame;
Dear charming nymph, neglected and decried,
My shame in crowds, my solitary pride;
Thou source of all my bliss and all my woe,

That found'st me poor at first, and keep'st me so;
Thou guide by which the nobler arts excel,
Thou nurse of every virtue, fare thee well!
Farewell! and oh! where'er thy voice be tried,
On Torno's cliffs, or Pambamarca's side,
Whether where equinoctial fervours glow,
Or winter wraps the polar world in snow,
Still let thy voice, prevailing over time,
Redress the rigours of th' inclement clime;
Aid slighted Truth with thy persuasive strain;
Teach erring man to spurn the rage of gain;
Teach him that states, of native strength possest,
Though very poor, may still be very blest;
That Trade's proud empire hastes to swift decay,
As ocean sweeps the labour'd mole away;
While self-dependent power can time defy
As rocks resist the billows and the sky.

311

The Traveller;

OR,

A Prospect of Society

Remote, unfriended, melancholy, slow,
Or by the lazy Scheldt, or wandering Po;
Or onward, where the rude Carinthian boor,
Against the houseless stranger shuts the door;
Or where Campania's plain forsaken lies,
A weary waste expanding to the skies:
Where'er I roam, whatever realms to see,
My heart untravell'd fondly turns to thee;
Still to my brother turns, with ceaseless pain,
And drags at each remove a lengthening chain.

Eternal blessings crown my earliest friend,
And round his dwelling guardian saints attend:
Bless'd be that spot, where cheerful guests retire
To pause from toil, and trim their ev'ning fire;

Bless'd that abode, where want and pain repair,
And every stranger finds a ready chair;
Bless'd be those feasts with simple plenty crown'd,
Where all the ruddy family around
Laugh at the jests or pranks that never fail,
Or sigh with pity at some mournful tale,
Or press the bashful stranger to his food,
And learn the luxury of doing good.

But me, not destin'd such delights to share,
My prime of life in wand'ring spent and care,
Impell'd, with steps unceasing, to pursue
Some fleeting good, that mocks me with the view
That, like the circle bounding earth and skies,
Allures from far, yet, as I follow, flies;
My fortune leads to traverse realms alone,
And find no spot of all the world my own.

Even now, where Alpine solitudes ascend,
I sit me down a pensive hour to spend;
And, plac'd on high above the storm's career,
Look downward where an hundred realms appear;
Lakes, forests, cities, plain, extending wide,
The pomp of kings, the shepherd's humbler pride.

When thus Creation's charms around combine,
Amidst the store, should thankless pride repine?
Say, should the philosophic mind disdain
That good, which makes each humbler bosom vain?
Let school-taught pride dissemble all it can,
These little things are great to little man;
And wiser he, whose sympathetic mind
Exults in all the good of all mankind.
Ye glitt'ring towns, with wealth and splendour crown'd,
Ye fields, where summer spreads profusion round,
Ye lakes, whose vessels catch the busy gale,
Ye bending swains, that dress the flow'ry vale,
For me your tributary stores combine;
Creation's heir, the world, the world is mine!

As some lone miser visiting his store,
Bends at his treasure, counts, re-counts it o'er;
Hoards after hoards his rising raptures fill,
Yet still he sighs, for hoards are wanting still:
Thus to my breast alternate passions rise,
Pleas'd with each good that heaven to man supplies:
Yet oft a sigh prevails, and sorrows fall,
To see the hoard of human bliss so small;
And oft I wish, amidst the scene, to find
Some spot to real happiness consign'd,
Where my worn soul, each wand'ring hope at rest
May gather bliss to see my fellows bless'd.

But where to find that happiest spot below,
Who can direct, when all pretend to know?
The shudd'ring tenant of the frigid zone
Boldly proclaims that happiest spot his own,
Extols the treasures of his stormy seas,
And his long nights of revelry and ease;
The naked negro, panting at the line,
Boasts of his golden sands and palmy wine,
Basks in the glare, or stems the tepid wave,
And thanks his Gods for all the good they gave.
Such is the patriot's boast, where'er we roam,
His first, best country ever is, at home.
And yet, perhaps, if countries we compare,
And estimate the blessings which they share,
Though patriots flatter, still shall wisdom find
An equal portion dealt to all mankind,
As different good, by Art or Nature given,
To different nations makes their blessings even.

Nature, a mother kind alike to all,
Still grants her bliss at Labour's earnest call;
With food as well the peasant is supplied
On Idra's cliffs as Arno's shelvy side;
And though the rocky-crested summits frown,
These rocks, by custom, turn to beds of down.
From Art more various are the blessings sent;
Wealth, commerce, honour, liberty, content.

Yet these each other's power so strong contest,
That either seems destructive of the rest.
Where wealth and freedom reign contentment fails,
And honour sinks where commerce long prevails.
Hence every state, to one lov'd blessing prone,
Conforms and models life to that alone.
Each to the favourite happiness attends,
And spurns the plan that aims at other ends;
Till, carried to excess in each domain,
This favourite good begets peculiar pain.

But let us try these truths with closer eyes,
And trace them through the prospect as it lies:
Here for a while my proper cares resign'd,
Here let me sit in sorrow for mankind,
Like yon neglected shrub at random cast,
That shades the steep, and sighs at every blast.

Far to the right where Apennine ascends,
Bright as the summer, Italy extends;
Its uplands sloping deck the mountain's side,
Woods over woods in gay theatric pride;
While oft some temple's mould'ring tops between
With venerable grandeur mark the scene.

Could Nature's bounty satisfy the breast,
The sons of Italy were surely blest.
Whatever fruits in different climes were found,
That proudly rise, or humbly court the ground;
Whatever blooms in torrid tracts appear,
Whose bright succession decks the varied year;
Whatever sweets salute the northern sky
With vernal lives that blossom but to die;
These, here disporting, own the kindred soil,
Nor ask luxuriance from the planter's toil;
While sea-born gales their gelid wings expand
To winnow fragrance round the smiling land.

But small the bliss that sense alone bestows,
And sensual bliss is all the nation knows.

In florid beauty groves and fields appear,
Man seems the only growth that dwindles here.
Contrasted faults through all his manners reign,
Though poor, luxurious; though submissive, vain,
Though grave, yet trifling; zealous, yet untrue;
And e'en in penance planning sins anew.
All evils here contaminate the mind
That opulence departed leaves behind;
For wealth was theirs, not far remov'd the date,
When commerce proudly flourish'd through the state;
At her command the palace learn'd to rise,
Again the long-fall'n column sought the skies;
The canvas glow'd beyond e'en Nature warm,
The pregnant quarry teem'd with human form;
Till, more unsteady than the southern gale,
Commerce on other shores display'd her sail;
While nought remain'd of all that riches gave,
But towns unmann'd, and lords without a slave;
And late the nation found with fruitless skill
Its former strength was but plethoric ill.

Yet still the loss of wealth is here supplied
By arts, the splendid wrecks of former pride;
From these the feeble heart and long-fall'n mind
An easy compensation seem to find.
Here may be seen, in bloodless pomp array'd,
The paste-board triumph and the cavalcade;
Processions form'd for piety and love,
A mistress or a saint in every grove.
By sports like these are all their cares beguil'd,
The sports of children satisfy the child;
Each nobler aim, represt by long control,
Now sinks at last, or feebly mans the soul;
While low delights, succeeding fast behind,
In happier meanness occupy the mind:
As in those domes, where Cæsars once bore
sway,
Defac'd by time and tottering in decay,
There in the ruin, heedless of the dead,
The shelter-seeking peasant builds his shed,

And wond'ring man could want the larger pile,
Exults, and owns his cottage with a smile.

My soul, turn from them, turn we to survey
Where rougher climes a nobler race display,
Where the bleak Swiss their stormy mansions tread,
And force a churlish soil for scanty bread;
No product here the barren hills afford,
But man and steel, the soldier and his sword.
No vernal blooms their torpid rocks array,
But winter ling'ring chills the lap of May;
No Zephyr fondly sues the mountain's breast,
But meteors glare, and stormy glooms invest.

Yet still, ev'n here, content can spread a charm,
Redress the clime, and all its rage disarm.
Though poor the peasant's hut, his feasts though small,
He sees his little lot the lot of all;
Sees no contiguous palace rear its head
To shame the meanness of his humble shed;
No costly lord the sumptuous banquet deal,
To make him loathe his vegetable meal;
But calm, and bred in ignorance and toil,
Each wish contracting, fits him to the soil.
Cheerful at morn he wakes from short repose,
Breasts the keen air, and carols as he goes;
With patient angle trolls the finny deep,
Or drives his venturous ploughshare to the steep,
Or seeks the den where snow-tracks mark the way,
And drags the struggling savage into day.
At night returning, every labour sped,
He sits him down the monarch of a shed;
Smiles by his cheerful fire, and round surveys
His children's looks, that brighten at the blaze;
While his lov'd partner, boastful of her hoard,
Displays her cleanly platter on the board:
And haply too some pilgrim, thither led,
With many a tale repays the nightly bed.

Thus every good his native wilds impart,
Imprints the patriot passion on his heart,
And ev'n those ills, that round his mansion rise,
Enhance the bliss his scanty fund supplies.
Dear is that shed to which his soul conforms,
And dear that hill which lifts him to the storms;
And as a child, when scaring sounds molest,
Clings close and closer to the mother's breast,
So the loud torrent, and the whirlwind's roar,
But bind him to his native mountains more.

Such are the charms to barren states assigned;
Their wants but few, their wishes all confin'd.
Yet let them only share the praises due,
If few their wants, their pleasures are but few;
For every want that stimulates the breast
Becomes a source of pleasure when redrest.
Whence from such lands each pleasing science flies,
That first excites desire, and then supplies;
Unknown to them, when sensual pleasures cloy,
To fill the languid pause with finer joy;
Unknown those powers that raise the soul to flame,
Catch every nerve, and vibrate through the frame.
Their level life is but a smould'ring fire,
Unquench'd by want, unfann'd by strong desire;
Unfit for raptures, or, if raptures cheer
On some high festival of once a year,
In wild excess the vulgar breast takes fire,
Till, buried in debauch, the bliss expire.

But not their joys alone thus coarsely flow:
Their morals, like their pleasures, are but low,
For, as refinement stops, from sire to son
Unalter'd, unimprov'd, the manners run;
And love's and friendship's finely pointed dart
Fall blunted from each indurated heart.
Some sterner virtues o'er the mountain's breast
May sit, like falcons cow'ring on the nest;
But all the gentler morals, such as play
Through life's more cultur'd walks, and charm the way,

These, far dispers'd, on timorous pinions fly,
To sport and flutter in a kinder sky.

To kinder skies, where gentler manners reign,
I turn; and France displays her bright domain.
Gay sprightly land of mirth and social ease,
Pleas'd with thyself, whom all the world can please,
How often have I led thy sportive choir,
With tuneless pipe, beside the murmuring Loire?
Where shading elms along the margin grew,
And freshen'd from the wave the zephyr flew;
And haply, though my harsh touch, faltering still,
But mock'd all tune, and marr'd the dancer's skill;
Yet would the village praise my wondrous power,
And dance, forgetful of the noontide hour.
Alike all ages. Dames of ancient days
Have led their children through the mirthful maze,
And the gay grandsire, skill'd in gestic lore,
Has frisk'd beneath the burthen of threescore.

So blest a life these thoughtless realms display,
Thus idly busy rolls their world away:
Theirs are those arts that mind to mind endear,
For honour forms the social temper here:
Honour, that praise which real merit gains,
Or even imaginary worth obtains,
Here passes current; paid from hand to hand,
It shifts in splendid traffic round the land:
From courts, to camps, to cottages it strays,
And all are taught an avarice of praise.
They please, are pleas'd, they give to get esteem,
Till seeming blest, they grow to what they seem.

But while this softer art their bliss supplies,
It gives their follies also room to rise;
For praise too dearly lov'd, or warmly sought,
Enfeebles all internal strength of thought;
And the weak soul, within itself unblest,
Leans for all pleasure on another's breast.
Hence ostentation here, with tawdry art,

Pants for the vulgar praise which fools impart;
Here vanity assumes her pert grimace,
And trims her robes of frieze with copper lace;
Here beggar pride defrauds her daily cheer,
To boast one splendid banquet once a year;
The mind still turns where shifting fashion draws,
Nor weighs the solid worth of self-applause.

To men of other minds my fancy flies,
Embosom'd in the deep where Holland lies.
Methinks her patient sons before me stand,
Where the broad ocean leans against the land,
And, sedulous to stop the coming tide,
Lift the tall rampire's artificial pride.
Onward, methinks, and diligently slow,
The firm-connected bulwark seems to grow;
Spreads its long arms amidst the watery roar,
Scoops out an empire, and usurps the shore:
While the pent ocean rising o'er the pile,
Sees an amphibious world beneath him smile;
The slow canal, the yellow-blossom'd vale,
The willow-tufted bank, the gliding sail,
The crowded mart, the cultivated plain,—
A new creation rescued from his reign.

Thus, while around the wave-subjected soil
Impels the native to repeated toil,
Industrious habits in each bosom reign,
And industry begets a love of gain.
Hence all the good from opulence that springs,
With all those ills superfluous treasure brings,
Are here displayed. Their much lov'd wealth imparts
Convenience, plenty, elegance, and arts;
But view them closer, craft and fraud appear,
Ev'n liberty itself is barter'd here.
At gold's superior charms all freedom flies,
The needy sell it, and the rich man buys;
A land of tyrants, and a den of slaves,
Here wretches seek dishonourable graves,
And calmly bent, to servitude conform,
Dull as their lakes that slumber in the storm.

Heavens! how unlike their Belgic sires of old!
Rough, poor, content, ungovernably bold;
War in each breast, and freedom on each brow;
How much unlike the sons of Britain now!

Fir'd at the sound, my genius spreads her wing,
And flies where Britain courts the western spring;
Where lawns extend that scorn Arcadian pride,
And brighter streams than fam'd Hydaspes glide.
There all around the gentlest breezes stray,
There gentle music melts on every spray;
Creation's mildest charms are there combin'd,
Extremes are only in the master's mind!
Stern o'er each bosom Reason holds her state,
With daring aims irregularly great,
Pride in their port, defiance in their eye,
I see the lords of human kind pass by,
Intent on high designs, a thoughtful band,
By forms unfashion'd, fresh from Nature's hand;
Fierce in their native hardiness of soul,
True to imagin'd right, above control,
While ev'n the peasant boasts these rights to scan,
And learns to venerate himself as man.

Thine, Freedom, thine the blessings pictur'd here,
Thine are those charms that dazzle and endear;
Too bless'd, indeed, were such without alloy,
But foster'd ev'n by Freedom, ills annoy:
That independence Britons prize too high,
Keeps man from man, and breaks the social tie;
The self-dependent lordlings stand alone,
All claims that bind and sweeten life unknown;
Here by the bonds of nature feebly held,
Minds combat minds, repelling and repell'd.
Ferments arise, imprison'd factions roar,
Repress'd ambition struggles round her shore,
Till over-wrought, the general system feels
Its motions stop, or phrenzy fires the wheels.

Nor this the worst. As nature's ties decay,
As duty, love, and honour fail to sway,
Fictitious bonds, the bonds of wealth and law,
Still gather strength, and force unwilling awe.
Hence all obedience bows to these alone,
And talent sinks, and merit weeps unknown;
Till time may come, when stripp'd of all her charms,
The land of scholars, and the nurse of arms,
Where noble stems transmit the patriot flame,
Where kings have toil'd, and poets wrote for fame,
One sink of level avarice shall lie,
And scholars, soldiers, kings, unhonour'd die.

Yet think not, thus when Freedom's ills I state,
I mean to flatter kings, or court the great;
Ye powers of truth, that bid my soul aspire,
Far from my bosom drive the low desire;
And thou, fair Freedom, taught alike to feel
The rabble's rage, and tyrant's angry steel;
Thou transitory flower, alike undone
By proud contempt, or favour's fostering sun,
Still may thy blooms the changeful clime endure!
I only would repress them to secure:
For just experience tells, in every soil,
That those who think must govern those that toil;
And all that freedom's highest aims can reach,
Is but to lay proportion'd loads on each.
Hence, should one order disproportion'd grow,
Its double weight must ruin all below.

O then how blind to all that earth requires,
Who think it freedom when a part aspires!
Calm is my soul, nor apt to rise in arms,
Except when fast-approaching danger warms:
But when contending chiefs blockade the throne,
Contracting regal power to stretch their own,
When I behold a factious band agree
To call it freedom when themselves are free;
Each wanton judge new penal statutes draw,
Laws grind the poor, and rich men rule the law;

The wealth of climes, where savage nations roam,
Pillag'd from slaves to purchase slaves at home;
Fear, pity, justice, indignation start,
Tear off reserve, and bare my swelling heart;
Till half a patriot, half a coward grown,
I fly from petty tyrants to the throne.

Yes, brother, curse with me that baleful hour,
When first ambition struck at regal power;
And thus polluting honour in its source,
Gave wealth to sway the mind with double force.
Have we not seen, round Britain's peopled shore,
Her useful sons exchanged for useless ore?
Seen all her triumphs but destruction haste,
Like flaring tapers brightening as they waste;
Seen opulence, her grandeur to maintain,
Lead stern depopulation in her train,
And over fields where scatter'd hamlets rose,
In barren solitary pomp repose?
Have we not seen at pleasure's lordly call,
The smiling long-frequented village fall?
Beheld the duteous son, the sire decay'd,
The modest matron, and the blushing maid,
Forc'd from their homes, a melancholy train,
To traverse climes beyond the western main;
Where wild Oswego spreads her swamps around,
And Niagara stuns with thund'ring sound?

Even now, perhaps, as there some pilgrim strays
Through tangled forests, and through dangerous ways;
Where beasts with man divided empire claim,
And the brown Indian marks with murderous aim;
There, while above the giddy tempest flies,
And all around distressful yells arise,
The pensive exile, bending with his woe,
To stop too fearful, and too faint to go,
Casts a long look where England's glories shine,
And bids his bosom sympathise with mine.

Vain, very vain, my weary search to find
That bliss which only centres in the mind:

Why have I stray'd from pleasure and repose,
To seek a good each government bestows?
In every government, though terrors reign,
Though tyrant kings, or tyrant laws restrain,
How small, of all that human hearts endure,
That part which laws or kings can cause or cure!
Still to ourselves in every place consign'd,
Our own felicity we make or find:
With secret course, which no loud storms annoy,
Glides the smooth current of domestic joy.
The lifted axe, the agonising wheel,
Luke's iron crown, and Damien's bed of steel,
To men remote from power but rarely known,
Leave reason, faith, and conscience, all our own.

ROBERT GRAHAM OF GARTMORE

[*1735-1797*]

312

If Doughty Deeds

If doughty deeds my lady please
  Right soon I'll mount my steed;
And strong his arm, and fast his seat
  That bears frae me the meed.
I'll wear thy colours in my cap,
  Thy picture at my heart;
And he that bends not to thine eye
  Shall rue it to his smart!
    Then tell me how to woo thee, Love;
      O tell me how to woo thee!
    For thy dear sake, nae care I'll take
      Tho' ne'er another trow me.
If gay attire delight thine eye
  I'll dight me in array;
I'll tend thy chamber door all night,
  And squire thee all the day.
If sweetest sounds can win thine ear,
  These sounds I'll strive to catch;

Thy voice I'll steal to woo thysell,
That voice that nane can match.

But if fond love thy heart can gain,
I never broke a vow;
Nae maiden lays her skaith to me,
I never loved but you.
For you alone I ride the ring,
For you I wear the blue;
For you alone I strive to sing,
O tell me how to woo!
Then tell me how to woo thee, Love;
O tell me how to woo thee!
For thy dear sake, nae care I'll take,
Tho' ne'er another trow me.

ADAM AUSTIN

[1726(?)-1774]

313

For Lack of Gold

For lack of gold she's left me, O,
And of all that's dear bereft me, O;
She me forsook for Athole's duke,
And to endless woe she has left me, O.
A star and garter have more art
Than youth, a true and faithful heart;
For empty titles we must part,
And for glittering show she's left me, O.

No cruel fair shall ever move
My injured heart again to love;
Through distant climates I must rove,
Since Jeanie she has left me, O.
Ye powers above, I to your care
Give up my faithless, lovely fair;
Your choicest blessings be her share,
Though she's for ever left me, O!

WILLIAM COWPER

[*1731-1800*]

314

Loss of the Royal George

Toll for the Brave!
The brave that are no more!
All sunk beneath the wave
Fast by their native shore!

Eight hundred of the brave
Whose courage well was tried,
Had made the vessel heel
And laid her on her side.

A land-breeze shook the shrouds
And she was overset;
Down went the Royal George,
With all her crew complete.

Toll for the brave!
Brave Kempenfelt is gone;
His last sea-fight is fought,
His work of glory done.

It was not in the battle;
No tempest gave the shock;
She sprang no fatal leak,
She ran upon no rock.

His sword was in its sheath,
His fingers held the pen,
When Kempenfelt went down
With twice four hundred men.

Weigh the vessel up
Once dreaded by our foes!
And mingle with our cup
The tears that England owes.

Her timbers yet are sound,
And she may float again
Full charged with England's thunder,
And plough the distant main:

But Kempenfelt is gone,
His victories are o'er;
And he and his eight hundred
Shall plough the wave no more.

315

To a Young Lady

Sweet stream, that winds through yonder glade,
Apt emblem of a virtuous maid—
Silent and chaste she steals along,
Far from the world's gay busy throng:
With gentle yet prevailing force,
Intent upon her destined course;
Graceful and useful all she does,
Blessing and blest where'er she goes;
Pure-bosom'd as that watery glass,
And Heaven reflected in her face.

316

The Poplar Field

The poplars are fell'd, farewell to the shade
And the whispering sound of the cool colonnade;
The winds play no longer and sing in the leaves,
Nor Ouse on his bosom their image receives.

Twelve years have elapsed since I first took a view
Of my favourite field, and the bank where they grew:
And now in the grass behold they are laid,
And the tree is my seat that once lent me a shade.

The blackbird has fled to another retreat
Where the hazels afford him a screen from the heat;
And the scene where his melody charm'd me before
Resounds with his sweet-flowing ditty no more.

My fugitive years are all hasting away,
And I must ere long lie as lowly as they,
With a turf on my breast and a stone at my head,
Ere another such grove shall arise in its stead.

'Tis a sight to engage me, if anything can,
To muse on the perishing pleasures of man;
Short-lived as we are, our enjoyments, I see,
Have a still shorter date; and die sooner than we.

317 THE SOLITUDE OF ALEXANDER SELKIRK

I AM monarch of all I survey;
My right there is none to dispute;
From the centre all round to the sea
I am lord of the fowl and the brute.
O Solitude! where are the charms
That sages have seen in thy face?
Better dwell in the midst of alarms,
Than reign in this horrible place.

I am out of humanity's reach,
I must finish my journey alone,
Never hear the sweet music of speech;
I start at the sound of my own.
The beasts that roam over the plain
My form with indifference see;
They are so unacquainted with man,
Their tameness is shocking to me.

Society, Friendship, and Love
Divinely bestow'd upon man,
O, had I the wings of a dove
How soon would I taste you again!
My sorrows I then might assuage
In the ways of religion and truth;
Might learn from the wisdom of age,
And be cheer'd by the sallies of youth.

Ye winds that have made me your sport,
Convey to this desolate shore
Some cordial endearing report
Of a land I shall visit no more:
My friends, do they now and then send
A wish or a thought after me?
O tell me I yet have a friend,
Though a friend I am never to see.

How fleet is a glance of the mind!
Compared with the speed of its flight,
The tempest itself lags behind,
And the swift-wingèd arrows of light.
When I think of my own native land
In a moment I seem to be there;
But alas! recollection at hand
Soon hurries me back to despair.

But the sea-fowl is gone to her nest,
The beast is laid down in his lair;
Even here is a season of rest,
And I to my cabin repair.
There's mercy in every place,
And mercy, encouraging thought!
Gives even affliction a grace
And reconciles man to his lot.

318 To Mary Unwin

Mary! I want a lyre with other strings,
Such aid from heaven as some have feign'd they drew,
An eloquence scarce given to mortals, new
And undebased by praise of meaner things,

That ere through age or woe I shed my wings
I may record thy worth with honour due,
In verse as musical as thou art true,
And that immortalizes whom it sings:—

But thou hast little need. There is a Book
By seraphs writ with beams of heavenly light,
On which the eyes of God not rarely look,

A chronicle of actions just and bright—
There all thy deeds, my faithful Mary, shine;
And since thou own'st that praise, I spare thee mine.

319 To the Same

The twentieth year is well-nigh past
Since first our sky was overcast;
Ah would that this might be the last!
My Mary!

Thy spirits have a fainter flow,
I see thee daily weaker grow—
'Twas my distress that brought thee low,
My Mary!

Thy needles, once a shining store,
For my sake restless heretofore,
Now rust disused, and shine no more;
My Mary!

For though thou gladly wouldst fulfil
The same kind office for me still,
Thy sight now seconds not thy will,
My Mary!

But well thou play'dst the housewife's part,
And all thy threads with magic art
Have wound themselves about this heart,
My Mary!

Thy indistinct expressions seem
Like language utter'd in a dream;
Yet me they charm, whate'er the theme,
My Mary!

Thy silver locks, once auburn bright,
Are still more lovely in my sight
Than golden beams of orient light,
My Mary!

For could I view nor them nor thee,
What sight worth seeing could I see?
The sun would rise in vain for me,
My Mary!

Partakers of thy sad decline,
Thy hands their little force resign;
Yet, gently press'd, press gently mine,
My Mary!

Such feebleness of limbs thou prov'st
That now at every step thou mov'st
Upheld by two; yet still thou lov'st,
My Mary!

And still to love, though press'd with ill,
In wintry age to feel no chill,
With me is to be lovely still,
My Mary!

But ah! by constant heed I know
How oft the sadness that I show
Transforms thy smiles to looks of wo
My Mary!

And should my future lot be cast
With much resemblance of the past,
Thy worn-out heart will break at last—
My Mary!

320 BOADICEA: AN ODE

WHEN the British warrior queen,
Bleeding from the Roman rods,
Sought, with an indignant mien,
Counsel of her country's gods,

Sage beneath a spreading oak
  Sat the Druid, hoary chief;
Every burning word he spoke
  Full of rage, and full of grief.

'Princess! if our aged eyes
  Weep upon thy matchless wrongs,
'Tis because resentment ties
  All the terrors of our tongues.

'Rome shall perish—write that word
  In the blood that she has spilt;
Perish, hopeless and abhorred,
  Deep in ruin as in guilt.

'Rome, for empire far renowned,
  Tramples on a thousand states;
Soon her pride shall kiss the ground—
  Hark! the Gaul is at her gates!

'Other Romans shall arise,
  Heedless of a soldier's name;
Sounds, not arms, shall win the prize—
  Harmony the path to fame.

'Then the progeny that springs
  From the forests of our land,
Armed with thunder, clad with wings,
  Shall a wider world command.

'Regions Cæsar never knew
  Thy posterity shall sway,
Where his eagles never flew,
  None invincible as they.'

Such the bard's prophetic words,
  Pregnant with celestial fire,
Bending, as he swept the chords
  Of his sweet but awful lyre.

She, with all a monarch's pride,
  Felt them in her bosom glow;
Rushed to battle, fought, and died;
  Dying, hurled them at the foe.

'Ruffians, pitiless as proud,
  Heaven awards the vengeance due;
Empire is on us bestowed,
  Shame and ruin wait for you.'

321

The Castaway

Obscurest night involved the sky,
  The Atlantic billows roared,
When such a destined wretch as I,
  Washed headlong from on board,
Of friends, of hope, of all bereft,
His floating home for ever left.

No braver chief could Albion boast
  Than he with whom he went,
Nor ever ship left Albion's coast
  With warmer wishes sent.
He loved them both, but both in vain,
Nor him beheld, nor her again.

Not long beneath the whelming brine,
  Expert to swim, he lay;
Nor soon he felt his strength decline,
  Or courage die away;
But waged with death a lasting strife,
Supported by despair of life.

He shouted: nor his friends had failed
  To check the vessel's course,
But so the furious blast prevailed,
  That, pitiless perforce,
They left their outcast mate behind,
And scudded still before the wind.

Some succour yet they could afford;
  And such as storms allow,
The cask, the coop, the floated cord,
  Delayed not to bestow.
But he (they knew) nor ship nor shore,
Whate'er they gave, should visit more.

Nor, cruel as it seemed, could he
  Their haste himself condemn,
Aware that flight, in such a sea,
  Alone could rescue them;
Yet bitter felt it still to die
Deserted, and his friends so nigh.

He long survives, who lives an hour
  In ocean, self-upheld;
And so long he, with unspent power,
  His destiny repelled;
And ever, as the minutes flew,
Entreated help, or cried 'Adieu!'

At length, his transient respite past,
  His comrades, who before
Had heard his voice in every blast,
  Could catch the sound no more:
For then, by toil subdued, he drank
The stifling wave, and then he sank.

No poet wept him; but the page
  Of narrative sincere,
That tells his name, his worth, his age,
  Is wet with Anson's tear:
And tears by bards or heroes shed
Alike immortalize the dead.

I therefore purpose not, or dream,
  Descanting on his fate,
To give the melancholy theme
  A more enduring date:
But misery still delights to trace
Its semblance in another's case.

No voice divine the storm allayed,
  No light propitious shone,
When, snatched from all effectual aid,
  We perished, each alone:
But I beneath a rougher sea,
And whelmed in deeper gulfs than he.

322 THE SHRUBBERY

O HAPPY shades! to me unblest!
  Friendly to peace, but not to me!
How ill the scene that offers rest,
  And heart that cannot rest, agree!

This glassy stream, that spreading pine,
  Those alders quivering to the breeze,
Might soothe a soul less hurt than mine,
  And please, if anything could please.

But fixed unalterable Care
  Foregoes not what she feels within,
Shows the same sadness everywhere,
  And slights the season and the scene.

For all that pleased in wood or lawn,
  While Peace possessed these silent bowers,
Her animating smile withdrawn,
  Has lost its beauties and its powers.

The saint or moralist should tread
  This moss-grown alley, musing, slow;
They seek like me the secret shade,
  But not, like me, to nourish woe!

Me fruitful scenes and prospects waste,
  Alike admonish not to roam;
These tell me of enjoyments past,
  And those of sorrows yet to come.

323 On the Receipt of My Mother's Picture Out of Norfolk

Oh that those lips had language! Life has passed
With me but roughly since I heard thee last.
Those lips are thine—thy own sweet smile I see,
The same that oft in childhood solaced me;
Voice only fails, else how distinct they say,
'Grieve not, my child, chase all thy fears away!'
The meek intelligence of those dear eyes
(Blessed be the art that can immortalize,
The art that baffles Time's tyrannic claim
To quench it) here shines on me still the same.
  Faithful remembrancer of one so dear,
O welcome guest, though unexpected here!
Who bidst me honour with an artless song,
Affectionate, a mother lost so long,
I will obey, not willingly alone,
But gladly, as the precept were her own:
And, while that face renews my filial grief,
Fancy shall weave a charm for my relief,
Shall steep me in Elysian reverie,
A momentary dream that thou art she.
  My mother! when I learnt that thou wast dead,
Say, wast thou conscious of the tears I shed?
Hovered thy spirit o'er thy sorrowing son,
Wretch even then, life's journey just begun?
Perhaps thou gavest me, though unfelt, a kiss:
Perhaps a tear, if souls can weep in bliss—
Ah, that maternal smile! It answers—Yes.
I heard the bell toll on thy burial day,
I saw the hearse that bore thee slow away,
And, turning from my nursery window, drew
A long, long sigh, and wept a last adieu!
But was it such?—It was.—Where thou art gone
Adieus and farewells are a sound unknown.
May I but meet thee on that peaceful shore,
The parting word shall pass my lips no more!
Thy maidens, grieved themselves at my concern,

Oft gave me promise of thy quick return.
What ardently I wished I long believed,
And, disappointed still, was still deceived.
By expectation every day beguiled,
Dupe of *to-morrow* even from a child.
Thus many a sad to-morrow came and went,
Till, all my stock of infant sorrow spent,
I learnt at last submission to my lot;
But, though I less deplored thee, ne'er forgot.
  Where once we dwelt our name is heard no more,
Children not thine have trod my nursery floor;
And where the gardener Robin, day by day,
Drew me to school along the public way,
Delighted with my bauble coach, and wrapped
In scarlet mantle warm, and velvet capped,
'Tis now become a history little known,
That once we called the pastoral house our own.
Short-lived possession! but the record fair
That memory keeps, of all thy kindness there,
Still outlives many a storm that has effaced
A thousand other themes less deeply traced.
The nightly visits to my chamber made,
That thou mightst know me safe and warmly laid;
Thy morning bounties ere I left my home,
The biscuit, or confectionary plum;
The fragrant waters on my cheek bestowed
By thy own hand, till fresh they shone and glowed;
All this, and more endearing still than all,
Thy constant flow of love, that knew no fall,
Ne'er roughened by those cataracts and brakes
That humour interposed too often makes;
All this still legible in memory's page,
And still to be so to my latest age,
Adds joy to duty, makes me glad to pay
Such honours to thee as my numbers may;
Perhaps a frail memorial, but sincere,
Not scorned in heaven, though little noticed here.
  Could Time, his flight reversed, restore the hours,
When, playing with thy vesture's tissued flowers,
The violet, the pink, and jessamine,

I pricked them into paper with a pin
(And thou wast happier than myself the while,
Wouldst softly speak, and stroke my head and smile),
Could these few pleasant days again appear,
Might one wish bring them, would I wish them here?
I would not trust my heart—the dear delight
Seems so to be desired, perhaps I might.—
But no—what here we call our life is such
So little to be loved, and thou so much,
That I should ill requite thee to constrain
Thy unbound spirit into bonds again.
 Thou, as a gallant bark from Albion's coast
(The storms all weathered and the ocean crossed)
Shoots into port at some well-havened isle,
Where spices breathe, and brighter seasons smile,
There sits quiescent on the floods that show
Her beauteous form reflected clear below,
While airs impregnated with incense play
Around her, fanning light her streamers gay;
So thou, with sails how swift! hast reached the shore,
'Where tempests never beat nor billows roar,'
And thy loved consort on the dangerous tide
Of life long since has anchored by thy side.
But me, scarce hoping to attain that rest,
Always from port withheld, always distressed—
Me howling blasts drive devious, tempest tost,
Sails ripped, seams opening wide, and compass lost,
And day by day some current's thwarting force
Sets me more distant from a prosperous course.
Yet, oh, the thought that thou art safe, and he!
That thought is joy, arrive what may to me.
My boast is not, that I deduce my birth
From loins enthroned and rulers of the earth;
But higher far my proud pretensions rise—
The son of parents passed into the skies!
And now, farewell!—Time unrevoked has run
His wonted course, yet what I wished is done.
By contemplation's help, not sought in vain,
I seemed to have lived my childhood o'er again;
To have renewed the joys that once were mine,

Without the sin of violating thine:
And, while the wings of Fancy still are free,
And I can view this mimic show of thee,
Time has but half succeeded in his theft—
Thyself removed, thy power to soothe me left.

324 THE DIVERTING HISTORY OF JOHN GILPIN

JOHN GILPIN was a citizen
Of credit and renown,
A train-band captain eke was he
Of famous London town.

John Gilpin's spouse said to her dear,
'Though wedded we have been
These twice ten tedious years, yet we
No holiday have seen.

'To-morrow is our wedding-day,
And we will then repair
Unto the Bell at Edmonton,
All in a chaise and pair.

'My sister, and my sister's child,
Myself, and children three,
Will fill the chaise; so you must ride
On horseback after we.'

He soon replied, 'I do admire
Of womankind but one,
And you are she, my dearest dear,
Therefore it shall be done.

'I am a linen-draper bold,
As all the world doth know,
And my good friend the calender
Will lend his horse to go.'

Quoth Mrs. Gilpin, 'That's well said;
And for that wine is dear,
We will be furnished with our own,
Which is both bright and clear.'

John Gilpin kissed his loving wife;
O'erjoyed was he to find,
That though on pleasure she was bent,
She had a frugal mind.

The morning came, the chaise was brought,
But yet was not allowed
To drive up to the door, lest all
Should say that she was proud.

So three doors off the chaise was stayed,
Where they did all get in;
Six precious souls, and all agog
To dash through thick and thin.

Smack went the whip, round went the wheels,
Were never folk so glad,
The stones did rattle underneath,
As if Cheapside were mad.

John Gilpin at his horse's side
Seized fast the flowing mane,
And up he got, in haste to ride,
But soon came down again;

For saddle-tree scarce reached had he,
His journey to begin,
When, turning round his head, he saw
Three customers come in.

So down he came; for loss of time,
Although it grieved him sore,
Yet loss of pence, full well he knew,
Would trouble him much more.

'Twas long before the customers
  Were suited to their mind,
When Betty screaming came down stairs,
  'The wine is left behind!'

'Good lack,' quoth he—'yet bring it me,
  My leathern belt likewise,
In which I bear my trusty sword,
  When I do exercise.'

Now Mistress Gilpin (careful soul!)
  Had two stone bottles found,
To hold the liquor that she loved,
  And keep it safe and sound.

Each bottle had a curling ear,
  Through which the belt he drew,
And hung a bottle on each side,
  To make his balance true.

Then over all, that he might be
  Equipped from top to toe,
His long red cloak, well brushed and neat,
  He manfully did throw.

Now see him mounted once again
  Upon his nimble steed,
Full slowly pacing o'er the stones,
  With caution and good heed.

But finding soon a smoother road
  Beneath his well-shod feet,
The snorting beast began to trot,
  Which galled him in his seat.

So, 'Fair and softly,' John he cried,
  But John he called in vain;
That trot became a gallop soon,
  In spite of curb and rein.

So stooping down as needs he must
  Who cannot sit upright,
He grasped the mane with both his hands,
  And eke with all his might.

His horse, who never in that sort
  Had handled been before,
What thing upon his back had got
  Did wonder more and more.

Away went Gilpin, neck or nought;
  Away went hat and wig;
He little dreamt, when he set out,
  Of running such a rig.

The wind did blow, the cloak did fly,
  Like streamer long and gay,
Till, loop and button failing both,
  At last it flew away.

Then might all people well discern
  The bottles he had slung;
A bottle swinging at each side,
  As hath been said or sung.

The dogs did bark, the children screamed,
  Up flew the windows all;
And every soul cried out, 'Well done!'
  As loud as he could bawl.

Away went Gilpin—who but he?
  His fame soon spread around;
'He carries weight! He rides a race!'
  ''Tis for a thousand pound!'

And still, as fast as he drew near,
  'Twas wonderful to view,
How in a trice the turnpike-men
  Their gates wide open threw.

And now, as he went bowing down
  His reeking head full low,
The bottles twain behind his back
  Were shattered at a blow.

Down ran the wine into the road,
  Most piteous to be seen,
Which made his horse's flanks to smoke
  As they had basted been.

But still he seemed to carry weight,
  With leathern girdle braced;
For all might see the bottle-necks
  Still dangling at his waist.

Thus all through merry Islington
  These gambols he did play,
Until he came unto the Wash
  Of Edmonton so gay;

And there he threw the Wash about
  On both sides of the way,
Just like unto a trundling mop,
  Or a wild goose at play.

At Edmonton his loving wife
  From the balcony spied
Her tender husband, wondering much
  To see how he did ride.

'Stop, stop, John Gilpin!—Here's the house!'
  They all at once did cry;
'The dinner waits, and we are tired;'—
  Said Gilpin—'So am I!'

But yet his horse was not a whit
  Inclined to tarry there!
For why?—his owner had a house
  Full ten miles off at Ware.

So like an arrow swift he flew,
  Shot by an archer strong;
So did he fly—which brings me to
  The middle of my song.

Away went Gilpin, out of breath,
  And sore against his will,
Till at his friend the calender's
  His horse at last stood still.

The calender, amazed to see
  His neighbour in such trim,
Laid down his pipe, flew to the gate,
  And thus accosted him:

'What news? what news? your tidings tell;
  Tell me you must and shall—
Say why bareheaded you are come,
  Or why you come at all?'

Now Gilpin had a pleasant wit,
  And loved a timely joke;
And thus unto the calender
  In merry guise he spoke:

'I came because your horse would come,
  And, if I well forebode,
My hat and wig will soon be here,—
  They are upon the road.'

The calender, right glad to find
  His friend in merry pin,
Returned him not a single word,
  But to the house went in;

Whence straight he came with hat and wig;
  A wig that flowed behind,
A hat not much the worse for wear,
  Each comely in its kind.

He held them up, and in his turn
  Thus showed his ready wit,
'My head is twice as big as yours,
  They therefore needs must fit.

'But let me scrape the dirt away
  That hangs upon your face;
And stop and eat, for well you may
  Be in a hungry case.'

Said John, 'It is my wedding day,
  And all the world would stare,
If wife should dine at Edmonton,
  And I should dine at Ware.'

So turning to his horse, he said,
  'I am in haste to dine;
'Twas for your pleasure you came here,
  You shall go back for mine.'

Ah, luckless speech, and bootless boast!
  For which he paid full dear;
For, while he spake, a braying ass
  Did sing most loud and clear;

Whereat his horse did snort, as he
  Had heard a lion roar,
And galloped off with all his might,
  As he had done before.

Away went Gilpin, and away
  Went Gilpin's hat and wig;
He lost them sooner than at first;
  For why?—they were too big.

Now Mistress Gilpin, when she saw
  Her husband posting down
Into the country far away,
  She pulled out half a crown;

And thus unto the youth she said
  That drove them to the Bell,
'This shall be yours, when you bring back
  My husband safe and well.'

The youth did ride, and soon did meet
  John coming back again:
Whom in a trice he tried to stop,
  By catching at his rein;

But not performing what he meant,
  And gladly would have done,
The frighted steed he frighted more,
  And made him faster run.

Away went Gilpin, and away
  Went postboy at his heels,
The postboy's horse right glad to miss
  The lumbering of the wheels.

Six gentlemen upon the road,
  Thus seeing Gilpin fly,
With postboy scampering in the rear,
  They raised the hue and cry:

'Stop thief! stop thief!—a highwayman!'
  Not one of them was mute;
And all and each that passed that way
  Did join in the pursuit.

And now the turnpike gates again
  Flew open in short space;
The toll-men thinking, as before,
  That Gilpin rode a race.

And so he did, and won it too,
  For he got first to town;
Nor stopped till where he had got up
  He did again get down.

Now let us sing, Long live the King!
And Gilpin, long live he!
And when he next doth ride abroad
May I be there to see!

RICHARD BRINSLEY SHERIDAN

[1751-1816]

325 DRINKING SONG

HERE'S to the maiden of bashful fifteen,
Here's to the widow of fifty;
Here's to the flaunting extravagant quean,
And here's to the housewife that's thrifty;

Chorus. *Let the toast pass,*
Drink to the lass,
I'll warrant she'll prove an excuse for the glass.

Here's to the charmer, whose dimples we prize,
And now to the maid who has none, sir,
Here's to the girl with a pair of blue eyes,
And here's to the nymph with but one, sir.
Let the toast pass, etc.

Here's to the maid with a bosom of snow,
And to her that's as brown as a berry;
Here's to the wife with a face full of woe,
And now to the girl that is merry:
Let the toast pass, etc.

For let 'em be clumsy, or let 'em be slim,
Young or ancient, I care not a feather;
So fill a pint bumper quite up to the brim,
And let us e'en toast them together.

Chorus. *Let the toast pass,*
Drink to the lass,
I'll warrant she'll prove an excuse for the glass.

ANNA LAETITIA BARBAULD

[*1743-1825*]

326

LIFE

LIFE! I know not what thou art,
But know that thou and I must part;
And when, or how, or where we met,
I own to me's a secret yet.
But this I know, when thou art fled,
Where'er they lay these limbs, this head,
No clod so valueless shall be
As all that then remains of me.

O whither, whither, dost thou fly?
Where bend unseen thy trackless course?
  And in this strange divorce,
Ah, tell where I must seek this compound I?
To the vast ocean of empyreal flame
  From whence thy essence came
Dost thou thy flight pursue, when freed
From matter's base encumbering weed?
  Or dost thou, hid from sight,
  Wait, like some spell-bound knight,
Through blank oblivious years th' appointed hour
To break thy trance and reassume thy power?
Yet canst thou without thought or feeling be?
O say, what art thou, when no more thou'rt thee?

Life! we have been long together,
Through pleasant and through cloudy weather;
  'Tis hard to part when friends are dear;
  Perhaps 'twill cost a sigh, a tear;—
  Then steal away, give little warning,
      Choose thine own time;
Say not Good-night, but in some brighter clime
      Bid me Good-morning!

ISOBEL PAGAN (?)

[1741 (?)-1821]

327 CA' THE YOWES TO THE KNOWES

CA' the yowes[1] to the knowes,[2]
Ca' them where the heather grows,
Ca' them where the burnie[3] rows,[4]
My bonnie dearie.

As I gaed down the water side,
There I met my shepherd lad;
He row'd[5] me sweetly in his plaid,
And he ca'd me his dearie.

'Will ye gang down the water side,
And see the waves sae sweetly glide
Beneath the hazels spreading wide?
The moon it shines fu' clearly.'

'I was bred up at nae sic school,
My shepherd lad, to play the fool,
And a' the day to sit in dool,
And naebody to see me.'

'Ye sall get gowns and ribbons meet,
Cauf-leather shoon upon your feet,
And in my arms ye'se lie and sleep,
And ye sall be my dearie.'

'If ye'll but stand to what ye've said,
I'se gang wi' you, my shepherd lad,
And ye may row me in your plaid,
And I sall be your dearie.'

'While waters wimple to the sea,
While day blinks in the lift[6] sae hie,
Till clay-cauld death sall blin' my e'e,
Ye aye sall be my dearie!'

[1] Ewes. [2] Knolls. [3] Little stream. [4] Rolls. [5] Rolled. [6] Sky.

LADY ANNE LINDSAY

[*1750-1825*]

328 Auld Robin Gray

When the sheep are in the fauld,[1] and the kye[2] at hame,
And a' the warld to rest are gane,
The waes o' my heart fa' in showers frae my e'e,
While my gudeman lies sound by me.

Young Jamie lo'ed me weel, and sought me for his bride;
But saving a croun he had naething else beside:
To make the croun a pund, young Jamie gaed to sea;
And the croun and the pund were baith for me.

He hadna been awa' a week but only twa,
When my father brak his arm, and the cow was stown[3]
awa;
My mother she fell sick, and my Jamie at the sea—
And auld Robin Gray came a-courtin' me.

My father couldna work, and my mother couldna spin;
I toil'd day and night, but their bread I couldna win;
Auld Rob maintain'd them baith, and wi' tears in his e'e
Said, Jennie, for their sakes, O, marry me!

My heart it said nay; I look'd for Jamie back;
But the wind it blew high, and the ship it was a wrack;
His ship it was a wrack—why didna Jamie dee?
Or why do I live to cry, Wae's me?

My father urgit sair: my mother didna speak;
But she look'd in my face till my heart was like to break:
They gi'ed him my hand, but my heart was at the sea;
Sae auld Robin Gray he was gudeman to me.

I hadna been a wife a week but only four,
When mournfu' as I sat on the stane at the door,

[1] Fold. [2] Cows. [3] Stolen.

I saw my Jamie's wraith,[4] for I couldna think it he
Till he said, I'm come hame to marry thee.

O sair, sair did we greet,[5] and muckle[6] did we say;
We took but ae kiss, and I bad him gang away;
I wish that I were dead, but I'm no like to dee;
And why was I born to say, Wae's me!

I gang like a ghaist, and I carena to spin;
I daurna think on Jamie, for that wad be a sin;
But I'll do my best a gude wife aye to be,
For auld Robin Gray he is kind unto me.

THOMAS CHATTERTON

[*1752-1770*]

329 SONG FROM ÆLLA

O SING unto my roundelay,
O drop the briny tear with me;
Dance no more at holyday,
Like a running river be:
My love is dead,
Gone to his death-bed
All under the willow-tree.

Black his cryne[1] as the winter night,
White his rode[2] as the summer snow,
Red his face as the morning light,
Cold he lies in the grave below:
My love is dead,
Gone to his death-bed
All under the willow-tree.

Sweet his tongue as the throstle's note
Quick in dance as thought can be,
Deft his tabor, cudgel stout;

[4] Ghost. [5] Weep. [6] Much. [1] Hair. [2] Complexion.

O he lies by the willow-tree!
My love is dead,
Gone to his death-bed
All under the willow-tree.

Hark! the raven flaps his wing
In the brier'd dell below;
Hark! the death-owl loud doth sing
To the nightmares, as they go:
My love is dead,
Gone to his death-bed
All under the willow-tree.

See! the white moon shines on high;
Whiter is my true-love's shroud:
Whiter than the morning sky,
Whiter than the evening cloud:
My love is dead,
Gone to his death-bed
All under the willow-tree.

Here upon my true-love's grave
Shall the barren flowers be laid;
Not one holy saint to save
All the coldness of a maid:
My love is dead,
Gone to his death-bed
All under the willow-tree.

With my hands I'll dent[3] the briers
Round his holy corse to gre:[4]
Ouph[5] and fairy, light your fires,
Here my body still shall be:
My love is dead,
Gone to his death-bed
All under the willow-tree.

[3] Fasten. [4] Grow. [5] Elf.

CAROLINA OLIPHANT, LADY NAIRNE

[*1766-1845*]

330 ### THE LAND O' THE LEAL

I'M wearing awa', Jean,
Like snaw when its thaw, Jean,
I'm wearing awa'
To the land o' the leal.[1]
There's nae sorrow there, Jean,
There's neither cauld nor care, Jean,
The day is aye fair
In the land o' the leal.

Ye were aye leal and true, Jean,
Your task's ended noo, Jean,
And I'll welcome you
To the land o' the leal.
Our bonnie bairn's there, Jean,
She was baith guid and fair, Jean;
O we grudged her right sair
To the land o' the leal!

Then dry that tearfu' e'e, Jean,
My soul langs to be free, Jean,
And angels wait on me
To the land o' the leal.
Now fare ye weel, my ain Jean,
This warld's care is vain, Jean;
We'll meet and aye be fain
In the land o' the leal.

331 ### HE'S OWER THE HILLS THAT I LO'E WEEL

HE'S ower the hills that I lo'e weel,
He's ower the hills we daurna name;
He's ower the hills ayont Dunblane,
Wha soon will get his welcome hame.

[1] Loyal.

My faither's gane to fecht for him,
My brithers winna bide at hame;
My mither greets and prays for them,
And, 'deed, she thinks they're no to blame.

The Whigs may scoff, the Whigs may jeer,
But ah! that love maun be sincere
Which still keeps true whate'er betide,
And for his sake leaves a' beside.

His right these hills, his right these plains;
O'er Hieland hearts secure he reigns;
What lads e'er did our lads will do;
Were I a laddie I'd follow him too.

Sae noble a look, sae princely an air,
Sae gallant and bold, sae young and sae fair;
O did ye but see him ye'd do as we've done;
Hear him but once, to his standard you'll run.

He's ower the hills that I lo'e weel;
He's ower the hills we daurna name;
He's ower the hills ayont Dunblane,
Wha soon will get his welcome hame.

332

The Auld House

Oh, the auld house, the auld house!
What though the rooms were wee?
Oh, kind hearts were dwelling there,
And bairnies fu' o' glee!
The wild rose and the jessamine
Still hang upon the wa':
How mony cherished memories
Do they, sweet flowers, reca'!

Oh, the auld laird, the auld laird,
Sae canty, kind, and crouse!
How mony did he welcome to
His ain wee dear auld house!

And the leddy, too, sae genty,
  That sheltered Scotland's heir,
And clipt a lock wi' her ain hand
  Frae his lang yellow hair.

The mavis still doth sweetly sing,
  The blue-bells sweetly blaw;
The bonnie Earn's clear winding still
  But the auld house is awa'.
The auld house, the auld house!
  Deserted though ye be,
There ne'er can be a new house
  Will seem sae fair to me.

Still flourishing the auld pear tree,
  The bairnies liked to see;
And oh, how often they did speir
  When ripe they a' wad be!
The voices sweet, the wee bit feet
  Aye rinnin' here and there;
The merry shout—oh! whiles we greet
  To think we'll hear nae mair.

For they are a' wide scattered now,
  Some to the Indies gane,
And ane, alas! to her lang hame;
  Not here will meet again.
The kirkyaird! the kirkyaird!
  Wi' flowers o' every hue,
Sheltered by the holly's shade,
  And the dark sombre yew.

The setting sun, the setting sun,
  How glorious it gaed doun!
The cloudy splendour raised our hearts
  To cloudless skies abune.
The auld dial, the auld dial,
  It tauld how time did pass;
The wintry winds ha'e dung it doun,
  Now hid 'mang weeds and grass.

333 THE LAIRD O' COCKPEN

THE Laird o' Cockpen, he's proud and he's great
His mind is ta'en up wi' things o' the State:
He wanted a wife, his braw house to keep;
But favour wi' wooin' was fashious[1] to seek.

Down by the dyke[2]-side a lady did dwell;
At his table-head he thought she'd look well—
McClish's ae[3] daughter o' Clavers-ha' Lee,
A penniless lass wi' a lang pedigree.

His wig was weel pouther'd[4] and as gude as new;
His waistcoat was white, his coat it was blue;
He put on a ring, a sword, and cocked hat,—
And wha could refuse the Laird wi' a' that!

He took the grey mare, and rade cannily,[5]
And rapped at the yett[6] o' Clavers-ha' Lee:
'Gae tell Mistress Jean to come speedily ben,—
She's wanted to speak to the Laird o' Cockpen.'

Mistress Jean was makin' the elder-flower wine:
'And what brings the Laird at sic a like time?'
She put aff her apron and on her silk goun,
Her mutch[7] wi' red ribbons, and gaed awa doun.

And when she cam' ben he bowed fu' low;
And what was his errand he soon let her know.
Amazed was the Laird when the lady said 'Na';—
And wi' a laigh[8] curtsey she turn'd awa'.

Dumfounder'd was he; but nae sigh did he gi'e,
He mounted his mare, and rade cannily;
And aften he thought as he gaed through the glen,
'She's daft[9] to refuse the Laird o' Cockpen!'

[1] Troublesome. [2] Stone wall. [3] One. [4] Powdered. [5] Cautiously. [6] Gate. [7] Cap. [8] Low. [9] Mad.

And now that the Laird his exit had made,
Mistress Jean she reflected on what she had said;
'Oh, for ane I'll get better its waur[10] I'll get ten,
I was daft to refuse the Laird o' Cockpen.'

Next time that the Laird and the lady were seen,
They were gaun arm-in-arm to the kirk on the green;
Now she sits in the ha' like a weel-tappit hen,
But as yet there's nae chickens appeared at Cockpen.

334 The Rowan Tree

O ROWAN[1] tree, O rowan tree! thou'lt aye be dear to me!
Intwined thou art wi' mony ties o' hame and infancy.
Thy leaves were aye the first o' spring, thy flowers the simmer's pride;
There wasna sic[2] a bonnie tree in a' the country side.
O rowan tree!

How fair wert thou in simmer time, wi' a' thy clusters white,
How rich and gay thy autumn dress, wi' berries red and bright!
On thy fair stem were mony names which now nae mair I see,
But they're engraven on my heart—forgot they ne'er can be!
O rowan tree!

We sat aneath thy spreading shade, the bairnies round thee ran,
They pu'd thy bonnie berries red, and necklaces they strang.
My mother! O I see her still, she smiled our sports to see,
Wi' little Jeanie on her lap, and Jamie at her knee.
O rowan tree!

O there arose my father's prayer, in holy evening's calm;
How sweet was then my mother's voice in the Martyr's psalm!

[10] Worse. [1] Mountain ash. [2] Such.

Now a' are gane! we meet na mair aneath the rowan tree!
But hallowed thoughts around thee twine o' hame and infancy.
O rowan tree!

335 Wha'll Be King But Charlie?

The news frae Moidart cam' yestreen,[1]
Will soon gar mony ferlie;[2]
For ships o' war hae just come in,
And landit Royal Charlie.

Come thro' the heather, around him gather,
Ye're a' the welcomer early;
Around him cling wi' a' your kin;
For wha'll be king but Charlie?
Come thro' the heather, around him gather,
Come Ronald, come Donald, come a' thegither[3]
And crown your rightfu', lawfu' king!
For wha'll be king but Charlie?

The Hieland clans, wi' sword in hand,
Frae John o' Groats to Airlie,
Hae to a man declared to stand
Or fa' wi' Royal Charlie.

The Lowlands a', baith great an sma',
Wi' mony a lord and laird, hae
Declar'd for Scotia's king an' law,
An' speir[4] ye wha but Charlie.

There's ne'er a lass in a' the lan,
But vows baith late and early,
She'll ne'er to man gie heart or han',
Wha wadna fecht for Charlie.

Then here's a health to Charlie's cause,
And be't complete an' early;
His very name our heart's blood warms;
To arms for Royal Charlie!

[1] Last night. [2] Wonder. [3] Together. [4] Ask.

Come thro' the heather, around him gather,
  Ye're a' the welcomer early;
Around him cling wi' a' your kin;
  For wha'll be king but Charlie?
Come thro' the heather, around him gather,
Come Ronald, come Donald, come a' thegither,
And crown your rightfu', lawfu' king!
  For wha'll be king but Charlie?

336

Charlie Is My Darling

'Twas on a Monday morning,
  Right early in the year,
When Charlie came to our town,
  The young Chevalier.

O Charlie is my darling,
My darling, my darling—
O Charlie is my darling,
The young Chevalier!

As he cam' marching up the street,
  The pipes played loud and clear,
And a' the folk cam' running out
  To meet the Chevalier.
    O Charlie is my darling, etc.

Wi' Hieland bonnets on their heads,
  And claymores bright and clear,
They cam' to fight for Scotland's right,
  And the young Chevalier.
    O Charlie is my darling, etc.

They've left their bonnie Hieland hills,
  Their wives and bairnies dear,
To draw the sword for Scotland's lord,
  The young Chevalier.
    O Charlie is my darling, etc.

O, there were mony beating hearts,
And mony a hope and fear,
And mony were the prayers put up
For the young Chevalier.

O Charlie is my darling,
My darling, my darling—
O Charlie is my darling,
The young Chevalier!

ALEXANDER ROSS

[*1699-1784*]

337 Wooed and Married and A'

The bride cam' out o' the byre,
And O, as she dighted[1] her cheeks,
'Sirs, I'm to be married the-night,
And ha'e neither blankets nor sheets—
Ha'e neither blankets nor sheets,
Nor scarce a coverlet too;
The bride that has a' thing to borrow,
Has e'en right meikle[2] ado!'

Wooed and married and a'!
Married and wooed and a'!
And was she na very weel aff
That was wooed and married and a'?

Out spake the bride's father
As he cam' in frae the pleugh,
'O haud your tongue, my dochter,
And ye'se[3] get gear[4] eneugh.
The stirk[5] stands i' the tether,
And our braw bawsint yade[6]
Will carry hame your corn:—
What wad ye be at, ye jade?'

[1] Wiped. [2] Much. [3] You shall. [4] Property. [5] Steer.
[6] Fine white-faced mare.

Out spake the bride's mither:
 'What, deil, needs a' this pride?
I hadna a plack[7] in my pouch
 That night I was a bride.
My gown was linsey-wolsey,
 And ne'er a sark[8] ava;
And ye ha'e ribbons and buskin's[9]
 Mae[10] than ane or twa.'

Out spake the bride's brither
 As he cam' in wi' the kye:[11]
'Puir Willie wad ne'er ha'e ta'en ye
 Had he kent ye as weel as I.
For ye're baith proud and saucy,
 And no for a puir man's wife;
Gin[12] I canna get a better
 I'se ne'er tak' ane i' my life!'

Out spake the bride's sister
 As she cam' in frae the byre;
'Oh, gin I were but married,
 It's a' that I desire!
But we puir folk maun live,
 And do the best we can;
I dinna ken what I should want
 If I could get but a man!'

JOHN SKINNER

[*1721-1807*]

338 TULLOCHGORUM

COME, gi'es sang, Montgom'rie cried,
And lay your disputes a' aside;
What signifies for folks to chide
 For what was done before them?
Let Whig and Tory a' agree,
Whig and Tory, Whig and Tory,

[7] Four-pence Scots. [8] Chemise. [9] Ornaments. [10] More. [11] Cows. [12] If.

Whig and Tory a' agree
  To drop their whigmigmorum;
Let Whig and Tory a' agree
To spend this night in mirth and glee,
And cheerfu' sing, alang wi' me,
  The reel o' Tullochgorum.

O Tullochgorum's my delight;
It gars us a' in ane unite;
And ony sumph that keeps up spite,
  In conscience I abhor him.
Blithe and merry we'll be a',
Blithe and merry, blithe and merry,
Blithe and merry we'll be a'
  And mak' a cheerfu' quorum.
For blithe and merry we'll be a'
As lang as we ha'e breath to draw,
And dance, till we be like to fa',
  The reel o' Tullochgorum.

What needs there be sae great a fraise
Wi' dringin', dull Italian lays?
I wadna gi'e our ain strathspeys
  For half a hunder score o' them.
They're dowf and dowie at the best,
Dowf and dowie, dowf and dowie,
Dowf and dowie at the best,
  Wi' a' their variorum.
They're dowf and dowie at the best,
Their *allegros* and a' the rest;
They canna please a Scottish taste
  Compared wi' Tullochgorum.

Let worldly worms their minds oppress
Wi' fears o' want and double cess,
And sullen sots themsel's distress
  Wi' keeping up decorum.
Shall we sae sour and sulky sit?
Sour and sulky, sour and sulky,
Sour and sulky shall we sit,

Like auld philosophorum?
Shall we sae sour and sulky sit,
Wi' neither sense, nor mirth, nor wit,
Nor ever rise to shake a fit
To the reel o' Tullochgorum?

May choicest blessings aye attend
Each honest, open-hearted friend,
And calm and quiet be his end,
And a' that's gude watch o'er him!
May peace and plenty be his lot,
Peace and plenty, peace and plenty,
Peace and plenty be his lot,
And dainties a great store o' them!
May peace and plenty be his lot,
Unstained by ony vicious spot,
And may he never want a groat,
That's fond o' Tullochgorum!

But for the discontented fool,
Wha wants to be oppression's tool,
May envy gnaw his rotten soul,
And discontent devour him!
May dule and sorrow be his chance,
Dule and sorrow, dule and sorrow,
Dule and sorrow be his chance,
And nane say 'Wae's me for him!'
May dule and sorrow be his chance,
And a' the ills that come frae France,
Whae'er he be that winna dance
The reel o' Tullochgorum!

MICHAEL BRUCE

[1746-1767]

339

To the Cuckoo

Hail! beauteous Stranger of the wood!
Attendant on the Spring!
Now heav'n repairs thy rural seat,
And woods thy welcome sing.

Soon as the daisy decks the green,
  Thy certain voice we hear:
Hast thou a star to guide thy path,
  Or mark the rolling year?

Delightful visitant! with thee
  I hail the time of flow'rs,
When heav'n is fill'd with music sweet
  Of birds among the bow'rs.

The schoolboy wand'ring in the wood
  To pull the flow'rs so gay,
Starts, thy curious voice to hear,
  And imitates thy lay.

Soon as the pea puts on the bloom,
  Thou fly'st thy vocal vale,
An annual guest, in other lands,
  Another Spring to hail.

Sweet bird! thy bow'r is ever green,
  Thy sky is ever clear;
Thou hast no sorrow in thy song,
  No winter in thy year!

Alas! sweet bird! not so my fate,
  Dark scowling skies I see
Fast gathering round, and fraught with woe
  And wintry years to me.

O could I fly, I'd fly with thee:
  We'd make, with social wing,
Our annual visit o'er the globe,
  Companions of the Spring.

GEORGE HALKET

[*d. 1756(?)*]

340

Logie o' Buchan

O Logie o' Buchan, O Logie the laird,
They ha'e ta'en awa' Jamie, that delved in the yaird,
Wha played on the pipe and the viol sae sma',
They ha'e ta'en awa' Jamie, the flower o' them a'!

He said, 'Think na lang, lassie, though I gang awa'!'
He said, 'Think na lang, lassie, though I gang awa'!'
For simmer is coming, cauld winter's awa',
And I'll come and see thee in spite o' them a'!'

Though Sandy has ousen, has gear, and has kye,
A house and a hadden, and siller forbye;
Yet I'd tak' mine ain lad, wi' his staff in his hand,
Before I'd ha'e him, wi' the houses and land.

My daddy looks sulky, my minnie looks sour;
They frown upon Jamie because he is poor;
Though I lo'e them as weel as a dochter should do,
They're nae hauf sae dear to me, Jamie, as you.

I sit on my creepie, I spin at my wheel,
And think on the laddie that lo'ed me sae weel:
He had but a sixpence, he brak' it in twa,
And gi'ed me the hauf o't when he gaed awa'.

Then haste ye back, Jamie, and bide na awa'!
Then haste ye back, Jamie, and bide na awa'!
The simmer is coming, cauld winter's awa',
And ye'll come and see me in spite o' them a'.

WILLIAM HAMILTON OF BANGOUR

[*1704-1754*]

341

The Braes of Yarrow

'Busk ye, busk ye, my bonnie, bonnie bride!
Busk ye, busk ye, my winsome marrow!
Busk ye, busk ye, my bonnie, bonnie bride!
And think nae mair on the braes of Yarrow!'

'Where got ye that bonnie, bonnie bride?
Where got ye that winsome marrow?'
'I got her where I durst not well be seen—
Pu'ing the birks on the braes of Yarrow.'

'Weep not, weep not, my bonnie, bonnie bride!
Weep not, weep not, my winsome marrow!
Nor let thy heart lament to leave
Pu'ing the birks on the braes of Yarrow.'

'Why does she weep, thy bonnie, bonnie bride?
Why does she weep, thy winsome marrow?
And why dare ye nae mair weel be seen
Pu'ing the birks on the braes of Yarrow?'

'Lang maun she weep, lang maun she, maun she weep,
Lang maun she weep with dule and sorrow;
And lang maun I nae weel be seen
Pu'ing the birks on the braes of Yarrow.

'For she has tint her lover, lover dear—
Her lover dear, the cause of sorrow;
And I have slain the comeliest swain
That ever pu'ed birks on the braes of Yarrow.

'Why runs thy stream O Yarrow, Yarrow, reid?
Why on thy braes is heard the voice of sorrow?
And why yon melancholious weeds
Hung on the bonnie birks of Yarrow.

'What's yonder floats on the rueful, rueful flood?
What's yonder floats? O dule and sorrow!
'Tis he, the comely swain I slew
Upon the duleful braes of Yarrow.

'Wash, O wash his wounds, his wounds in tears,
His wounds in tears of dule and sorrow;
And wrap his limbs in mourning weeds,
And lay him on the braes of Yarrow.

'Then build, then build, ye sisters, sisters sad,
Ye sisters sad, his tomb with sorrow:
And weep around, in woeful wise,
His hapless fate on the braes of Yarrow.

'Curse ye, curse ye, his useless, useless shield,
My arm that wrought the deed of sorrow,
The fatal spear that pierced his breast—
His comely breast on the braes of Yarrow!

'Did I not warn thee not to, not to love,
And warn from fight? But, to my sorrow,
Too rashly bold, a stronger arm
Thou met'st, and fell on the braes of Yarrow.'

'Sweet smells the birk, green grows, green grows the grass,
Yellow on Yarrow's braes the gowan;
Fair hangs the apple frae the rock,
Sweet the wave of Yarrow flowing!'

'Flows Yarrow sweet? As sweet, as sweet flows Tweed;
As green its grass, its gowan as yellow;
As sweet smells on its braes the birk,
The apple from its rocks as mellow.

'Fair was thy love, fair, fair indeed thy love;
In flowery bands thou didst him fetter:
Though he was fair, and well beloved again
Than me, he never loved thee better.

'Busk ye then, busk, my bonnie, bonnie bride!
  Busk, ye, busk ye, my winsome marrow!
Busk ye, and lo'e me on the banks of Tweed,
  And think nae mair on the braes of Yarrow!'

'How can I busk, a bonnie, bonnie bride?
  How can I busk, a winsome marrow?
How lo'e him on the banks of Tweed
  That slew my love on the braes of Yarrow!

'O Yarrow fields, may never, never rain
  Nor dew thy tender blossoms cover!
For there was basely slain my love—
  My love as he had not been a lover.

'The boy put on his robes, his robes of green,
  His purple vest—'twas my ain sewing:
Ah, wretched me! I little, little knew
  He was in these to meet his ruin!

'The boy took out his milk-white, milk-white steed,
  Unheedful of my dule and sorrow;
But ere the to-fall of the night
  He lay a corpse on the braes of Yarrow.

'Much I rejoiced, that woeful, woeful day;
  I sang, my voice the woods returning;
But lang ere night the spear was flown
  That slew my love and left me mourning.

'What can my barbarous, barbarous father do,
  But with his cruel rage pursue me?
My lover's blood is on thy spear;
  How canst thou, barbarous man, then woo me?

'My happy sisters may be, may be proud—
  With cruel and ungentle scoffin'
May bid me seek, on Yarrow's braes,
  My lover nailed in his coffin.

'My brother Douglas may upbraid,
And strive with threat'ning words to move me:
My lover's blood is on thy spear,
How canst thou ever bid me love thee?

'Yes, yes, prepare the bed, the bed of love!
With bridal sheets my body cover!
Unbar, ye bridal maids, the door;
Let in the expected husband lover!

'But who the expected husband, husband is?
His hands, methinks, are bathed in slaughter.
Ah me! what ghastly spectre's yon,
Comes in his pale shroud bleeding after?

'Pale as he is, here lay him, lay him down;
O lay his cold head on my pillow:
Take aff, take aff these bridal weeds,
And crown my careful head with willow.

'Pale though thou art, yet best, yet best beloved!
Oh! could my warmth to life restore thee,
Ye'd lie all night between my breasts!
No youth lay ever there before thee.

'Pale, pale indeed! O lovely, lovely youth!
Forgive, forgive so foul a slaughter;
And lie all night between my breasts!
No youth shall ever lie there after.'

'Return, return, O mournful, mournful bride!
Return, and dry thy useless sorrow!
Thy lover heeds nought of thy sighs—
He lies a corpse on the braes of Yarrow."

HECTOR MacNEIL

[*1746-1818*]

342 I Lo'ed Ne'er a Laddie but Ane

I lo'ed ne'er a laddie but ane,
He lo'es na a lassie but me;
He's willing to mak' me his ain,
And his ain I am willing to be.
He coft[1] me a rokelay[2] o' blue,
And a pair o' mittens o' green;
He vowed that he'd ever be true,
And I plighted my troth yestreen.

Let ithers brag weel o' their gear,[3]
Their land and their lordly degree;
I carena for aught but my dear,
For he's ilka thing lordly to me.
His words are sae sugared, sae sweet,
His sense drives ilk[4] fear far awa';
I listen, puir fool, and I greet,
Yet how sweet are the tears as they fa'!

'Dear lassie,' he cries wi' a jeer,
'Ne'er heed what the auld anes will say:
Though we've little to brag o', ne'er fear,
What's gowd to a heart that is wae?
Our laird has baith honours and wealth,
Yet see how he's dwining[5] wi' care;
Now we, though we've naething but health,
Are cantie[6] and leal[7] evermair.

'O Menie, the heart that is true
Has something mair costly than gear;
Ilk e'en it has naething to rue,
Ilk morn it has naething to fear.

[1] Bought. [2] A short cloak. [3] Possessions. [4] Each. [5] Pining. [6] Cheerful. [7] Loyal.

Ye warldlings, gae hoard up your store,
  And tremble for fear aught ye tyne;[8]
Guard your treasures wi' lock, bar, and door,
  While here in my arms I lock mine!'

He ends wi' a kiss and a smile—
  Wae's me, can I tak' it amiss?
My laddie's unpractised in guile,
  He's free aye to daut[9] and to kiss.
Ye lasses wha' lo'e to torment
  Your wooers wi' fause scorn and strife,
Play your pranks; I ha'e gi'en my consent,
  And this night I am Jamie's for life.

343 Come Under My Plaidie

'Come under my plaidie, the night's gaun to fa';
Come in frae the cauld blast, the drift, and the snaw:
Come under my plaidie, and sit down beside me,
There's room in't, dear lassie, believe me, for twa.
Come under my plaidie, and sit down beside me,
I'll hap[1] ye frae every cauld blast that can blaw:
Oh, come under my plaidie, and sit down beside me!
There's room in't, dear lassie, believe me, for twa.'

'Gae 'wa wi' your plaidie, auld Donald, gae 'wa!
I fearna the cauld blast, the drift, nor the snaw;
Gae 'wa wi' your plaidie; I'll no sit beside ye,
Ye may be a gutcher,[2] auld Donald, gae 'wa.
I'm gaun to meet Johnnie—he's young and he's bonnie;
He's been at Meg's bridal, fu' trig[3] and fu' braw:[4]
Oh, nane dances sae lightly, sae gracefu', sae tightly;
His cheek's like the new rose, his brow's like the snaw.'

'Dear Marion, let that flee stick fast to the wa';
Your Jock's but a gowk,[5] and has naething ava;
The hale[6] o' his pack he has now on his back:
He's thretty, and I am but threescore and twa.

[8] Loss. [9] Pet. [1] Wrap. [2] Grandfather. [3] Neat. [4] Fine. [5] Fool. [6] Whole.

Be frank now and kindly: I'll busk[7] ye aye finely,
To kirk or to market there'll few gang sae braw;
A bien[8] house to bide in, a chaise for to ride in,
And flunkies to 'tend ye as aft as ye ca'.'

'My father's aye tauld me, my mither an a',
Ye'd mak' a gude husband, and keep me aye braw:
It's true I lo'e Johnnie—he's gude and he's bonnie,
But, wae's me! ye ken he has naething ava.
I ha'e little tocher:[9] you've made a good offer:
I'm now mair than twenty—my time is but sma';
Sae, gi'e me your plaidie, I'll creep in beside ye,
I thocht ye'd been aulder than threescore and twa.'

She crap in ayont him, aside the stane wa'.
Where Johnnie was list'nin, and heard her tell a';
The day was appointed: his proud heart it dunted,[10]
And strack 'gainst his side as if bursting in twa.
He wandered hame weary: the night it was dreary;
And, thowless,[11] he tint[12] his gate 'mang the deep snaw:
The owlet was screamin'; while Johnnie cried, 'Women
Wad marry Auld Nick if he'd keep them aye braw!'

SIR WILLIAM JONES

[*1746-1794*]

344

An Ode

In Imitation of Alcaeus

What constitutes a State?
Not high-raised battlement or laboured mound,
Thick wall or moated gate,
Not cities proud with spires and turrets crowned;
Not bays and broad-armed ports,
Where, laughing at the storm, rich navies ride;
Not starred and spangled courts,

[7] Dress. [8] Comfortable. [9] Dowry. [10] Throbbed violently.
[11] Enfeebled. [12] Lost.

Where low-browed baseness wafts perfume to pride.
No:—men, high-minded men,
With powers as far above dull brutes endued
In forest, brake, or den,
As beasts excel cold rocks and brambles rude;
Men, who their duties know,
But know their rights, and, knowing, dare maintain,
Prevent the long-aimed blow,
And crush the tyrant while they rend the chain:
These constitute a State,
And sovereign Law, that State's collected will,
O'er thrones and globes elate,
Sits Empress, crowning good, repressing ill.
Smit by her sacred frown,
The fiend, Dissension, like a vapour sinks,
And e'en the all-dazzling crown
Hides her faint rays, and at her bidding shrinks.
Such was this heaven-loved isle,
Than Lesbos fairer and the Cretan shore!
No more shall Freedom smile?
Shall Britons languish, and be men no more?
Since all must life resign,
Those sweet rewards, which decorate the brave,
'Tis folly to decline,
And steal inglorious to the silent grave.

345 On Parent Knees a Naked New-born Child

On parent knees, a naked new-born child,
Weeping thou sat'st while all around thee smiled:
So live, that sinking to thy life's last sleep,
Calm thou may'st smile, whilst all around thee weep.

SUSANNA BLAMIRE

[*1747-1794*]

346 And Ye Shall Walk in Silk Attire

And ye shall walk in silk attire,
And siller[1] hae to spare,

[1] Money.

Gin ye'll consent to be his bride,
Nor think o' Donald mair.
Oh, wha wad buy a silken goun
Wi' a puir broken heart?
Or what's to me a siller croun,
Gin frae my love I part?

The mind wha's every wish is pure
Far dearer is to me;
And ere I'm forced to break my faith,
I'll lay me doun and dee:
For I ha'e pledged my virgin troth
Brave Donald's fate to share;
And he has gi'en to me his heart,
Wi' a' its virtues rare.

His gentle manners wan my heart,
He gratefu' took the gift;
Could I but think to tak' it back,
It wad be waur[2] than theft.
For langest life can ne'er repay
The love he bears to me;
And ere I'm forced to break my troth
I'll lay me doun and dee.

ANNE HUNTER

[*1742-1821*]

347 My Mother Bids Me Bind My Hair

My mother bids me bind my hair
With bands of rosy hue,
Tie up my sleeves with ribbons rare,
And lace my bodice blue.

'For why,' she cries, 'sit still and weep,
While others dance and play?'
Alas! I scarce can go or creep
While Lubin is away.

[2] Worse.

'Tis sad to think the days are gone
  When those we love were near;
I sit upon this mossy stone
  And sigh when none can hear.

And while I spin my flaxen thread,
  And sing my simple lay,
The village seems asleep or dead,
  Now Lubin is away.

JOHN DUNLOP

[*1755-1820*]

348 THE YEAR THAT'S AWA'

HERE'S to the year that's awa'!
  We will drink it in strong and in sma';
And here's to ilk bonnie young lassie we lo'ed,
  While swift flew the year that's awa'
      And here's to ilk, etc.

Here's to the sodger who bled,
  And the sailor who bravely did fa';
Their fame is alive though their spirits are fled
  On the wings o' the year that's awa'.
      Their fame is alive, etc.

Here's to the friends we can trust
  When storms of adversity blaw;
May they live in our song and be nearest our hearts,
  Nor depart like the year that's awa'.
      May they live, etc.

SAMUEL ROGERS

[*1763-1855*]

349

A Wish

Mine be a cot beside the hill;
A bee-hive's hum shall soothe my ear;
A willowy brook, that turns a mill,
With many a fall shall linger near.

The swallow, oft, beneath my thatch,
Shall twitter from her clay-built nest;
Oft shall the pilgrim lift the latch,
And share my meal, a welcome guest.

Around my ivy'd porch shall spring
Each fragrant flower that drinks the dew;
And Lucy, at her wheel, shall sing
In russet gown and apron blue.

The village-church among the trees,
Where first our marriage-vows were given,
With merry peals shall swell the breeze,
And point with taper spire to heaven.

350

The Sleeping Beauty

Sleep on, and dream of Heaven awhile—
Tho' shut so close thy laughing eyes,
Thy rosy lips still wear a smile
And move, and breathe delicious sighs!

Ah, now soft blushes tinge her cheeks
And mantle o'er her neck of snow:
Ah, now she murmurs, now she speaks
What most I wish—and fear to know!

She starts, she trembles, and she weeps!
Her fair hands folded on her breast:
—And now, how like a saint she sleeps!
A seraph in the realms of rest!

Sleep on secure! Above controul
Thy thoughts belong to Heaven and thee:
And may the secret of thy soul
Remain within its sanctuary!

WILLIAM BLAKE

[*1757-1827*]

351

The Tiger

Tiger, tiger, burning bright
In the forests of the night,
What immortal hand or eye
Could frame thy fearful symmetry?

In what distant deeps or skies
Burnt the fire of thine eyes?
On what wings dare he aspire?
What the hand dare seize the fire?

And what shoulder and what art
Could twist the sinews of thy heart?
And, when thy heart began to beat,
What dread hand and what dread feet?

What the hammer? What the chain?
In what furnace was thy brain?
What the anvil? What dread grasp
Dare its deadly terrors clasp?

When the stars threw down their spears,
And water'd heaven with their tears,
Did He smile His work to see?
Did He who made the lamb make thee?

Tiger, tiger, burning bright
In the forests of the night,
What immortal hand or eye
Dare frame thy fearful symmetry?

352

Ah! Sun-Flower

Ah, sun-flower! weary of time,
Who countest the steps of the Sun;
Seeking after that sweet golden clime,
Where the traveller's journey is done;

Where the Youth pined away with desire,
And the pale Virgin shrouded in snow,
Arise from their graves, and aspire
Where my sun-flower wishes to go.

353

To Spring

O thou with dewy locks, who lookest down
Through the clear windows of the morning, turn
Thine angel eyes upon our western isle,
Which in full choir hails thy approach, O Spring!

The hills tell one another, and the listening
Valleys hear; all our longing eyes are turn'd
Up to thy bright pavilions: issue forth
And let thy holy feet visit our clime!

Come o'er the eastern hills, and let our winds
Kiss thy perfumèd garments; let us taste
Thy morn and evening breath; scatter thy pearls
Upon our lovesick land that mourns for thee.

O deck her forth with thy fair fingers; pour
Thy soft kisses on her bosom; and put
Thy golden crown upon her languish'd head,
Whose modest tresses are bound up for thee.

354

Reeds of Innocence

Piping down the valleys wild,
Piping songs of pleasant glee,
On a cloud I saw a child,
And he laughing said to me:

'Pipe a song about a Lamb!'
So I piped with merry cheer.
'Piper, pipe that song again;'
So I piped: he wept to hear.

'Drop thy pipe, thy happy pipe;
Sing thy songs of happy cheer!'
So I sung the same again,
While he wept with joy to hear.

'Piper, sit thee down and write
In a book that all may read.'
So he vanish'd from my sight;
And I pluck'd a hollow reed,

And I made a rural pen,
And I stain'd the water clear,
And I wrote my happy songs
Every child may joy to hear.

355

Night

The sun descending in the west,
The evening star does shine;
The birds are silent in their nest,
And I must seek for mine.
The moon, like a flower
In heaven's high bower,
With silent delight
Sits and smiles on the night.

Farewell, green fields and happy grove,
  Where flocks have took delight:
Where lambs have nibbled, silent move
  The feet of angels bright;
    Unseen they pour blessing
    And joy without ceasing
    On each bud and blossom,
    On each sleeping bosom.

They look in every thoughtless nest
  Where birds are cover'd warm;
They visit caves of every beast,
  To keep them all from harm:
    If they see any weeping
    That should have been sleeping,
    They pour sleep on their head,
    And sit down by their bed.

When wolves and tigers howl for prey,
  They pitying stand and weep,
Seeking to drive their thirst away
  And keep them from the sheep.
    But, if they rush dreadful,
    The angels, most heedful,
    Receive each mild spirit,
    New worlds to inherit.

And there the lion's ruddy eyes
  Shall flow with tears of gold:
And pitying the tender cries,
  And walking round the fold:
    Saying, 'Wrath by His meekness,
    And, by His health, sickness,
    Are driven away
    From our immortal day.

'And now beside thee, bleating lamb,
  I can lie down and sleep,
Or think on Him who bore thy name,
  Graze after thee, and weep.

For, wash'd in life's river,
My bright mane for ever
Shall shine like the gold
As I guard o'er the fold.'

356

Auguries of Innocence

To see a world in a grain of sand,
And a heaven in a wild flower,
Hold infinity in the palm of your hand,
And eternity in an hour.

A robin redbreast in a cage
Puts all heaven in a rage.
A dove-house fill'd with doves and pigeons
Shudders hell thro' all its regions.
A dog starv'd at his master's gate
Predicts the ruin of the state.
A horse misused upon the road
Calls to heaven for human blood.
Each outcry of the hunted hare
A fibre from the brain does tear.
A skylark wounded in the wing,
A cherubim does cease to sing.
The game-cock clipt and arm'd for fight
Does the rising sun affright.

Every wolf's and lion's howl
Raises from hell a human soul.
The wild deer, wand'ring here and there,
Keeps the human soul from care.
The lamb misus'd breeds public strife,
And yet forgives the butcher's knife.
The bat that flits at close of eve
Has left the brain that won't believe.
The owl that calls upon the night
Speaks the unbeliever's fright.
He who shall hurt the little wren
Shall never be belov'd by men.

He who the ox to wrath has mov'd
Shall never be by woman lov'd.
The wanton boy that kills the fly
Shall feel the spider's enmity.
He who torments the chafer's sprite
Weaves a bower in endless night.
The caterpillar on the leaf
Repeats to thee thy mother's grief.
Kill not the moth nor butterfly,
For the last judgment draweth nigh.
He who shall train the horse to war
Shall never pass the polar bar.
The beggar's dog and widow's cat,
Feed them and thou wilt grow fat.
The gnat that sings his summer's song
Poison gets from slander's tongue.
The poison of the snake and newt
Is the sweat of envy's foot.
The poison of the honey bee
Is the artist's jealousy.

The prince's robes and beggar's rags
Are toadstools on the miser's bags.
A truth that's told with bad intent
Beats all the lies you can invent.
It is right it should be so;
Man was made for joy and woe;
And when this we rightly know,
Thro' the world we safely go.
Joy and woe are woven fine,
A clothing for the soul divine.
Under every grief and pine
Runs a joy with silken twine.
The babe is more than swaddling bands;
Throughout all these human lands
Tools were made, and born were hands,
Every farmer understands.
Every tear from every eye
Becomes a babe in eternity;
This is caught by females bright,

And return'd to its own delight.
The bleat, the bark, bellow, and roar,
Are waves that beat on heaven's shore.
The babe that weeps the rod beneath
Writes revenge in realms of death.
The beggar's rags, fluttering in air,
Does to rags the heavens tear.
The soldier, arm'd with sword and gun,
Palsied strikes the summer's sun.
The poor man's farthing is worth more
Than all the gold on Afric's shore.
One mite wrung from the lab'rer's hands
Shall buy and sell the miser's lands;
Or, if protected from on high,
Does that whole nation sell and buy.
He who mocks the infant's faith
Shall be mock'd in age and death.
He who shall teach the child to doubt
The rotting grave shall ne'er get out.
He who respects the infant's faith
Triumphs over hell and death.
The child's toys and the old man's reasons
Are the fruits of the two seasons.
The questioner, who sits so sly,
Shall never know how to reply.
He who replies to words of doubt
Doth put the light of knowledge out.
The strongest poison ever known
Came from Caesar's laurel crown.
Nought can deform the human race
Like to the armour's iron brace.
When gold and gems adorn the plow
To peaceful arts shall envy bow.
A riddle, or the cricket's cry,
Is to doubt a fit reply.
The emmet's inch and eagle's mile
Make lame philosophy to smile.
He who doubts from what he sees
Will ne'er believe, do what you please.
If the sun and moon should doubt

They'd immediately go out.
To be in a passion you good may do,
But no good if a passion is in you.
The whore and gambler, by the state
Licensed, build that nation's fate.
The harlot's cry from street to street
Shall weave old England's winding-sheet.
The winner's shout, the loser's curse,
Dance before dead England's hearse.
Every night and every morn
Some to misery are born,
Every morn and every night
Some are born to sweet delight.
Some are born to sweet delight,
Some are born to endless night.
We are led to believe a lie
When we see not thro' the eye,
Which was born in a night to perish in a night,
When the soul slept in beams of light.
God appears, and God is light,
To those poor souls who dwell in night;
But does a human form display
To those who dwell in realms of day.

357 NURSE'S SONG

WHEN the voices of children are heard on the green,
And laughing is heard on the hill,
My heart is at rest within my breast,
And everything else is still.

'Then come home, my children, the sun is gone down,
And the dews of night arise;
Come, come, leave off play, and let us away
Till the morning appears in the skies.'

'No, no, let us play, for it is yet day,
And we cannot go to sleep;
Besides, in the sky the little birds fly,
And the hills are all cover'd with sheep.'

'Well, well, go and play till the light fades away,
  And then go home to bed.'
The little ones leapèd and shoutèd and laugh'd
  And all the hills echoèd.

358 HOLY THURSDAY

'TWAS on a Holy Thursday, their innocent faces clean,
The children walking two and two, in red and blue and green,
Grey headed beadles walk'd before, with wands as white as snow,
Till unto the high dome of Paul's they like Thames' waters flow.

O what a multitude they seem'd, these flowers of London town!
Seated in companies, they sit with radiance all their own.
The hum of multitudes was there, but multitudes of lambs,
Thousands of little boys and girls raising their innocent hands.

Now like a mighty wind they raise to heaven the voice of song,
Or like harmonious thunderings the seats of heaven among.
Beneath them sit the agèd men, wise guardians of the poor;
Then cherish pity, lest you drive an angel from your door.

359 THE DIVINE IMAGE

To Mercy, Pity, Peace, and Love
All pray in their distress;
And to these virtues of delight
Return their thankfulness.

For Mercy, Pity, Peace, and Love
Is God, our father dear,
And Mercy, Pity, Peace, and Love
Is Man, his child and care.

For Mercy has a human heart,
Pity a human face,
And Love, the human form divine,
And Peace, the human dress.

Then every man, of every clime,
That prays in his distress,
Prays to the human form divine,
Love, Mercy, Pity, Peace.

And all must love the human form,
In heathen, Turk, or Jew;
Where Mercy, Love and Pity dwell,
There God is dwelling too.

360 SONG

FRESH from the dewy hill, the merry year
Smiles on my head and mounts his flaming car;
Round my young brows the laurel wreathes a shade,
And rising glories beam around my head.

My feet are wing'd, while o'er the dewy lawn,
I meet my maiden risen like the morn:
Oh bless those holy feet, like angel's feet;
Oh bless those limbs, beaming with heav'nly light.

Like as an angel glitt'ring in the sky
In times of innocence and holy joy;
The joyful shepherd stops his grateful song
To hear the music of an angel's tongue.

So when she speaks, the voice of heaven I hear;
So when we walk, nothing impure comes near;
Each field seems Eden, and each calm retreat
Each village seems the haunt of holy feet.

But that sweet village where my black-ey'd maid
Closes her eyes in sleep beneath night's shade,
Whene'er I enter, more than mortal fire
Burns in my soul, and does my song inspire.

JOHN COLLINS

[*d. 1808 (?)*]

361 TO-MORROW

In the downhill of life, when I find I'm declining,
May my fate no less fortunate be
Than a snug elbow-chair can afford for reclining,
And a cot that o'erlooks the wide sea;
With an ambling pad-pony to pace o'er the lawn,
While I carol away idle sorrow,
And blithe as the lark that each day hails the dawn
Look forward with hope for to-morrow.

With a porch at my door, both for shelter and shade too,
As the sun-shine or rain may prevail;
And a small spot of ground for the use of the spade too,
With a barn for the use of the flail:
A cow for my dairy, a dog for my game,
And a purse when a friend wants to borrow;
I'll envy no nabob his riches or fame,
Nor what honours may wait him to-morrow.

From the bleak northern blast may my cot be completely
Secured by a neighbouring hill;
And at night may repose steal upon me more sweetly
By the sound of a murmuring rill:
And while peace and plenty I find at my board,
With a heart free from sickness and sorrow,
With my friends may I share what today may afford,
And let them spread the table to-morrow.

And when I at last must throw off this frail covering,
Which I've worn for three-score years and ten,
On the brink of the grave I'll not seek to keep hovering,
Nor my thread wish to spin o'er again:
But my face in the glass I'll serenely survey,
And with smiles count each wrinkle and furrow;
And this old worn-out stuff which is threadbare today,
May become everlasting to-morrow.

ROBERT TANNAHILL

[*1774-1810*]

362 JESSIE, THE FLOWER O' DUNBLANE

THE sun has gane down o'er the lofty Benlomond,
And left the red clouds to preside o'er the scene,
While lanely I stray in the calm simmer gloamin'
To muse on sweet Jessie, the flower o' Dunblane.
How sweet is the brier, wi' its saft faulding blossom,
And sweet is the birk, wi' its mantle o' green;
Yet sweeter and fairer, and dear to this bosom,
Is lovely young Jessie, the flower o' Dunblane.

She's modest as ony, and blythe as she's bonny;
For guileless simplicity marks her its ain;
And far be the villain, divested o' feeling,
Wha'd blight, in its bloom, the sweet flower o' Dunblane.
Sing on, thou sweet mavis, thy hymn to the e'ening,
Thou'rt dear to the echoes of Calderwood glen;
Sae dear to this bosom, sae artless and winning,
Is charming young Jessie, the flower o' Dunblane

How lost were my days till I met wi' my Jessie,
The sports o' the city seemed foolish and vain;
I ne'er saw a nymph I would ca' my dear lassie,
Till charm'd wi' sweet Jessie, the flower o' Dunblane.
Though mine were the station o' loftiest grandeur,
Amidst its profusion I'd languish in pain;
And reckon as naething the height o' its splendour,
If wanting sweet Jessie, the flower o' Dunblane.

363 GLOOMY WINTER'S NOW AWA'

GLOOMY winter's now awa',
Saft the westlan' breezes blaw,
'Mang the birks o' Stanley-shaw
The mavis sings fu' cheerie, O!

Sweet the crawflower's early bell
Decks Gleniffer's dewy dell,
Blooming like thy bonnie sel',
My young, my artless dearie, O!

Come, my lassie, let us stray
O'er Glenkilloch's sunny brae,
Blithely spend the gowden day
'Midst joys that never weary, O!
Towering o'er the Newton wuds,
Laverocks[1] fan the snaw-white cluds,
Siller saughs,[2] wi' downy buds,
Adorn the banks sae briery, O!

Round the sylvan fairy nooks
Feath'ry breckans[3] fringe the rocks,
'Neath the brae the burnie jouks,[4]
And ilka[5] thing is cheerie, O!
Trees may bud, and birds may sing,
Flowers may bloom, and verdure spring,
Joy to me they canna bring,
Unless wi' thee, my dearie, O!

WILLIAM WORDSWORTH

[*1770-1850*]

364 Ode on Intimations of Immortality from Recollections of Early Childhood

There was a time when meadow, grove, and stream,
The earth, and every common sight
To me did seem
Apparell'd in celestial light,
The glory and the freshness of a dream.
It is not now as it has been of yore;—
Turn wheresoe'er I may,
By night or day,
The things which I have seen I now can see no more!

[1] Larks. [2] Silver willows. [3] Brakes. [4] Dodges. [5] Each.

The rainbow comes and goes,
And lovely is the rose;
The moon doth with delight
Look round her when the heavens are bare;
Waters on a starry night
Are beautiful and fair;
The sunshine is a glorious birth;
But yet I know, where'er I go,
That there hath pass'd away a glory from the earth.

Now, while the birds thus sing a joyous song,
And while the young lambs bound
As to the tabor's sound,
To me alone there came a thought of grief:
A timely utterance gave that thought relief,
And I again am strong.
The cataracts blow their trumpets from the steep,—
No more shall grief of mine the season wrong:
I hear the echoes through the mountains throng,
The winds come to me from the fields of sleep,
And all the earth is gay;
Land and sea
Give themselves up to jollity,
And with the heart of May
Doth every beast keep holiday;—
Thou child of joy
Shout round me, let me hear thy shouts, thou happy
Shepherd-boy!

Ye blesséd creatures, I have heard the call
Ye to each other make; I see
The heavens laugh with you in your jubilee;
My heart is at your festival,
My head hath its coronal,
The fulness of your bliss, I feel—I feel it all.
O evil day! if I were sullen
While Earth herself is adorning
This sweet May morning;
And the children are culling
On every side,

In a thousand valleys far and wide,
Fresh flowers; while the sun shines warm,
And the babe leaps up on his mother's arm:—
I hear, I hear, with joy I hear!
—But there's a tree, of many, one,
A single field which I have look'd upon,

Both of them speak of something that is gone:
The pansy at my feet
Doth the same tale repeat:
Whither is fled the visionary gleam?
Where is it now, the glory and the dream?

Our birth is but a sleep and a forgetting;
The Soul that rises with us, our life's Star,
Hath had elsewhere its setting
And cometh from afar;
Not in entire forgetfulness,
And not in utter nakedness,
But trailing clouds of glory do we come
From God, who is our home:
Heaven lies about us in our infancy!
Shades of the prison-house begin to close
Upon the growing boy,
But he beholds the light, and whence it flows,
He sees it in his joy;
The youth, who daily farther from the east
Must travel, still is Nature's priest,
And by the vision splendid
Is on his way attended;
At length the man perceives it die away,
And fade into the light of common day.

Earth fills her lap with pleasures of her own;
Yearnings she hath in her own natural kind,
And, even with something of a mother's mind
And no unworthy aim,
The homely nurse doth all she can
To make her foster-child, her inmate, Man,
Forget the glories he hath known
And that imperial palace whence he came.

Behold the Child among his new-born blisses,
A six years' darling of a pigmy size!
See, where 'mid work of his own hand he lies,
Fretted by sallies of his mother's kisses,
With light upon him from his father's eyes!
See, at his feet, some little plan or chart,
Some fragment from his dream of human life
Shaped by himself with newly-learnéd art;
A wedding or a festival,
A mourning or a funeral;
And this hath now his heart,
And unto this he frames his song:
Then will he fit his tongue
To dialogues of business, love, or strife;
But it will not be long
Ere this be thrown aside,
And with new joy and pride
The little actor cons another part;
Filling from time to time his 'humorous stage
With all the Persons, down to palsied Age,
That life brings with her in her equipage;
As if his whole vocation
Were endless imitation.

Thou, whose exterior semblance doth belie
Thy soul's immensity;
Thou best philosopher, who yet dost keep
Thy heritage, thou eye among the blind,
That, deaf and silent, read'st the eternal deep,
Haunted for ever by the eternal Mind,—
Mighty Prophet! Seer blest!
On whom those truths do rest
Which we are toiling all our lives to find;
Thou, over whom thy immortality
Broods like the day, a master o'er a slave,
A presence which is not to be put by;
Thou little child, yet glorious in the might
Of heaven-born freedom on thy being's height,
Why with such earnest pains dost thou provoke
The years to bring the inevitable yoke,

Thus blindly with thy blessedness at strife?
Full soon thy soul shall have her earthly freight,
And custom lie upon thee with a weight
Heavy as frost, and deep almost as life!

O joy! that in our embers
Is something that doth live,
That Nature yet remembers
What was so fugitive!
The thought of our past years in me doth breed
Perpetual benediction: not indeed
For that which is most worthy to be blest,
Delight and liberty, the simple creed
Of childhood, whether busy or at rest,
With new-fledged hope still fluttering in his breast:
—Not for these I raise
The song of thanks and praise;
But for those obstinate questionings
Of sense and outward things,
Fallings from us, vanishings,
Blank misgivings of a creature
Moving about in worlds not realized,
High instincts, before which our mortal nature
Did tremble like a guilty thing surprised:
But for those first affections,
Those shadowy recollections,
Which, be they what they may,
Are yet the fountain-light of all our day,
Are yet a master-light of all our seeing;
Uphold us—cherish—and have power to make
Our noisy years seem moments in the being
Of the eternal silence: truths that wake,
To perish never;
Which neither listlessness, nor mad endeavour,
Nor man nor boy,
Nor all that is at enmity with joy,
Can utterly abolish or destroy!
Hence, in a season of calm weather
Though inland far we be,
Our souls have sight of that immortal sea

Which brought us hither;
Can in a moment travel thither—
And see the children sport upon the shore,
And hear the mighty waters rolling evermore.

Then sing, ye birds, sing, sing a joyous song!
And let the young lambs bound
As to the tabor's sound!
We, in thought, will join your throng
Ye that pipe and ye that play,
Ye that through your hearts to-day
Feel the gladness of the May!
What though the radiance which was once so bright
Be now for ever taken from my sight,
Though nothing can bring back the hour
Of splendour in the grass, of glory in the flower;
We will grieve not, rather find
Strength in what remains behind,
In the primal sympathy
Which having been must ever be,
In the soothing thoughts that spring
Out of human suffering,
In the faith that looks through death,
In years that bring the philosophic mind.

And O, ye Fountains, Meadows, Hills, and Groves,
Forbode not any severing of our loves!
Yet in my heart of hearts I feel your might;
I only have relinquish'd one delight
To live beneath your more habitual sway;
I love the brooks which down their channels fret
Even more than when I tripp'd lightly as they;
The innocent brightness of a new-born day
Is lovely yet;
The clouds that gather round the setting sun
Do take a sober colouring from an eye
That hath kept watch o'er man's mortality;
Another race hath been, and other palms are won.

Thanks to the human heart by which we live,
Thanks to its tenderness, its joys and fears,
To me the meanest flower that blows can give
Thoughts that do often lie too deep for tears.

365 My Heart Leaps Up

My heart leaps up when I behold
A rainbow in the sky:
So was it when my life began,
So is it now I am a man,
So be it when I shall grow old
Or let me die!
The Child is father of the Man:
And I could wish my days to be
Bound each to each by natural piety.

366 The Two April Mornings

We walk'd along, while bright and red
Uprose the morning sun;
And Matthew stopp'd, he look'd, and said
'The will of God be done!'

A village schoolmaster was he,
With hair of glittering gray;
As blithe a man as you could see
On a spring holiday.

And on that morning, through the grass
And by the steaming rills
We travell'd merrily, to pass
A day among the hills.

'Our work,' said I, 'was well begun;
Then from thy breast what thought,
Beneath so beautiful a sun,
So sad a sigh has brought?'

A second time did Matthew stop;
And fixing still his eye
Upon the eastern mountain-top,
To me he made reply:

'Yon cloud with that long purple cleft
Brings fresh into my mind
A day like this, which I have left
Full thirty years behind.

'And just above yon slope of corn
Such colours, and no other,
Were in the sky that April morn
Of this the very brother.

'With rod and line I sued the sport
Which that sweet season gave,
And coming to the church, stopp'd short
Beside my daughter's grave.

'Nine summers had she scarcely seen,
The pride of all the vale;
And then she sang:—she would have been
A very nightingale.

'Six feet in earth my Emma lay;
And yet I loved her more—
For so it seem'd,—than till that day
I e'er had loved before.

'And turning from her grave, I met,
Beside the churchyard yew,
A blooming Girl, whose hair was wet
With points of morning dew.

'A basket on her head she bare;
Her brow was smooth and white:
To see a child so very fair,
It was a pure delight!

'No fountain from its rocky cave
E'er tripp'd with foot so free;
She seem'd as happy as a wave
That dances on the sea.

'There came from me a sigh of pain
Which I could ill confine;
I look'd at her, and look'd again:
And did not wish her mine!'

—Matthew is in his grave, yet now
Methinks I see him stand
As at that moment, with a bough
Of wilding in his hand.

367

The Fountain

A Conversation

We talk'd with open heart, and tongue
Affectionate and true,
A pair of friends, though I was young,
And Matthew seventy-two.

We lay beneath a spreading oak,
Beside a mossy seat;
And from the turf a fountain broke
And gurgled at our feet.

'Now, Matthew!' said I, 'let us match
This water's pleasant tune
With some old border-song, or catch
That suits a summer's noon.

'Or of the church-clock and the chimes
Sing here beneath the shade
That half-mad thing of witty rhymes
Which you last April made!'

In silence Matthew lay, and eyed
The spring beneath the tree;
And thus the dear old man replied,
The gray-hair'd man of glee:

'No check, no stay, this Streamlet fears,
How merrily it goes!
'Twill murmur on a thousand years
And flow as now it flows.

'And here, on this delightful day,
I cannot choose but think
How oft, a vigorous man, I lay
Beside this fountain's brink.

'My eyes are dim with childish tears,
My heart is idly stirr'd,
For the same sound is in my ears
Which in those days I heard.

'Thus fares it still in our decay:
And yet the wiser mind
Mourns less for what Age takes away,
Than what it leaves behind.

'The blackbird amid leafy trees,
The lark above the hill,
Let loose their carols when they please,
Are quiet when they will.

'With Nature never do they wage
A foolish strife; they see
A happy youth, and their old age
Is beautiful and free:

'But we are press'd by heavy laws;
And often, glad no more,
We wear a face of joy, because
We have been glad of yore.

'If there be one who need bemoan
His kindred laid in earth,
The household hearts that were his own,—
It is the man of mirth.

'My days, my friend, are almost gone,
My life has been approved,
And many love me; but by none
Am I enough beloved.'

'Now both himself and me he wrongs,
The man who thus complains!
I live and sing my idle songs
Upon these happy plains:

'And Matthew, for thy children dead
I'll be a son to thee!'
At this he grasp'd my hand and said,
'Alas! that cannot be.'

We rose up from the fountain-side;
And down the smooth descent
Of the green sheep-track did we glide,
And through the wood we went;

And ere we came to Leonard's rock
He sang those witty rhymes
About the crazy old church-clock,
And the bewilder'd chimes.

368 Written in March

While resting on the Bridge at the foot of Brother's Water

The cock is crowing,
The stream is flowing,
The small birds twitter,
The lake doth glitter,
The green field sleeps in the sun;

The oldest and youngest
Are at work with the strongest;
The cattle are grazing,
Their heads never raising;
There are forty feeding like one!

Like an army defeated
The Snow hath retreated,
And now doth fare ill
On the top of the bare hill;
The Ploughboy is whooping—anon—anon:
There's joy in the mountains;
There's life in the fountains;
Small clouds are sailing,
Blue sky prevailing;
The rain is over and gone!

369 Nature and the Poet

Suggested by a Picture of Peele Castle in a Storm, painted by Sir George Beaumont

I was thy neighbour once, thou rugged Pile!
Four summer weeks I dwelt in sight of thee:
I saw thee every day; and all the while
Thy form was sleeping on a glassy sea.

So pure the sky, so quiet was the air!
So like, so very like, was day to day!
Whene'er I look'd, thy image still was there;
It trembled, but it never pass'd away.

How perfect was the calm! It seem'd no sleep,
No mood, which season takes away, or brings:
I could have fancied that the mighty Deep
Was even the gentlest of all gentle things.

Ah! then if mine had been the painter's hand
To express what then I saw; and add the gleam,
The light that never was on sea or land,
The consecration, and the Poet's dream,—

I would have planted thee, thou hoary pile,
Amid a world how different from this!
Beside a sea that could not cease to smile;
On tranquil land, beneath a sky of bliss.

A picture had it been of lasting ease,
Elysian quiet, without toil or strife;
No motion but the moving tide, a breeze,
Or merely silent Nature's breathing life.

Such, in the fond illusion of my heart,
Such picture would I at that time have made;
And seen the soul of truth in every part,
A steadfast peace that might not be betray'd.

So once it would have been,—'tis so no more;
I have submitted to a new control:
A power is gone, which nothing can restore;
A deep distress hath humanized my soul.

Not for a moment could I now behold
A smiling sea, and be what I have been:
The feeling of my loss will ne'er be old;
This, which I know, I speak with mind serene.

Then, Beaumont, Friend! who would have been the friend
If he had lived, of him whom I deplore,
This work of thine I blame not, but commend;
This sea in anger, and that dismal shore.

O 'tis a passionate work!—yet wise and well,
Well chosen is the spirit that is here;
That hulk which labours in the deadly swell,
This rueful sky, this pageantry of fear!

And this huge Castle, standing here sublime,
I love to see the look with which it braves,
—Cased in the unfeeling armour of old time—
The lightning, the fierce wind and trampling waves.

—Farewell, farewell the heart that lives alone,
Housed in a dream, at distance from the Kind!
Such happiness, wherever it be known
Is to be pitied; for 'tis surely blind.

But welcome fortitude, and patient cheer,
And frequent sights of what is to be borne!
Such sights, or worse, as are before me here:—
Not without hope we suffer and we mourn.

370 Ruth: Or the Influences of Nature

When Ruth was left half desolate
Her father took another mate;
And Ruth, not seven years old,
A slighted child, at her own will
Went wandering over dale and hill,
In thoughtless freedom bold.

And she had made a pipe of straw,
And music from that pipe could draw
Like sounds of wind and floods;
Had built a bower upon the green,
As if she from her birth had been
An infant of the woods.

Beneath her father's roof, alone
She seem'd to live; her thoughts her own;
Herself her own delight:
Pleased with herself, nor sad nor gay,
She passed her time; and in this way
Grew up to woman's height.

There came a youth from Georgia's shore—
A military casque he wore
With splendid feathers drest;
He brought them from the Cherokees;
The feathers nodded in the breeze
And made a gallant crest.

From Indian blood you deem him sprung:
But no! he spake the English tongue
And bore a soldier's name;
And, when America was free
From battle and from jeopardy,
He 'cross the ocean came.

With hues of genius on his cheek,
In finest tones the youth could speak:
—While he was yet a boy
The moon, the glory of the sun,
And streams that murmur as they run
Had been his dearest joy.

He was a lovely youth! I guess
The panther in the wilderness
Was not so fair as he;
And when he chose to sport and play,
No dolphin ever was so gay
Upon the tropic sea.

Among the Indians he had fought;
And with him many tales he brought
Of pleasure and of fear;
Such tales as, told to any maid
By such a youth, in the green shade,
Were perilous to hear.

He told of girls, a happy rout!
Who quit their fold with dance and shout,
Their pleasant Indian town,
To gather strawberries all day long;
Returning with a choral song
When daylight is gone down.

He spake of plants that hourly change
Their blossoms, through a boundless range
Of intermingling hues;
With budding, fading, faded flowers,
They stand the wonder of the bowers
From morn to evening dews.

He told of the Magnolia, spread
High as a cloud, high over head!
The cypress and her spire;
—Of flowers that with one scarlet gleam
Cover a hundred leagues, and seem
To set the hills on fire.

The youth of green savannahs spake,
And many an endless, endless lake
With all its fairy crowds
Of islands, that together lie
As quietly as spots of sky
Among the evening clouds.

'And,' then he said, 'how sweet it were
A fisher or a hunter there,
In sunshine or in shade
To wander with an easy mind,
And build a household fire, and find
A home in every glade!

'What days and what bright years! Ah me!
Our life were life indeed, with Thee
So pass'd in quiet bliss;
And all the while,' said he, 'to know
That we were in a world of woe,
On such an earth as this!'

And then he sometimes interwove
Fond thoughts about a father's love,
'For there,' said he, 'are spun
Around the heart such tender ties,
That our own children to our eyes
Are dearer than the sun.

Sweet Ruth! and could you go with me
My helpmate in the woods to be,
Our shed at night to rear;
Or run, my own adopted bride,
A sylvan huntress at my side,
And drive the flying deer!

Beloved Ruth!'—No more he said.
The wakeful Ruth at midnight shed
A solitary tear:
She thought again—and did agree
With him to sail across the sea,
And drive the flying deer.

'And now, as fitting is and right,
We in the church our faith will plight,
A husband and a wife.'
Even so they did; and I may say
That to sweet Ruth that happy day
Was more than human life.

Through dream and vision did she sink,
Delighted all the while to think
That, on those lonesome floods
And green savannahs, she should share
His board with lawful joy, and bear
His name in the wild woods.

But, as you have before been told,
This Stripling, sportive, gay, and bold,
And with his dancing crest
So beautiful, through savage lands
Had roam'd about, with vagrant bands
Of Indians in the West.

The wind, the tempest roaring high,
The tumult of a tropic sky
Might well be dangerous food
For him, a youth to whom was given
So much of earth—so much of heaven,
And such impetuous blood.

Whatever in those climes he found
Irregular in sight or sound
Did to his mind impart
A kindred impulse, seem'd allied
To his own powers, and justified
The workings of his heart.

Nor less, to feed voluptuous thought,
The beauteous forms of Nature wrought,—
Fair trees and gorgeous flowers;
The breezes their own languor lent;
The stars had feelings, which they sent
Into those favour'd bowers.

Yet, in his worst pursuits, I ween
That sometimes there did intervene
Pure hopes of high intent:
For passions link'd to forms so fair
And stately, needs must have their share
Of noble sentiment.

But ill he lived, much evil saw,
With men to whom no better law
Nor better life was known;
Deliberately and undeceived
Those wild men's vices he received,
And gave them back his own.

His genius and his moral frame
Were thus impair'd, and he became
The slave of low desires;
A man who without self-control
Would seek what the degraded soul
Unworthily admires.

And yet he with no feign'd delight
Had woo'd the maiden, day and night
Had loved her, night and morn:
What could he less than love a maid
Whose heart with so much nature play'd—
So kind and so forlorn?

Sometimes most earnestly he said,
'O Ruth! I have been worse than dead;
False thoughts, thoughts bold and vain
Encompass'd me on every side
When I, in confidence and pride,
Had cross'd the Atlantic main.

Before me shone a glorious world
Fresh as a banner bright, unfurl'd
To music suddenly:
I look'd upon those hills and plains,
And seem'd as if let loose from chains
To live at liberty!

No more of this—for now, by thee,
Dear Ruth! more happily set free,
With nobler zeal I burn;
My soul from darkness is released
Like the whole sky when to the east
The morning doth return.

Full soon that better mind was gone;
No hope, no wish remain'd, not one,—
They stirr'd him now no more;
New objects did new pleasure give,
And once again he wish'd to live
As lawless as before.

Meanwhile, as thus with him it fared,
They for the voyage were prepared,
And went to the sea-shore:
But, when they thither came, the youth
Deserted his poor bride, and Ruth
Could never find him more.

God help thee, Ruth!—Such pains she had
That she in half a year was mad
And in a prison housed;
And there, exulting in her wrongs
Among the music of her songs
She fearfully caroused.

Yet sometimes milder hours she knew,
Nor wanted sun, nor rain, nor dew,
Nor pastimes of the May,
—They all were with her in her cell;
And a clear brook with cheerful knell
Did o'er the pebbles play.

When Ruth three seasons thus had lain,
There came a respite to her pain;
She from her prison fled;
But of the vagrant none took thought;
And where it liked her best she sought
Her shelter and her bread.

Among the fields she breathed again:
The master-current of her brain
Ran permanent and free;
And, coming to the banks of Tone,
There did she rest; and dwell alone
Under the greenwood tree.

The engines of her pain, the tools
That shaped her sorrow, rocks and pools,
And airs that gently stir
The vernal leaves—she loved them still,
Nor ever tax'd them with the ill
Which had been done to her.

A barn her Winter bed supplies;
But, till the warmth of Summer skies
And Summer days is gone,
(And all do in this tale agree)
She sleeps beneath the greenwood tree,
And other home hath none.

An innocent life, yet far astray!
And Ruth will, long before her day,
Be broken down and old.
Sore aches she needs must have! but less
Of mind, than body's wretchedness,
From damp, and rain, and cold.

If she is prest by want of food
She from her dwelling in the wood
Repairs to a road-side;
And there she begs at one steep place,
Where up and down with easy pace
The horsemen-travellers ride.

That oaten pipe of hers is mute
Or thrown away: but with a flute
Her loneliness she cheers;
This flute, made of a hemlock stalk,
At evening in his homeward walk
The Quantock woodman hears.

I, too, have pass'd her on the hills
Setting her little water-mills
By spouts and fountains wild—
Such small machinery as she turn'd
Ere she had wept, ere she had mourn'd,
A young and happy child!

Farewell! and when thy days are told,
Ill-fated Ruth! in hallow'd mould
Thy corpse shall buried be;
For thee a funeral bell shall ring,
And all the congregation sing
A Christian psalm for thee.

371 A Lesson

There is a flower, the Lesser Celandine,
That shrinks like many more from cold and rain,
And the first moment that the sun may shine,
Bright as the sun himself, 'tis out again!

When hailstones have been falling, swarm on swarm,
Or blasts the green field and the trees distrest,
Oft have I seen it muffled up from harm
In close self-shelter, like a thing at rest.

But lately, one rough day, this flower I past,
And recognized it, though an alter'd form,
Now standing forth an offering to the blast,
And buffeted at will by rain and storm.

I stopp'd and said, with inly-mutter'd voice,
'It doth not love the shower, nor seek the cold;
This neither is its courage nor its choice,
But its necessity in being old.

'The sunshine may not cheer it, nor the dew;
It cannot help itself in its decay;
Stiff in its members, wither'd, changed of hue,'—
And, in my spleen, I smiled that it was gray.

To be a prodigal's favourite—then, worse truth,
A miser's pensioner—behold our lot!
O Man! that from thy fair and shining youth
Age might but take the things Youth needed not!

372 MICHAEL

A Pastoral Poem

IF from the public way you turn your steps
Up the tumultuous brook of Greenhead Ghyll,
You will suppose that with an upright path
Your feet must struggle; in such bold ascent
The pastoral mountains front you, face to face.
But, courage! for around that boisterous brook
The mountains have all opened out themselves,
And made a hidden valley of their own.
No habitation can be seen; but they
Who journey thither find themselves alone
With a few sheep, with rocks and stones, and kites
That overhead are sailing in the sky.
It is in truth an utter solitude;
Nor should I have made mention of this Dell
But for one object which you might pass by,
Might see and notice not. Beside the brook
Appears a struggling heap of unhewn stones!
And to that simple object appertains
A story—unenriched with strange events,
Yet not unfit, I deem, for the fireside,

Or for the summer shade. It was the first
Of those domestic tales that spake to me
Of shepherds, dwellers in the valleys, men
Whom I already loved;—not verily
For their own sakes, but for the fields and hills
Where was their occupation and abode.
And hence this Tale, while I was yet a Boy
Careless of books, yet having felt the power
Of Nature, by the gentle agency
Of natural objects, led me on to feel
For passions that were not my own, and think
(At random and imperfectly indeed)
On man, the heart of man, and human life.
Therefore, although it be a history
Homely and rude, I will relate the same
For the delight of a few natural hearts;
And, with yet fonder feeling, for the sake
Of youthful Poets, who among these hills
Will be my second self when I am gone.
  Upon the forest-side in Grasmere Vale
There dwelt a Shepherd, Michael was his name;
An old man, stout of heart, and strong of limb.
His bodily frame had been from youth to age
Of an unusual strength: his mind was keen,
Intense, and frugal, apt for all affairs,
And in his shepherd's calling he was prompt
And watchful more than ordinary men.
Hence had he learned the meaning of all winds,
Of blasts of every tone; and, oftentimes,
When others heeded not, he heard the South
Make subterraneous music, like the noise
Of bagpipers on distant Highland hills.
The Shepherd, at such warning, of his flock
Bethought him, and he to himself would say,
'The winds are now devising work for me!'
And, truly, at all times, the storm, that drives
The traveller to a shelter, summoned him
Up to the mountains: he had been alone
Amid the heart of many thousand mists,
That came to him, and left him, on the heights.

So lived he till his eightieth year was past.
And grossly that man errs, who should suppose
That the green valleys, and the streams and rocks,
Were things indifferent to the Shepherd's thoughts.
Fields, where with cheerful spirits he had breathed
The common air; hills, which with vigorous step
He had so often climbed; which had impressed
So many incidents upon his mind
Of hardship, skill or courage, joy or fear;
Which, like a book, preserved the memory
Of the dumb animals, whom he had saved,
Had fed or sheltered, linking to such acts
The certainty of honourable gain;
Those fields, those hills—what could they less? had laid
Strong hold on his affections, were to him
A pleasurable feeling of blind love,
The pleasure which there is in life itself.

His days had not been passed in singleness.
His Helpmate was a comely matron, old—
Though younger than himself full twenty years.
She was a woman of a stirring life,
Whose heart was in her house; two wheels she had
Of antique form; this large, for spinning wool;
That small, for flax; and if one wheel had rest
It was because the other was at work.
The Pair had but one inmate in their house,
An only Child, who had been born to them
When Michael, telling o'er his years, began
To deem that he was old,—in shepherd's phrase,
With one foot in the grave. This only Son,
With two brave sheep-dogs tried in many a storm,
The one of an inestimable worth,
Made all their household. I may truly say,
That they were as a proverb in the vale
For endless industry. When day was gone,
And from their occupations out of doors
The Son and Father were come home, even then,
Their labour did not cease; unless when all
Turned to the cleanly supper-board, and there,

Each with a mess of pottage and skimmed milk,
Sat round the basket piled with oaten cakes,
And their plain home-made cheese. Yet when the meal
Was ended, Luke (for so the son was named)
And his old Father both betook themselves
To such convenient work as might employ
Their hands by the fireside; perhaps to card
Wool for the Housewife's spindle, or repair
Some injury done to sickle, flail, or scythe,
Or other implement of house or field.
Down from the ceiling, by the chimney's edge,
That in our ancient uncouth country style
With huge and black projection overbrowed
Large space beneath, as duly as the light
Of day grew dim the Housewife hung a lamp;
An aged utensil, which had performed
Service beyond all others of its kind.
Early at evening did it burn—and late,
Surviving comrade of uncounted hours,
Which, going by from year to year, had found,
And left, the couple neither gay perhaps
Nor cheerful, yet with objects and with hopes,
Living a life of eager industry.
And now, when Luke had reached his eighteenth year,
There by the light of this old lamp they sate,
Father and Son, while far into the night
The Housewife plied her own peculiar work,
Making the cottage through the silent hours
Murmur as with the sound of summer flies.
This light was famous in its neighbourhood,
And was a public symbol of the life
That thrifty Pair had lived. For, as it chanced,
Their cottage on a plot of rising ground
Stood single, with large prospect, north and south,
High into Easedale, up to Dunmail-Raise,
And westward to the village near the lake;
And from this constant light, so regular
And so far seen, the House itself, by all
Who dwelt within the limits of the vale,
Both old and young, was named THE EVENING STAR.

Thus living on through such a length of years,
The Shepherd, if he loved himself, must needs
Have loved his Helpmate; but to Michael's heart
This son of his old age was yet more dear—
Less from instinctive tenderness, the same
Fond spirit that blindly works in the blood of all—
Than that a child, more than all other gifts
That earth can offer to declining man,
Brings hope with it, and forward-looking thoughts,
And stirrings of inquietude, when they
By tendency of nature needs must fail.
Exceeding was the love he bare to him,
His heart and his heart's joy! For oftentimes
Old Michael, while he was a babe in arms,
Had done him female service, not alone
For pastime and delight, as is the use
Of fathers, but with patient mind enforced
To acts of tenderness; and he had rocked
His cradle, as with a woman's gentle hand.

And, in a later time, ere yet the Boy
Had put on boy's attire, did Michael love,
Albeit of a stern unbending mind,
To have the young-one in his sight, when he
Wrought in the field, or on his shepherd's stool
Sate with a fettered sheep before him stretched
Under the large old oak, that near his door
Stood single, and, from matchless depth of shade,
Chosen for the Shearer's covert from the sun,
Thence in our rustic dialect was called
The CLIPPING TREE, a name which yet it bears.
There, while they two were sitting in the shade,
With others round them, earnest all and blithe,
Would Michael exercise his heart with looks
Of fond correction and reproof bestowed
Upon the Child, if he disturbed the sheep
By catching at their legs, or with his shouts
Scared them, while they lay still beneath the shears.

And when by Heaven's good grace the boy grew up
A healthy Lad, and carried in his cheek
Two steady roses that were five years old;

Then Michael from a winter coppice cut
With his own hand a sapling, which he hooped
With iron, making it throughout in all
Due requisites a perfect shepherd's staff,
And gave it to the Boy; wherewith equipt
He as a watchman oftentimes was placed
At gate or gap, to stem or turn the flock;
And, to his office prematurely called,
There stood the urchin, as you will divine,
Something between a hindrance and a help;
And for this cause not always, I believe,
Receiving from his Father hire of praise;
Though nought was left undone which staff, or voice,
Or looks, or threatening gestures, could perform.
But soon as Luke, full ten years old, could stand
Against the mountain blasts; and to the heights,
Not fearing toil, nor length of weary ways,
He with his Father daily went, and they
Were as companions, why should I relate
That objects which the Shepherd loved before
Were dearer now? that from the Boy there came
Feelings and emanations—things which were
Light to the sun and music to the wind;
And that the old Man's heart seemed born again?
Thus in his Father's sight the Boy grew up:
And now, when he had reached his eighteenth year,
He was his comfort and his daily hope.

While in this sort the simple household lived
From day to day, to Michael's ear there came
Distressful tidings. Long before the time
Of which I speak, the Shepherd had been bound
In surety for his brother's son, a man
Of an industrious life, and ample means;
But unforeseen misfortunes suddenly
Had prest upon him; and old Michael now
Was summoned to discharge the forfeiture,
A grievous penalty, but little less
Than half his substance. This unlooked-for claim,
At the first hearing, for a moment took

More hope out of his life than he supposed
That any old man ever could have lost.
As soon as he had armed himself with strength
To look his trouble in the face, it seemed
The Shepherd's sole resource to sell at once
A portion of his patrimonial fields.
Such was his first resolve; he thought again,
And his heart failed him. 'Isabel,' said he,
Two evenings after he had heard the news,
'I have been toiling more than seventy years,
And in the open sunshine of God's love
Have we all lived; yet if these fields of ours
Should pass into a stranger's hand, I think
That I could not lie quiet in my grave.
Our lot is a hard lot; the sun himself
Has scarcely been more diligent than I;
And I have lived to be a fool at last
To my own family. An evil man
That was, and made an evil choice, if he
Were false to us; and if he were not false,
There are ten thousand to whom loss like this
Had been no sorrow. I forgive him;—but
'Twere better to be dumb than to talk thus.
  When I began, my purpose was to speak
Of remedies and of a cheerful hope.
Our Luke shall leave us, Isabel; the land
Shall not go from us, and it shall be free;
He shall possess it, free as is the wind
That passes over it. We have, thou know'st,
Another kinsman—he will be our friend
In this distress. He is a prosperous man,
Thriving in trade—and Luke to him shall go,
And with his kinsman's help and his own thrift
He quickly will repair this loss, and then
He may return to us. If here he stay,
What can be done? Where every one is poor,
What can be gained?
                    At this the old Man paused,
And Isabel sat silent, for her mind
Was busy, looking back into past times.

There's Richard Bateman, thought she to herself,
He was a parish boy—at the church-door
They made a gathering for him, shillings, pence
And halfpennies, wherewith the neighbours bought
A basket, which they filled with pedlar's wares;
And, with this basket on his arm, the lad
Went up to London, found a master there,
Who, out of many, chose the trusty boy
To go and overlook his merchandise
Beyond the seas; where he grew wondrous rich,
And left estates and monies to the poor,
And, at his birthplace, built a chapel floored
With marble which he sent from foreign lands.
These thoughts, and many others of like sort,
Passed quickly through the mind of Isabel,
And her face brightened. The old Man was glad,
And thus resumed:—'Well, Isabel! this scheme
These two days, has been meat and drink to me.
Far more than we have lost is left us yet.
—We have enough—I wish indeed that I
Were younger;—but this hope is a good hope.
—Make ready Luke's best garments, of the best
Buy for him more, and let us send him forth
To-morrow, or the next day, or to-night:
—If he *could* go, the Boy should go to-night.'
  Here Michael ceased, and to the fields went forth
With a light heart. The Housewife for five days
Was restless morn and night, and all day long
Wrought on with her best fingers to prepare
Things needful for the journey of her son.
But Isabel was glad when Sunday came
To stop her in her work: for, when she lay
By Michael's side, she through the last two nights
Heard him, how he was troubled in his sleep:
And when they rose at morning she could see
That all his hopes were gone. That day at noon
She said to Luke, while they two by themselves
Were sitting at the door, 'Thou must not go:
We have no other Child but thee to lose,
None to remember—do not go away,

For if thou leave thy Father he will die.'
The Youth made answer with a jocund voice;
And Isabel, when she had told her fears,
Recovered heart. That evening her best fare
Did she bring forth, and all together sat
Like happy people round a Christmas fire.
 With daylight Isabel resumed her work;
And all the ensuing week the house appeared
As cheerful as a grove in Spring: at length
The expected letter from their kinsman came,
With kind assurances that he would do
His utmost for the welfare of the Boy;
To which, requests were added, that forthwith
He might be sent to him. Ten times or more
The letter was read over; Isabel
Went forth to show it to the neighbours round;
Nor was there at that time on English land
A prouder heart than Luke's. When Isabel
Had to her house returned, the old Man said,
'He shall depart to-morrow.' To this word
The Housewife answered, talking much of things
Which, if at such short notice he should go,
Would surely be forgotten. But at length
She gave consent, and Michael was at ease.
 Near the tumultuous brook of Greenhead Ghyll,
In that deep valley, Michael had designed
To build a Sheepfold; and, before he heard
The tidings of his melancholy loss,
For this same purpose he had gathered up
A heap of stones, which by the streamlet's edge
Lay thrown together, ready for the work.
With Luke that evening thitherward he walked;
And soon as they had reached the place he stopped.
And thus the old Man spake to him:—'My Son,
To-morrow thou wilt leave me: with full heart
I look upon thee, for thou art the same
That wert a promise to me ere thy birth,
And all thy life hast been my daily joy.
I will relate to thee some little part
Of our two histories; 'twill do thee good

When thou art from me, even if I should touch
On things thou canst not know of.—After thou
First cam'st into the world—as oft befalls
To new-born infants—thou didst sleep away
Two days, and blessings from thy Father's tongue
Then fell upon thee. Day by day passed on,
And still I loved thee with increasing love.
Never to living ear came sweeter sounds
Than when I heard thee by our own fireside
First uttering, without words, a natural tune:
While thou, a feeding babe, didst in thy joy
Sing at thy Mother's breast. Month followed month,
And in the open fields my life was passed
And on the mountains; else I think that thou
Hadst been brought up upon thy Father's knees.
But we were playmates, Luke: among these hills,
As well thou knowest, in us the old and young
Have played together, nor with me didst thou
Lack any pleasure which a boy can know.'
Luke had a manly heart; but at these words
He sobbed aloud. The old Man grasped his hand,
And said, 'Nay, do not take it so—I see
That these are things of which I need not speak.
—Even to the utmost I have been to thee
A kind and a good Father: and herein
I but repay a gift which I myself
Received at others' hand; for, though now old
Beyond the common life of man, I still
Remember them who loved me in my youth.
Both of them sleep together; here they lived,
As all their Forefathers had done; and when
At length their time was come, they were not loth
To give their bodies to the family mould.
I wished that thou shouldst live the life they lived:
But, 'tis a long time to look back, my Son
And see so little gained from threescore years.
These fields were burthened when they came to me;
Till I was forty years of age, not more
Than half of my inheritance was mine.
I toiled and toiled; God blessed me in my work,

And till these three weeks past the land was free.
—It looks as if it never could endure
Another Master. Heaven forgive me, Luke,
If I judge ill for thee, but it seems good
That thou shouldst go.'
At this the old Man paused;
Then, pointing to the stones near which they stood,
Thus, after a short silence, he resumed:
'This was a work for us; and now, my Son,
It is a work for me. But, lay one stone—
Here, lay it for me, Luke, with thine own hands.
Nay, Boy, be of good hope;—we both may live
To see a better day. At eighty-four
I still am strong and hale;—do thou thy part;
I will do mine.—I will begin again
With many tasks that were resigned to thee:
Up to the heights, and in among the storms,
Will I without thee go again, and do
All works which I was wont to do alone,
Before I knew thy face.—Heaven bless thee, Boy!
Thy heart these two weeks has been beating fast
With many hopes; it should be so—yes—yes—
I knew that thou couldst never have a wish
To leave me, Luke: thou hast been bound to me
Only by links of love: when thou art gone,
What will be left to us!—But, I forget
My purposes: Lay now the corner-stone,
As I requested; and hereafter, Luke,
When thou art gone away, should evil men
Be thy companions, think of me, my Son,
And of this moment; hither turn thy thoughts,
And God will strengthen thee: amid all fear
And all temptations, Luke, I pray that thou
May'st bear in mind the life thy Fathers lived,
Who, being innocent, did for that cause
Bestir them in good deeds. Now, fare thee well—
When thou return'st, thou in this place wilt see
A work which is not here: a covenant
'Twill be between us; but, whatever fate
Befall thee, I shall love thee to the last,

And bear thy memory with me to the grave.'
The Shepherd ended here; and Luke stooped down,
And, as his Father had requested, laid
The first stone of the Sheepfold. At the sight
The old Man's grief broke from him; to his heart
He pressed his Son, he kissèd him and wept;
And to the house together they returned.
—Hushed was that House in peace, or seeming peace,
Ere the Night fell:—with morrow's dawn the Boy
Began his journey, and when he had reached
The public way, he put on a bold face;
And all the neighbours, as he passed their doors,
Came forth with wishes and with farewell prayers,
That followed him till he was out of sight.
A good report did from their kinsman come,
Of Luke and his well-doing: and the Boy
Wrote loving letters, full of wondrous news,
Which, as the Housewife phrased it, were throughout
'The prettiest letters that were ever seen.'
Both parents read them with rejoicing hearts.
So, many months passed on: and once again
The Shepherd went about his daily work
With confident and cheerful thoughts; and now
Sometimes when he could find a leisure hour
He to that valley took his way, and there
Wrought at the Sheepfold. Meantime Luke began
To slacken in his duty; and, at length,
He in the dissolute city gave himself
To evil courses: ignominy and shame
Fell on him, so that he was driven at last
To seek a hiding-place beyond the seas.
There is a comfort in the strength of love;
'Twill make a thing endurable, which else
Would overset the brain, or break the heart:
I have conversed with more than one who well
Remember the old Man, and what he was
Years after he had heard this heavy news.
His bodily frame had been from youth to age
Of an unusual strength. Among the rocks
He went, and still looked up to sun and cloud,

And listened to the wind; and, as before,
Performed all kinds of labour for his sheep,
And for the land, his small inheritance.
And to that hollow dell from time to time
Did he repair, to build the Fold of which
His flock had need. 'Tis not forgotten yet
The pity which was then in every heart
For the old Man—and 'tis believed by all
That many and many a day he thither went,
And never lifted up a single stone.
There, by the Sheepfold, sometimes was he seen
Sitting alone, or with his faithful Dog,
Then old, beside him, lying at his feet.
The length of full seven years, from time to time,
He at the building of this Sheepfold wrought,
And left the work unfinished when he died.
Three years, or little more, did Isabel
Survive her Husband: at her death the estate
Was sold, and went into a stranger's hand.
The Cottage which was named the EVENING STAR
Is gone—the ploughshare has been through the ground
On which it stood; great changes have been wrought
In all the neighbourhood:—yet the oak is left
That grew beside their door; and the remains
Of the unfinished Sheepfold may be seen
Beside the boisterous brook of Greenhead Ghyll.

373

YARROW UNVISITED

[1803]

FROM Stirling Castle we had seen
The mazy Forth unravell'd,
Had trod the banks of Clyde and Tay,
And with the Tweed had travell'd;
And when we came to Clovenford,
Then said my 'winsome Marrow,'
'Whate'er betide, we'll turn aside,
And see the Braes of Yarrow.'

'Let Yarrow folk, frae Selkirk town,
Who have been buying, selling,
Go back to Yarrow, 'tis their own,
Each maiden to her dwelling!
On Yarrow's banks let herons feed,
Hares couch, and rabbits burrow;
But we will downward with the Tweed,
Nor turn aside to Yarrow.

'There's Galla Water, Leader Haughs,
Both lying right before us;
And Dryburgh, where with chiming Tweed
The lintwhites sing in chorus;
There's pleasant Teviotdale, a land
Made blythe with plough and harrow:
Why throw away a needful day
To go in search of Yarrow?

'What's Yarrow but a river bare
That glides the dark hills under?
There are a thousand such elsewhere
As worthy of your wonder.'
—Strange words they seem'd of slight and
scorn;
My true-love sigh'd for sorrow,
And look'd me in the face, to think
I thus could speak of Yarrow!

'O green,' said I, 'are Yarrow's holms.
And sweet is Yarrow flowing!
Fair hangs the apple frae the rock,
But we will leave it growing.
O'er hilly path and open strath
We'll wander Scotland thorough;
But, though so near, we will not turn
Into the dale of Yarrow.

'Let beeves and home-bred kine partake
The sweets of Burn-mill meadow;
The swan on still Saint Mary's Lake

Float double, swan and shadow!
We will not see them; will not go
To-day, nor yet to-morrow;
Enough if in our hearts we know
There's such a place as Yarrow.

'Be Yarrow stream unseen, unknown;
It must, or we shall rue it:
We have a vision of our own,
Ah! why should we undo it?
The treasured dreams of times long past,
We'll keep them, winsome Marrow!
For when we're there, although 'tis fair,
'Twill be another Yarrow!

'If care with freezing years should come
And wandering seem but folly,—
Should we be loth to stir from home,
And yet be melancholy;
Should life be dull, and spirits low,
'Twill soothe us in our sorrow
That earth has something yet to show,
The bonny Holms of Yarrow!'

374

Yarrow Visited

[*September, 1814*]

And is this—Yarrow?—This the stream
Of which my fancy cherish'd
So faithfully, a waking dream,
An image that hath perish'd?
O that some minstrel's harp were near
To utter notes of gladness
And chase this silence from the air,
That fills my heart with sadness.

Yet why?—a silvery current flows
With uncontroll'd meanderings;
Nor have these eyes by greener hills

Been soothed, in all my wanderings.
And, through her depths, Saint Mary's Lake
Is visibly delighted;
For not a feature of those hills
Is in the mirror slighted.

A blue sky bends o'er Yarrow Vale,
Save where that pearly whiteness
Is round the rising sun diffused,
A tender hazy brightness;
Mild dawn of promise! that excludes
All profitless dejection;
Though not unwilling here to admit
A pensive recollection.

Where was it that the famous Flower
Of Yarrow Vale lay bleeding?
His bed perchance was yon smooth mound
On which the herd is feeding:
And haply from this crystal pool
Now peaceful as the morning,
The water-Wraith ascended thrice,
And gave his doleful warning.

Delicious is the Lay that sings
The haunts of happy lovers,
The path that leads them to the grove,
The leafy grove that covers:
And pity sanctifies the verse
That paints, by strength of sorrow,
The unconquerable strength of love;
Bear witness, rueful Yarrow!

But thou that didst appear so fair
To fond imagination
Dost rival in the light of day
Her delicate creation:
Meek loveliness is round thee spread,
A softness still and holy:
The grace of forest charms decay'd,
And pastoral melancholy.

That region left, the vale unfolds
Rich groves of lofty stature,
With Yarrow winding through the pomp
Of cultivated Nature;
And rising from those lofty groves
Behold a ruin hoary,
The shatter'd front of Newark's Towers,
Renown'd in Border story.

Fair scenes for childhood's opening bloom,
For sportive youth to stray in,
For manhood to enjoy his strength,
And age to wear away in!
Yon cottage seems a bower of bliss,
A covert for protection
Of studious ease and generous cares
And every chaste affection!

How sweet on this autumnal day
The wild-wood fruits to gather,
And on my true-love's forehead plant
A crest of blooming heather!
And what if I enwreathed my own?
'Twere no offence to reason;
The sober hills thus deck their brows
To meet the wintry season.

I see—but not by sight alone,
Loved Yarrow, have I won thee;
A ray of Fancy still survives—
Her sunshine plays upon thee!
Thy ever-youthful waters keep
A course of lively pleasure;
And gladsome notes my lips can breathe
Accordant to the measure.

The vapours linger round the heights,
They melt, and soon must vanish;
One hour is theirs, nor more is mine—
Sad thought! which I would banish,

But that I know, where'er I go,
Thy genuine image, Yarrow!
Will dwell with me, to heighten joy
And cheer my mind in sorrow.

375

Yarrow Revisited

The gallant Youth, who may have gained,
  Or seeks, a 'winsome Marrow,'
Was but an Infant in the lap
  When first I looked on Yarrow;
Once more, by Newark's Castle-gate
  Long left without a warder,
I stood, looked, listened, and with Thee,
  Great Minstrel of the Border!

Grave thoughts ruled wide on that sweet
    day,
  Their dignity installing
In gentle bosoms, while sere leaves
  Were on the bough, or falling;
But breezes played, and sunshine gleamed—
  The forest to embolden;
Reddened the fiery hues, and shot
  Transparence through the golden.

For busy thoughts the Stream flowed on
  In foamy agitation;
And slept in many a crystal pool
  For quiet contemplation:
No public and no private care
  The freeborn mind enthralling,
We made a day of happy hours,
  Our happy days recalling.

Brisk Youth appeared, the Morn of youth,
  With freaks of graceful folly—
Life's temperate Noon, her sober Eve,
  Her Night not melancholy;

Past, present, future, all appeared
  In harmony united,
Like guests that meet, and some from far,
  By cordial love invited.

And if, as Yarrow, through the woods
  And down the meadow ranging,
Did meet us with unaltered face,
  Though we were changed and changing;
If, *then,* some natural shadows spread
  Our inward prospect over,
The soul's deep valley was not slow
  Its brightness to recover.

Eternal blessings on the Muse,
  And her divine employment!
The blameless Muse, who trains her Sons
  For hope and calm enjoyment;
Albeit sickness, lingering yet,
  Has o'er their pillow brooded;
And Care waylays their steps—a Sprite
  Not easily eluded.

For thee, O SCOTT! compelled to change
  Green Eildon-hill and Cheviot
For warm Vesuvio's vine-clad slopes,
  And leave thy Tweed and Tiviot
For mild Sorrento's breezy waves;
  May classic Fancy, linking
With native Fancy her fresh aid,
  Preserve thy heart from sinking!

Oh! while they minister to thee,
  Each vying with the other,
May Health return to mellow Age
  With Strength, her venturous brother;
And Tiber, and each brook and rill
  Renowned in song and story,
With unimagined beauty shine,
  Nor lose one ray of glory!

For Thou, upon a hundred streams,
  By tales of love and sorrow,
Of faithful love, undaunted truth,
  Hast shed the power of Yarrow;
And streams unknown, hills yet unseen,
  Wherever they invite Thee,
At parent Nature's grateful call,
  With gladness must requite Thee.

A gracious welcome shall be thine,
  Such looks of love and honour
As thy own Yarrow gave to me
  When first I gazed upon her;
Beheld what I had feared to see,
  Unwilling to surrender
Dreams treasured up from early days,
  The holy and the tender.

And what, for this frail world, were all
  That mortals do or suffer,
Did no responsive harp, no pen,
  Memorial tribute offer?
Yea, what were mighty Nature's self?
  Her features, could they win us,
Unhelped by the poetic voice
  That hourly speaks within us?

Nor deem that localized Romance
  Plays false with our affections;
Unsanctifies our tears—made sport
  For fanciful dejections;
Ah, no! the visions of the past
  Sustain the heart in feeling
Life as she is—our changeful Life,
  With friends and kindred dealing.

Bear witness, Ye, whose thoughts that day
  In Yarrow's groves were centred;
Who through the silent portal arch
  Of mouldering Newark enter'd;

And clomb the winding stair that once
  Too timidly was mounted
By the 'last Minstrel,' (not the last!)
  Ere he his Tale recounted.

Flow on for ever, Yarrow Stream!
  Fulfil thy pensive duty,
Well pleased that future Bards should chant
  For simple hearts thy beauty;
To dream-light dear while yet unseen,
  Dear to the common sunshine,
And dearer still, as now I feel,
  To memory's shadowy moonshine!

376 LINES

Composed a Few Miles Above Tintern Abbey, on Revisiting the Banks of the Wye During a Tour July 13, 1798

FIVE years have past; five summers, with the length
Of five long winters! and again I hear
These waters, rolling from their mountain-springs
With a soft inland murmur.—Once again
Do I behold these steep and lofty cliffs,
That on a wild secluded scene impress
Thoughts of more deep seclusion; and connect
The landscape with the quiet of the sky.
The day is come when I again repose
Here, under this dark sycamore, and view
These plots of cottage-ground, these orchard-tufts,
Which at this season, with their unripe fruits,
Are clad in one green hue, and lose themselves
'Mid groves and copses. Once again I see
These hedge-rows, hardly hedge-rows, little lines
Of sportive wood run wild: these pastoral farms,
Green to the very door; and wreaths of smoke
Sent up, in silence, from among the trees!
With some uncertain notice, as might seem
Of vagrant dwellers in the houseless woods,
Or of some Hermit's cave, where by his fire

The Hermit sits alone.
These beauteous forms,
Through a long absence, have not been to me
As is a landscape to a blind man's eye:
But oft, in lonely rooms, and 'mid the din
Of towns and cities, I have owed to them
In hours of weariness, sensations sweet,
Felt in the blood, and felt along the heart;
And passing even into my purer mind,
With tranquil restoration:—feelings too
Of unremembered pleasure: such, perhaps,
As have no slight or trivial influence
On that best portion of a good man's life,
His little, nameless, unremembered, acts
Of kindness and of love. Nor less, I trust,
To them I may have owed another gift,
Of aspect more sublime; that blessed mood,
In which the burthen of the mystery,
In which the heavy and the weary weight
Of all this unintelligible world,
Is lightened:—that serene and blessed mood,
In which the affections gently lead us on,—
Until, the breath of this corporeal frame
And even the motion of our human blood
Almost suspended, we are laid asleep
In body, and become a living soul:
While with an eye made quiet by the power
Of harmony, and the deep power of joy,
We see into the life of things.
If this
Be but a vain belief, yet, oh! how oft,
In darkness, and amid the many shapes
Of joyless daylight; when the fretful stir
Unprofitable, and the fever of the world,
Have hung upon the beatings of my heart,
How oft, in spirit, have I turned to thee,
O sylvan Wye! thou wanderer thro' the woods,
How often has my spirit turned to thee!
And now, with gleams of half-extinguished thought,
With many recognitions dim and faint,

And somewhat of a sad perplexity,
The picture of the mind revives again:
While here I stand, not only with the sense
Of present pleasure, but with pleasing thoughts
That in this moment there is life and food
For future years. And so I dare to hope,
Though changed, no doubt, from what I was when first
I came among these hills; when like a roe
I bounded o'er the mountains, by the sides
Of the deep rivers, and the lonely streams,
Wherever nature led: more like a man
Flying from something that he dreads, than one
Who sought the thing he loved. For nature then
(The coarser pleasures of my boyish days,
And their glad animal movements all gone by)
To me was all in all.—I cannot paint
What then I was. The sounding cataract
Haunted me like a passion: the tall rock,
The mountain, and the deep and gloomy wood,
Their colours and their forms, were then to me
An appetite; a feeling and a love,
That had no need of a remoter charm,
By thought supplied, nor any interest
Unborrowed from the eye.—That time is past,
And all its aching joys are now no more,
And all its dizzy raptures. Not for this
Faint I, nor mourn nor murmur; other gifts
Have followed; for such loss, I would believe,
Abundant recompence. For I have learned
To look on nature, not as in the hour
Of thoughtless youth; but hearing oftentimes
The still, sad music of humanity,
Nor harsh nor grating, though of ample power
To chasten and subdue. And I have felt
A presence that disturbs me with the joy
Of elevated thoughts: a sense sublime
Of something far more deeply interfused,
Whose dwelling is the light of setting suns,
And the round ocean and the living air,
And the blue sky, and in the mind of man:

A motion and a spirit, that impels
All thinking things, all objects of all thought,
And rolls through all things. Therefore am I still
A lover of the meadows and the woods,
And mountains; and of all that we behold
From this green earth; of all the mighty world
Of eye and ear,—both what they half create,
And what perceive; well pleased to recognise
In nature and the language of the sense,
The anchor of my purest thoughts, the nurse,
The guide, the guardian of my heart, and soul
Of all my moral being.

Nor perchance,
If I were not thus taught, should I the more
Suffer my genial spirits to decay:
For thou art with me here upon the banks
Of this fair river; thou, my dearest Friend,
My dear, dear Friend; and in thy voice I catch
The language of my former heart, and read
My former pleasures in the shooting lights
Of thy wild eyes. Oh! yet a little while
May I behold in thee what I was once,
My dear, dear Sister! and this prayer I make
Knowing that Nature never did betray
The heart that loved her; 'tis her privilege
Through all the years of this our life, to lead
From joy to joy: for she can so inform
The mind that is within us, so impress
With quietness and beauty, and so feed
With lofty thoughts, that neither evil tongues,
Rash judgments, nor the sneers of selfish men,
Nor greetings where no kindness is, nor all
The dreary intercourse of daily life,
Shall e'er prevail against us, or disturb
Our cheerful faith, that all which we behold
Is full of blessings. Therefore let the moon
Shine on thee in thy solitary walk;
And let the misty mountain winds be free
To blow against thee: and, in after years,
When these wild ecstasies shall be matured

Into a sober pleasure; when thy mind
Shall be a mansion for all lovely forms,
Thy memory be as a dwelling-place
For all sweet sounds and harmonies; oh! then,
If solitude, or fear, or pain, or grief,
Should be thy portion, with what healing thoughts
Of tender joy wilt thou remember me,
And these my exhortations! Nor, perchance—
If I should be where I no more can hear
Thy voice, nor catch from thy wild eyes those
gleams
Of past existence,—wilt thou then forget
That on the banks of this delightful stream
We stood together; and that I, so long
A worshipper of Nature, hither came
Unwearied in that service: rather say
With warmer love, oh! with far deeper zeal
Of holier love. Nor wilt thou then forget,
That after many wanderings, many years
Of absence, these steep woods and lofty cliffs,
And this green pastoral landscape, were to me
More dear, both for themselves and for thy sake!

377 THE DAFFODILS

I WANDER'D lonely as a cloud
That floats on high o'er vales and hills,
When all at once I saw a crowd,
A host of golden daffodils,
Beside the lake, beneath the trees
Fluttering and dancing in the breeze.

Continuous as the stars that shine
And twinkle on the milky way,
They stretch'd in never-ending line
Along the margin of a bay:
Ten thousand saw I at a glance
Tossing their heads in sprightly dance.

The waves beside them danced, but they
Out-did the sparkling waves in glee:—
A Poet could not but be gay
In such a jocund company!
I gazed—and gazed—but little thought
What wealth the show to me had brought;

For oft, when on my couch I lie
In vacant or in pensive mood,
They flash upon that inward eye
Which is the bliss of solitude;
And then my heart with pleasure fills,
And dances with the daffodils.

378

To the Daisy

With little here to do or see
Of things that in the great world be,
Sweet Daisy! oft I talk to thee
    For thou art worthy,
Thou unassuming commonplace
Of Nature, with that homely face,
And yet with something of a grace
    Which love makes for thee!

Oft on the dappled turf at ease
I sit and play with similes,
Loose types of things through all degrees,
    Thoughts of thy raising;
And many a fond and idle name
I give to thee, for praise or blame
As is the humour of the game,
    While I am gazing.

A nun demure, of lowly port;
Or sprightly maiden, of Love's court,
In thy simplicity the sport
    Of all temptations;

A queen in crown of rubies drest;
A starveling in a scanty vest;
Are all, as seems to suit thee best,
Thy appellations.

A little Cyclops, with one eye
Staring to threaten and defy,
That thought comes next—and instantly
The freak is over,
The shape will vanish, and behold!
A silver shield with boss of gold
That spreads itself, some fairy bold
In fight to cover.

I see thee glittering from afar—
And then thou art a pretty star,
Not quite so fair as many are
In heaven above thee!
Yet like a star, with glittering crest,
Self-poised in air thou seem'st to rest;—
May peace come never to his nest
Who shall reprove thee!

Sweet Flower! for by that name at last
When all my reveries are past
I call thee, and to that cleave fast,
Sweet silent Creature!
That breath'st with me in sun and air,
Do thou, as thou art wont, repair
My heart with gladness, and a share
Of thy meek nature!

379

To the Cuckoo

O blithe new-comer! I have heard,
I hear thee and rejoice:
O Cuckoo! shall I call thee bird,
Or but a wandering Voice?

While I am lying on the grass
Thy twofold shout I hear;
From hill to hill it seems to pass,
At once far off and near.

Though babbling only to the vale
Of sunshine and of flowers,
Thou bringest unto me a tale
Of visionary hours.

Thrice welcome, darling of the Spring!
Even yet thou art to me
No bird, but an invisible thing,
A voice, a mystery;

The same whom in my school-boy days
I listen'd to; that Cry
Which made me look a thousand ways
In bush, and tree, and sky.

To seek thee did I often rove
Through woods and on the green;
And thou wert still a hope, a love;
Still long'd for, never seen!

And I can listen to thee yet;
Can lie upon the plain
And listen, till I do beget
That golden time again.

O blessèd Bird! the earth we pace
Again appears to be
An unsubstantial, fairy place,
That is fit home for Thee!

380

The Green Linnet

Beneath these fruit-tree boughs that shed
Their snow-white blossoms on my head,
With brightest sunshine round me spread
Of Spring's unclouded weather,

In this sequester'd nook how sweet
To sit upon my orchard-seat!
And flowers and birds once more to greet,
My last year's friends together.

One have I mark'd, the happiest guest
In all this covert of the blest:
Hail to Thee, far above the rest
In joy of voice and pinion!
Thou, Linnet! in thy green array
Presiding Spirit here to-day
Dost lead the revels of the May,
And this is thy dominion.

While birds, and butterflies, and flowers,
Make all one band of paramours,
Thou, ranging up and down the bowers
Art sole in thy employment;
A Life, a Presence like the air,
Scattering thy gladness without care,
Too blest with any one to pair,
Thyself thy own enjoyment.

Amid yon tuft of hazel trees
That twinkle to the gusty breeze,
Behold him perch'd in ecstasies
Yet seeming still to hover;
There, where the flutter of his wings
Upon his back and body flings
Shadows and sunny glimmerings,
That cover him all over.

My dazzled sight he oft deceives—
A brother of the dancing leaves;
Then flits, and from the cottage-eaves
Pours forth his song in gushes,
As if by that exulting strain
He mock'd and treated with disdain
The voiceless Form he chose to feign,
While fluttering in the bushes.

381

Written in Early Spring

I heard a thousand blended notes
While in a grove I sate reclined,
In that sweet mood when pleasant thoughts
Bring sad thoughts to the mind.

To her fair works did Nature link
The human soul that through me ran;
And much it grieved my heart to think
What Man has made of Man.

Through primrose tufts, in that sweet bower,
The periwinkle trail'd its wreaths;
And 'tis my faith that every flower
Enjoys the air it breathes.

The birds around me hopp'd and play'd,
Their thoughts I cannot measure,—
But the least motion which they made
It seem'd a thrill of pleasure.

The budding twigs spread out their fan
To catch the breezy air;
And I must think, do all I can,
That there was pleasure there.

If this belief from heaven be sent,
If such be Nature's holy plan,
Have I not reason to lament
What Man has made of Man?

382

To the Skylark

Ethereal minstrel! pilgrim of the sky!
Dost thou despise the earth where cares abound?
Or while the wings aspire, are heart and eye

Both with thy nest upon the dewy ground?
Thy nest which thou canst drop into at will,
Those quivering wings composed, that music still!

To the last point of vision, and beyond
Mount, daring warbler!—that love-prompted strain
—'Twixt thee and thine a never-failing bond—
Thrills not the less the bosom of the plain:
Yet might'st thou seem, proud privilege! to sing
All independent of the leafy Spring.

Leave to the nightingale her shady wood;
A privacy of glorious light is thine,
Whence thou dost pour upon the world a flood
Of harmony, with instinct more divine;
Type of the wise, who soar, but never roam—
True to the kindred points of Heaven and Home.

383 The Affliction of Margaret

Where art thou, my beloved Son,
Where art thou, worse to me than dead!
O find me, prosperous or undone!
Or if the grave be now thy bed,
Why am I ignorant of the same
That I may rest; and neither blame
Nor sorrow may attend thy name?

Seven years, alas! to have received
No tidings of an only child—
To have despair'd, have hoped, believed,
And been for evermore beguiled,—
Sometimes with thoughts of very bliss!
I catch at them, and then I miss;
Was ever darkness like to this?

He was among the prime in worth,
An object beauteous to behold;
Well born, well bred; I sent him forth
Ingenuous, innocent, and bold:

If things ensued that wanted grace
As hath been said, they were not base;
And never blush was on my face.

Ah! little doth the young-one dream
When full of play and childish cares,
What power is in his wildest scream
Heard by his mother unawares!
He knows it not, he cannot guess;
Years to a mother bring distress;
But do not make her love the less.

Neglect me! no, I suffer'd long
From that ill thought; and being blind
Said 'Pride shall help me in my wrong:
Kind mother have I been, as kind
As ever breathed:' and that is true;
I've wet my path with tears like dew,
Weeping for him when no one knew.

My Son, if thou be humbled, poor,
Hopeless of honour and of gain,
O! do not dread thy mother's door;
Think not of me with grief and pain:
I now can see with better eyes;
And worldly grandeur I despise
And fortune with her gifts and lies.

Alas! the fowls of heaven have wings,
And blasts of heaven will aid their flight;
They mount—how short a voyage brings
The wanderers back to their delight!
Chains tie us down by land and sea;
And wishes, vain as mine, may be
All that is left to comfort thee.

Perhaps some dungeon hears thee groan
Maim'd, mangled by inhuman men;
Or thou upon a desert thrown
Inheritest the lion's den;

Or hast been summon'd to the deep
Thou, thou, and all thy mates, to keep
An incommunicable sleep.

I look for ghosts: but none will force
Their way to me; 'tis falsely said
That there was ever intercourse
Between the living and the dead;
For surely then I should have sight
Of him I wait for day and night
With love and longings infinite.

My apprehensions come in crowds;
I dread the rustling of the grass;
The very shadows of the clouds
Have power to shake me as they pass;
I question things, and do not find
One that will answer to my mind;
And all the world appears unkind.

Beyond participation lie
My troubles, and beyond relief:
If any chance to heave a sigh
They pity me, and not my grief.
Then come to me, my Son, or send
Some tidings that my woes may end!
I have no other earthly friend.

384 Simon Lee the Old Huntsman

In the sweet shire of Cardigan,
Not far from pleasant Ivor Hall,
An old man dwells, a little man,
I've heard he once was tall.
Full five-and-thirty years he lived
A running huntsman merry;
And still the centre of his cheek
Is red as a ripe cherry.

No man like him the horn could sound,
And hill and valley rang with glee,
When Echo bandied, round and round,
The halloo of Simon Lee.
In those proud days he little cared
For husbandry or tillage;
To blither tasks did Simon rouse
The sleepers of the village.

He all the country could outrun,
Could leave both man and horse behind;
And often, ere the chase was done,
He reel'd and was stone-blind.
And still there's something in the world
At which his heart rejoices;
For when the chiming hounds are out,
He dearly loves their voices.

But O the heavy change!—bereft
Of health, strength, friends and kindred, see
Old Simon to the world is left
In liveried poverty:
His master's dead, and no one now
Dwells in the Hall of Ivor;
Men, dogs, and horses, all are dead;
He is the sole survivor.

And he is lean and he is sick,
His body, dwindled and awry,
Rests upon ankles swoln and thick;
His legs are thin and dry.
He has no son, he has no child,
His wife, an aged woman,
Lives with him, near the waterfall,
Upon the village common.

Beside their moss-grown hut of clay,
Not twenty paces from the door,
A scrap of land they have, but they
Are poorest of the poor.

This scrap of land he from the heath
Enclosed when he was stronger;
But what avails the land to them
Which he can till no longer?

Oft, working by her husband's side,
Ruth does what Simon cannot do;
For she, with scanty cause for pride,
Is stouter of the two.
And, though you with your utmost skill
From labour could not wean them,
'Tis little, very little, all
That they can do between them.

Few months of life has he in store
As he to you will tell,
For still, the more he works, the more
Do his weak ankles swell.
My gentle reader, I perceive
How patiently you've waited,
And now I fear that you expect
Some tale will be related.

O reader! had you in your mind
Such stores as silent thought can bring,
O gentle reader! you would find
A tale in everything.
What more I have to say is short,
And you must kindly take it:
It is no tale; but, should you think,
Perhaps a tale you'll make it.

One summer-day I chanced to see
This old man doing all he could
To unearth the root of an old tree,
A stump of rotten wood.
The mattock totter'd in his hand;
So vain was his endeavour
That at the root of the old tree
He might have work'd for ever.

'You're overtask'd, good Simon Lee,
Give me your tool,' to him I said;
And at the word right gladly he
Received my proffer'd aid.
I struck, and with a single blow
The tangled root I sever'd,
At which the poor old man so long
And vainly had endeavour'd.

The tears into his eyes were brought,
And thanks and praises seem'd to run
So fast out of his heart, I thought
They never would have done.
—I've heard of hearts unkind, kind deeds
With coldness still returning;
Alas! the gratitude of men
Hath oftener left me mourning.

385

Ode to Duty

Stern Daughter of the voice of God!
O Duty! if that name thou love
Who art a light to guide, a rod
To check the erring, and reprove;
Thou who art victory and law
When empty terrors overawe;
From vain temptations dost set free,
And calm'st the weary strife of frail humanity!

There are who ask not if thine eye
Be on them; who, in love and truth
Where no misgiving is, rely
Upon the genial sense of youth:
Glad hearts! without reproach or blot,
Who do thy work, and know it not:
O! if through confidence misplaced
They fail, thy saving arms, dread Power! around
them cast.

Serene will be our days and bright
And happy will our nature be
When love is an unerring light,
And joy its own security.
And they a blissful course may hold
Ev'n now, who, not unwisely bold,
Live in the spirit of this creed;
Yet find that other strength according to their need.

I, loving freedom, and untried,
No sport of every random gust,
Yet being to myself a guide,
Too blindly have reposed my trust:
And oft, when in my heart was heard
Thy timely mandate, I deferr'd
The task, in smoother walks to stray;
But thee I now would serve more strictly, if I may.

Through no disturbance of my soul
Or strong compunction in me wrought,
I supplicate for thy controul,
But in the quietness of thought:
Me this uncharter'd freedom tires;
I feel the weight of chance-desires:
My hopes no more must change their name;
I long for a repose tha. ever is the same.

Stern lawgiver! yet thou dost wear
The Godhead's most benignant grace;
Nor know we anything so fair
As is the smile upon thy face:
Flowers laugh before thee on their beds,
And fragrance in thy footing treads;
Thou dost preserve the Stars from wrong;
And the most ancient Heavens, through thee, are
fresh and strong.

To humbler functions, awful Power!
I call thee: I myself commend
Unto thy guidance from this hour;

O let my weakness have an end!
Give unto me, made lowly wise,
The spirit of self-sacrifice;
The confidence of reason give;
And in the light of Truth thy bondman let me live.

386 She Was a Phantom of Delight

She was a phantom of delight
When first she gleam'd upon my sight;
A lovely apparition, sent
To be a moment's ornament;
Her eyes as stars of twilight fair;
Like Twilight's, too, her dusky hair;
But all things else about her drawn
From May-time and the cheerful dawn;
A dancing shape, an image gay,
To haunt, to startle, and waylay.

I saw her upon nearer view,
A spirit, yet a woman too!
Her household motions light and free,
And steps of virgin-liberty;
A countenance in which did meet
Sweet records, promises as sweet;
A creature not too bright or good
For human nature's daily food,
For transient sorrows, simple wiles,
Praise, blame, love, kisses, tears, and smiles.

And now I see with eye serene
The very pulse of the machine;
A being breathing thoughtful breath,
A traveller between life and death:
The reason firm, the temperate will,
Endurance, foresight, strength, and skill;
A perfect woman, nobly plann'd
To warn, to comfort, and command;
And yet a Spirit still, and bright
With something of angelic light.

387 To the Highland Girl of Inversneyde

Sweet Highland Girl, a very shower
Of beauty is thy earthly dower!
Twice seven consenting years have shed
Their utmost bounty on thy head:
And these gray rocks, this household lawn,
These trees—a veil just half withdrawn,
This fall of water that doth make
A murmur near the silent lake,
This little bay, a quiet road
That holds in shelter thy abode;
In truth together ye do seem
Like something fashion'd in a dream;
Such forms as from their covert peep
When earthly cares are laid asleep!
But O fair Creature! in the light
Of common day, so heavenly bright
I bless Thee, Vision as thou art,
I bless thee with a human heart:
God shield thee to thy latest years!
I neither know thee nor thy peers:
And yet my eyes are fill'd with tears.

With earnest feeling I shall pray
For thee when I am far away;
For never saw I mien or face
In which more plainly I could trace
Benignity and home-bred sense
Ripening in perfect innocence.
Here scatter'd, like a random seed,
Remote from men, Thou dost not need
The embarrass'd look of shy distress,
And maidenly shamefacédness:
Thou wear'st upon thy forehead clear
The freedom of a mountaineer:
A face with gladness overspread,
Soft smiles, by human kindness bred;
And seemliness complete, that sways

Thy courtesies, about thee plays;
With no restraint, but such as springs
From quick and eager visitings
Of thoughts that lie beyond the reach
Of thy few words of English speech:
A bondage sweetly brook'd, a strife
That gives thy gestures grace and life!
So have I, not unmoved in mind,
Seen birds of tempest-loving kind,
Thus beating up against the wind.

What hand but would a garland cull
For thee who art so beautiful?
O happy pleasure! here to dwell
Beside thee in some heathy dell;
Adopt your homely ways, and dress,
A shepherd, thou a shepherdess!
But I could frame a wish for thee
More like a grave reality:
Thou art to me but as a wave
Of the wild sea: and I would have
Some claim upon thee, if I could,
Though but of common neighbourhood.
What joy to hear thee, and to see!
Thy elder brother I would be,
Thy father, anything to thee.
Now thanks to Heaven! that of its grace
Hath led me to this lonely place:
Joy have I had; and going hence
I bear away my recompense.
In spots like these it is we prize
Our memory, feel that she hath eyes:
Then why should I be loth to stir?
I feel this place was made for her;
To give new pleasure like the past,
Continued long as life shall last.
Nor am I loth, though pleased at heart,
Sweet Highland Girl! from thee to part;
For I, methinks, till I grow old
As fair before me shall behold

As I do now, the cabin small,
The lake, the bay, the waterfall;
And Thee, the spirit of them all!

388

The Solitary Reaper

Behold her, single in the field,
Yon solitary Highland Lass!
Reaping and singing by herself;
Stop here, or gently pass!
Alone she cuts and binds the grain,
And sings a melancholy strain;
O listen! for the vale profound
Is overflowing with the sound.

No nightingale did ever chaunt
More welcome notes to weary bands
Of travellers in some shady haunt,
Among Arabian sands:
No sweeter voice was ever heard
In spring-time from the cuckoo-bird,
Breaking the silence of the seas
Among the farthest Hebrides.

Will no one tell me what she sings?
Perhaps the plaintive numbers flow
For old, unhappy, far-off things,
And battles long ago:
Or is it some more humble lay,
Familiar matter of to-day?
Some natural sorrow, loss, or pain,
That has been, and may be again!

Whate'er the theme, the maiden sang
As if her song could have no ending;
I saw her singing at her work,
And o'er the sickle bending;

I listen'd, till I had my fill;
And, as I mounted up the hill,
The music in my heart I bore
Long after it was heard no more.

389 THE REVERIE OF POOR SUSAN

AT the corner of Wood Street, when daylight appears,
Hangs a Thrush that sings loud, it has sung for three years:
Poor Susan has pass'd by the spot, and has heard
In the silence of morning the song of the bird.

'Tis a note of enchantment; what ails her? She sees
A mountain ascending, a vision of trees;
Bright volumes of vapour through Lothbury glide,
And a river flows on through the vale of Cheapside.

Green pastures she views in the midst of the dale
Down which she so often has tripp'd with her pail;
And a single small cottage, a nest like a dove's,
The one only dwelling on earth that she loves.

She looks, and her heart is in heaven: but they fade,
The mist and the river, the hill and the shade;
The stream will not flow, and the hill will not rise,
And the colours have all pass'd away from her eyes.

390 TO TOUSSAINT L'OUVERTURE

TOUSSAINT, the most unhappy man of men!
Whether the whistling Rustic tend his plough
Within thy hearing, or thy head be now
Pillowed in some deep dungeon's earless den;—
O miserable Chieftain! where and when
Wilt thou find patience? Yet die not; do thou
Wear rather in thy bonds a cheerful brow:
Though fallen thyself, never to rise again,

Live, and take comfort. Thou hast left behind
  Powers that will work for thee; air, earth, and skies;
There's not a breathing of the common wind
  That will forget thee; thou hast great allies;
Thy friends are exultations, agonies,
  And love, and man's unconquerable mind.

391 Character of the Happy Warrior

Who is the happy Warrior? Who is he
What every man in arms should wish to be?
—It is the generous Spirit, who, when brought
Among the tasks of real life, hath wrought
Upon the plan that pleased his childish thought:
Whose high endeavours are an inward light
That makes the path before him always bright:
Who, with a natural instinct to discern
What knowledge can perform, is diligent to learn;
Abides by this resolve, and stops not there,
But makes his moral being his prime care;
Who, doomed to go in company with Pain,
And Fear, and Bloodshed, miserable train!
Turns his necessity to glorious gain;
In face of these doth exercise a power
Which is our human nature's highest dower;
Controls them and subdues, transmutes, bereaves
Of their bad influence, and their good receives:
By objects, which might force the soul to abate
Her feeling, rendered more compassionate;
Is placable—because occasions rise
So often that demand such sacrifice;
More skilful in self-knowledge, even more pure,
As tempted more; more able to endure,
As more exposed to suffering and distress;
Thence, also, more alive to tenderness.
—'Tis he whose law is reason; who depends
Upon that law as on the best of friends;
Whence, in a state where men are tempted still
To evil for a guard against worse ill,

And what in quality or act is best
Doth seldom on a right foundation rest,
He labours good on good to fix, and owes
To virtue every triumph that he knows:
—Who, if he rise to station of command,
Rises by open means; and there will stand
On honourable terms, or else retire,
And in himself possess his own desire;
Who comprehends his trust, and to the same
Keeps faithful with a singleness of aim;
And therefore does not stoop, nor lie in wait
For wealth, or honours, or for worldly state,
Whom they must follow; on whose head must fall,
Like showers of manna, if they come at all:
Whose power shed round him in the common strife,
Or mild concerns of ordinary life,
A constant influence, a peculiar grace;
But who, if he be called upon to face
Some awful moment to which Heaven has joined
Great issues, good or bad for human kind,
Is happy as a Lover; and attired
With sudden brightness, like a Man inspired;
And, through the heat of conflict, keeps the law
In calmness made, and sees what he foresaw:
Or if an unexpected call succeed,
Come when it will, is equal to the need:
—He who, though thus endued as with a sense
And faculty for storm and turbulence,
Is yet a Soul whose master-bias leans
To homefelt pleasures and to gentle scenes;
Sweet images! which, whereso'er he be,
Are at his heart; and such fidelity
It is his darling passion to approve;
More brave for this, that he hath much to love:—
'Tis, finally, the Man, who, lifted high,
Conspicuous object in a Nation's eye,
Or left unthought-of in obscurity,—
Who, with a toward or untoward lot,
Prosperous or adverse, to his wish or not,
Plays, in the many games of life, that one

Where what he most doth value must be won.
Whom neither shape of danger can dismay,
Nor thought of tender happiness betray;
Who, not content that former worth stand fast,
Looks forward, persevering to the last,
From well to better, daily self-surpast:
Who, whether praise of him must walk the earth
For ever, and to noble deeds give birth,
Or he must fall to sleep without his fame,
And leave a dead unprofitable name,
Finds comfort in himself and in his cause;
And, while the mortal mist is gathering, draws
His breath in confidence of Heaven's applause:
This is the happy Warrior; this is he
Whom every Man in arms should wish to be.

392 Resolution and Independence

There was a roaring in the wind all night;
The rain came heavily and fell in floods;
But now the sun is rising calm and bright;
The birds are singing in the distant woods;
Over his own sweet voice the Stock-dove broods;
The Jay makes answer as the Magpie chatters;
And all the air is filled with pleasant noise of waters.

All things that love the sun are out of doors;
The sky rejoices in the morning's birth;
The grass is bright with rain-drops;—on the moors
The hare is running races in her mirth;
And with her feet she from the plashy earth
Raises a mist, that, glittering in the sun,
Runs with her all the way, wherever she doth run.

I was a Traveller then upon the moor,
I saw the hare that raced about with joy;
I heard the woods and distant waters roar;
Or heard them not, as happy as a boy;

The pleasant season did my heart employ:
My old remembrances went from me wholly;
And all the ways of men, so vain and melancholy.

But, as it sometimes chanceth, from the might
Of joys in minds that can no further go,
As high as we have mounted in delight
In our dejection do we sink as low;
To me that morning did it happen so;
And fears and fancies thick upon me came;
Dim sadness—and blind thoughts, I knew not, nor could name.

I heard the sky-lark warbling in the sky;
And I bethought me of the playful hare:
Even such a happy Child of earth am I:
Even as these blissful creatures do I fare;
Far from the world I walk, and from all care;
But there may come another day to me—
Solitude, pain of heart, distress, and poverty.

My whole life I have lived in pleasant thought,
As if life's business were a summer mood;
As if all needful things would come unsought
To genial faith, still rich in genial good;
But how can He expect that others should
Build for him, sow for him, and at his call
Love him, who for himself will take no heed at all?

I thought of Chatterton, the marvellous Boy,
The sleepless Soul that perished in his pride;
Of Him who walked in glory and in joy
Following his plough, along the mountain-side:
By our own spirits are we deified:
We Poets in our youth begin in gladness;
But thereof come in the end despondency and madness.

Now, whether it were by peculiar grace,
A leading from above, a something given,
Yet it befell, that, in this lonely place,

When I with these untoward thoughts had striven,
Beside a pool bare to the eye of heaven
I saw a man before me unawares:
The oldest man he seemed that ever wore grey hairs.

As a huge stone is sometimes seen to lie
Couched on the bald top of an eminence;
Wonder to all who do the same espy,
By what means it could thither come, and whence;
So that it seems a thing endued with sense:
Like a sea-beast crawled forth, that on a shelf
Of rock or sand reposeth, there to sun itself;

Such seemed this Man, not all alive nor dead,
Nor all asleep—in his extreme old age:
His body was bent double, feet and head
Coming together in Life's pilgrimage;
As if some dire constraint of pain, or rage
Of sickness felt by him in times long past,
A more than human weight upon his frame had cast.

Himself he propped, limbs, body, and pale face,
Upon a long grey staff of shaven wood:
And, still as I drew near with gentle pace,
Upon the margin of that moorish flood
Motionless as a cloud the old man stood;
That heareth not the loud winds when they call;
And moveth altogether, if it move at all.

At length, himself unsettling, he the pond
Stirred with his staff, and fixedly did look
Upon the muddy water, which he conned,
As if he had been reading in a book:
And now a stranger's privilege I took;
And, drawing to his side, to him did say,
'This morning gives us promise of a glorious day.'

A gentle answer did the old Man make,
In courteous speech which forth he slowly drew:
And him with further words I thus bespake,

'What occupation do you there pursue?
This is a lonesome place for one like you.'
Ere he replied, a flash of mild surprise
Broke from the sable orbs of his yet-vivid eyes.

His words came feebly, from a feeble chest,
But each in solemn order followed each,
With something of a lofty utterance drest—
Choice word and measured phrase, above the reach
Of ordinary men; a stately speech;
Such as grave Livers do in Scotland use,
Religious men, who give to God and man their dues.

He told, that to these waters he had come
To gather leeches, being old and poor:
Employment hazardous and wearisome!
And he had many hardships to endure:
From pond to pond he roamed, from moor to moor:
Housing, with God's good help, by choice or chance;
And in this way he gained an honest maintenance,

The old Man still stood talking by my side;
But now his voice to me was like a stream
Scarce heard; nor word from word could I divide:
And the whole body of the man did seem
Like one whom I had met with in a dream;
Or like a man from some far region sent,
To give me human strength, by apt admonishment

My former thoughts returned: the fear that kills
And hope that is unwilling to be fed;
Cold, pain, and labour, and all fleshly ills:
And mighty Poets in their misery dead.
—Perplexed, and longing to be comforted,
My question eagerly did I renew,
'How is it that you live, and what is it you do?'

He with a smile did then his words repeat:
And said, that, gathering leeches, far and wide
He travelled; stirring thus about his feet

The waters of the pools where they abide.
‘Once I could meet with them on every side;
But they have dwindled long by slow decay;
Yet still I persevere, and find them where I may.’

While he was talking thus, the lonely place,
The old Man’s shape, and speech—all troubled me:
In my mind’s eye I seemed to see him pace
About the weary moors continually,
Wandering about alone and silently.
While I these thoughts within myself pursued,
He, having made a pause, the same discourse renewed.

And soon with this he other matter blended,
Cheerfully uttered, with demeanour kind,
But stately in the main; and when he ended,
I could have laughed myself to scorn to find
In that decrepit Man so firm a mind.
‘God,’ said I, ‘be my help and stay secure;
I’ll think of the leech-gatherer on the lonely moor!’

393 LAODAMIA

‘WITH sacrifice before the rising morn
Vows have I made by fruitless hope inspired;
And from the infernal Gods, ’mid shades forlorn
Of night, my slaughtered Lord have I required:
Celestial pity I again implore;—
Restore him to my sight—great Jove, restore!’

So speaking, and by fervent love endowed
With faith, the Suppliant heavenward lifts her hands
While, like the sun emerging from a cloud,
Her countenance brightens—and her eye expands;
Her bosom heaves and spreads, her stature grows;
And she expects the issue in repose.

O terror! what hath she perceived?—O joy!
What doth she look on?—whom doth she behold?
Her Hero slain upon the beach of Troy?

His vital presence? his corporeal mould?
It is—if sense deceive her not—'tis He!
And a God leads him, wingèd Mercury!

Mild Hermes spake—and touched her with his wand
That calms all fear; 'Such grace hath crowned thy
prayer,
Laodamia! that at Jove's command
Thy Husband walks the paths of upper air:
He comes to tarry with thee three hours' space;
Accept the gift, behold him face to face!'

Forth sprang the impassioned Queen her Lord to clasp:
Again that consummation she essayed;
But unsubstantial Form eludes her grasp
As often as that eager grasp was made.
The Phantom parts—but parts to reunite,
And re-assume his place before her sight.

'Protesilàus, lo! thy guide is gone!
Confirm, I pray, the vision with thy voice:
This is our palace,—yonder is thy throne;
Speak, and the floor thou tread'st on will rejoice.
Not to appal me have the gods bestowed
This precious boon; and blest a sad abode.'

'Great Jove, Laodamia! doth not leave
His gifts imperfect:—Spectre though I be,
I am not sent to scare thee or deceive;
But in reward of thy fidelity.
And something also did my worth obtain;
For fearless virtue bringeth boundless gain.

'Thou knowest, the Delphic oracle foretold
That the first Greek who touched the Trojan strand
Should die; but me the threat could not withhold:
A generous cause a victim did demand;
And forth I leapt upon the sandy plain;
A self-devoted chief—by Hector slain.'

'Supreme of Heroes—bravest, noblest, best!
Thy matchless courage I bewail no more,
Which then, when tens of thousands were deprest
By doubt, propelled thee to the fatal shore;
Thou found'st—and I forgive thee—here thou art—
A nobler counsellor than my poor heart.

'But thou, though capable of sternest deed,
Wert kind as resolute, and good as brave;
And he, whose power restores thee, hath decreed
Thou should'st elude the malice of the grave:
Redundant are thy locks, thy lips as fair
As when their breath enriched Thessalian air.

'No Spectre greets me,—no vain shadow this;
Come, blooming Hero, place thee by my side!
Give, on this well-known couch, one nuptial kiss
To me, this day, a second time thy bride!'
Jove frowned in heaven: the conscious Parsæ threw
Upon those roseate lips a Stygian hue.

'This visage tells thee that my doom is past:
Nor should the change be mourned, even if the joys
Of sense were able to return as fast
And surely as they vanish. Earth destroys
Those raptures duly—Erebus disdains:
Calm pleasures there abide—majestic pains.

'Be taught, O faithful Consort, to control
Rebellious passion: for the Gods approve
The depth, and not the tumult, of the soul;
A fervent, not ungovernable, love.
Thy transports moderate; and meekly mourn
When I depart, for brief is my sojourn—'

'Ah, wherefore?—Did not Hercules by force
Wrest from the guardian Monster of the tomb
Alcestis, a reanimated corse,
Given back to dwell on earth in vernal bloom?
Medea's spells dispersed the weight of years,
And Æson stood a youth 'mid youthful peers.

'The Gods to us are merciful—and they
Yet further may relent: for mightier far
Than strength of nerve and sinew, or the sway
Of magic potent over sun and star,
Is love, though oft to agony distrest,
And though his favourite seat be feeble woman's breast.

'But if thou goest, I follow—' 'Peace!' he said—
She looked upon him and was calmed and cheered;
The ghastly colour from his lips had fled;
In his deportment, shape, and mien, appeared
Elysian beauty, melancholy grace,
Brought from a pensive though a happy place.

He spake of love, such love as Spirits feel
In worlds whose course is equable and pure;
No fears to beat away—no strife to heal—
The past unsighed for, and the future sure;
Spake of heroic arts in graver mood
Revived, with finer harmony pursued:

Of all that is most beauteous—imaged there
In happier beauty; more pellucid streams,
An ampler ether, a diviner air,
And fields invested with purpureal gleams;
Climes which the sun, who sheds the brightest day
Earth knows, is all unworthy to survey.

Yet there the Soul shall enter which hath earned
That privilege by virtue—'Ill,' said he,
'The end of man's existence I discerned,
Who from ignoble games and revelry
Could draw, when we had parted, vain delight
While tears were thy best pastime,—day and night:

'And while my youthful peers, before my eyes,
(Each hero following his peculiar bent)
Prepared themselves for glorious enterprise
By martial sports,—or, seated in the tent,
Chieftains and kings in council were detained;
What time the fleet at Aulis lay enchained.

'The wished-for wind was given:—I then revolved
The oracle, upon the silent sea;
And, if no worthier led the way, resolved
That, of a thousand vessels, mine should be
The foremost prow in pressing to the strand,—
Mine the first blood that tinged the Trojan sand.

'Yet bitter, oft-times bitter, was the pang
When of thy loss I thought, belovèd Wife!
On thee too fondly did my memory hang,
And on the joys we shared in mortal life,—
The paths which we had trod—these fountains, flowers,
My new-planned cities, and unfinished towers.

'But should suspense permit the Foe to cry,
'Behold, they tremble!—haughty their array,
Yet of their number no one dares to die!'—
In soul I swept the indignity away:
Old frailties then recurred:—but lofty thought,
In act embodied, my deliverance wrought.

'And Thou, though strong in love, art all too weak
In reason, in self-government too slow;
I counsel thee by fortitude to seek
Our blest reunion in the shades below.
The invisible world with thee hath sympathized:
Be thy affections raised and solemnized.

'Learn, by a mortal yearning, to ascend
Seeking a higher object. Love was given,
Encouraged, sanctioned, chiefly for that end:
For this the passion to excess was driven—
That self might be annulled: her bondage prove
The fetters of a dream, opposed to love.'—

Aloud she shrieked! for Hermes reappears!
Round the dear Shade she would have clung—'tis vain:
The hours are past—too brief had they been years;
And him no mortal effort can detain:

Swift, toward the realms that know not earthly day,
He through the portal takes his silent way,
And on the palace floor a lifeless corse She lay.

Thus, all in vain exhorted and reproved,
She perished; and, as for a wilful crime,
By the just Gods whom no weak pity moved,
Was doomed to wear out her appointed time,
Apart from happy Ghosts—that gather flowers
Of blissful quiet 'mid unfading bowers.

Yet tears to human suffering are due;
And mortal hopes defeated and o'erthrown
Are mourned by man, and not by man alone,
As fondly he believes.—Upon the side
Of Hellespont (such faith was entertained)
A knot of spiry trees for ages grew
From out the tomb of him for whom she died;
And ever, when such stature they had gained
That Ilium's walls were subject to their view,
The trees' tall summits withered at the sight;
A constant interchange of growth and blight!

394

We Are Seven

A simple Child,
That lightly draws its breath,
And feels its life in every limb,
What should it know of death?

I met a little cottage Girl:
She was eight years old, she said;
Her hair was thick with many a curl
That clustered round her head.

She had a rustic, woodland air,
And she was wildly clad:
Her eyes were fair, and very fair;
—Her beauty made me glad.

'Sisters and brothers, little Maid,
How many may you be?'
'How many? Seven in all,' she said,
And wondering looked at me.

'And where are they? I pray you tell.'
She answered, 'Seven are we;
And two of us at Conway dwell,
And two are gone to sea.

'Two of us in the church-yard lie,
My sister and my brother;
And, in the church-yard cottage, I
Dwell near them with my mother.'

'You say that two at Conway dwell,
And two are gone to sea,
Yet ye are seven!—I pray you tell,
Sweet Maid, how this may be.'

Then did the little maid reply,
'Seven boys and girls are we;
Two of us in the church-yard lie,
Beneath the church-yard tree.'

'You run above, my little Maid,
Your limbs they are alive;
If two are in the church-yard laid,
Then ye are only five.'

'Their graves are green, they may be seen,'
The little Maid replied,
'Twelve steps or more from my mother's door,
And they are side by side.

'My stockings there I often knit,
My kerchief there I hem;
And there upon the ground I sit,
And sing a song to them.

'And often after sun-set, Sir,
When it is light and fair,
I take my little porringer,
And eat my supper there.

'The first that died was sister Jane;
In bed she moaning lay,
Till God released her of her pain;
And then she went away.

'So in the church-yard she was laid;
And, when the grass was dry,
Together round her grave we played,
My brother John and I.

'And when the ground was white with snow,
And I could run and slide,
My brother John was forced to go,
And he lies by her side.'

'How many are you, then,' said I,
'If they two are in heaven?'
Quick was the little Maid's reply,
'O Master! we are seven.'

'But they are dead; those two are dead!
Their spirits are in heaven!'
'Twas throwing words away; for still
The little Maid would have her will,
And said. 'Nay, we are seven!'

395

Lucy

I

She dwelt among the untrodden ways
  Beside the springs of Dove;
A maid whom there were none to praise,
  And very few to love.

A violet by a mossy stone
  Half-hidden from the eye!
—Fair as a star, when only one
  Is shining in the sky.

She lived unknown, and few could know
  When Lucy ceased to be;
But she is in her grave, and, O!
  The difference to me!

II

I travell'd among unknown men
  In lands beyond the sea;
Nor, England! did I know till then
  What love I bore to thee.

'Tis past, that melancholy dream!
  Nor will I quit thy shore
A second time, for still I seem
  To love thee more and more.

Among thy mountains did I feel
  The joy of my desire;
And she I cherish'd turn'd her wheel
  Beside an English fire.

Thy mornings show'd, thy nights conceal'd
  The bowers where Lucy play'd;
And thine too is the last green field
  That Lucy's eyes survey'd.

III

Three years she grew in sun and shower;
Then Nature said, 'A lovelier flower
On earth was never sown:
This child I to myself will take;
She shall be mine, and I will make
A lady of my own.

'Myself will to my darling be
Both law and impulse: and with me
The girl, in rock and plain,
In earth and heaven, in glade and bower,
Shall feel an overseeing power
To kindle or restrain.

'She shall be sportive as the fawn
That wild with glee across the lawn
Or up the mountain springs;
And her's shall be the breathing balm,
And her's the silence and the calm
Of mute insensate things.

'The floating clouds their state shall lend
To her; for her the willow bend;
Nor shall she fail to see
E'en in the motions of the storm
Grace that shall mould the maiden's form
By silent sympathy.

'The stars of midnight shall be dear
To her; and she shall lean her ear
In many a secret place
Where rivulets dance their wayward round,
And beauty born of murmuring sound
Shall pass into her face.

'And vital feelings of delight
Shall rear her form to stately height,
Her virgin bosom swell;
Such thoughts to Lucy I will give
Where she and I together live
Here in this happy dell.'

Thus Nature spake—The work was done—
How soon my Lucy's race was run!
She died, and left to me
This heath, this calm and quiet scene;
The memory of what has been,
And never more will be.

IV

A slumber did my spirit seal;
  I had no human fears:
She seem'd a thing that could not feel
  The touch of earthly years.

No motion has she now, no force;
  She neither hears nor sees;
Roll'd round in earth's diurnal course
  With rocks, and stones, and trees.

396

The Inner Vision

Most sweet it is with unuplifted eyes
To pace the ground, if path there be or none
While a fair region round the Traveller lies
Which he forbears again to look upon;

Pleased rather with some soft ideal scene
The work of Fancy, or some happy tone
Of meditation, slipping in between
The beauty coming and the beauty gone.

—If Thought and Love desert us, from that day
Let us break off all commerce with the Muse:
With Thought and Love companions of our way—

Whate'er the senses take or may refuse,—
The Mind's internal heaven shall shed her dews
Of inspiration on the humblest lay.

397

By the Sea

It is a beauteous evening, calm and free;
The holy time is quiet as a nun
Breathless with adoration; the broad sun
Is sinking down in its tranquillity;

The gentleness of heaven is on the Sea:
Listen! the mighty being is awake,
And doth with his eternal motion make
A sound like thunder—everlastingly.

Dear child! dear girl! that walkest with me here,
If thou appear untouch'd by solemn thought
Thy nature is not therefore less divine:

Thou liest in Abraham's bosom all the year,
And worship'st at the Temple's inner shrine,
God being with thee when we know it not.

398

Upon Westminster Bridge

Sept. 3, 1802

Earth has not anything to show more fair:
Dull would he be of soul who could pass by
A sight so touching in its majesty:
This City now doth like a garment wear

The beauty of the morning: silent, bare,
Ships, towers, domes, theatres, and temples lie
Open unto the fields, and to the sky,
All bright and glittering in the smokeless air.

Never did sun more beautifully steep
In his first splendour valley, rock, or hill;
Ne'er saw I, never felt, a calm so deep!

The river glideth at his own sweet will:
Dear God! the very houses seem asleep;
And all that mighty heart is lying still!

399

To a Distant Friend

Why art thou silent? Is thy love a plant
Of such weak fibre that the treacherous air
Of absence withers what was once so fair?
Is there no debt to pay, no boon to grant?

Yet have my thoughts for thee been vigilant,
Bound to thy service with unceasing care—
The mind's least generous wish a mendicant
For nought but what thy happiness could spare.

Speak!—though this soft warm heart, once free to hold
A thousand tender pleasures, thine and mine,
Be left more desolate, more dreary cold

Than a forsaken bird's-nest fill'd with snow
'Mid its own bush of leafless eglantine—
Speak, that my torturing doubts their end may know!

400

Desideria

Surprized by joy—impatient as the wind—
I turn'd to share the transport—O with whom
But Thee—deep buried in the silent tomb,
That spot which no vicissitude can find?

Love, faithful love recall'd thee to my mind
But how could I forget thee? Through what power
Even for the least division of an hour
Have I been so beguiled as to be blind

To my most grievous loss—That thought's return
Was the worst pang that sorrow ever bore
Save one, one only, when I stood forlorn,

Knowing my heart's best treasure was no more;
That neither present time, nor years unborn
Could to my sight that heavenly face restore.

401

We Must be Free or Die

It is not to be thought of that the flood
Of British freedom, which, to the open sea
Of the world's praise, from dark antiquity
Hath flowed, 'with pomp of waters, unwithstood,'

Roused though it be full often to a mood
Which spurns the check of salutary bands,
That this most famous Stream in bogs and sands
Should perish; and to evil and to good
Be lost for ever. In our halls is hung
Armoury of the invincible knights of old:
We must be free or die, who speak the tongue
That Shakespeare spoke: the faith and morals hold
Which Milton held.—In everything we are sprung
Of Earth's first blood, have titles manifold.

402 England and Switzerland

[*1802*]

Two Voices are there, one is of the Sea,
One of the Mountains, each a mighty voice:
In both from age to age thou didst rejoice,
They were thy chosen music, Liberty!

There came a tyrant, and with holy glee
Thou fought'st against him,—but hast vainly striven:
Thou from thy Alpine holds at length art driven
Where not a torrent murmurs heard by thee.

—Of one deep bliss thine ear hath been bereft;
Then cleave, O cleave to that which still is left—
For high-soul'd Maid, what sorrow would it be

That Mountain floods should thunder as before,
And Ocean bellow from his rocky shore,
And neither awful Voice be heard by Thee!

403 On the Extinction of the Venetian Republic

Once did She hold the gorgeous East in fee
And was the safeguard of the West; the worth
Of Venice did not fall below her birth,
Venice, the eldest child of liberty.

She was a maiden city, bright and free;
No guile seduced, no force could violate;
And when she took unto herself a mate,
She must espouse the everlasting Sea.

And what if she had seen those glories fade,
Those titles vanish, and that strength decay,—
Yet shall some tribute of regret be paid

When her long life hath reach'd its final day:
Men are we, and must grieve when even the shade
Of that which once was great has pass'd away.

404

London, MDCCCII

O Friend! I know not which way I must look
For comfort, being, as I am, opprest
To think that now our life is only drest
For show; mean handi-work of craftsman, cook,

Or groom!—We must run glittering like a brook
In the open sunshine, or we are unblest;
The wealthiest man among us is the best:
No grandeur now in nature or in book

Delights us. Rapine, avarice, expense,
This is idolatry; and these we adore:
Plain living and high thinking are no more:

The homely beauty of the good old cause
Is gone; our peace, our fearful innocence,
And pure religion breathing household laws.

405

The Same

Milton! thou shouldst be living at this hour:
England hath need of thee: she is a fen
Of stagnant waters: altar, sword, and pen,
Fireside, the heroic wealth of hall and bower,

Have forfeited their ancient English dower
Of inward happiness. We are selfish men:
O! raise us up, return to us again;
And give us manners, virtue, freedom, power.

Thy soul was like a Star, and dwelt apart:
Thou hadst a voice whose sound was like the sea,
Pure as the naked heavens, majestic, free;

So didst thou travel on life's common way
In cheerful godliness; and yet thy heart
The lowliest duties on herself did lay.

406 When I Have Borne

When I have borne in memory what has tamed
Great nations; how ennobling thoughts depart
When men change swords for ledgers, and desert
The student's bower for gold,—some fears unnamed

I had, my Country!—am I to be blamed?
Now, when I think of thee, and what thou art,
Verily, in the bottom of my heart
Of those unfilial fears I am ashamed.

For dearly must we prize thee; we who find
In thee a bulwark for the cause of men;
And I by my affection was beguiled:

What wonder if a Poet now and then,
Among the many movements of his mind,
Felt for thee as a lover or a child!

407 The World is Too Much With Us

The World is too much with us; late and soon,
Getting and spending, we lay waste our powers;
Little we see in Nature that is ours;
We have given our hearts away, a sordid boon!

This Sea that bares her bosom to the moon,
The winds that will be howling at all hours
And are up-gather'd now like sleeping flowers,
For this, for every thing, we are out of tune;

It moves us not.—Great God! I'd rather be
A Pagan suckled in a creed outworn,—
So might I, standing on this pleasant lea,

Have glimpses that would make me less forlorn;
Have sight of Proteus rising from the sea;
Or hear old Triton blow his wreathéd horn.

408 Within King's College Chapel, Cambridge

Tax not the royal Saint with vain expense,
With ill-match'd aims the Architect who plann'd
(Albeit labouring for a scanty band
Of white-robed Scholars only) this immense

And glorious work of fine intelligence!
—Give all thou canst; high Heaven rejects the lore
Of nicely-calculated less or more:—
So deem'd the man who fashion'd for the sense

These lofty pillars, spread that branching roof
Self-poised, and scoop'd into ten thousand cells
Where light and shade repose, where music dwells

Lingering and wandering on as loth to die—
Like thoughts whose very sweetness yieldeth proof
That they were born for immortality.

409 Valedictory Sonnet to the River Duddon

I thought of Thee, my partner and my guide,
As being past away.—Vain sympathies!
For, backward, Duddon! as I cast my eyes,
I see what was, and is, and will abide;

Still glides the Stream, and shall for ever glide;
The Form remains, the Function never dies;
While we, the brave, the mighty, and the wise,
We Men, who in our morn of youth defied
The elements, must vanish;—be it so!
Enough, if something from our hands have power
To live, and act, and serve the future hour;
And if, as toward the silent tomb we go, [dower,
Through love, through hope, and faith's transcendent
We feel that we are greater than we know.

410 Composed at Neidpath Castle, the Property of Lord Queensberry

[*1803*]

Degenerate Douglas! oh, the unworthy lord!
Whom mere despite of heart could so far please
And love of havoc, (for with such disease
Fame taxes him,) that he could send forth word

To level with the dust a noble horde,
A brotherhood of venerable trees,
Leaving an ancient dome, and towers like these,
Beggar'd and outraged!—Many hearts deplored

The fate of those old trees; and oft with pain
The traveller at this day will stop and gaze
On wrongs, which Nature scarcely seems to heed:

For shelter'd places, bosoms, nooks, and bays,
And the pure mountains, and the gentle Tweed,
And the green silent pastures, yet remain.

411 Admonition to a Traveller

Yes, there is holy pleasure in thine eye!
—The lovely cottage in the guardian nook
Hath stirr'd thee deeply; with its own dear brook,
Its own small pasture, almost its own sky!

But covet not the abode; O do not sigh
As many do, repining while they look;
Intruders who would tear from Nature's book
This precious leaf with harsh impiety:

—Think what the home must be if it were thine,
Even thine, though few thy wants!—Roof, window, door,
The very flowers are sacred to the Poor,

The roses to the porch which they entwine:
Yea, all that now enchants thee, from the day
On which it should be touch'd would melt away!

412 To Sleep

A flock of sheep that leisurely pass by
One after one; the sound of rain, and bees
Murmuring; the fall of rivers, winds and seas,
Smooth fields, white sheets of water, and pure sky;—

I've thought of all by turns, and still I lie
Sleepless; and soon the small birds' melodies
Must hear, first utter'd from my orchard trees,
And the first cuckoo's melancholy cry.

Even thus last night, and two nights more I lay,
And could not win thee, Sleep! by any stealth:
So do not let me wear to-night away:

Without Thee what is all the morning's wealth?
Come, blesséd barrier between day and day,
Dear mother of fresh thoughts and joyous health!

413 The Sonnet

I

Nuns fret not at their convent's narrow room;
And hermits are contented with their cells;
  And students with their pensive citadels;
Maids at the wheel, the weaver at his loom,

Sit blithe and happy; bees that soar for bloom,
  High as the highest peak of Furness-fells,
  Will murmur by the hour in foxglove bells:
In truth the prison, unto which we doom
Ourselves, no prison is: and hence for me,
  In sundry moods, 'twas pastime to be bound
  Within the Sonnet's scanty plot of ground;
Pleased if some souls (for such there needs must be)
Who have felt the weight of too much liberty,
  Should find brief solace there, as I have found.

II

Scorn not the Sonnet; Critic, you have frown'd,
Mindless of its just honours; with this key
  Shakespeare unlock'd his heart; the melody
Of this small lute gave ease to Petrarch's wound;
A thousand times this pipe did Tasso sound;
  With it Camöens sooth'd an exile's grief;
  The Sonnet glitter'd a gay myrtle leaf
Amid the cypress with which Dante crown'd
His visionary brow: a glow-worm lamp,
  It cheer'd mild Spenser, call'd from Faery-land
To struggle through dark ways; and, when a damp
  Fell round the path of Milton, in his hand
The Thing became a trumpet; whence he blew
Soul-animating strains—alas, too few!

WILLIAM LISLE BOWLES

[*1762-1850*]

414 Dover Cliffs

On these white cliffs, that calm above the flood
Uplift their shadowy heads, and at their feet
Scarce hear the surge that has for ages beat,
Sure many a lonely wanderer has stood;
And while the distant murmur met his ear,
And o'er the distant billows the still eve
Sailed slow, has thought of all his heart must leave

To-morrow; of the friends he loved most dear;
Of social scenes from which he wept to part.
But if, like me, he knew how fruitless all
The thoughts that would full fain the past recall;
Soon would he quell the risings of his heart,
And brave the wild winds and unhearing tide,
The world his country, and his God his guide.

SAMUEL TAYLOR COLERIDGE

[*1772-1834*]

415 The Rime of the Ancient Mariner

IN SEVEN PARTS

Argument.—How a Ship having passed the Line was driven by storms to the cold Country towards the South Pole; and how from thence she made her course to the tropical Latitude of the Great Pacific Ocean; and of the strange things that befell; and in what manner the Ancyent Marinere came back to his own Country. [1798.]

Part I

An ancient Mariner meeteth three Gallants bidden to a wedding-feast, and detaineth one

It is an ancient Mariner,
And he stoppeth one of three.
"By thy long grey beard and glittering eye,
Now wherefore stopp'st thou me?

"The Bridegroom's doors are opened wide,
And I am next of kin;
The guests are met, the feast is set:
May'st hear the merry din."

He holds him with his skinny hand,
"There was a ship," quoth he.
"Hold off! unhand me, grey-beard loon!"
Eftsoons his hand dropt he.

The Wedding-Guest is spell-bound by the eye of the old seafaring man, and constrained to hear his tale

He holds him with his glittering eye—
The Wedding-Guest stood still,
And listens like a three years' child:
The Mariner hath his will.

The Wedding-Guest sat on a stone:
He cannot choose but hear;
And thus spake on that ancient man,
The bright-eyed Mariner.

"The ship was cheered, the harbour cleared,
Merrily did we drop
Below the kirk, below the hill,
Below the lighthouse top.

The Mariner tells how the ship sailed southward with a good wind and fair weather, till it reached the line

"The sun came up upon the left,
Out of the sea came he!
And he shone bright, and on the right
Went down into the sea.

"Higher and higher every day,
Till over the mast at noon—"
The Wedding-Guest here beat his breast,
For he heard the loud bassoon.

The Wedding-Guest heareth the bridal music; but the Mariner continueth his tale

The bride hath paced into the hall,
Red as a rose is she;
Nodding their heads before her goes
The merry minstrelsy.

The Wedding-Guest he beat his breast,
Yet he cannot choose but hear;
And thus spake on that ancient man,
The bright-eyed Mariner.

The ship driven by a storm toward the south pole

"And now the Storm-blast came, and he
Was tyrannous and strong:
He struck with his o'ertaking wings,
And chased us south along.

"With sloping masts and dipping prow,
As who pursued with yell and blow
Still treads the shadow of his foe,

And forward bends his head,
The ship drove fast, loud roared the blast,
And southward aye we fled.

"And now there came both mist and snow,
And it grew wondrous cold:
And ice, mast-high, came floating by,
As green as emerald.

The land of ice, and of fearful sounds where no living thing was to be seen

"And through the drifts the snowy clifts
Did send a dismal sheen:
Nor shapes of men nor beasts we ken—
The ice was all between.

"The ice was here, the ice was there,
The ice was all around:
It cracked and growled, and roared and howled,
Like noises in a swound!

Till a great sea-bird, called the Albatross, came through the snow-fog, and was received with great joy and hospitality

"At length did cross an Albatross,
Thorough the fog it came;
As if it had been a Christian soul,
We hailed it in God's name.

"It ate the food it ne'er had eat,
And round and round it flew.
The ice did split with a thunder-fit;
The helmsman steered us through!

And lo! the Albatross proveth a bird of good omen, and followeth the ship as it returned northward through fog and floating ice

"And a good south wind sprung up behind;
The Albatross did follow,
And every day, for food or play,
Came to the mariners' hollo!

"In mist or cloud, on mast or shroud,
It perched for vespers nine;
Whiles all the night, through fog-smoke white,
Glimmered the white moon-shine."

"God save thee, ancient Mariner!
From the fiends, that plague thee thus!—
Why look'st thou so?"—With my cross-bow
I shot the Albatross.

The ancient Mariner inhospitably killeth the pious bird of good omen

Part II

The Sun now rose upon the right:
Out of the sea came he,
Still hid in mist, and on the left
Went down into the sea.

And the good south wind still blew behind,
But no sweet bird did follow,
Nor any day for food or play
Came to the mariners' hollo!

And I had done a hellish thing,
And it would work 'em woe:
For all averred, I had killed the bird
That made the breeze to blow.
Ah wretch! said they, the bird to slay,
That made the breeze to blow!

His shipmates cry out against the ancient Mariner, for killing the bird of good luck

Nor dim nor red, like God's own head,
The glorious Sun uprist:
Then all averred, I had killed the bird
That brought the fog and mist.
'Twas right, said they, such birds to slay,
That bring the fog and mist.

But when the fog cleared off, they justify the same, and thus make themselves accomplices in the crime

The fair breeze blew, the white foam flew,
The furrow followed free;
We were the first that ever burst
Into that silent sea.

The fair breeze continues; the ship enters the Pacific Ocean, and sails northward, even till it reaches the Line

Down dropt the breeze, the sails dropt down,
'Twas sad as sad could be;
And we did speak only to break
The silence of the sea!

The ship hath been suddenly becalmed

All in a hot and copper sky,
The bloody Sun, at noon,
Right up above the mast did stand,
No bigger than the Moon.

Day after day, day after day,
We stuck, nor breath nor motion;
As idle as a painted ship
Upon a painted ocean.

And the Albatross begins to be avenged

Water, water, every where,
And all the boards did shrink;
Water, water, every where
Nor any drop to drink.

The very deep did rot: O Christ!
That ever this should be!
Yea, slimy things did crawl with legs
Upon the slimy sea.

About, about, in reel and rout
The death-fires danced at night;
The water, like a witch's oils,
Burnt green, and blue and white.

A Spirit had followed them; one of the invisible inhabitants of this planet, neither departed souls nor angels; concerning whom the learned Jew, Josephus, and the Platonic Constantinopolitan, Michael Psellus, may be consulted. They are very numerous, and there is no climate or element without one or more

And some in dreams assurèd were
Of the Spirit that plagued us so,
Nine fathom deep he had followed us
From the land of mist and snow.

And every tongue, through utter drought,
Was withered at the root;
We could not speak, no more than if
We had been choked with soot.

The shipmates, in their sore distress, would fain throw the whole guilt on the ancient Mariner: in sign whereof they hang the dead sea-bird round his neck

Ah! well a-day! what evil looks
Had I from old and young!
Instead of the cross, the Albatross
About my neck was hung.

Part III

There passed a weary time. Each throat
Was parched, and glazed each eye.
A weary time! a weary time!
How glazed each weary eye,
When looking westward, I beheld
A something in the sky.

The ancient Mariner beholdeth a sign in the element afar off

At first it seemed a little speck,
And then it seemed a mist;
It moved and moved, and took at last
A certain shape, I wist.

A speck, a mist, a shape, I wist!
And still it neared and neared:
As if it dodged a water-sprite,
It plunged and tacked and veered.

With throats unslaked, with black lips baked,
We could nor laugh nor wail;
Through utter drought all dumb we stood!
I bit my arm, I sucked the blood,
And cried, A sail! a sail!

At its nearer approach, it seemeth him to be a ship; and at a dear ransom he freeth his speech from the bonds of thirst

With throats unslaked, with black lips baked,
Agape they heard me call:
Gramercy! they for joy did grin,
And all at once their breath drew in,
As they were drinking all.

A flash of joy;

See! see! (I cried) she tacks no more!
Hither to work us weal;
Without a breeze, without a tide,
She steadies with upright keel!

And horror follows. For can it be a ship that comes onward without wind or tide?

The western wave was all a-flame.
The day was well nigh done!
Almost upon the western wave

Rested the broad bright Sun;
When that strange shape drove suddenly
Betwixt us and the Sun.

It seemeth him but the skeleton of a ship

And straight the Sun was flecked with bars,
(Heaven's Mother send us grace!)
As if through a dungeon-grate he peered
With broad and burning face.

Alas! (thought I, and my heart beat loud)
How fast she nears and nears!
Are those her sails that glance in the Sun,
Like restless gossameres?

And its ribs are seen as bars on the face of the setting Sun. The Spectre-Woman and her Deathmate, and no other on board the skeleton-ship

Are those her ribs through which the Sun
Did peer, as through a grate?
And is that Woman all her crew?
Is that a Death? and are there two?
Is Death that woman's mate?

Her lips were red, her looks were free,
Her locks were yellow as gold:
Her skin was as white as leprosy,
The Night-mare Life-in-Death was she,
Who thicks man's blood with cold.

Like vessel, like crew!

Death and Life-in-Death have diced for the ship's crew, and she (the latter) winneth the ancient Mariner

The naked hulk alongside came,
And the twain were casting dice;
"The game is done! I've won! I've won!"
Quoth she, and whistles thrice.

No twilight within the courts of the sun

The Sun's rim dips; the stars rush out:
At one stride comes the dark;
With far-heard whisper, o'er the sea,
Off shot the spectre-bark.

At the rising of the Moon,

We listened and looked sideways up!
Fear at my heart, as at a cup,
My life-blood seemed to sip!
The stars were dim, and thick the night,

The steersman's face by his lamp gleamed white;
From the sails the dew did drip—
Till clomb above the eastern bar
The horned Moon, with one bright star
Within the nether tip.

One after one, by the star-dogged Moon,
Too quick for groan or sigh,
Each turned his face with a ghastly pang,
And cursed me with his eye.

One after another,

Four times fifty living men,
(And I heard nor sigh nor groan)
With heavy thump, a lifeless lump,
They dropped down one by one.

His shipmates drop down dead

The souls did from their bodies fly,—
They fled to bliss or woe!
And every soul, it passed me by,
Like the whizz of my cross-bow!

But Life-in-Death begins her work on the ancient Mariner

PART IV

"I fear thee, ancient Mariner!
I fear thy skinny hand!
And thou art long, and lank. and brown,
As is the ribbed sea-sand.

The Wedding-Guest feareth that a Spirit is talking to him;

"I fear thee and thy glittering eye,
And thy skinny hand, so brown."—
Fear not, fear not, thou Wedding-Guest!
This body dropt not down.

But the ancient Mariner assureth him of his bodily life, and proceedeth to relate his horrible penance

Alone, alone, all, all alone,
Alone on a wide wide sea!
And never a saint took pity on
My soul in agony.

He despiseth the creatures of the calm

The many men, so beautiful!
And they all dead did lie:
And a thousand thousand slimy things
Lived on; and so did I.

And envieth that they should live, and so many lie dead

I looked upon the rotting sea,
And drew my eyes away;
I looked upon the rotting deck,
And there the dead men lay.

I looked to heaven, and tried to pray;
But or ever a prayer had gusht,
A wicked whisper came, and made
My heart as dry as dust.

I closed my lids, and kept them close,
And the balls like pulses beat;
For the sky and the sea, and the sea and the sky
Lay like a load on my weary eye,
And the dead were at my feet.

But the curse liveth for him in the eye of the dead men

The cold sweat melted from their limbs,
Nor rot nor reek did they:
The look with which they looked on me
Had never passed away.

An orphan's curse would drag to hell
A spirit from on high;
But oh! more horrible than that
Is the curse in a dead man's eye!
Seven days, seven nights, I saw that curse,
And yet I could not die.

In his loneliness and fixedness he yearneth towards the journeying Moon, and the stars that still sojourn, yet still move onward; and everywhere the blue sky belongs to them, and is their appointed rest, and their native country and their

The moving Moon went up the sky,
And no where did abide:
Softly she was going up,
And a star or two beside—

Her beams bemocked the sultry main,
Like April hoar-frost spread;

But where the ship's huge shadow lay,
The charmed water burnt alway
A still and awful red.

own natural homes, which they enter unannounced, as lords that are certainly expected and yet there is a silent joy at their arrival

Beyond the shadow of the ship,
I watched the water-snakes:
They moved in tracks of shining white,
And when they reared, the elfish light
Fell off in hoary flakes.

By the light of the Moon he beholdeth God's creatures of the great calm

Within the shadow of the ship
I watched their rich attire:
Blue, glossy green, and velvet black,
They coiled and swam; and every track
Was a flash of golden fire.

O happy living things! no tongue
Their beauty might declare:
A spring of love gushed from my heart,
And I blessed them unaware:
Sure my kind saint took pity on me,
And I blessed them unaware.

Their beauty and their happiness

He blesseth them in his heart

The selfsame moment I could pray;
And from my neck so free
The Albatross fell off, and sank
Like lead into the sea.

The spell begins to break

Part V

Oh sleep! it is a gentle thing,
Beloved from pole to pole!
To Mary Queen the praise be given!
She sent the gentle sleep from Heaven,
That slid into my soul.

The silly buckets on the deck,
That had so long remained,
I dreamt that they were filled with dew;
And when I awoke, it rained.

By grace of the holy Mother, the ancient Mariner is refreshed with rain

My lips were wet, my throat was cold,
My garments all were dank;
Sure I had drunken in my dreams,
And still my body drank.

I moved, and could not feel my limbs:
I was so light—almost
I thought that I had died in sleep,
And was a blessed ghost.

He heareth sounds and seeth strange sights and commotions in the sky and the element

And soon I heard a roaring wind:
It did not come anear;
But with its sound it shook the sails,
That were so thin and sere.

The upper air burst into life!
And a hundred fire-flags sheen,
To and fro they were hurried about!
And to and fro, and in and out,
The wan stars danced between.

And the coming wind did roar more loud,
And the sails did sigh like sedge;
And the rain poured down from one black cloud;
The Moon was at its edge.

The thick black cloud was cleft, and still
The Moon was at its side:
Like waters shot from some high crag,
The lightning fell with never a jag,
A river steep and wide.

The bodies of the ship's crew are inspired, and the ship moves on;

The loud wind never reached the ship,
Yet now the ship moved on!
Beneath the lightning and the Moon
The dead men gave a groan.

They groaned, they stirred, they all uprose,
Nor spake, nor moved their eyes;
It had been strange, even in a dream,
To have seen those dead men rise.

The helmsman steered, the ship moved on;
Yet never a breeze up blew;
The mariners all 'gan work the ropes,
Where they were wont to do;
They raised their limbs like lifeless tools—
We were a ghastly crew.

The body of my brother's son
Stood by me, knee to knee:
The body and I pulled at one rope
But he said nought to me.

"I fear thee, ancient Mariner!"
Be calm, thou Wedding-Guest!
'Twas not those souls that fled in pain,
Which to their corses came again,
But a troop of spirits blest:

But not by the souls of the men, nor by dæmons of earth or middle air, but by a blessed troop of angelic spirits, sent down by the invocation of the guardian saint

For when it dawned—they dropped their arms,
And clustered round the mast;
Sweet sounds rose slowly through their mouths,
And from their bodies passed.

Around, around, flew each sweet sound,
Then darted to the Sun;
Slowly the sounds came back again,
Now mixed, now one by one.

Sometimes a-dropping from the sky
I heard the sky-lark sing;
Sometimes all little birds that are,
How they seemed to fill the sea and air
With their sweet jargoning!

And now 'twas like all instruments,
Now like a lonely flute;
And now it is an angel's song,
That makes the heavens be mute.

It ceased; yet still the sails made on
A pleasant noise till noon,
A noise like of a hidden brook
In the leafy month of June,
That to the sleeping woods all night
Singeth a quiet tune.

Till noon we quietly sailed on,
Yet never a breeze did breathe:
Slowly and smoothly went the ship,
Moved onward from beneath.

The lonesome Spirit from the south-pole carries on the ship as far as the Line, in obedience to the angelic troop, but still requireth vengeance

Under the keel nine fathom deep,
From the land of mist and snow,
The spirit slid: and it was he
That made the ship to go.
The sails at noon left off their tune,
And the ship stood still also.

The Sun, right up above the mast,
Had fixed her to the ocean:
But in a minute she 'gan stir,
With a short uneasy motion—
Backwards and forwards half her length
With a short uneasy motion.

Then like a pawing horse let go,
She made a sudden bound:
It flung the blood into my head,
And I fell down in a swound.

The Polar Spirit's fellow-dæmons, the invisible inhabitants of the element, take part in his wrong; and two of them relate, one to the other, that penance long and heavy for the ancient Mariner hath been accorded to the Polar Spirit, who returneth southward

How long in that same fit I lay,
I have not to declare;
But ere my living life returned,
I heard and in my soul discerned
Two voices in the air.

"Is it he?" quoth one, "Is this the man?
By him who died on cross,
With his cruel bow he laid full low
The harmless Albatross.

"The spirit who bideth by himself
In the land of mist and snow,
He loved the bird that loved the man
Who shot him with his bow."

The other was a softer voice,
As soft as honey-dew:
Quoth he, "The man hath penance done,
And penance more will do."

Part VI

FIRST VOICE

"But tell me, tell me! speak again,
Thy soft response renewing—
What makes that ship drive on so fast?
What is the ocean doing?"

SECOND VOICE

"Still as a slave before his lord,
The ocean hath no blast;
His great bright eye most silently
Up to the moon is cast—

"If he may know which way to go;
For she guides him smooth or grim.
See, brother, see! how graciously
She looketh down on him."

FIRST VOICE

The Mariner hath been cast into a trance; for the angelic power causeth the vessel to drive northward faster than human life could endure

"But why drives on that ship so fast,
Without or wave or wind?"

SECOND VOICE

"The air is cut away before,
And closes from behind.

"Fly, brother, fly! more high, more high!
Or we shall be belated:
For slow and slow that ship will go,
When the Mariner's trance is abated."

The supernatural motion is retarded; the Mariner awakes, and his penance begins anew

I woke, and we were sailing on
As in a gentle weather:
'Twas night, calm night, the moon was high,
The dead men stood together.

All stood together on the deck,
For a charnel-dungeon fitter:
All fixed on me their stony eyes,
That in the Moon did glitter.

The pang, the curse, with which they died,
Had never passed away:
I could not draw my eyes from theirs,
Nor turn them up to pray.

The curse is finally expiated

And now this spell was snapt: once more
I viewed the ocean green,
And looked far forth, yet little saw
Of what had else been seen—

Like one, that on a lonesome road
Doth walk in fear and dread,
And having once turned round walks on,
And turns no more his head;
Because he knows, a frightful fiend
Doth close behind him tread.

But soon there breathed a wind on me,
Nor sound nor motion made:
Its path was not upon the sea,
In ripple or in shade.

It raised my hair, it fanned my cheek
Like a meadow-gale of spring—
It mingled strangely with my fears,
Yet it felt like a welcoming.

Swiftly, swiftly flew the ship,
Yet she sailed softly too:
Sweetly, sweetly blew the breeze—
On me alone it blew.

Oh! dream of joy! is this indeed
The light-house top I see?
Is this the hill? is this the kirk?
Is this mine own countree?

And the ancient Mariner beholdeth his native country

We drifted o'er the harbour-bar,
And I with sobs did pray—
O let me be awake, my God!
Or let me sleep alway.

The harbour-bay was clear as glass,
So smoothly it was strewn!
And on the bay the moonlight lay,
And the shadow of the Moon.

The rock shone bright, the kirk no less,
That stands above the rock:
The moonlight steeped in silentness
The steady weathercock.

And the bay was white with silent light
Till rising from the same,
Full many shapes, that shadows were,
In crimson colours came.

The Angelic spirits leave the dead bodies,

A little distance from the prow
Those crimson shadows were:
I turned my eyes upon the deck—
Oh, Christ! what saw I there!

And appear in their own forms of light

Each corse lay flat, lifeless and flat.
And, by the holy rood!
A man all light, a seraph-man,
On every corse there stood.

This seraph-band, each waved his hand:
It was a heavenly sight!
They stood as signals to the land,
Each one a lovely light;

This seraph-band, each waved his hand,
No voice did they impart—
No voice; but oh! the silence sank
Like music on my heart.

But soon I heard the dash of oars,
I heard the Pilot's cheer;
My head was turned perforce away,
And I saw a boat appear.

The Pilot and the Pilot's boy,
I heard them coming fast:
Dear Lord in Heaven! it was a joy
The dead men could not blast.

I saw a third—I heard his voice:
It is the Hermit good!
He singeth loud his godly hymns
That he makes in the wood.
He'll shrieve my soul, he'll wash away
The Albatross's blood.

Part VII

The Hermit of the Wood

This Hermit good lives in that wood
Which slopes down to the sea.
How loudly his sweet voice he rears!
He loves to talk with marineres
That come from a far countree.

He kneels at morn, and noon, and eve—
He hath a cushion plump:
It is the moss that wholly hides
The rotted old oak-stump.

The skiff-boat neared: I heard them talk,
"Why, this is strange, I trow!
Where are those lights so many and fair,
That signal made but now?"

"Strange, by my faith!" the Hermit said—
"And they answered not our cheer!
The planks looked warped! and see those sails,
How thin they are and sere!
I never saw aught like to them,
Unless perchance it were

Approacheth the ship with wonder

"Brown skeletons of leaves that lag
My forest-brook along;
When the ivy-tod is heavy with snow,
And the owlet whoops to the wolf below,
That eats the she-wolf's young."

"Dear Lord! it hath a fiendish look—
(The Pilot made reply)
I am a-feared"—"Push on, push on!"
Said the Hermit cheerily.

The boat came closer to the ship,
But I nor spake nor stirred;
The boat came close beneath the ship,
And straight a sound was heard.

Under the water it rumbled on,
Still louder and more dread:
It reached the ship, it split the bay;
The ship went down like lead.

The ship suddenly sinketh

Stunned by that loud and dreadful sound,
Which sky and ocean smote,
Like one that hath been seven days drowned
My body lay afloat;
But swift as dreams, myself I found
Within the Pilot's boat.

The ancient Mariner is saved in the Pilot's boat

Upon the whirl, where sank the ship,
The boat spun round and round;
And all was still, save that the hill
Was telling of the sound.

I moved my lips—the Pilot shrieked
And fell down in a fit;
The holy Hermit raised his eyes,
And prayed where he did sit.

I took the oars: the Pilot's boy,
Who now doth crazy go,
Laughed loud and long, and all the while
His eyes went to and fro.
"Ha! ha!" quoth he, "full plain I see,
The Devil knows how to row."

And now, all in my own countree,
I stood on the firm land!
The Hermit stepped forth from the boat,
And scarcely he could stand.

The ancient Mariner earnestly entreateth the Hermit to shrieve him; and the penance of life falls on him

"O shrieve me, shrieve me, holy man!"
The Hermit crossed his brow.
"Say quick," quoth he, "I bid thee say—
What manner of man art thou?"

Forthwith this frame of mine was wrenched
With a woful agony,
Which forced me to begin my tale;
And then it left me free.

And ever and anon throughout his future life an agony constraineth him to travel from land to land,

Since then, at an uncertain hour,
That agony returns:
And till my ghastly tale is told,
This heart within me burns.

I pass, like night, from land to land;
I have strange power of speech;

That moment that his face I see,
I know the man that must hear me:
To him my tale I teach.

What loud uproar bursts from that door!
The wedding-guests are there:
But in the garden-bower the bride
And bride-maids singing are:
And hark the little vesper bell
Which biddeth me to prayer!

O Wedding-Guest! this soul hath been
Alone on a wide wide sea:
So lonely 'twas, that God himself
Scarce seemed there to be.

O sweeter than the marriage-feast,
'Tis sweeter far to me,
To walk together to the kirk
With a goodly company!—

To walk together to the kirk,
And all together pray,
While each to his great Father bends,
Old men, and babes, and loving friends
And youths and maidens gay!

Farewell, farewell! but this I tell
To thee, thou Wedding-Guest!
He prayeth well, who loveth well
Both man and bird and beast.

And to teach, by his own example, love and reverence to all things that God made and loveth

He prayeth best, who loveth best
All things both great and small;
For the dear God who loveth us,
He made and loveth all.

The Mariner, whose eye is bright,
Whose beard with age is hoar,
Is gone: and now the Wedding-Guest
Turned from the bridegroom's door.

He went like one that hath been stunned,
And is of sense forlorn:
A sadder and a wiser man,
He rose the morrow morn.

416 KUBLA KHAN

IN Xanadu did Kubla Khan
  A stately pleasure-dome decree:
Where Alph, the sacred river, ran
Through caverns measureless to man
  Down to a sunless sea.
So twice five miles of fertile ground
With walls and towers were girdled round:
And here were gardens bright with sinuous rills,
Where blossomed many an incense-bearing tree
And here were forests ancient as the hills,
Enfolding sunny spots of greenery.

But oh! that deep romantic chasm which slanted
Down the green hill athwart a cedarn cover!
A savage place! as holy and enchanted
As e'er beneath a waning moon was haunted
By woman wailing for her demon-lover!
And from this chasm, with ceaseless turmoil seething,
As if this earth in fast thick pants were breathing,
A mighty fountain momently was forced;
Amid whose swift half-intermitted burst
Huge fragments vaulted like rebounding hail,
Or chaffy grain beneath the thresher's flail:
And 'mid these dancing rocks at once and ever
It flung up momently the sacred river.
Five miles meandering with a mazy motion
Through wood and dale the sacred river ran,
Then reached the caverns measureless to man,
And sank in tumult to a lifeless ocean:
And 'mid this tumult Kubla heard from far
Ancestral voices prophesying war!

The shadow of the dome of pleasure
Floated midway on the waves;
Where was heard the mingled measure
From the fountain and the caves.
It was a miracle of rare device,
A sunny pleasure-dome with caves of ice!

A damsel with a dulcimer
In a vision once I saw:
It was an Abyssinian maid,
And on her dulcimer she played,
Singing of Mount Abora.
Could I revive within me
Her symphony and song,
To such a deep delight 'twould win me,
That with music loud and long,
I would build that dome in air,
That sunny dome! those caves of ice!
And all who heard should see them there,
And all should cry, Beware! Beware!
His flashing eyes, his floating hair!
Weave a circle round him thrice,
And close your eyes with holy dread,
For he on honey-dew hath fed,
And drunk the milk of Paradise.

417

Youth and Age

Verse, a breeze 'mid blossoms straying,
Where Hope clung feeding, like a bee—
Both were mine! Life went a-maying
With Nature, Hope, and Poesy,
When I was young!
When I was young?—Ah, woful when!
Ah! for the change 'twixt Now and Then!
This breathing house not built with hands,
This body that does me grievous wrong,
O'er aery cliffs and glittering sands
How lightly then it flash'd along:

Like those trim skiffs, unknown of yore,
On winding lakes and rivers wide,
That ask no aid of sail or oar,
That fear no spite of wind or tide!
Nought cared this body for wind or weather
When Youth and I lived in't together.

Flowers are lovely; Love is flower-like;
Friendship is a sheltering tree;
O! the joys, that came down shower-like,
Of Friendship, Love, and Liberty,
Ere I was old!
Ere I was old? Ah woful Ere,
Which tells me, Youth's no longer here.
O Youth! for years so many and sweet,
'Tis known that Thou and I were one,
I'll think it but a fond conceit—
It cannot be, that Thou art gone!
Thy vesper-bell hath not yet toll'd:—
And thou wert aye a masker bold!
What strange disguise hast now put on
To make believe that Thou art gone?
I see these locks in silvery slips,
This drooping gait, this alter'd size:
But Springtide blossoms on thy lips,
And tears take sunshine from thine eyes!
Life is but Thought: so think I will
That Youth and I are housemates still.

Dew-drops are the gems of morning,
But the tears of mournful eve!
Where no hope is, life's a warning
That only serves to make us grieve
When we are old:
—That only serves to make us grieve
With oft and tedious taking-leave,
Like some poor nigh-related guest
That may not rudely be dismist,
Yet hath out-stay'd his welcome while.
And tells the jest without the smile.

418

Love

All thoughts, all passions, all delights,
Whatever stirs this mortal frame,
All are but ministers of Love,
  And feed his sacred flame.

Oft in my waking dreams do I
Live o'er again that happy hour,
When midway on the mount I lay,
  Beside the ruin'd tower.

The moonshine stealing o'er the scene
Had blended with the lights of eve;
And she was there, my hope, my joy,
  My own dear Genevieve!

She lean'd against the armèd man,
The statue of the armèd knight;
She stood and listen'd to my lay,
  Amid the lingering light.

Few sorrows hath she of her own,
My hope! my joy! my Genevieve!
She loves me best, whene'er I sing
  The songs that make her grieve.

I play'd a soft and doleful air,
I sang an old and moving story—
An old rude song, that suited well
  That ruin wild and hoary.

She listen'd with a flitting blush,
With downcast eyes and modest grace;
For well she knew, I could not choose
  But gaze upon her face.

I told her of the Knight that wore
Upon his shield a burning brand;
And that for ten long years he woo'd
  The Lady of the Land.

I told her how he pined: and ah!
The deep, the low, the pleading tone
With which I sang another's love
Interpreted my own.

She listen'd with a flitting blush,
With downcast eyes and modest grace;
And she forgave me, that I gazed
Too fondly on her face!

But when I told the cruel scorn
That crazed that bold and lovely Knight,
And that he cross'd the mountain-woods,
Nor rested day nor night;

That sometimes from the savage den,
And sometimes from the darksome shade
And sometimes starting up at once
In green and sunny glade

There came and look'd him in the face
An angel beautiful and bright;
And that he knew it was a Fiend,
This miserable Knight!

And that unknowing what he did,
He leap'd amid a murderous band,
And saved from outrage worse than death
The Lady of the Land;

And how she wept, and clasp'd his knees;
And how she tended him in vain;
And ever strove to expiate
The scorn that crazed his brain;

And that she nursed him in a cave,
And how his madness went away,
When on the yellow forest-leaves
A dying man he lay;

—His dying words—but when I reach'd
That tenderest strain of all the ditty,
My faltering voice and pausing harp
Disturb'd her soul with pity!

All impulses of soul and sense
Had thrill'd my guileless Genevieve;
The music and the doleful tale,
The rich and balmy eve;

And hopes, and fears that kindle hope,
An undistinguishable throng,
And gentle wishes long subdued,
Subdued and cherish'd long!

She wept with pity and delight,
She blush'd with love, and virgin shame;
And like the murmur of a dream,
I heard her breathe my name.

Her bosom heaved—she stepp'd aside,
As conscious of my look she stept—
Then suddenly, with timorous eye
She fled to me and wept.

She half enclosed me with her arms,
She press'd me with a meek embrace;
And bending back her head, look'd up,
And gazed upon my face.

'Twas partly love, and partly fear,
And partly 'twas a bashful art
That I might rather feel, than see,
The swelling of her heart.

I calm'd her fears, and she was calm,
And told her love with virgin pride;
And so I won my Genevieve,
My bright and beauteous Bride.

419 Hymn Before Sunrise, in the Vale of Chamouni

Hast thou a charm to stay the morning-star
In his deep course? So long he seems to pause
On thy bald awful head, O sovran Blanc!
The Arve and Arveiron at thy base
Rave ceaselessly; but thou, most awful Form!
Risest from forth thy silent sea of pines,
How silently! Around thee and above
Deep is the air and dark, substantial, black,
An ebon mass: methinks thou piercest it,
As with a wedge! But when I look again,
It is thine own calm home, thy crystal shrine,
Thy habitation from eternity!
O dread and silent Mount! I gazed upon thee,
Till thou, still present to the bodily sense,
Didst vanish from my thought: entranced in prayer
I worshipped the Invisible alone.

Yet, like some sweet beguiling melody,
So sweet, we know not we are listening to it,
Thou, the meanwhile, wast blending with my Thought,
Yea, with my Life and Life's own secret joy:
Till the dilating Soul, enrapt, transfused,
Into the mighty vision passing—there
As in her natural form, swelled vast to Heaven.

Awake, my soul! not only passive praise
Thou owest! not alone these swelling tears,
Mute thanks and secret ecstasy! Awake,
Voice of sweet song! Awake, my heart, awake!
Green vales and icy cliffs, all join my Hymn.

Thou first and chief, sole sovereign of the Vale!
O struggling with the darkness all the night,
And visited all night by troops of stars,
Or when they climb the sky or when they sink:
Companion of the morning-star at dawn,

Thyself Earth's rosy star, and of the dawn
Co-herald: wake, O wake, and utter praise!
Who sank thy sunless pillars deep in Earth?
Who fill'd thy countenance with rosy light?
Who made thee parent of perpetual streams?

And you, ye five wild torrents fiercely glad!
Who called you forth from night and utter death,
From dark and icy caverns called you forth,
Down those precipitous, black, jagged rocks,
For ever shattered and the same for ever?
Who gave you your invulnerable life,
Your strength, your speed, your fury, and your joy,
Unceasing thunder and eternal foam?
And who commanded (and the silence came),
Here let the billows stiffen, and have rest?

Ye Ice-falls! ye that from the mountain's brow
Adown enormous ravines slope amain—
Torrents, methinks, that heard a mighty voice,
And stopped at once amid their maddest plunge!
Motionless torrents! silent cataracts!
Who made you glorious as the gates of Heaven
Beneath the keen full moon? Who bade the sun
Clothe you with rainbows? Who, with living flowers
Of loveliest blue, spread garlands at your feet?—
God! let the torrents, like a shout of nations,
Answer! and let the ice-plains echo, God!
God! sing ye meadow-streams with gladsome voice!
Ye pine-groves, with your soft and soul-like sounds!
And they too have a voice, yon piles of snow,
And in their perilous fall shall thunder, God!

Ye living flowers that skirt the eternal frost!
Ye wild goats sporting round the eagle's nest!
Ye eagles, play-mates of the mountain-storm!
Ye lightnings, the dread arrows of the clouds!
Ye signs and wonders of the element!
Utter forth God, and fill the hills with praise!

Thou too, hoar Mount! with thy sky-pointing peaks,
Oft from whose feet the avalanche, unheard,
Shoots downward, glittering through the pure serene
Into the depth of clouds, that veil thy breast—
Thou too again, stupendous Mountain! thou
That as I raise my head, awhile bowed low
In adoration, upward from thy base
Slow travelling with dim eyes suffused with tears,
Solemnly seemest, like a vapoury cloud,
To rise before me—Rise, O ever rise,
Rise like a cloud of incense from the Earth!
Thou kingly Spirit throned among the hills,
Thou dread ambassador from Earth to Heaven,
Great Hierarch! tell thou the silent sky,
And tell the stars, and tell yon rising sun,
Earth, with her thousand voices, praises God.

420 CHRISTABEL

PART THE FIRST

'Tis the middle of night by the castle clock,
And the owls have awakened the crowing cock;
Tu—whit!——Tu—whoo!
And hark, again! the crowing cock,
How drowsily it crew!

Sir Leoline, the Baron rich,
Hath a toothless mastiff bitch;
From her kennel beneath the rock
Maketh answer to the clock,
Four for the quarters, and twelve for the hour;
Ever and aye, by shine and shower,
Sixteen short howls, not over loud;
Some say, she sees my lady's shroud.

Is the night chilly and dark?
The night is chilly, but not dark.
The thin gray cloud is spread on high,
It covers but not hides the sky.

The moon is behind, and at the full;
And yet she looks both small and dull.
The night is chill, the cloud is gray:
'Tis a month before the month of May,
And the Spring comes slowly up this way.

The lovely lady, Christabel,
Whom her father loves so well,
What makes her in the wood so late,
A furlong from the castle gate?
She had dreams all yesternight—
Of her own betrothed knight;
And she in the midnight wood will pray
For the weal of her lover that's far away.

She stole along, she nothing spoke,
The sighs she heaved were soft and low,
And naught was green upon the oak
But moss and rarest mistletoe:
She kneels beneath the huge oak-tree,
And in silence prayeth she.

The lady sprang up suddenly,
The lovely lady, Christabel!
It moaned as near, as near can be,
But what it is she cannot tell.—
On the other side it seems to be,
Of the huge, broad-breasted, old oak-tree.

The night is chill; the forest bare;
Is it the wind that moaneth bleak?
There is not wind enough in the air
To move away the ringlet curl
From the lovely lady's cheek—
There is not wind enough to twirl
The one red leaf, the last of its clan,
That dances as often as dance it can,
Hanging so light, and hanging so high,
On the topmost twig that looks up at the sky.

Hush, beating heart of Christabel!
Jesu, Maria, shield her well!
She folded her arms beneath her cloak,
And stole to the other side of the oak.
  What sees she there?

There she sees a damsel bright
Drest in a silken robe of white,
That shadowy in the moonlight shone:
The neck that made that white robe wan,
Her stately neck, and arms were bare;
Her blue-veined feet unsandalled were,
And wildly glittered here and there
The gems entangled in her hair.
I guess, 'twas frightful there to see—
A lady so richly clad as she—
  Beautiful exceedingly!

Mary mother, save me now!
(Said Christabel,) And who art thou?

The lady strange made answer meet,
And her voice was faint and sweet:—
Have pity on my sore distress,
I scarce can speak for weariness:
Stretch forth thy hand, and have no fear!
Said Christabel, How camest thou here?
And the lady, whose voice was faint and sweet,
Did thus pursue her answer meet:—

My sire is of a noble line,
And my name is Geraldine:
Five warriors seized me yestermorn,
Me, even me, a maid forlorn:
They choked my cries with force and fright,
And tied me on a palfrey white.
The palfrey was as fleet as wind,
And they rode furiously behind.
They spurred amain, their steeds were white:
And once we crossed the shade of night.

As sure as Heaven shall rescue me,
I have no thought what men they be;
Nor do I know how long it is
(For I have lain entranced I wis)
Since one, the tallest of the five,
Took me from the palfrey's back,
A weary woman, scarce alive.
Some muttered words his comrades spoke:
He placed me underneath this oak;
He swore they would return with haste;
Whither they went I cannot tell—
I thought I heard, some minutes past,
Sounds as of a castle bell.
Stretch forth thy hand (thus ended she),
And help a wretched maid to flee.

Then Christabel stretched forth her hand,
And comforted fair Geraldine:
O well, bright dame! may you command
The service of Sir Leoline;
And gladly our stout chivalry
Will he send forth and friends withal
To guide and guard you safe and free
Home to your noble father's hall.

She rose: and forth with steps they passed
That strove to be, and were not, fast.
Her gracious stars the lady blest,
And thus spake on sweet Christabel:
All our household are at rest,
The hall as silent as the cell;
Sir Leoline is weak in health,
And may not well awakened be,
But we will move as if in stealth,
And I beseech your courtesy,
This night, to share your couch with me.

They crossed the moat, and Christabel
Took the key that fitted well;
A little door she opened straight,

All in the middle of the gate,
The gate that was ironed within and without,
Where an army in battle array had marched out,
The lady sank, belike through pain,
And Christabel with might and main
Lifted her up, a weary weight,
Over the threshold of the gate:
Then the lady rose again,
And moved, as she were not in pain.

So free from danger, free from fear,
They crossed the court: right glad they were.
And Christabel devoutly cried
To the lady by her side,
Praise we the Virgin all divine
Who hath rescued thee from thy distress!
Alas, alas! said Geraldine,
I cannot speak for weariness.
So free from danger, free from fear,
They crossed the court: right glad they were.

Outside her kennel, the mastiff old
Lay fast asleep, in moonshine cold.
The mastiff old did not awake,
Yet she an angry moan did make!
And what can ail the mastiff bitch?
Never till now she uttered yell
Beneath the eye of Christabel.
Perhaps it is the owlet's scritch:
For what can ail the mastiff bitch?

They passed the hall, that echoes still,
Pass as lightly as you will!
The brands were flat, the brands were dying,
Amid their own white ashes lying;
But when the lady passed, there came
A tongue of light, a fit of flame;
And Christabel saw the lady's eye,
And nothing else saw she thereby,
Save the boss of the shield of Sir Leoline tall,

Which hung in a murky old niche in the wall.
O softly tread, said Christabel,
My father seldom sleepeth well.

Sweet Christabel her feet doth bare,
And jealous of the listening air
They steal their way from stair to stair,
Now in the glimmer, and now in gloom,
And now they pass the Baron's room,
As still as death, with stifled breath!
And now have reached her chamber door;
And now doth Geraldine press down
The rushes of the chamber floor.

The moon shines dim in the open air,
And not a moonbeam enters there.
But they without its light can see
The chamber carved so curiously,
Carved with figures strange and sweet,
All made out of the carver's brain,
For a lady's chamber meet:
The lamp with twofold silver chain
Is fastened to an angel's feet.

The silver lamp burns dead and dim;
But Christabel the lamp will trim.
She trimmed the lamp, and made it bright,
And left it swinging to and fro,
While Geraldine, in wretched plight,
Sank down upon the floor below.

O weary lady, Geraldine,
I pray you, drink this cordial wine!
It is a wine of virtuous powers;
My mother made it of wild flowers.

And will your mother pity me,
Who am a maiden most forlorn?
Christabel answered—Woe is me!
She died the hour that I was born.

I have heard the gray-haired friar tell
How on her death-bed she did say,
That she should hear the castle-bell
Strike twelve upon my wedding-day.
O mother dear! that thou wert here!
I would, said Geraldine, she were!

But soon with altered voice, said she—
'Off, wandering mother! Peak and pine!
I have power to bid thee flee.'
Alas! what ails poor Geraldine?
Why stares she with unsettled eye?
Can she the bodiless dead espy?
And why with hollow voice cries she,
'Off, woman, off! this hour is mine—
Though thou her guardian spirit be,
Off, woman, off! 'tis given to me.'

Then Christabel knelt by the lady's side,
And raised to heaven her eyes so blue—
'Alas!' said she, 'this ghastly ride—
Dear lady! it hath wildered you!
The lady wiped her moist cold brow,
And faintly said, ''Tis over now!'

Again the wild-flower wine she drank:
Her fair large eyes 'gan glitter bright,
And from the floor whereon she sank,
The lofty lady stood upright:
She was most beautiful to see,
Like a lady of a far countrée.

And thus the lofty lady spake—
'All they who live in the upper sky,
Do love you, holy Christabel!
And you love them, and for their sake
And for the good which me befel,
Even I in my degree will try,
Fair maiden, to requite you well.
But now unrobe yourself; for I

Must pray, ere yet in bed I lie.'
Quoth Christabel, So let it be!
And as the lady bade, did she.
Her gentle limbs did she undress,
And lay down in her loveliness.

But through her brain of weal and woe
So many thoughts moved to and fro,
That vain it were her lids to close;
So half-way from the bed she rose,
And on her elbow did recline
To look at the lady Geraldine.

Beneath the lamp the lady bowed,
And slowly rolled her eyes around;
Then drawing in her breath aloud,
Like one that shuddered, she unbound
The cincture from beneath her breast:
Her silken robe, and inner vest,
Dropt to her feet, and full in view,
Behold! her bosom and half her side—
A sight to dream of, not to tell!
O shield her! shield sweet Christabel!

Yet Geraldine nor speaks nor stirs;
Ah! what a stricken look was hers!
Deep from within she seems half-way
To lift some weight with sick assay,
And eyes the maid and seeks delay;
Then suddenly, as one defied,
Collects herself in scorn and pride,
And lay down by the Maiden's side!—
And in her arms the maid she took,
Ah wel-a-day!
And with low voice and doleful look
These words did say:
'In the touch of this bosom there worketh a spell,
Which is lord of thy utterance, Christabel!
Thou knowest to-night, and wilt know to-morrow,
This mark of my shame, this seal of my sorrow;

But vainly thou warrest,
For this is alone in
Thy power to declare,
That in the dim forest
Thou heard'st a low moaning,
And found'st a bright lady, surpassingly fair;
And didst bring her home with thee in love and in charity,
To shield and shelter her from the damp air.'

The Conclusion to Part the First

It was a lovely sight to see
The lady Christabel, when she
Was praying at the old oak-tree;
Amid the jagged shadows
Of mossy leafless boughs,
Kneeling in the moonlight,
To make her gentle vows;
Her slender palms together prest,
Heaving sometimes on her breast;
Her face resigned to bliss or bale—
Her face, oh call it fair not pale,
And both blue eyes more bright than clear,
Each about to have a tear.

With open eyes (ah woe is me!)
Asleep, and dreaming fearfully,
Fearfully dreaming, yet, I wis,
Dreaming that alone, which is—
O sorrow and shame! Can this be she,
The lady, who knelt at the old oak tree?
And lo! the worker of these harms,
That holds the maiden in her arms,
Seems to slumber still and mild,
As a mother with her child.

A star hath set, a star hath risen,
O Geraldine! since arms of thine
Have been the lovely lady's prison.
O Geraldine! one hour was thine—

Thou'st had thy will! By tairn and rill,
The night-birds all that hour were still.
But now they are jubilant anew,
From cliff and tower, tu—whoo! tu—whoo!
Tu—whoo! tu—whoo! from wood and fell!

And see! the lady Christabel!
Gathers herself from out her trance;
Her limbs relax, her countenance
Grows sad and soft; the smooth thin lids
Close o'er her eyes; and tears she sheds—
Large tears that leave the lashes bright!
And oft the while she seems to smile
As infants at a sudden light!

Yea, she doth smile, and she doth weep,
Like a youthful hermitess,
Beauteous in a wilderness,
Who, praying always, prays in sleep,
And, if she move unquietly,
Perchance, 'tis but the blood so free
Comes back and tingles in her feet.
No doubt, she hath a vision sweet.
What if her guardian spirit 'twere,
What if she knew her mother near?
But this she knows, in joys and woes,
That saints will aid if men will call:
For the blue sky bends over all!

Part the Second

Each matin bell, the Baron saith,
Knells us back to a world of death.
These words Sir Leoline first said,
When he rose and found his lady dead;
These words Sir Leoline will say
Many a morn to his dying day!

And hence the custom and law began
That still at dawn the sacristan,
Who duly pulls the heavy bell,

Five and forty beads must tell
Between each stroke—a warning knell,
Which not a soul can choose but hear
From Bratha Head to Wyndermere.

Saith Bracy the bard, So let it knell!
And let the drowsy sacristan
Still count as slowly as he can!
There is no lack of such, I ween,
As well fill up the space between.
In Langdale Pike and Witch's Lair,
And Dungeon-ghyll so foully rent,
With ropes of rock and bells of air
Three sinful sextons' ghosts are pent,
Who all give back, one after t'other,
The death-note to their living brother;
And oft too, by the knell offended,
Just as their one! two! three! is ended,
The devil mocks the doleful tale
With a merry peal from Borrowdale.

The air is still! through mist and cloud
That merry peal comes ringing loud;
And Geraldine shakes off her dread,
And rises lightly from the bed;
Puts on her silken vestments white,
And tricks her hair in lovely plight,
And nothing doubting of her spell
Awakens the lady Christabel.
'Sleep you, sweet lady Christabel?
I trust that you have rested well?

And Christabel awoke and spied
The same who lay down by her side—
O rather say, the same whom she
Raised up beneath the old oak tree!
Nay, fairer yet! and yet more fair!
For she belike hath drunken deep
Of all the blessedness of sleep!
And while she spake, her looks, her air,
Such gentle thankfulness declare,

That (so it seemed) her girded vests
Grew tight beneath her heaving breasts.
'Sure I have sinn'd!' said Christabel,
'Now heaven be praised if all be well!'
And in low faltering tones, yet sweet,
Did she the lofty lady greet
With such perplexity of mind
As dreams too lively leave behind.

So quickly she rose, and quickly arrayed
Her maiden limbs, and having prayed
That He, who on the cross did groan,
Might wash away her sins unknown
She forthwith led fair Geraldine
To meet her sire, Sir Leoline.
The lovely maid and the lady tall
Are pacing both into the hall,
And pacing on through page and groom,
Enter the Baron's presence-room.

The Baron rose, and while he prest
His gentle daughter to his breast,
With cheerful wonder in his eyes
The lady Geraldine espies,
And gave such welcome to the same,
As might beseem so bright a dame!

But when he heard the lady's tale,
And when she told her father's name,
Why waxed Sir Leoline so pale,
Murmuring o'er the name again,
Lord Roland de Vaux of Tryermaine?

Alas! they had been friends in youth;
But whispering tongues can poison truth;
And constancy lives in realms above;
And life is thorny; and youth is vain;
And to be wroth with one we love
Doth work like madness in the brain.
And thus it chanced, as I divine,

With Roland and Sir Leoline.
Each spake words of high disdain
And insult to his heart's best brother:
They parted—ne'er to meet again!
But never either found another
To free the hollow heart from paining—
They stood aloof, the scars remaining,
Like cliffs which had been rent asunder;
A dreary sea now flows between.
But neither heat, nor frost, nor thunder,
Shall wholly do away, I ween,
The marks of that which once hath been.

Sir Leoline, a moment's space,
Stood gazing on the damsel's face:
And the youthful Lord of Tryermaine
Came back upon his heart again.
O then the Baron forgot his age,
His noble heart swelled high with rage;
He swore by the wounds in Jesu's side
He would proclaim it far and wide,
With trump and solemn heraldry,
That they, who thus had wronged the dame
Were base as spotted infamy!
'And if they dare deny the same,
My herald shall appoint a week,
And let the recreant traitors seek
My tourney court—that there and then
I may dislodge their reptile souls
From the bodies and forms of men!'
He spake: his eye in lightning rolls!
For the lady was ruthlessly seized; and he kenned
In the beautiful lady the child of his friend!

And now the tears were on his face,
And fondly in his arms he took
Fair Geraldine, who met the embrace,
Prolonging it with joyous look.
Which when she viewed, a vision fell
Upon the soul of Christabel,

The vision of fear, the touch and pain!
She shrunk and shuddered, and saw again—
(Ah, woe is me! Was it for thee,
Thou gentle maid! such sights to see?)

Again she saw that bosom old,
Again she felt that bosom cold,
And drew in her breath with a hissing sound:
Whereat the Knight turned wildly round
And nothing saw but his own sweet maid
With eyes upraised, as one that prayed.
The touch, the sight, had passed away,
And in its stead that vision blest,
Which comforted her after-rest,
While in the lady's arms she lay,
Had put a rapture in her breast.
And on her lips and o'er her eyes
Spread smiles like light!
With new surprise,
'What ails then my beloved child?'
The Baron said—His daughter mild
Made answer, 'All will yet be well!'
I ween, she had no power to tell
Aught else: so mighty was the spell.
Yet he, who saw this Geraldine,
Had deemed her sure a thing divine.
Such sorrow with such grace she blended,
As if she feared she had offended
Sweet Christabel, that gentle maid!
And with such lowly tones she prayed
She might be sent without delay
Home to her father's mansion.
'Nay!
Nay, by my soul!' said Leoline.
'Ho! Bracy the bard, the charge be thine!
Go thou, with music sweet and loud,
And take two steeds with trappings proud,
And take the youth whom thou lov'st best
To bear thy harp, and learn thy song,
And clothe you both in solemn vest,

And over the mountains haste along,
Lest wandering folk, that are abroad
Detain you on the valley road.
'And when he has crossed the Irthing flood,
My merry bard! he hastes, he hastes
Up Knorren Moor, through Halegarth Wood,
And reaches soon that castle good
Which stands and threatens Scotland's wastes.

'Bard Bracy! bard Bracy! your horses are fleet,
Ye must ride up the hall, your music so sweet,
More loud than your horses' echoing feet!
And loud and loud to Lord Roland call,
Thy daughter is safe in Langdale hall!
Thy beautiful daughter is safe and free—
Sir Leoline greets thee thus through me.
He bids thee come without delay
With all thy numerous array;
And take thy lovely daughter home;
And he will meet thee on the way
With all his numerous array
White with their panting palfreys' foam:
And, by mine honour! I will say,
That I repent me of the day
When I spake words of fierce disdain
To Roland de Vaux of Tryermaine!—
—For since that evil hour hath flown,
Many a summer's sun hath shone;
Yet ne'er found I a friend again
Like Roland de Vaux of Tryermaine.'

The lady fell, and clasped his knees,
Her face upraised, her eyes o'erflowing;
And Bracy replied, with faltering voice,
His gracious hail on all bestowing:
'Thy words, thou sire of Christabel,
Are sweeter than my harp can tell;
Yet might I gain a boon of thee,
This day my journey should not be,
So strange a dream hath come to me;

That I had vowed with music loud
To clear yon wood from thing unblest,
Warn'd by a vision in my rest!
For in my sleep I saw that dove,
That gentlest bird, whom thou dost love,
And call'st by thy own daughter's name—
Sir Leoline! I saw the same,
Fluttering, and uttering fearful moan,
Among the green herbs in the forest alone.
Which when I saw and when I heard,
I wonder'd what might ail the bird;
For nothing near it could I see, [tree.
Save the grass and green herbs underneath the old

'And in my dream, methought, I went
To search out what might there be found;
And what the sweet bird's trouble meant,
That thus lay fluttering on the ground.
I went and peered, and could descry
No cause for her distressful cry;
But yet for her dear lady's sake
I stooped, methought, the dove to take,
When lo! I saw a bright green snake
Coiled around its wings and neck.
Green as the herbs on which it couched,
Close by the dove's its head it crouched;
And with the dove it heaves and stirs,
Swelling its neck as she swelled hers!
I woke; it was the midnight hour,
The clock was echoing in the tower;
But though my slumber was gone by,
This dream it would not pass away—
It seems to live upon my eye!
And thence I vowed this self-same day
With music strong and saintly song
To wander through the forest bare,
Lest aught unholy loiter there.'

Thus Bracy said: the Baron, the while,
Half-listening heard him with a smile;

Then turn'd to Lady Geraldine,
His eyes made up of wonder and love;
And said in courtly accents fine,
'Sweet maid, Lord Roland's beauteous dove,
With arms more strong than harp or song,
Thy sire and I will crush the snake!'
He kissed her forehead as he spake,
And Geraldine in maiden wise
Casting down her large bright eyes,
With blushing cheek and courtesy fine
She turned her from Sir Leoline;
Softly gathering up her train,
That o'er her right arm fell again;
And folded her arms across her chest,
And couched her head upon her breast,
And looked askance at Christabel—
Jesu, Maria, shield her well!

A snake's small eye blinks dull and shy,
And the lady's eyes they shrunk in her head,
Each shrunk up to a serpent's eye,
And with somewhat of malice, and more of dread,
At Christabel she look'd askance!—
One moment—and the sight was fled!
But Christabel in dizzy trance
Stumbling on the unsteady ground
Shuddered aloud, with a hissing sound;
And Geraldine again turned round,
And like a thing that sought relief,
Full of wonder and full of grief,
She rolled her large bright eyes divine
Wildly on Sir Leoline.

The maid, alas! her thoughts are gone,
She nothing sees—no sight but one!
The maid, devoid of guile and sin,
I know not how, in fearful wise,
So deeply had she drunken in
That look, those shrunken serpent eyes,
That all her features were resigned

To this sole image in her mind:
And passively did imitate
That look of dull and treacherous hate!
And thus she stood, in dizzy trance,
Still picturing that look askance
With forced unconscious sympathy
Full before her father's view—
As far as such a look could be
In eyes so innocent and blue!
And when the trance was o'er, the maid
Paused awhile, and inly prayed:
Then falling at the Baron's feet,
'By my mother's soul do I entreat
That thou this woman send away!'
She said: and more she could not say:
For what she knew she could not tell,
O'er-mastered by the mighty spell.

Why is thy cheek so wan and wild,
Sir Leoline? Thy only child
Lies at thy feet, thy joy, thy pride,
So fair, so innocent, so mild;
The same, for whom thy lady died!
O, by the pangs of her dear mother
Think thou no evil of thy child!
For her, and thee, and for no other,
She prayed the moment ere she died:
Prayed that the babe for whom she died,
Might prove her dear lord's joy and pride!
  That prayer her deadly pangs beguiled,
    Sir Leoline!
  And wouldst thou wrong thy only child,
    Her child and thine?

Within the Baron's heart and brain
If thoughts, like these, had any share,
They only swelled his rage and pain,
And did but work confusion there.
His heart was cleft with pain and rage,
His cheeks they quivered, his eyes were wild,

Dishonour'd thus in his old age;
Dishonour'd by his only child,
And all his hospitality
To the insulted daughter of his friend
By more than woman's jealousy
Brought thus to a disgraceful end—
He rolled his eye with stern regard
Upon the gentle minstrel bard,
And said in tones abrupt, austere—
'Why, Bracy! dost thou loiter here?
I bade thee hence!' The bard obeyed;
And turning from his own sweet maid,
The aged knight, Sir Leoline,
Led forth the lady Geraldine!

The Conclusion to Part the Second

A little child, a limber elf,
Singing, dancing, to itself,
A fairy thing with red round cheeks,
That always finds, and never seeks,
Makes such a vision to the sight
As fills a father's eyes with light;
And pleasures flow in so thick and fast
Upon his heart, that he at last
Must needs express his love's excess
With words of unmeant bitterness.
Perhaps 'tis pretty to force together
Thoughts so all unlike each other;
To mutter and mock a broken charm,
To dally with wrong that does no harm.
Perhaps 'tis tender too and pretty
At each wild word to feel within
A sweet recoil of love and pity.
And what, if in a world of sin
(O sorrow and shame should this be true!)
Such giddiness of heart and brain
Comes seldom save from rage and pain,
So talks as it's most used to do.

421

Dejection: an Ode

Late, late yestreen I saw the new Moon,
With the old Moon in her arms;
And I fear, I fear, my master dear!
We shall have a deadly storm.
Ballad of Sir Patrick Spence

I

Well! If the Bard was weather-wise, who made
The grand old ballad of Sir Patrick Spence,
This night, so tranquil now, will not go hence
Unroused by winds, that ply a busier trade
Than those which mould yon cloud in lazy flakes,
Or the dull sobbing draft, that moans and rakes
Upon the strings of this Æolian lute,
Which better far were mute.
For lo! the New-moon winter-bright!
And overspread with phantom light,
(With swimming phantom light o'erspread
But rimmed and circled by a silver thread)
I see the old Moon in her lap, foretelling
The coming-on of rain and squally blast,
And oh! that even now the gust were swelling,
And the slant night-shower driving loud and fast!
Those sounds which oft have raised me, whilst they awed
And sent my soul abroad,
Might now perhaps their wonted impulse give,
Might startle this dull pain, and make it move and live!

II

A grief without a pang, void, dark, and drear,
A stifled, drowsy, unimpassioned grief,
Which finds no natural outlet, no relief,
In word, or sigh, or tear—
O Lady! in this wan and heartless mood,
To other thoughts by yonder throstle woo'd,
All this long eve, so balmy and serene,

Have I been gazing on the western sky,
  And its peculiar tint of yellow green;
And still I gaze—and with how blank an eye!
And those thin clouds above, in flakes and bars,
That give away their motion to the stars:
Those stars, that glide behind them or between,
Now sparkling, now bedimmed, but always seen;
Yon crescent Moon, as fixed as if it grew
In its own cloudless, starless lake of blue;
I see them all so excellently fair,
I see, not feel, how beautiful they are!

III

    My genial spirits fail;
    And what can these avail
To lift the smothering weight from off my breast?
    It were a vain endeavour,
    Though I should gaze for ever
On that green light that lingers in the west;
I may not hope from outward forms to win
The passion and the life, whose fountains are within.

IV

O Lady! we receive but what we give,
And in our life alone does Nature live;
Ours is her wedding-garment, ours her shroud!
  And would we aught behold, of higher worth,
Than that inanimate cold world allowed
To the poor loveless ever-anxious crowd,
  Ah! from the soul itself must issue forth
A light, a glory, a fair luminous cloud
    Enveloping the Earth—
And from the soul itself must there be sent
  A sweet and potent voice, of its own birth,
Of all sweet sounds the life and element!

V

O pure of heart! thou need'st not ask of me
What this strong music in the soul may be!
What, and wherein it doth exist,
This light, this glory, this fair luminous mist,
This beautiful and beauty-making power.
  Joy, virtuous Lady! Joy that ne'er was given,
Save to the pure, and in their purest hour,
Life, and life's effluence, cloud at once and shower,
Joy, Lady! is the spirit and the power,
Which wedding Nature to us gives in dower,
  A new Earth and new Heaven,
Undreamt of by the sensual and the proud—
Joy is the sweet voice, Joy the luminous cloud—
    We in ourselves rejoice!
And thence flows all that charms or ear or sight,
  All melodies the echoes of that voice,
All colours a suffusion from that light.

VI

There was a time when, though my path was rough,
  This joy within me dallied with distress,
And all misfortunes were but as the stuff
  Whence Fancy made me dreams of happiness:
For hope grew round me, like the twining vine,
And fruits, and foliage, not my own, seemed mine.
But now afflictions bow me down to earth:
Nor care I that they rob me of my mirth;
    But oh! each visitation
Suspends what nature gave me at my birth,
  My shaping spirit of Imagination.
For not to think of what I needs must feel
  But to be still and patient, all I can;
And haply by abstruse research to steal
  From my own nature all the natural man—
  This was my sole resource, my only plan;
Till that which suits a part infects the whole,
And now is almost grown the habit of my soul.

VII

Hence, viper thoughts, that coil around my mind,
Reality's dark dream!
I turn from you, and listen to the wind,
Which long has raved unnoticed. What a scream
Of agony by torture lengthened out
That lute sent forth! Thou Wind, that rav'st without,
Bare crag, or mountain-tairn, or blasted tree,
Or pine-grove whither woodman never clomb,
Or lonely house, long held the witches' home,
Methinks were fitter instruments for thee,
Mad Lutanist! who in this month of showers,
Of dark-brown gardens, and of peeping flowers,
Mak'st Devils' yule, with worse than wintry song,
The blossoms, buds, and timorous leaves among.
Thou Actor, perfect in all tragic sounds!
Thou mighty Poet, even to frenzy bold!
What tell'st thou now about?
'Tis of the rushing of an host in rout,
With groans of trampled men, with smarting wounds—
At once they groan with pain and shudder with the cold!
But hush! there is a pause of deepest silence!
And all that noise, as of a rushing crowd,
With groans, and tremulous shudderings—all is over—
It tells another tale, with sounds less deep and loud!
A tale of less affright,
And tempered with delight,
As Otway's self had framed the tender lay.
'Tis of a little child,
Upon a lonesome wild,
Not far from home, but she hath lost her way;
And now moans low in bitter grief and fear,
And now screams loud, and hopes to make her mother hear.

VIII

'Tis midnight, but small thoughts have I of sleep:
Full seldom may my friend such vigils keep!
Visit her, gentle Sleep! with wings of healing,

And may this storm be but a mountain-birth,
May all the stars hang bright above her dwelling,
Silent as though they watched the sleeping Earth!
With light heart may she rise,
Gay fancy, cheerful eyes.
Joy lift her spirit, joy attune her voice;
To her may all things live, from pole to pole,
Their life the eddying of her living soul!
O simple spirit, guided from above,
Dear Lady! friend devoutest of my choice,
Thus may'st thou ever, evermore rejoice.

ROBERT SOUTHEY

[1774-1843]

422

After Blenheim

It was a summer evening,
Old Kaspar's work was done,
And he before his cottage door
Was sitting in the sun;
And by him sported on the green
His little grandchild Wilhelmine.

She saw her brother Peterkin
Roll something large and round
Which he beside the rivulet
In playing there had found;
He came to ask what he had found
That was so large and smooth and round.

Old Kaspar took it from the boy
Who stood expectant by;
And then the old man shook his head,
And with a natural sigh
''Tis some poor fellow's skull,' said he,
'Who fell in the great victory.

'I find them in the garden,
  For there's many here about;
And often when I go to plough
  The ploughshare turns them out.
For many thousand men,' said he,
'Were slain in that great victory.'

'Now tell us what 'twas all about,'
  Young Peterkin he cries;
And little Wilhelmine looks up
  With wonder-waiting eyes;
'Now tell us all about the war,
And what they fought each other for.'

'It was the English,' Kaspar cried,
  'Who put the French to rout;
But what they fought each other for
  I could not well make out.
But every body said,' quoth he,
'That 'twas a famous victory.

'My father lived at Blenheim then,
  Yon little stream hard by;
They burnt his dwelling to the ground,
  And he was forced to fly:
So with his wife and child he fled,
Nor had he where to rest his head.

'With fire and sword the country round
  Was wasted far and wide,
And many a childing mother then
  And newborn baby died:
But things like that, you know, must be
At every famous victory.

'They say it was a shocking sight
  After the field was won;
For many thousand bodies here
  Lay rotting in the sun:
But things like that, you know, must be
After a famous victory.

'Great praise the Duke of Marlbro' won
And our good Prince Eugene;'
'Why 'twas a very wicked thing!'
Said little Wilhelmine;
'Nay . . nay . . my little girl,' quoth he,
'It was a famous victory.

'And every body praised the Duke
Who this great fight did win.'
'But what good came of it at last?'
Quoth little Peterkin:—
'Why that I cannot tell,' said he,
'But 'twas a famous victory.'

423

The Scholar

My days among the Dead are past;
Around me I behold,
Where'er these casual eyes are cast,
The mighty minds of old:
My never-failing friends are they,
With whom I converse day by day.

With them I take delight in weal
And seek relief in woe;
And while I understand and feel
How much to them I owe,
My cheeks have often been bedew'd
With tears of thoughtful gratitude.

My thoughts are with the Dead; with them
I live in long-past years,
Their virtues love, their faults condemn,
Partake their hopes and fears,
And from their lessons seek and find
Instruction with an humble mind.

My hopes are with the Dead; anon
My place with them will be,
And I with them shall travel on

Through all Futurity;
Yet leaving here a name, I trust,
That will not perish in the dust.

CHARLES LAMB

[1775-1834]

424 The Old Familiar Faces

I HAVE had playmates, I have had companions
In my days of childhood, in my joyful school-days;
All, all are gone, the old familiar faces.

I have been laughing, I have been carousing,
Drinking late, sitting late, with my bosom cronies;
All, all are gone, the old familiar faces.

I loved a Love once, fairest among women:
Closed are her doors on me, I must not see her—
All, all are gone, the old familiar faces.

I have a friend, a kinder friend has no man:
Like an ingrate, I left my friend abruptly;
Left him, to muse on the old familiar faces.

Ghost-like I paced round the haunts of my childhood,
Earth seem'd a desert I was bound to traverse,
Seeking to find the old familiar faces.

Friend of my bosom, thou more than a brother,
Why wert not thou born in my father's dwelling?
So might we talk of the old familiar faces,

How some they have died, and some they have left me,
And some are taken from me; all are departed;
All, all are gone, the old familiar faces.

425

Hester

WHEN maidens such as Hester die
Their place ye may not well supply,
Though ye among a thousand try
With vain endeavour.
A month or more hath she been dead,
Yet cannot I by force be led
To think upon the wormy bed
And her together.

A springy motion in her gait,
A rising step, did indicate
Of pride and joy no common rate
That flush'd her spirit:
I know not by what name beside
I shall it call: if 'twas not pride,
It was a joy to that allied
She did inherit.

Her parents held the Quaker rule,
Which doth the human feeling cool;
But she was train'd in Nature's school,
Nature had blest her.
A waking eye, a prying mind,
A heart that stirs, is hard to bind;
A hawk's keen sight ye cannot blind,
Ye could not Hester.

My sprightly neighbour! gone before
To that unknown and silent shore,
Shall we not meet, as heretofore
Some summer morning—
When from thy cheerful eyes a ray
Hath struck a bliss upon the day,
A bliss that would not go away,
A sweet fore-warning?

426 On an Infant Dying as Soon as Born

I saw where in the shroud did lurk
A curious frame of Nature's work;
A flow'ret crushéd in the bud,
A nameless piece of Babyhood,
Was in her cradle-coffin lying;
Extinct, with scarce the sense of dying:
So soon to exchange the imprisoning womb
For darker closets of the tomb!
She did but ope an eye, and put
A clear beam forth, then straight up shut
For the long dark: ne'er more to see
Through glasses of mortality,
Riddle of destiny, who can show
What thy short visit meant, or know
What thy errand here below?
Shall we say, that Nature blind
Check'd her hand, and changed her mind
Just when she had exactly wrought
A finish'd pattern without fault?
Could she flag, or could she tire,
Or lack'd she the Promethean fire
(With her nine moons' long workings sicken'd)
That should thy little limbs have quicken'd?
Limbs so firm, they seem'd to assure
Life of health, and days mature:
Woman's self in miniature!
Limbs so fair, they might supply
(Themselves now but cold imagery)
The sculptor to make Beauty by.
Or did the stern-eyed Fate descry
That babe or mother, one must die;
So in mercy left the stock
And cut the branch; to save the shock
Of young years widow'd, and the pain
When Single State comes back again
To the lone man who, reft of wife,
Thenceforward drags a maiméd life?

The economy of Heaven is dark,
And wisest clerks have miss'd the mark
Why human buds, like this, should fall,
More brief than fly ephemeral
That has his day; while shrivell'd crones
Stiffen with age to stocks and stones;
And crabbed use the conscience sears
In sinners of an hundred years.
—Mother's prattle, mother's kiss,
Baby fond, thou ne'er wilt miss:
Rites, which custom does impose,
Silver bells, and baby clothes;
Coral redder than those lips
Which pale death did late eclipse;
Music framed for infants' glee,
Whistle never tuned for thee;
Though thou want'st not, thou shalt have them,
Loving hearts were they which gave them.
Let not one be missing; nurse,
See them laid upon the hearse
Of infant slain by doom perverse.
Why should kings and nobles have
Pictured trophies to their grave,
And we, churls, to thee deny
Thy pretty toys with thee to lie—
A more harmless vanity?

SIR WALTER SCOTT

[1771-1832]

427

THE OUTLAW

O BRIGNALL banks are wild and fair,
  And Greta woods are green,
And you may gather garlands there
  Would grace a summer-queen.
And as I rode by Dalton-Hall
  Beneath the turrets high,

A Maiden on the castle-wall
  Was singing merrily:
'O Brignall Banks are fresh and fair,
  And Greta woods are green;
I'd rather rove with Edmund there
  Than reign our English queen.'

'If, Maiden, thou wouldst wend with me,
  To leave both tower and town,
Thou first must guess what life lead we
  That dwell by dale and down.
And if thou canst that riddle read,
  As read full well you may,
Then to the greenwood shalt thou speed
  As blithe as Queen of May.'
Yet sung she, 'Brignall banks are fair,
  And Greta woods are green;
I'd rather rove with Edmund there
  Than reign our English queen.

'I read you, by your bugle-horn
  And by your palfrey good,
I read you for a ranger sworn
  To keep the king's greenwood.'
'A Ranger, lady, winds his horn,
  And 'tis at peep of light;
His blast is heard at merry morn,
  And mine at dead of night.'
Yet sung she, 'Brignall banks are fair,
  And Greta woods are gay;
I would I were with Edmund there
  To reign his Queen of May!

'With burnish'd brand and musketoon
  So gallantly you come,
I read you for a bold Dragoon
  That lists the tuck of drum.'
'I list no more the tuck of drum,
  No more the trumpet hear;

But when the beetle sounds his hum
  My comrades take the spear.
And O! though Brignall banks be fair
  And Greta woods be gay,
Yet mickle must the maiden dare
  Would reign my Queen of May!

'Maiden! a nameless life I lead,
  A nameless death I'll die;
The fiend whose lantern lights the mead
  Were better mate than I!
And when I'm with my comrades met
  Beneath the greenwood bough,—
What once we were we all forget,
  Nor think what we are now.'

Chorus

'Yet Brignall banks are fresh and fair,
  And Greta woods are green,
And you may gather garlands there
  Would grace a summer-queen.'

428

To a Lock of Hair

THY hue, dear pledge, is pure and bright
As in that well-remember'd night
When first thy mystic braid was wove,
And first my Agnes whisper'd love.

Since then how often hast thou prest
The torrid zone of this wild breast,
Whose wrath and hate have sworn to dwell
With the first sin that peopled hell;
A breast whose blood's a troubled ocean,
Each throb the earthquake's wild commotion!
O if such clime thou canst endure
Yet keep thy hue unstain'd and pure,
What conquest o'er each erring thought

Of that fierce realm had Agnes wrought!
I had not wander'd far and wide
With such an angel for my guide;
Nor heaven nor earth could then reprove me
If she had lived and lived to love me.

Not then this world's wild joys had been
To me one savage hunting scene,
My sole delight the headlong race
And frantic hurry of the chase;
To start, pursue, and bring to bay,
Rush in, drag down, and rend my prey,
Then—from the carcass turn away!
Mine ireful mood had sweetness tamed,
And soothed each wound which pride inflamed:—
Yes, God and man might now approve me
If thou hadst lived and lived to love me!

429 Jock of Hazeldean

'Why weep ye by the tide, ladie?
Why weep ye by the tide?
I'll wed ye to my youngest son,
And ye sall be his bride:
And ye sall be his bride, ladie,
Sae comely to be seen'—
But aye she loot the tears down fa'
For Jock of Hazeldean.

'Now let this wilfu' grief be done,
And dry that cheek so pale;
Young Frank is chief of Errington
And lord of Langley-dale;
His step is first in peaceful ha',
His sword in battle keen'—
But aye she loot the tears down fa'
For Jock of Hazeldean.

'A chain of gold ye sall not lack,
  Nor braid to bind your hair,
Nor mettled hound, nor managed hawk,
  Nor palfrey fresh and fair;
And you the foremost o' them a'
  Shall ride our forest-queen '—
But aye she loot the tears down fa'
  For Jock of Hazeldean.

The kirk was deck'd at morning-tide,
  The tapers glimmer'd fair;
The priest and bridegroom wait the bride,
  And dame and knight are there:
They sought her baith by bower and ha'
  The ladie was not seen!
She's o'er the Border, and awa'
  Wi' Jock of Hazeldean.

430

Eleu Loro

WHERE shall the lover rest
  Whom the fates sever
From his true maiden's breast
  Parted for ever?
Where, through groves deep and high
  Sounds the far billow,
Where early violets die
  Under the willow.
    Eleu loro
  Soft shall be his pillow.

There through the summer day
  Cool streams are laving:
There, while the tempests sway,
  Scarce are boughs waving;
There thy rest shalt thou take,
  Parted for ever,
Never again to wake

Never, O never!
Eleu loro
Never, O never!

Where shall the traitor rest,
He, the deceiver,
Who could win maiden's breast,
Ruin, and leave her?
In the lost battle,
Borne down by the flying,
Where mingles war's rattle
With groans of the dying;
Eleu loro
There shall he be lying.

Her wing shall the eagle flap
O'er the falsehearted;
His warm blood the wolf shall lap
Ere life be parted:
Shame and dishonour sit
By his grave ever;
Blessing shall hallow it
Never, O never!
Eleu loro
Never, O never!

431

A SERENADE

AH! County Guy, the hour is nigh
The sun has left the lea,
The orange-flower perfumes the bower,
The breeze is on the sea.
The lark, his lay who trill'd all day,
Sits hush'd his partner nigh;
Breeze, bird, and flower confess the hour,
But where is County Guy?

The village maid steals through the shade
Her shepherd's suit to hear;

To Beauty shy, by lattice high,
  Sings high-born Cavalier.
The star of Love, all stars above,
  Now reigns o'er earth and sky,
And high and low the influence know—
  But where is County Guy?

432

The Rover

A WEARY lot is thine, fair maid,
  A weary lot is thine!
To pull the thorn thy brow to braid,
  And press the rue for wine.
A lightsome eye, a soldier's mien
  A feather of the blue,
A doublet of the Lincoln green—
  No more of me you knew
      My Love!
No more of me you knew.

'This morn is merry June, I trow,
  The rose is budding fain;
But she shall bloom in winter snow
  Ere we two meet again.'
He turn'd his charger as he spake
  Upon the river shore,
He gave the bridle-reins a shake,
  Said 'Adieu for evermore
      My Love!
And adieu for evermore.'

433

The Maid of Neidpath

O LOVERS' eyes are sharp to see,
  And lovers' ears in hearing;
And love, in life's extremity,
  Can lend an hour of cheering.
Disease had been in Mary's bower
  And slow decay from mourning,

Though now she sits on Neidpath's tower
  To watch her Love's returning.

All sunk and dim her eyes so bright,
  Her form decay'd by pining,
Till through her wasted hand, at night,
  You saw the taper shining.
By fits a sultry hectic hue
  Across her cheek was flying;
By fits so ashy pale she grew
  Her maidens thought her dying.

Yet keenest powers to see and hear
  Seem'd in her frame residing;
Before the watch-dog prick'd his ear
  She heard her lover's riding;
Ere scarce a distant form was kenn'd
  She knew and waved to greet him,
And o'er the battlement did bend
  As on the wing to meet him.

He came—he pass'd—an heedless gaze
  As o'er some stranger glancing:
Her welcome, spoke in faltering phrase,
  Lost in his courser's prancing—
The castle-arch, whose hollow tone
  Returns each whisper spoken,
Could scarcely catch the feeble moan
  Which told her heart was broken.

434

Gathering Song of Donald the Black

Pibroch of Donuil Dhu
  Pibroch of Donuil
Wake thy wild voice anew,
  Summon Clan Conuil.
Come away, come away,
  Hark to the summons!
Come in your war-array,
  Gentles and commons.

Come from deep glen, and
  From mountain so rocky;
The war-pipe and pennon
  Are at Inverlocky.
Come every hill-plaid, and
  True heart that wears one,
Come every steel blade, and
  Strong hand that bears one.

Leave untended the herd,
  The flock without shelter;
Leave the corpse uninterr'd,
  The bride at the altar;
Leave the deer, leave the steer,
  Leave nets and barges:
Come with your fighting gear,
  Broadswords and targes.

Come as the winds come, when
  Forests are rended,
Come as the waves come, when
  Navies are stranded:
Faster come, faster come,
  Faster and faster,
Chief, vassal, page and groom,
  Tenant and master.

Fast they come, fast they come;
  See how they gather!
Wide waves the eagle plume
  Blended with heather.
Cast your plaids, draw your blades,
  Forward each man set!
Pibroch of Donuil Dhu
  Knell for the onset!

435

Border Ballad

MARCH, march, Ettrick and Teviotdale,
Why the deil dinna ye march forward in order!
March, march, Eskdale and Liddesdale,
All the Blue Bonnets are bound for the Border.
Many a banner spread,
Flutters above your head,
Many a crest that is famous in story.
Mount and make ready then,
Sons of the mountain glen,
Fight for the Queen and our old Scottish glory.

Come from the hills where your hirsels are grazing,
Come from the glen of the buck and the roe;
Come to the crag where the beacon is blazing,
Come with the buckler, the lance, and the bow.
Trumpets are sounding,
War-steeds are bounding,
Stand to your arms and march in good order;
England shall many a day
Tell of the bloody fray,
When the Blue Bonnets came over the Border.

436

The Pride of Youth

PROUD Maisie is in the wood,
Walking so early;
Sweet Robin sits on the bush
Singing so rarely.

'Tell me, thou bonny bird,
When shall I marry me?'
—'When six braw gentlemen
Kirkward shall carry ye.'

'Who makes the bridal bed,
Birdie, say truly?'
—'The gray-headed sexton
That delves the grave duly.

'The glowworm o'er grave and stone
  Shall light thee steady;
The owl from the steeple sing,
  Welcome, proud lady.'

437

Coronach

He is gone on the mountain,
  He is lost to the forest,
Like a summer-dried fountain,
  When our need was the sorest.
The font reappearing
  From the raindrops shall borrow,
But to us comes no cheering,
  To Duncan no morrow!

The hand of the reaper
  Takes the ears that are hoary,
But the voice of the weeper
  Wails manhood in glory.
The autumn winds rushing
  Waft the leaves that are serest,
But our flower was in flushing
  When blighting was nearest.

Fleet foot on the correi,
  Sage counsel in cumber,
Red hand in the foray,
  How sound is thy slumber!
Like the dew on the mountain,
  Like the foam on the river
Like the bubble on the fountain,
  Thou art gone, and for ever.

438

Lucy Ashton's Song

Look not thou on beauty's charming;
Sit thou still when kings are arming;
Taste not when the wine-cup glistens;
Speak not when the people listens;

Stop thine ear against the singer;
From the red gold keep thy finger;
Vacant heart and hand and eye,
Easy live and quiet die.

439

Answer

Sound, sound the clarion, fill the fife!
  To all the sensual world proclaim,
One crowded hour of glorious life
  Is worth an age without a name.

440

Rosabelle

O listen, listen, ladies gay!
  No haughty feat of arms I tell;
Soft is the note, and sad the lay
  That mourns the lovely Rosabelle.

'Moor, moor the barge, ye gallant crew!
  And, gentle lady, deign to stay!
Rest thee in Castle Ravensheuch,
  Nor tempt the stormy firth to-day.

'The blackening wave is edged with white;
  To inch and rock the sea-mews fly;
The fishers have heard the Water-Sprite,
  Whose screams forebode that wreck is nigh.

'Last night the gifted Seer did view
  A wet shroud swathed round ladye gay;
Then stay thee, Fair, in Ravensheuch;
  Why cross the gloomy firth to-day?'

''Tis not because Lord Lindesay's heir
  Tonight at Roslin leads the ball,
But that my lady-mother there
  Sits lonely in her castle-hall.

''Tis not because the ring they ride,
  And Lindesay at the ring rides well,
But that my sire the wine will chide
  If 'tis not fill'd by Rosabelle.'

—O'er Roslin all that dreary night
  A wondrous blaze was seen to gleam;
'Twas broader than the watch-fire's light,
  And redder than the bright moonbeam.

It glared on Roslin's castled rock,
  It ruddied all the copse-wood glen;
'Twas seen from Dryden's groves of oak,
  And seen from cavern'd Hawthornden.

Seem'd all on fire that chapel proud
  Where Roslin's chiefs uncoffin'd lie,
Each Baron, for a sable shroud,
  Sheathed in his iron panoply.

Seem'd all on fire within, around,
  Deep sacristy and altar's pale;
Shone every pillar foliage-bound,
  And glimmer'd all the dead men's mail.

Blazed battlement and pinnet high,
  Blazed every rose-carved buttress fair—
So still they blaze, when fate is nigh
  The lordly line of high Saint Clair.

There are twenty of Roslin's barons bold
  Lie buried within that proud chapelle;
Each one the holy vault doth hold
  But the sea holds lovely Rosabelle!

And each Saint Clair was buried there
  With candle, with book, and with knell;
But the sea-caves rung, and the wild winds sung
  The dirge of lovely Rosabelle.

441

Hunting Song

Waken, lords and ladies gay,
On the mountain dawns the day;
All the jolly chase is here
With hawk and horse and hunting-spear;
Hounds are in their couples yelling,
Hawks are whistling, horns are knelling,
Merrily merrily mingle they,
'Waken, lords and ladies gay.'

Waken, lords and ladies gay,
The mist has left the mountain gray,
Springlets in the dawn are steaming,
Diamonds on the brake are gleaming;
And foresters have busy been
To track the buck in thicket green;
Now we come to chant our lay
'Waken, lords and ladies gay.'

'Waken, lords and ladies gay,
To the greenwood haste away;
We can show you where he lies,
Fleet of foot and tall of size;
We can show the marks he made
When 'gainst the oak his antlers fray'd;
You shall see him brought to bay;
'Waken, lords and ladies gay.'

Louder, louder chant the lay,
Waken, lords and ladies gay!
Tell them youth and mirth and glee
Run a course as well as we;
Time, stern huntsman! who can baulk,
Stanch as hound and fleet as hawk;
Think of this, and rise with day
Gentle lords and ladies gay!

442 LOCHINVAR

OH! young Lochinvar is come out of the west,
Through all the wide Border his steed was the best;
And save his good broadsword he weapons had none.
He rode all unarmed and he rode all alone.
So faithful in love and so dauntless in war,
There never was knight like the young Lochinvar.

He stayed not for brake and he stopped not for stone,
He swam the Eske river where ford there was none,
But ere he alighted at Netherby gate
The bride had consented, the gallant came late:
For a laggard in love and a dastard in war
Was to wed the fair Ellen of brave Lochinvar.

So boldly he entered the Netherby Hall,
Among bridesmen, and kinsmen, and brothers, and all:
Then spoke the bride's father, his hand on his sword,—
For the poor craven bridegroom said never a word,—
'Oh! come ye in peace here, or come ye in war,
Or to dance at our bridal, young Lord Lochinvar?'—

'I long wooed your daughter, my suit you denied;
Love swells like the Solway, but ebbs like its tide—
And now am I come, with this lost love of mine,
To lead but one measure, drink one cup of wine.
There are maidens in Scotland more lovely by far,
That would gladly be bride to the young Lochinvar.'

The bride kissed the goblet; the knight took it up,
He quaffed off the wine, and he threw down the cup,
She looked down to blush, and she looked up to sigh,
With a smile on her lips and a tear in her eye.
He took her soft hand ere her mother could bar,—
'Now tread we a measure!' said young Lochinvar.

So stately his form, and so lovely her face,
That never a hall such a galliard did grace;

While her mother did fret, and her father did fume,
And the bridegroom stood dangling his bonnet and plume;
And the bride-maidens whispered ''Twere better by far
To have matched our fair cousin with young Lochinvar.'

One touch to her hand and one word in her ear,
When they reached the hall-door, and the charger stood near;
So light to the coupe the fair lady he swung,
So light to the saddle before her he sprung!
'She is won! we are gone, over bank, bush, and scaur;
They'll have fleet steeds that follow,' quoth young Lochinvar.

There was mounting 'mong Graemes of the Netherby clan;
Fosters, Fenwicks, and Musgraves, they rode and they ran:
There was racing and chasing on Canobie Lee,
But the lost bride of Netherby ne'er did they see.
So daring in love and so dauntless in war,
Have ye e'er heard of gallant like young Lochinvar?

443 BONNY DUNDEE

To the Lords of Convention 'twas Claver'se who spoke.
'Ere the King's crown shall fall there are crowns to be broke;
So let each Cavalier who loves honour and me,
Come follow the bonnet of Bonny Dundee.
    Come fill up my cup, come fill up my can,
    Come saddle your horses, and call up your men;
    Come open the West Port and let me gang free,
    And it's room for the bonnets of Bonny Dundee!'

Dundee he is mounted, he rides up the street,
The bells are rung backward, the drums they are beat;
But the Provost, douce man, said, 'Just e'en let him be,
The Gude Town is weel quit of that Deil of Dundee.'
    Come fill up my cup, etc.

As he rode down the sanctified bends of the Bow,
Ilk carline was flyting and shaking her pow;

But the young plants of grace they looked couthie and slee,
Thinking luck to thy bonnet, thou Bonny Dundee!
Come fill up my cup, etc.

With sour-featured Whigs the Grass-market was crammed,
As if half the West had set tryst to be hanged;
There was spite in each look, there was fear in each e'e,
As they watched for the bonnets of Bonny Dundee.
Come fill up my cup, etc.

These cowls of Kilmarnock had spits and had spears,
And lang-hafted gullies to kill cavaliers;
But they shrunk to close-heads and the causeway was free,
At the toss of the bonnet of Bonny Dundee.
Come fill up my cup, etc.

He spurred to the foot of the proud Castle rock,
And with the gay Gordon he gallantly spoke;
'Let Mons Meg and her marrows speak twa words or three,
For the love of the bonnet of Bonny Dundee.'
Come fill up my cup, etc.

The Gordon demands of him which way he goes—
'Where'er shall direct me the shade of Montrose!
Your Grace in short space shall hear tidings of me,
Or that low lies the bonnet of Bonny Dundee.
Come fill up my cup, etc.

'There are hills beyond Pentland and lands beyond Forth,
If there's lords in the Lowlands, there's chiefs in the North;
There are wild Duniewassals three thousand times three,
Will cry *hoigh!* for the bonnet of Bonny Dundee.
Come fill up my cup, etc.

'There's brass on the target of barkened bull-hide;
There's steel in the scabbard that dangles beside;
The brass shall be burnished, the steel shall flash free,
At the toss of the bonnet of Bonny Dundee.
Come fill up my cup, etc.

'Away to the hills, to the caves, to the rocks—
Ere I own an usurper, I'll couch with the fox;
And tremble, false Whigs, in the midst of your glee,
You have not seen the last of my bonnet and me!'
Come fill up my cup, etc.

He waved his proud hand the trumpets were blown,
The kettle-drums clashed and the horsemen rode on,
Till on Ravelston's cliffs and on Clermiston's lee
Died away the wild war-notes of Bonny Dundee.
Come fill up my cup, come fill up my can,
Come saddle the horses, and call up the men,
Come open your gates, and let me gae free,
For it's up with the bonnets of Bonny Dundee!

444 DATUR HORA QUIETI

THE sun upon the lake is low,
The wild birds hush their song,
The hills have evening's deepest glow,
Yet Leonard tarries long.
Now all whom varied toil and care
From home and love divide,
In the calm sunset may repair
Each to the loved one's side.

The noble dame, on turret high,
Who waits her gallant knight,
Looks to the western beam to spy
The flash of armour bright.
The village maid, with hand on brow
The level ray to shade,
Upon the footpath watches now
For Colin's darkening plaid.

Now to their mates the wild swans row,
By day they swam apart,
And to the thicket wanders slow
The hind beside the hart.

The woodlark at his partner's side
Twitters his closing song—
All meet whom day and care divide,
But Leonard tarries long!

445 HERE'S A HEALTH TO KING CHARLES

BRING the bowl which you boast,
Fill it up to the brim;
'Tis to him we love most,
And to all who love him.
Brave gallants, stand up,
And avaunt ye, base carles!
Were there death in the cup,
Here's a health to King Charles.

Though he wanders through dangers,
Unaided, unknown,
Dependent on strangers,
Estranged from his own;
Though 'tis under our breath,
Amidst forfeits and perils,
Here's to honor and faith,
And a health to King Charles!

Let such honors abound
As the time can afford,
The knee on the ground,
And the hand on the sword;
But the time shall come round
When, 'mid Lords, Dukes, and Earls,
The loud trumpet shall sound,
Here's a health to King Charles!

446 HARP OF THE NORTH, FAREWELL!

HARP of the North, farewell! The hills grow dark,
On purple peaks a deeper shade descending;
In twilight copse the glow-worm lights her spark,
The deer, half-seen, are to the covert wending.

Resume thy wizard elm! the fountain lending,
 And the wild breeze, thy wilder minstrelsy;
Thy numbers sweet with nature's vespers blending,
 With distant echo from the fold and lea,
And herd-boy's evening pipe, and hum of housing bee.

Yet, once again, farewell, thou Minstrel Harp!
 Yet, once again, forgive my feeble sway,
And little reck I of the censure sharp
 May idly cavil at an idle lay.
Much have I owed thy strains on life's long way,
 Through secret woes the world has never known,
When on the weary night dawned wearier day,
 And bitterer was the grief devoured alone.—
That I o'erlive such woes, Enchantress! is thine own.

Hark! as my lingering footsteps slow retire,
 Some spirit of the Air has waked thy string!
'Tis now a seraph bold, with touch of fire,
 'Tis now the brush of Fairy's frolic wing.
Receding now, the dying numbers ring
 Fainter and fainter down the rugged dell;
And now the mountain breezes scarcely bring
 A wandering witch-note of the distant spell—
And now, 'tis silent all!—Enchantress, fare thee well!

JAMES HOGG

[*1770-1835*]

447 KILMENY

BONNIE Kilmeny gaed up the glen;
But it wasna to met Duneira's men,
Nor the rosy monk of the isle to see,
For Kilmeny was pure as pure could be.
It was only to hear the yorlin[1] sing,
And pu' the cress-flower round the spring;
The scarlet hypp and the hindberrye,[2]

[1] The yellow-hammer. [2] Bramble.

And the nut that hung frae the hazel tree;
For Kilmeny was pure as pure could be.
But lang may her minny[3] look o'er the wa',
And lang may she seek i' the green-wood shaw;
Lang the laird o' Duneira blame,
And lang, lang greet[4] or Kilmeny come hame!
When many a day had come and fled,
When grief grew calm, and hope was dead,
When mess for Kilmeny's soul had been sung,
When the bedesman had pray'd and the dead bell rung,
Late, late in gloamin' when all was still,
When the fringe was red on the Westlin[5] hill,
The wood was sere, the moon i' the wane,
The reek[6] o' the cot hung over the plain,
Like a little wee cloud in the world its lane;[7]
When the ingle[8] low'd[9] wi' an eiry leme,[10]
Late, late in the gloamin' Kilmeny came hame!

'Kilmeny, Kilmeny, where have you been?
Lang hae we sought baith holt[11] and den;
By linn,[12] by ford, and green-wood tree,
Yet you are halesome and fair to see.
Where gat you that joup[13] o' the lily scheen?
That bonnie snood[14] of the birk sae green?
And these roses, the fairest that ever were seen?
Kilmeny, Kilmeny, where have you been?'

Kilmeny look'd up with a lovely grace,
But nae smile was seen on Kilmeny's face;
As still was her look, and as still was her e'e,
As the stillness that lay on the emerant lea,
Or the mist that sleeps on a waveless sea.
For Kilmeny had been, she knew not where,
And Kilmeny had seen what she could not declare;
Kilmeny had been where the cock never crew,
Where the rain never fell, and the wind never blew.
But it seem'd as the harp of the sky had rung,
And the airs of heaven play'd round her tongue,

[3] Mother. [4] Weep. [5] Western. [6] Smoke. [7] Alone, by itself.
[8] Hearth. [9] Flamed. [10] Weird gleam. [11] Wood. [12] Waterfall.
[13] Mantle. [14] Hair-ribbon.

When she spake of the lovely forms she had seen,
And a land where sin had never been;
A land of love and a land of light,
Withouten sun, or moon, or night;
Where the river swa'd a living stream,
And the light a pure celestial beam;
The land of vision, it would seem,
A still, an everlasting dream.

In yon green-wood there is a waik,[15]
And in that waik there is a wene,[16]
And in that wene there is a maike,[17]
That neither has flesh, blood, nor bane;
And down in yon green-wood he walks his lane.

In that green wene Kilmeny lay,
Her bosom happ'd[18] wi' flowerets gay;
But the air was soft and the silence deep,
And bonnie Kilmeny fell sound asleep.
She kenn'd[19] nae mair, nor open'd her e'e,
Till waked by the hymns of a far countrye.
She 'waken'd on a couch of the silk sae slim,
All striped wi' the bars of the rainbow's rim;
And lovely beings round were rife,
Who erst had travell'd mortal life;
And aye they smiled and 'gan to speer,[20]
'What spirit has brought this mortal here?'—

'Lang have I journey'd, the world wide,'
A meek and reverend fere[21] replied;
'Baith night and day I have watch'd the fair,
Eident[22] a thousand years and mair.
Yes, I have watch'd o'er ilk[23] degree,
Wherever blooms femenitye;
But sinless virgin, free of stain
In mind and body, fand I nane.
Never, since the banquet of time,
Found I a virgin in her prime,

[15] Clearing. [16] Dwelling. [17] Creature. [18] Covered. [19] Knew. [20] Ask. [21] Fellow. [22] Diligently. [23] Every.

Till late this bonnie maiden I saw
As spotless as the morning snaw:
Full twenty years she has lived as free
As the spirits that sojourn in this countrye:
I have brought her away frae the snares of men,
That sin or death she never may ken.'—

They clasp'd her wrist and her hands sae fair,
They kiss'd her cheek and they kemed[24] her hair,
And round came many a blooming fere,
Saying, 'Bonnie Kilmeny, ye're welcome here!
Women are freed of the littand[25] scorn:
O blest be the day Kilmeny was born!
Now shall the land of the spirits see,
Now shall it ken what a woman may be!
Many a lang year, in sorrow and pain,
Many a lang year through the world we've gane,
Commission'd to watch fair womankind,
For it's they who nurice the immortal mind.
We have watch'd their steps as the dawning shone,
And deep in the green-wood walks alone;
By lily bower and silken bed,
The viewless tears have o'er them shed;
Have soothed their ardent minds to sleep,
Or left the couch of love to weep.
We have seen! we have seen! but the time must come,
And the angels will weep at the day of doom!

'O would the fairest of mortal kind
Aye keep the holy truths in mind,
That kindred spirits their motions see,
Who watch their ways with anxious e'e,
And grieve for the guilt of humanitye!
O, sweet to Heaven the maiden's prayer,
And the sigh that heaves a bosom sae fair!
And dear to Heaven the words of truth,
And the praise of virtue frae beauty's mouth!
And dear to the viewless forms of air,
The minds that kyth[26] as the body fair!

[24] Combed. [25] Shameful. [26] Show.

'O bonnie Kilmeny! free frae stain,
If ever you seek the world again,
That world of sin, of sorrow and fear,
O tell of the joys that are waiting here;
And tell of the signs you shall shortly see;
Of the times that are now, and the times that
shall be.'—
They lifted Kilmeny, they led her away,
And she walk'd in the light of a sunless day;
The sky was a dome of crystal bright,
The fountain of vision, and fountain of light:
The emerald fields were of dazzling glow,
And the flowers of everlasting blow.
Then deep in the stream her body they laid,
That her youth and beauty never might fade;
And they smiled on heaven, when they saw her lie
In the stream of life that wander'd bye.
And she heard a song, she heard it sung,
She kenn'd not where; but sae sweetly it rung,
It fell on the ear like a dream of the morn:
'O, blest be the day Kilmeny was born!
Now shall the land of the spirits see,
Now shall it ken what a woman may be!
The sun that shines on the world sae bright,
A borrow'd gleid[27] frae the fountain of light;
And the moon that sleeks the sky sae dun,
Like a gouden bow, or a beamless sun,
Shall wear away, and be seen nae mair,
And the angels shall miss them travelling the air.
But lang, lang after baith night and day,
When the sun and the world have elyed[28] away;
When the sinner has gane to his waesome doom,
Kilmeny shall smile in eternal bloom!'—

They bore her away, she wist not how,
For she felt not arm nor rest below;
But so swift they wain'd[29] her through the light,
'Twas like the motion of sound or sight;
They seem'd to split the gales of air,

[27] Beam. [28] Vanished. [29] Bore (?)

And yet nor gale nor breeze was there.
Unnumber'd groves below them grew,
They came, they pass'd, and backward flew,
Like floods of blossoms gliding on,
In moment seen, in moment gone.
O, never vales to mortal view
Appear'd like those o'er which they flew!
That land to human spirits given,
The lowermost vales of the storied heaven;
From thence they can view the world below,
And heaven's blue gates with sapphires glow,
More glory yet unmeet to know.
They bore her far to a mountain green,
To see what mortal never had seen;
And they seated her high on a purple sward,
And bade her heed what she saw and heard,
And note the changes the spirits wrought,
For now she lived in the land of thought.
She look'd, and she saw nor sun nor skies,
But a crystal dome of a thousand dyes:
She look'd, and she saw nae land aright,
But an endless whirl of glory and light:
And radiant beings went and came,
Far swifter than wind, or the linkèd flame.
She hid her e'en frae the dazzling view;
She look'd again, and the scene was new.

She saw a sun on a summer sky,
And clouds of amber sailing bye;
A lovely land beneath her lay,
And that land had glens and mountains gray;
And that land had valleys and hoary piles,
And marlèd[30] seas, and a thousand isles.
Its fields were speckled, its forests green,
And its lakes were all of the dazzling sheen,
Like magic mirrors, where slumbering lay
The sun and the sky and the cloudlet gray;
Which heaved and trembled, and gently swung,
On every shore they seem'd to be hung;

[30] Parti-colored.

For there they were seen on their downward plain
A thousand times and a thousand again;
In winding lake and placid firth,
Little peaceful heavens in the bosom of earth.
Kilmeny sigh'd and seem'd to grieve,
For she found her heart to that land did cleave;
She saw the corn wave on the vale,
She saw the deer run down the dale,
She saw the plaid and the broad claymore,
And the brows that the badge of freedom bore;
And she thought she had seen the land before.

She saw a lady sit on a throne,
The fairest that ever the sun shone on!
A lion lick'd her hand of milk,
And she held him in a leish of silk;
And a leifu'[31] maiden stood at her knee,
With a silver wand and melting e'e;
Her sovereign shield till love stole in,
And poison'd all the fount within.

Then a gruff untoward bedesman came,
And hundit the lion on his dame;
And the guardian maid wi' the dauntless e'e,
She dropp'd a tear, and left her knee;
And she saw till the queen frae the lion fled,
Till the bonniest flower of the world lay dead;
A coffin was set on a distant plain,
And she saw the red blood fall like rain;
Then bonnie Kilmeny's heart grew sair,
And she turn'd away, and could look nae mair.

Then the gruff grim carle[32] girn'd[33] amain,
And they trampled him down, but he rose again;
And he baited the lion to deeds of weir,[34]
Till he lapp'd the blood to the kingdom dear;
And weening his head was danger-preef,
When crown'd with the rose and clover leaf,
He gowl'd[35] at the carle, and chased him away

[31] Loyal. [32] Fellow. [33] Growled. [34] War. [35] Growled.

To feed wi' the deer on the mountain gray.
He gowl'd at the carle, and geck'd at Heaven,
But his mark was set, and his arles[36] given.
Kilmeny a while her e'en withdrew;
She look'd again, and the scene was new.
She saw before her fair unfurl'd
One half of all the glowing world,
Where oceans roll'd, and rivers ran,
To bound the aims of sinful man.
She saw a people, fierce and fell,
Burst frae their bounds like fiends of hell;
There lilies grew, and the eagle flew;
And she herkèd[37] on her ravening crew,
Till the cities and towers were wrapp'd in a blaze,
And the thunder it roar'd o'er the lands and the seas.
The widows they wail'd, and the red blood ran,
And she threaten'd an end to the race of man;
She never lened,[38] nor stood in awe,
Till caught by the lion's deadly paw.
O, then the eagle swink'd[39] for life,
And brainzell'd[40] up a mortal strife;
But flew she north, or flew she south,
She met wi' the gowl[41] o' the lion's mouth.

With a mooted[42] wing and waefu' maen,
The eagle sought her eiry again;
But lang may she cower in her bloody nest,
And lang, lang sleek her wounded breast,
Before she sey[43] another flight,
To play wi' the norland lion's might.

But to sing the sights Kilmeny saw,
So far surpassing nature's law,
The singer's voice wad sink away,
And the string of his harp wad cease to play.
But she saw till the sorrows of man were bye,
And all was love and harmony;
Till the stars of heaven fell calmly away,
Like flakes of snaw on a winter day.

[36] Earnest money; *fig.* a beating. [37] Urged. [38] Crouched. [39] Worked.
[40] Stirred. [41] Howl. [42] Moulted. [43] Try.

Then Kilmeny begg'd again to see
The friends she had left in her own countrye;
To tell of the place where she had been,
And the glories that lay in the land unseen;
To warn the living maidens fair,
The loved of Heaven, the spirits' care,
That all whose minds unmeled[44] remain
Shall bloom in beauty when time is gane.

With distant music, soft and deep,
They lull'd Kilmeny sound asleep;
And when she awaken'd, she lay her lane,
All happ'd with flowers, in the green-wood
wene.
When seven lang years had come and fled,
When grief was calm, and hope was dead;
When scarce was remember'd Kilmeny's name,
Late, late in a gloamin' Kilmeny came hame!
And O, her beauty was fair to see,
But still and steadfast was her e'e!
Such beauty bard may never declare,
For there was no pride nor passion there;
And the soft desire of maiden's e'en
In that mild face could never be seen.
Her seymar[45] was the lily flower,
And her cheek the moss-rose in the shower;
And her voice like the distant melodye,
That floats along the twilight sea.
But she loved to raike[46] the lanely glen,
And keepèd afar frae the haunts of men;
Her holy hymns unheard to sing,
To suck the flowers, and drink the spring.
But wherever her peaceful form appear'd,
The wild beasts of the hill were cheer'd;
The wolf play'd blythly round the field,
The lordly byson low'd and kneel'd;
The dun deer woo'd with manner bland,
And cower'd aneath her lily hand.
And when at even the woodlands rung,

[44] Unspotted. [45] Robe. [46] Wander.

When hymns of other worlds she sung
In ecstasy of sweet devotion,
O, then the glen was all in motion!
The wild beasts of the forest came,
Broke from their bughts[47] and faulds the tame,
And goved[48] around, charm'd and amazed;
Even the dull cattle croon'd and gazed,
And murmur'd and look'd with anxious pain
For something the mystery to explain.
The buzzard came with the throstle-cock;
The corby[49] left her houf[50] in the rock;
The blackbird alang wi' the eagle flew;
The hind came tripping o'er the dew;
The wolf and the kid their raike[51] began,
And the tod,[52] and the lamb, and the leveret ran;
The hawk and the hern attour[53] them hung,
And the merle and the mavis forhooy'd[24] their young;
And all in a peaceful ring were hurl'd;
It was like an Eve in a sinless world!

When a month and a day had come and gane,
Kilmeny sought the green-wood wene;
There laid her down on the leaves sae green,
And Kilmeny on earth was never mair seen.
But O, the words that fell from her mouth
Were words of wonder, and words of truth!
But all the land were in fear and dread,
For they kendna whether she was living or dead.
It wasna her hame, and she couldna remain;
She left this world of sorrow and pain,
And return'd to the land of thought again.

448 When the Kye Comes Hame

Come all ye jolly shepherds,
  That whistle through the glen,
I'll tell ye of a secret
  That courtiers dinna ken:

47 Pens. 48 Gazed. 49 Raven. 50 Haunt. 51 Ramble. 52 Fox. 53 Above. 54 Forsook.

What is the greatest bliss
  That the tongue o' man can name?
'Tis to woo a bonny lassie
  When the kye comes hame.
When the kye comes hame,
  When the kye comes hame,
'Tween the gloaming an' the mirk
    When the kye comes hame.

'Tis not beneath the coronet,
  Nor canopy of state,
'Tis not on couch of velvet,
  Nor arbour of the great—
'Tis beneath the spreading birk,
  In the glen without the name,
Wi' a bonny, bonny lassie,
  When the kye comes hame.

There the blackbird bigs his nest
  For the mate he loes to see,
And on the topmost bough,
  O, a happy bird is he;
Where he pours his melting ditty,
  And love is a' the theme,
And he'll woo his bonny lassie
  When the kye comes hame.

When the blewart bears a pearl,
  And the daisy turns a pea,
And the bonny lucken gowan
  Has fauldit up her e'e,
Then the laverock frae the blue lift
  Drops down, an' thinks nae shame
To woo his bonny lassie
  When the kye comes hame.

See yonder pawkie shepherd,
  That lingers on the hill,
His ewes are in the fauld,
  An' his lambs are lying still;

Yet he downa gang to bed,
  For his heart is in a flame,
To meet his bonny lassie
  When the kye comes hame.

When the little wee bit heart
  Rises high in the breast,
An' the little wee bit starn
  Rises red in the east,
O there's a joy sae dear,
  That the heart can hardly frame,
Wi' a bonny, bonny lassie,
  When the kye comes hame!

Then since all nature joins
  In this love without alloy,
O, wha wad prove a traitor
  To Nature's dearest joy?
Or wha wad choose a crown,
  Wi' its perils and its fame,
And *miss* his bonny lassie
  When the kye comes hame?
    When the kye comes hame,
    When the kye comes hame,
   'Tween the gloaming and the mirk,
    When the kye comes hame.

449

The Skylark

  Bird of the wilderness,
  Blythesome and cumberless,
Sweet be thy matin o'er moorland and lea!
  Emblem of happiness,
  Blest is thy dwelling-place—
O to abide in the desert with thee!

  Wild is thy lay and loud,
  Far in the downy cloud,
Love gives it energy, love gave it birth.

Where, on thy dewy wing,
Where art thou journeying?
Thy lay is in heaven, thy love is on earth.

O'er fell and fountain sheen,
O'er moor and mountain green,
O'er the red steamer that heralds the day,
Over the cloudlet dim,
Over the rainbow's rim,
Musical cherub, soar, singing, away!

Then, when the gloaming comes,
Low in the heather blooms,
Sweet will thy welcome and bed of love be!
Emblem of happiness,
Blest is thy dwelling-place—
O to abide in the desert with thee!

450 Lock the Door, Lariston

Lock the door, Lariston, lion of Liddisdale,
Lock the door, Lariston, Lowther come on,
The Armstrongs are flying,
The widows are crying,
The Castletown's burning, and Oliver's gone!

Lock the door, Lariston,—high on the weather-gleam,
See how the Saxon plumes bob on the sky,—
Yeoman and carbinier,
Bilman and halberdier;
Fierce is the foray, and far is the cry.

Bewcastle brandishes high his broad scimitar;
Ridley is riding his fleet-footed grey;
Hidley and Howard there,
Wandale and Windermere,—
Lock the door, Lariston; hold them at bay.

Why dost thou smile, noble Elliot of Lariston?
Why do the joy-candles gleam in thine eye?
    Thou bold Border ranger,
    Beware of thy danger;—
Thy foes are relentless, determined, and nigh.

Jock Elliot raised up his steel bonnet and lookit,
His hand grasped the sword with a nervous embrace;
    'Ah, welcome, brave foemen,
    On earth there are no men
More gallant to meet in the foray or chase!

'Little know you of the hearts I have hidden here;
Little know you of our moss-troopers' might—
    Lindhope and Sorbie true,
    Sundhope and Milburn too,
Gentle in manner, but lions in fight!

'I've Mangerton, Ogilvie, Raeburn, and Netherbie,
Old Sim of Whitram, and all his array;
    Come, all Northumberland,
    Teesdale and Cumberland,
Here at the Breaken tower end shall the fray.'

Scowl'd the broad sun o'er the links of green Liddisdale,
Red as the beacon-light tipp'd he the wold;
    Many a bold martial eye,
    Mirror'd that morning sky,
Never more oped on his orbit of gold!

Shrill was the bugle's note! dreadful the warriors'
        shout!
Lances and halberds in splinters were borne;
    Helmet and hauberk then
    Braved the claymore in vain,
    Buckler armlet in shivers were shorn.

See how they wane—the proud files of the Windermere!
Howard—ah! woe to thy hopes of the day!
Hear the wide welkin rend,
While the Scots' shouts ascend,
'Elliot of Lariston, Elliot for aye!'

ROBERT SURTEES

[*1779-1834*]

451 Barthram's Dirge

They shot him dead on the Nine-Stone rig,
Beside the Headless Cross,
And they left him lying in his blood,
Upon the moor and moss.

. . . .

They made a bier of the broken bough,
The sauch and the aspen gray,
And they bore him to the Lady Chapel.
And waked him there all day.

A lady came to that lonely bower
And threw her robes aside,
She tore her long yellow hair,
And knelt at Barthram's side.

She bath'd him in the Lady-Well
His wounds so deep and sair,
And she plaited a garland for his breast,
And a garland for his hair.

They rowed him in a lily sheet,
And bare him to his earth,
(And the Grey Friars sung the dead man's mass,
As they passed the Chapel Garth).

They buried him at the midnight,
(When the dew fell cold and still,
When the aspen grey forgot to play,
And the mist clung to the hill).

They dug his grave but a bare foot deep,
By the edge of the Nine-Stone Burn,
And they covered him o'er with the heather-flower,
The moss and the Lady fern.

A Grey Friar staid upon the grave,
And sang till the morning tide,
And a friar shall sing for Barthram's soul,
While Headless Cross shall bide.

THOMAS CAMPBELL

[*1777-1844*]

452 THE SOLDIER'S DREAM

OUR bugles sang truce, for the night-cloud had lower'd,
And the sentinel stars set their watch in the sky;
And thousands had sunk on the ground overpower'd;
The weary to sleep, and the wounded to die.

When reposing that night on my pallet of straw
By the wolf-scaring faggot that guarded the slain,
At the dead of the night a sweet Vision I saw;
And thrice ere the morning I dreamt it again.

Methought from the battle-field's dreadful array
Far, far, I had roam'd on a desolate track:
'Twas Autumn,—and sunshine arose on the way
To the home of my fathers, that welcomed me back.

I flew to the pleasant fields traversed so oft
In life's morning march, when my bosom was young;
I heard my own mountain-goats bleating aloft,
And knew the sweet strain that the corn-reapers sung.

Then pledged we the wine-cup, and fondly I swore
  From my home and my weeping friends never to part;
My little ones kiss'd me a thousand times o'er,
  And my wife sobb'd aloud in her fulness of heart.

'Stay—stay with us!—rest!—thou art weary and worn!'—
  And fain was their war-broken soldier to stay;—
But sorrow return'd with the dawning of morn,
  And the voice in my dreaming ear melted away.

453 To the Evening Star

Star that bringest home the bee,
And sett'st the weary labourer free!
If any star shed peace, 'tis Thou
  That send'st it from above.
Appearing when Heaven's breath and brow
  Are sweet as hers we love.

Come to the luxuriant skies,
Whilst the landscape's odours rise,
Whilst far-off lowing herds are heard
  And songs when toil is done,
From cottages whose smoke unstirr'd
  Curls yellow in the sun.

Star of love's soft interviews,
Parted lovers on thee muse;
Their remembrancer in Heaven
  Of thrilling vows thou art,
Too delicious to be riven
  By absence from the heart.

454 Ode to Winter

Germany, December, 1800

When first the fiery-mantled Sun
His heavenly race began to run,
Round the earth and ocean blue
His children four the Seasons flew:—

First, in green apparel dancing,
The young Spring smiled with angel-grace;
Rosy Summer next advancing,
Rush'd into her sire's embrace—
Her bright-hair'd sire, who bade her keep
For ever nearest to his smiles,
On Calpe's olive-shaded steep
Or India's citron-cover'd isles.
More remote, and buxom-brown,
The Queen of vintage bow'd before his throne;
A rich pomegranate gemm'd her crown,
A ripe sheaf bound her zone.

But howling Winter fled afar
To hills that prop the polar star;
And loves on deer-borne car to ride
With barren darkness at his side,
Round the shore where loud Lofoden
Whirls to death the roaring whale,
Round the hall where Runic Odin
Howls his war-song to the gale—
Save when adown the ravaged globe
He travels on his native storm,
Deflowering Nature's grassy robe
And trampling on her faded form;
Till light's returning Lord assume
The shaft that drives him to his northern field,
Of power to pierce his raven plume
And crystal-cover'd shield.

O, sire of storms! whose savage ear
The Lapland drum delights to hear,
When Frenzy with her bloodshot eye
Implores thy dreadful deity—
Archangel! Power of desolation!
Fast descending as thou art,
Say, hath mortal invocation
Spells to touch thy stony heart:
Then, sullen Winter! hear my prayer,
And gently rule the ruin'd year;

Nor chill the wanderer's bosom bare
  Nor freeze the wretch's falling tear:
To shuddering Want's unmantled bed
  Thy horror-breathing agues cease to lend,
And gently on the orphan head
  Of Innocence descend.

But chiefly spare, O king of clouds!
The sailor on his airy shrouds,
When wrecks and beacons strew the steep,
And spectres walk along the deep.
Milder yet thy snowy breezes
  Pour on yonder tented shores,
Where the Rhine's broad billow freezes
  Or the dark-brown Danube roars.
O, winds of Winter! list ye there
  To many a deep and dying groan?
Or start, ye demons of the midnight air,
  At shrieks and thunders louder than your own?
Alas! e'en your unhallow'd breath
  May spare the victim fallen low;
But Man will ask no truce to death,
  No bounds to human woe.

455 LORD ULLIN'S DAUGHTER

A CHIEFTAIN to the Highlands bound
Cries 'Boatman, do not tarry!
And I'll give thee a silver pound
To row us o'er the ferry!'

'Now who be ye, would cross Lochgyle,
This dark and stormy water?'
'O I'm the chief of Ulva's isle,
And this, Lord Ullin's daughter.

'And fast before her father's men
Three days we've fled together,
For should he find us in the glen,
My blood would stain the heather.

'His horsemen hard behind us ride—
Should they our steps discover,
Then who will cheer my bonny bride,
When they have slain her lover?'

Out spoke the hardy Highland wight,
'I'll go, my chief, I'm ready:
It is not for your silver bright,
But for your winsome lady:—

'And by my word! the bonny bird
In danger shall not tarry;
So though the waves are raging white
I'll row you o'er the ferry.'

By this the storm grew loud apace,
The water-wraith was shrieking;
And in the scowl of heaven each face
Grew dark as they were speaking.

But still as wilder blew the wind,
And as the night grew drearer,
Adown the glen rode armèd men,
Their trampling sounded nearer.

'O haste thee, haste!' the lady cries,
'Though tempests round us gather;
I'll meet the raging of the skies,
But not an angry father.'

The boat has left a stormy land,
A stormy sea before her,—
When, O! too strong for human hand
The tempest gather'd o'er her.

And still they row'd amidst the roar
Of waters fast prevailing:
Lord Ullin reach'd that fatal shore,—
His wrath was changed to wailing.

For, sore dismay'd, through storm and shade
His child he did discover:—
One lovely hand she stretch'd for aid,
And one was round her lover.

'Come back! come back!' he cried in grief,
'Across this stormy water:
And I'll forgive your Highland chief,
My daughter!—O, my daughter!'

'Twas vain: the loud waves lash'd the shore,
Return or aid preventing:
The waters wild went o'er his child,
And he was left lamenting.

456

The River of Life

The more we live, more brief appear
  Our life's succeeding stages:
A day to childhood seems a year,
  And years like passing ages.

The gladsome current of our youth,
  Ere passion yet disorders,
Steals lingering like a river smooth
  Along its grassy borders.

But as the care-worn cheeks grow wan,
  And sorrow's shafts fly thicker,
Ye Stars, that measure life to man,
  Why seem your courses quicker?

When joys have lost their bloom and breath
  And life itself is vapid,
Why, as we reach the Falls of Death,
  Feel we its tide more rapid?

It may be strange—yet who would change
  Time's course to slower speeding,
When one by one our friends have gone
  And left our bosoms bleeding?

Heaven gives our years of fading strength
  Indemnifying fleetness;
And those of youth, a seeming length,
  Proportion'd to their sweetness.

457

To the Evening Star

Gem of the crimson-colour'd Even,
Companion of retiring day,
Why at the closing gates of heaven,
Beloved Star, dost thou delay?

So fair thy pensile beauty burns
When soft the tear of twilight flows;
So due thy plighted love returns
To chambers brighter than the rose;

To Peace, to Pleasure, and to Love
So kind a star thou seem'st to be,
Sure some enamour'd orb above
Descends and burns to meet with thee!

Thine is the breathing, blushing hour
When all unheavenly passions fly,
Chased by the soul-subduing power
Of Love's delicious witchery.

O! sacred to the fall of day
Queen of propitious stars, appear,
And early rise, and long delay,
When Caroline herself is here!

Shine on her chosen green resort
Whose trees the sunward summit crown,
And wanton flowers, that well may court
An angel's feet to tread them down:—

Shine on her sweetly scented road
Thou star of evening's purple dome,
That lead'st the nightingale abroad,
And guid'st the pilgrim to his home.

Shine where my charmer's sweeter breath
Embalms the soft exhaling dew,
Where dying winds a sigh bequeath
To kiss the cheek of rosy hue:—

Where, winnow'd by the gentle air
Her silken tresses darkly flow
And fall upon her brow so fair,
Like shadows on the mountain snow.

Thus, ever thus, at day's decline
In converse sweet to wander far—
O bring with thee my Caroline.
And thou shalt be my Ruling Star!

458 The Maid of Neidpath

Earl March look'd on his dying child,
  And, smit with grief to view her—
The youth, he cried, whom I exiled
  Shall be restored to woo her.

She's at the window many an hour
  His coming to discover:
And he look'd up to Ellen's bower
  And she look'd on her lover—

But ah! so pale, he knew her not,
  Though her smile on him was dwelling—
And am I then forgot—forgot?
  It broke the heart of Ellen.

In vain he weeps, in vain he sighs,
  Her cheek is cold as ashes;
Nor love's own kiss shall wake those eyes
  To lift their silken lashes.

459

Ye Mariners of England

Ye Mariners of England
That guard our native seas!
Whose flag has braved, a thousand years,
The battle and the breeze!
Your glorious standard launch again
To match another foe:
And sweep through the deep,
While the stormy winds do blow;
While the battle rages loud and long
And the stormy winds do blow.

The spirits of your fathers
Shall start from every wave—
For the deck it was their field of fame,
And Ocean was their grave:
Where Blake and mighty Nelson fell
Your manly hearts shall glow,
As ye sweep through the deep,
While the stormy winds do blow;
While the battle rages loud and long
And the stormy winds do blow.

Britannia needs no bulwarks,
No towers along the steep;
Her march is o'er the mountain-waves,
Her home is on the deep.
With thunders from her native oak
She quells the floods below—
As they roar on the shore,
When the stormy winds do blow;
When the battle rages loud and long,
And the stormy winds do blow.

The meteor flag of England
Shall yet terrific burn;
Till danger's troubled night depart
And the star of peace return.

Then, then, ye ocean-warriors!
Our song and feast shall flow
To the fame of your name,
When the storm has ceased to blow;
When the fiery fight is heard no more,
And the storm has ceased to blow.

460

Battle of the Baltic

Of Nelson and the North
Sing the glorious day's renown,
When to battle fierce came forth
All the might of Denmark's crown,
And her arms along the deep proudly shone;
By each gun the lighted brand
In a bold determined hand,
And the Prince of all the land
Led them on.

Like leviathans afloat
Lay their bulwarks on the brine;
While the sign of battle flew
On the lofty British line:
It was ten of April morn by the chime:
As they drifted on their path
There was silence deep as death;
And the boldest held his breath
For a time.

But the might of England flush'd
To anticipate the scene;
And her van the fleeter rush'd
O'er the deadly space between.
'Hearts of oak!' our captains cried, when each gun
From its adamantine lips
Spread a death-shade round the ships,
Like the hurricane eclipse
Of the sun.

Again! again! again!
And the havoc did not slack,
Till a feeble cheer the Dane
To our cheering sent us back;—
Their shots along the deep slowly boom:—
Then ceased—and all is wail,
As they strike the shatter'd sail;
Or in conflagration pale
Light the gloom.

Out spoke the victor then
As he hail'd them o'er the wave,
'Ye are brothers! ye are men!
And we conquer but to save:—
So peace instead of death let us bring:
But yield, proud foe, thy fleet
With the crews, at England's feet,
And make submission meet
To our King.'

Then Denmark bless'd our chief
That he gave her wounds repose;
And the sounds of joy and grief
From her people wildly rose,
As death withdrew his shades from the day:
While the sun look'd smiling bright
O'er a wide and woeful sight,
Where the fires of funeral light
Died away.

Now joy, old England, raise!
For the tidings of thy might,
By the festal cities' blaze,
Whilst the wine-cup shines in light;
And yet amidst that joy and uproar,
Let us think of them that sleep
Full many a fathom deep
By thy wild and stormy steep,
Elsinore!

Brave hearts! to Britain's pride
Once so faithful and so true,
On the deck of fame that died,
With the gallant good Riou:
Soft sigh the winds of Heaven o'er their grave!
While the billow mournful rolls
And the mermaid's song condoles
Singing glory to the souls
Of the brave!

461

Hohenlinden

On Linden, when the sun was low,
All bloodless lay the untrodden snow;
And dark as winter was the flow
    Of Iser, rolling rapidly.

But Linden saw another sight,
When the drum beat at dead of night
Commanding fires of death to light
    The darkness of her scenery.

By torch and trumpet fast array'd
Each horseman drew his battle-blade,
And furious every charger neigh'd
    To join the dreadful revelry.

Then shook the hills with thunder riven;
Then rush'd the steed, to battle driven;
And louder than the bolts of Heaven
    Far flash'd the red artillery.

But redder yet that light shall glow
On Linden's hills of stainéd snow;
And bloodier yet the torrent flow
    Of Iser, rolling rapidly.

'Tis morn; but scarce yon level sun
Can pierce the war-clouds, rolling dun,
Where furious Frank and fiery Hun
    Shout in their sulphurous canopy.

The combat deepens. On, ye Brave
Who rush to glory, or the grave!
Wave, Munich, all thy banners wave,
And charge with all thy chivalry!

Few, few shall part, where many meet!
The snow shall be their winding-sheet,
And every turf beneath their feet
Shall be a soldier's sepulchre.

J. CAMPBELL

462 Freedom and Love

How delicious is the winning
Of a kiss at love's beginning,
When two mutual hearts are sighing
For the knot there's no untying!

Yet remember, 'midst your wooing
Love has bliss, but Love has ruing;
Other smiles may make you fickle,
Tears for other charms may trickle.

Love he comes and Love he tarries
Just as fate or fancy carries;
Longest stays, when sorest chidden;
Laughs and flies, when press'd and bidden.

Bind the sea to slumber stilly,
Bind its odour to the lily,
Bind the aspen ne'er to quiver,
Then bind Love to last for ever.

Love's a fire that needs renewal
Of fresh beauty for its fuel:
Love's wing moults when caged and captured,
Only free, he soars enraptured.

Can you keep the bee from ranging,
Or the ringdove's neck from changing?
No! nor fetter'd Love from dying
In the knot there's no untying.

ALLAN CUNNINGHAM

[*1784-1842*]

463 Hame, Hame, Hame

Hame, hame, hame, O hame fain wad I be—
O hame, hame, hame, to my ain countree!

When the flower is i' the bud and the leaf is on the tree,
The larks shall sing me hame in my ain countree;
Hame, hame, hame, O hame fain wad I be—
O hame, hame, hame, to my ain countree!

The green leaf o' loyaltie's beginning for to fa',
The bonnie White Rose it is withering an' a';
But I'll water 't wi' the blude of usurping tyrannie,
An' green it will graw in my ain countree.

O, there's nocht now frae ruin my country can save,
But the keys o' kind heaven, to open the grave;
That a' the noble martyrs wha died for loyaltie
May rise again an' fight for their ain countree.

The great now are gane, a' wha ventured to save,
The new grass is springing on the tap o' their grave;
But the sun through the mirk blinks blythe in my e'e,
'I'll shine on ye yet in your ain countree.'

Hame, hame, hame, O hame fain wad I be—
O hame, hame, hame, to my ain countree!

464 A Wet Sheet and a Flowing Sea

A wet sheet and a flowing sea,
A wind that follows fast
And fills the white and rustling sail
And bends the gallant mast;
And bends the gallant mast, my boys,
While like the eagle free
Away the good ship flies, and leaves
Old England on the lee.

O for a soft and gentle wind!
I heard a fair one cry;
But give to me the snoring breeze
And white waves heaving high;
And white waves heaving high, my lads,
The good ship tight and free—
The world of waters is our home,
And merry men are we.

There's tempest in yon hornéd moon,
And lightning in yon cloud;
But hark the music, mariners!
The wind is piping loud;
The wind is piping loud, my boys,
The lightning flashes free—
While the hollow oak our palace is,
Our heritage the sea.

GEORGE GORDON, LORD BYRON

[*1788-1824*]

465 Youth and Age

There's not a joy the world can give like that it takes away
When the glow of early thought declines in feeling's dull decay;

'Tis not on youth's smooth cheek the blush alone, which fades so fast,
But the tender bloom of heart is gone, ere youth itself be past.

Then the few whose spirits float above the wreck of happiness
Are driven o'er the shoals of guilt, or ocean of excess:
The magnet of their course is gone, or only points in vain
The shore to which their shiver'd sail shall never stretch again.

Then the mortal coldness of the soul like death itself comes down;
It cannot feel for others' woes, it dare not dream its own;
That heavy chill has frozen o'er the fountain of our tears,
And though the eye may sparkle still, 'tis where the ice appears.

Though wit may flash from fluent lips, and mirth distract the breast,
Through midnight hours that yield no more their former hope of rest;
'Tis but as ivy-leaves around the ruin'd turret wreathe,
All green and wildly fresh without, but worn and gray beneath.

O could I feel as I have felt, or be what I have been,
Or weep as I could once have wept o'er many a vanish'd scene,—
As springs in deserts found seem sweet, all brackish though they be,
So midst the wither'd waste of life, those tears would flow to me!

466 THE DESTRUCTION OF SENNACHERIB

THE Assyrian came down like the wolf on the fold,
And his cohorts were gleaming in purple and gold;
And the sheen of their spears was like stars on the sea,
When the blue wave rolls nightly on deep Galilee.

Like the leaves of the forest when Summer is green,
That host with their banners at sunset were seen:
Like the leaves of the forest when Autumn hath blown,
That host on the morrow lay withered and strown.

For the Angel of Death spread his wings on the blast,
And breathed in the face of the foe as he passed;
And the eyes of the sleepers waxed deadly and chill,
And their hearts but once heaved, and for ever grew still!

And there lay the steed with his nostril all wide,
But through it there rolled not the breath of his pride;
And the foam of his gasping lay white on the turf,
And cold as the spray of the rock-beating surf.

And there lay the rider distorted and pale,
With the dew on his brow, and the rust on his mail:
And the tents were all silent, the banners alone,
The lances unlifted, the trumpet unblown.

And the widows of Ashur are loud in their wail,
And the idols are broke in the temple of Baal;
And the might of the Gentile, unsmote by the sword,
Hath melted like snow in the glance of the Lord!

467

Elegy on Thyrza

And thou art dead, as young and fair
  As aught of mortal birth;
And forms so soft and charms so rare
  Too soon return'd to Earth!
Though Earth received them in her bed,
And o'er the spot the crowd may tread
  In carelessness or mirth,
There is an eye which could not brook
A moment on that grave to look.

I will not ask where thou liest low
  Nor gaze upon the spot;
There flowers or weeds at will may grow
  So I behold them not:

It is enough for me to prove
That what I loved, and long must love
  Like common earth can rot;
To me there needs no stone to tell
'Tis Nothing that I loved so well.

Yet did I love thee to the last,
  As fervently as thou
Who didst not change through all the past
  And canst not alter now.
The love where Death has set his seal
Nor age can chill, nor rival steal,
  Nor falsehood disavow:
And, what were worse, thou canst not see
Or wrong, or change, or fault in me.

The better days of life were ours;
  The worst can be but mine:
The sun that cheers, the storm that lours,
  Shall never more be thine.
The silence of that dreamless sleep
I envy now too much to weep;
  Nor need I to repine
That all those charms have pass'd away
I might have watch'd through long decay.

The flower in ripen'd bloom unmatch'd
  Must fall the earliest prey;
Though by no hand untimely snatch'd,
  The leaves must drop away.
And yet it were a greater grief
To watch it withering, leaf by leaf,
  Than see it pluck'd today;
Since earthly eye but ill can bear
To trace the change to foul from fair.

I know not if I could have borne
  To see thy beauties fade;
The night that follow'd such a morn
  Had worn a deeper shade:

Thy day without a cloud hath past,
And thou wert lovely to the last,
  Extinguish'd, not decay'd;
As stars that shoot along the sky
Shine brightest as they fall from high.

As once I wept, if I could weep,
  My tears might well be shed
To think I was not near, to keep
  One vigil o'er thy bed:
To gaze, how fondly! on thy face,
To fold thee in a faint embrace,
  Uphold thy drooping head;
And show that love, however vain,
Nor thou nor I can feel again.

Yet how much less it were to gain,
  Though thou hast left me free,
The loveliest things that still remain
  Than thus remember thee!
The all of thine that cannot die
Through dark and dread Eternity
  Returns again to me,
And more thy buried love endears
Than aught except its living years.

468

When We Two Parted

When we two parted
In silence and tears,
Half broken-hearted,
To sever for years,
Pale grew thy cheek and cold,
Colder thy kiss;
Truly that hour foretold
Sorrow to this!

The dew of the morning
Sunk chill on my brow;

It felt like the warning
Of what I feel now.
Thy vows are all broken,
And light is thy fame:
I hear thy name spoken
And share in its shame.

They name thee before me,
A knell to mine ear;
A shudder comes o'er me—
Why wert thou so dear?
They know not I knew thee
Who knew thee too well:
Long, long shall I rue thee
Too deeply to tell.

In secret we met:
In silence I grieve
That thy heart could forget,
Thy spirit deceive.
If I should meet thee
After long years,
How should I greet thee?—
With silence and tears.

469

For Music

There be none of Beauty's daughters
  With a magic like Thee;
And like music on the waters
  Is thy sweet voice to me:
When, as if its sound were causing
The charmed ocean's pausing,
The waves lie still and gleaming,
And the lull'd winds seem dreaming:

And the midnight moon is weaving
  Her bright chain o'er the deep,
Whose breast is gently heaving
  As an infant's asleep:

So the spirit bows before thee
To listen and adore thee;
With a full but soft emotion,
Like the swell of Summer's ocean.

470 SHE WALKS IN BEAUTY

SHE walks in beauty, like the night
Of cloudless climes and starry skies,
And all that's best of dark and bright
Meet in her aspect and her eyes;
Thus mellow'd to that tender light
Which heaven to gaudy day denies.

One shade the more, one ray the less,
Had half impair'd the nameless grace
Which waves in every raven tress
Or softly lightens o'er her face,
Where thoughts serenely sweet express
How pure, how dear their dwelling-place.

And on that cheek and o'er that brow
So soft, so calm, yet eloquent,
The smiles that win, the tints that glow
But tell of days in goodness spent,—
A mind at peace with all below,
A heart whose love is innocent.

471 ALL FOR LOVE

O TALK not to me of a name great in story;
The days of our youth are the days of our glory;
And the myrtle and ivy of sweet two-and-twenty
Are worth all your laurels, though ever so plenty.

What are garlands and crowns to the brow that is wrinkled?
'Tis but as a dead flower with May-dew besprinkled:
Then away with all such from the head that is hoary—
What care I for the wreaths that can only give glory?

Oh Fame!—if I e'er took delight in thy praises,
'Twas less for the sake of thy high-sounding phrases,
Than to see the bright eyes of the dear one discover
She thought that I was not unworthy to love her.

There chiefly I sought thee, there only I found thee;
Her glance was the best of the rays that surround thee;
When it sparkled o'er aught that was bright in my story,
I knew it was love, and I felt it was glory.

472

Elegy

O snatch'd away in beauty's bloom!
On thee shall press no ponderous tomb;
But on thy turf shall roses rear
Their leaves, the earliest of the year,
And the wild cypress wave in tender gloom:

And oft by yon blue gushing stream
Shall Sorrow lean her drooping head,
And feed deep thought with many a dream,
And lingering pause and lightly tread;
Fond wretch! as if her step disturb'd the dead.

Away! we know that tears are vain,
That Death nor heeds nor hears distress:
Will this unteach us to complain?
Or make one mourner weep the less?
And thou, who tell'st me to forget,
Thy looks are wan, thine eyes are wet.

473

To Augusta

Though the day of my destiny's over,
And the star of my fate hath declined,
Thy soft heart refused to discover
The faults which so many could find.
Though thy soul with my grief was acquainted,
It shrunk not to share it with me,
And the love which my spirit hath painted
It never hath found but in *thee*.

Then when nature around me is smiling,
  The last smile which answers to mine,
I do not believe it beguiling,
  Because it reminds me of thine;
And when winds are at war with the ocean,
  As the breasts I believed in with me,
If their billows excite an emotion,
  It is that they bear me from *thee*.

Though the rock of my last hope is shivered,
  And its fragments are sunk in the wave,
Though I feel that my soul is delivered
  To pain—it shall not be its slave.
There is many a pang to pursue me:
  They may crush, but they shall not contemn;
They may torture, but shall not subdue me;
  'Tis of *thee* that I think—not of them.

Though human, thou didst not deceive me,
  Though woman, thou didst not forsake,
Though loved, thou forborest to grieve me,
  Though slander'd, thou never couldst shake;
Though trusted, thou didst not disclaim me,
  Though parted, it was not to fly,
Though watchful, 'twas not to defame me,
  Nor, mute, that the world might belie.

Yet I blame not the world, nor despise it,
  Nor the war of the many with one;
If my soul was not fitted to prize it,
  'Twas folly not sooner to shun:
And if dearly that error hath cost me,
  And more than I once could foresee,
I have found that, whatever it lost me,
  It could not deprive me of *thee*.

From the wreck of the past, which hath perish'd,
  Thus much I at least may recall,
It hath taught me that what I most cherish'd
  Deserved to be dearest of all:

In the desert a fountain is springing,
In the wide waste there still is a tree,
And a bird in the solitude singing,
Which speaks to my spirit of *thee.*

474

Epistle to Augusta

My sister! my sweet sister! if a name
Dearer and purer were, it should be thine;
Mountains and seas divide us, but I claim
No tears, but tenderness to answer mine:
Go where I will, to me thou art the same—
A loved regret which I would not resign.
There yet are two things in my destiny,—
A world to roam through, and a home with thee.

The first were nothing—had I still the last,
It were the haven of my happiness;
But other claims and other ties thou hast,
And mine is not the wish to make them less.
A strange doom is thy father's son's, and past
Recalling, as it lies beyond redress;
Reversed for him our grandsire's fate of yore,—
He had no rest at sea, nor I on shore.

If my inheritance of storms hath been
In other elements, and on the rocks
Of perils, overlook'd or unforeseen,
I have sustain'd my share of worldly shocks,
The fault was mine; nor do I seek to screen
My errors with defensive paradox;
I have been cunning in mine overthrow,
The careful pilot of my proper woe.

Mine were my faults, and mine be their reward.
My whole life was a contest, since the day
That gave me being, gave me that which marr'd
The gift,—a fate, or will, that walk'd astray;

And I at times have found the struggle hard,
And thought of shaking off my bonds of clay:
But now I fain would for a time survive,
If but to see what next can well arrive.

Kingdoms and empires in my little day
I have outlived, and yet I am not old:
And when I look on this, the petty spray
Of my own years of trouble, which have roll'd
Like a wild bay of breakers, melts away:
Something—I know not what—does still uphold
A spirit of slight patience;—not in vain,
Even for its own sake, do we purchase pain.

Perhaps the workings of defiance stir
Within me,—or perhaps a cold despair,
Brought when ills habitually recur,—
Perhaps a kindlier clime, or purer air,
(For even to this may change of soul refer,
And with light armour we may learn to bear),
Have taught me a strange quiet, which was not
The chief companion of a calmer lot.

I feel almost at times as I have felt
In happy childhood; trees, and flowers, and brooks,
Which do remember me of where I dwelt
Ere my young mind was sacrificed to books,
Come as of yore upon me, and can melt
My heart with recognition of their looks;
And even at moments I could think I see
Some living thing to love—but none like thee.

Here are the Alpine landscapes which create
A fund for contemplation—to admire
Is a brief feeling of a trivial date;
But something worthier do such scenes inspire;
Here to be lonely is not desolate,
For much I view which I could most desire,
And, above all, a lake I can behold
Lovelier, not dearer, than our own of old.

Oh that thou wert but with me!—but I grow
The fool of my own wishes, and forget
The solitude, which I have vaunted so,
Has lost its praise in this but one regret;
There may be others which I less may show!—
I am not of the plaintive mood, and yet
I feel an ebb in my philosophy,
And the tide rising in my alter'd eye.

I did remind thee of our own dear Lake,
By the old Hall which may be mine no more.
Leman's is fair; but think not I forsake
The sweet remembrance of a dearer shore;
Sad havoc Time must with my memory make,
Ere *that* or *thou* can fade these eyes before;
Though, like all things which I have loved, they are
Resign'd for ever, or divided far.

The world is all before me; I but ask
Of Nature that with which she will comply—
It is but in her summer's sun to bask,
To mingle with the quiet of her sky,
To see her gentle face without a mask,
And never gaze on it with apathy.
She was my early friend, and now shall be
My sister—till I look again on thee.

I can reduce all feeling but this one;
And that I would not;—for at length I see
Such scenes as those wherein my life begun.
The earliest—even the only paths for me—
Had I but sooner learnt the crowd to shun,
I had been better than I now can be;
The passions which have torn me would have slept;
I had not suffer'd and *thou* hadst not wept.

With false Ambition what had I to do?
Little with Love, and least of all with Fame;
And yet they came unsought, and with me grew,
And made me all which they can make—a name.

Yet this was not the end I did pursue;
Surely I once beheld a nobler aim.
But all is over—I am one the more
To baffled millions which have gone before.

And for the future, this world's future may
From me demand but little of my care;
I have outlived myself by many a day;
Having survived so many things that were;
My years have been no slumber, but the prey
Of ceaseless vigils; for I had the share
Of life which might have fill'd a century,
Before its fourth in time had pass'd me by.

And for the remnant which may be to come
I am content; and for the past I feel
Not thankless,—for within the crowded sum
Of struggles, happiness at times would steal,
And for the present, I would not benumb
My feelings farther.—Nor shall I conceal
That with all this I still can look around,
And worship Nature with a thought profound.

For thee, my own sweet sister, in thy heart
I know myself secure, as thou in mine.
We were and are—I am, even as thou art—
Beings who ne'er each other can resign:
It is the same, together or apart,
From life's commencement to its slow decline
We are entwined—let death come slow or fast,
The tie which bound the first endures the last!

475

Maid of Athens

Maid of Athens, ere we part,
Give, oh, give me back my heart!
Or, since that has left my breast,
Keep it now, and take the rest!
Hear my vow, before I go,
Ζώη μοῦ, σάς ἀγαπῶ.

By those tresses unconfined,
Woo'd by each Ægean wind;
By those lids whose jetty fringe
Kiss thy soft cheeks' blooming tinge;
By those wild eyes like the roe,
Ζώη μοῦ, σάς ἀγαπῶ.

By that lip I long to taste;
By that zone-encircled waist;
By all the token-flowers that tell
What words can never speak so well;
By love's alternate joy and woe,
Ζώη μοῦ, σάς ἀγαπῶ.

Maid of Athens! I am gone:
Think of me, sweet! when alone.
Though I fly to Istambol,
Athens holds my heart and soul;
Can I cease to love thee? No!
Ζώη μοῦ, σάς ἀγαπῶ.

476 Darkness

I HAD a dream, which was not all a dream,
The bright sun was extinguish'd, and the stars
Did wander darkling in the eternal space,
Rayless, and pathless; and the icy earth
Swung blind and blackening in the moonless air
Morn came and went—and came, and brought no day,
And men forgot their passions in the dread
Of this their desolation: and all hearts
Were chill'd into a selfish prayer for light:
And they did live by watchfires—and the thrones,
The palaces of crowned kings—the huts,
The habitations of all things which dwell,
Were burnt for beacons; cities were consumed,
And men were gathered round their blazing homes
To look once more into each other's face
Happy were those who dwelt within the eye

Of the volcanoes, and their mountain-torch:
A fearful hope was all the world contained;
Forests were set on fire—but hour by hour
They fell and faded—and the crackling trunks
Extinguish'd with a crash—and all was black.
The brows of men by the despairing light
Wore an unearthly aspect, as by fits
The flashes fell upon them; some lay down
And hid their eyes and wept; and some did rest
Their chins upon their clenched hands and smiled;
And others hurried to and fro, and fed
Their funeral piles with fuel, and look'd up
With mad disquietude on the dull sky,
The pall of a past world; and then again
With curses cast them down upon the dust,
And gnash'd their teeth and howl'd: the wild birds shriek'd,
And, terrified, did flutter on the ground.
And flap their useless wings; the wildest brutes
Came tame and tremulous; and vipers crawl'd
And twined themselves among the multitude,
Hissing, but stingless—they were slain for food:
And War, which for a moment was no more,
Did glut himself again:—a meal was bought
With blood, and each sate sullenly apart
Gorging himself in gloom: no love was left;
All earth was but one thought—and that was death
Immediate and inglorious; and the pang
Of famine fed upon all entrails—men
Died, and their bones were tombless as their flesh;
The meagre by the meagre were devour'd,
Even dogs assail'd their masters, all save one,
And he was faithful to a corse, and kept
The birds and beasts and famish'd men at bay,
Till hunger clung them, or the dropping dead
Lured their lank jaws; himself sought out no food,
But with a piteous and perpetual moan,
And a quick desolate cry, licking the hand
Which answer'd not with a caress—he died.
The crowd was famish'd by degrees; but two
Of an enormous city did survive,

And they were enemies: they met beside
The dying embers of an altar-place,
Where had been heap'd a mass of holy things
For an unholy usage; they raked up,
And shivering scraped with their cold skeleton hands
The feeble ashes, and their feeble breath
Blew for a little life, and made a flame
Which was a mockery; then they lifted up
Their eyes as it grew lighter, and beheld
Each other's aspects—saw and shriek'd, and died—
Ev'n of their mutual hideousness they died,
Unknowing who he was upon whose brow
Famine had written Fiend. The world was void,
The populous, and the powerful was a lump,
Seasonless, herbless, treeless, manless, lifeless,
A lump of death—a chaos of hard clay.
The rivers, lakes, and ocean all stood still,
And nothing stirr'd within their silent depths;
Ships sailorless lay rotting on the sea,
And their masts fell down piecemeal; as they dropp'd,
They slept on the abyss without a surge—
The waves were dead; the tides were in their grave,
The Moon, their mistress, had expired before;
The winds were wither'd in the stagnant air,
And the clouds perish'd; Darkness had no need
Of aid from them—She was the Universe!

477 LONGING

THE castled crag of Drachenfels
Frowns o'er the wide and winding Rhine,
Whose breast of waters broadly swells
Between the banks which bear the vine.
And hills all rich with blossom'd trees,
And fields which promise corn and wine,
And scatter'd cities crowning these,
Whose far white walls along them shine,
Have strew'd a scene, which I should see
With double joy wert *thou* with me.

And peasant girls, with deep blue eyes,
And hands which offer early flowers,
Walk smiling o'er this paradise:
Above, the frequent feudal towers
Through green leaves lift their walls of gray;
And many a rock which steeply lowers,
And noble arch in proud decay,
Look o'er this vale of vintage-bowers;
But one thing want these banks of Rhine,—
Thy gentle hand to clasp in mine!

I send the lilies given to me;
Though long before thy hand they touch,
I know that they must wither'd be,
But yet reject them not as such;
For I have cherish'd them as dear,
Because they yet may meet thine eye,
And guide thy soul to mine even here,
When thou behold'st them, drooping nigh,
And know'st them gather'd by the Rhine,
And offer'd from my heart to thine!

The river nobly foams and flows,
The charm of this enchanted ground,
And all its thousand turns disclose
Some fresher beauty varying round:
The haughtiest breast its wish might bound
Through life to dwell delighted here;
Nor could on earth a spot be found
To nature and to me so dear,
Could thy dear eyes in following mine
Still sweeten more these banks of Rhine!

478

Fare Thee Well

Fare thee well! and if for ever,
Still for ever, fare *thee well:*
Even though unforgiving, never
'Gainst thee shall my heart rebel.

Would that breast were bared before thee
  Where thy head so oft hath lain,
While that placid sleep came o'er thee
  Which thou ne'er canst know again:

Would that breast, by thee glanced over,
  Every inmost thought could show!
Then thou wouldst at last discover
  'Twas not well to spurn it so.

Though the world for this commend thee—
  Though it smile upon the blow,
Even its praises must offend thee,
  Founded on another's woe:

Though my many faults defaced me,
  Could no other arm be found,
Than the one which once embraced me,
  To inflict a cureless wound?

Yet, oh yet, thyself deceive not;
  Love may sink by slow decay,
But by sudden wrench, believe not
  Hearts can thus be torn away:

Still thine own its life retaineth,
  Still must mine, though bleeding, beat;
And the undying thought which paineth
  Is—that we no more may meet.

These are words of deeper sorrow
  Than the wail above the dead;
Both shall live, but every morrow
  Wake us from a widow'd bed.

And when thou wouldst solace gather,
  When our child's first accents flow,
Wilt thou teach her to say 'Father!'
  Though his care she must forego?

When her little hands shall press thee,
When her lip to thine is press'd,
Think of him whose prayer shall bless thee,
Think of him thy love had bless'd!

Should her lineaments resemble
Those thou never more may'st see,
Then thy heart will softly tremble
With a pulse yet true to me.

All my faults perchance thou knowest,
All my madness none can know;
All my hopes, where'er thou goest,
Wither, yet with *thee* they go.

Every feeling hath been shaken;
Pride, which not a world could bow,
Bows to thee—by thee forsaken,
Even my soul forsakes me now:

But 'tis done—all words are idle—
Words from me are vainer still;
But the thoughts we cannot bridle
Force their way without the will.

Fare thee well! thus disunited,
Torn from every nearer tie,
Sear'd in heart, and lone, and blighted,
More than this I scarce can die.

479 THE PRISONER OF CHILLON

My hair is gray, but not with years,
Nor grew it white
In a single night,
As men's have grown from sudden fears;
My limbs are bow'd, though not with toil,
But rusted with a vile repose,
For they have been a dungeon's spoil,
And mine has been the fate of those

To whom the goodly earth and air
Are bann'd, and barr'd—forbidden fare;
But this was for my father's faith
I suffer'd chains and courted death;
That father perish'd at the stake
For tenets he would not forsake;
And for the same his lineal race
In darkness found a dwelling-place.
We were seven—who now are one,
  Six in youth, and one in age,
Finish'd as they had begun,
  Proud of Persecution's rage;
One in fire, and two in field
Their belief with blood have seal'd,
Dying as their father died,
For the God their foes denied;
Three were in a dungeon cast,
Of whom this wreck is left the last.

There are seven pillars of Gothic mould,
In Chillon's dungeons deep and old,
There are seven columns, massy and gray,
Dim with a dull imprison'd ray,
A sunbeam which hath lost its way,
And through the crevice and the cleft
Of the thick wall is fallen and left;
Creeping o'er the floor so damp,
Like a marsh's meteor lamp.
And in each pillar there is a ring,
  And in each ring there is a chain;
That iron is a cankering thing,
  For in these limbs its teeth remain,
With marks that will not wear away,
Till I have done with this new day,
Which now is painful to these eyes,
Which have not seen the sun so rise
For years—I cannot count them o'er,
I lost their long and heavy score,
When my last brother droop'd and died,
And I lay living by his side.

They chain'd us each to a column stone,
And we were three—yet, each alone;
We could not move a single pace,
We could not see each other's face,
But with that pale and livid light
That made us strangers in our sight:
And thus together—yet apart,
Fetter'd in hand, but join'd in heart,
'T was still some solace, in the dearth
Of the pure elements of earth,
To hearken to each other's speech,
And each turn comforter to each
With some new hope, or legend old,
Or song heroically bold;
But even these at length grew cold,
Our voices took a dreary tone,
An echo of the dungeon stone,
  A grating sound, not full and free,
  As they of yore were wont to be;
  It might be fancy, but to me
They never sounded like our own.

I was the eldest of the three,
  And to uphold and cheer the rest
  I ought to do—and did my best;
And each did well in his degree.
  The youngest, whom my father loved,
Because our mother's brow was given
To him, with eyes as blue as heaven—
  For him my soul was sorely moved;
And truly might it be distress'd
To see such bird in such a nest;
For he was beautiful as day
  (When day was beautiful to me
  As to young eagles, being free)—
  A polar day, which will not see
A sunset till its summer's gone,
  Its sleepless summer of long light,
The snow-clad offspring of the sun:
  And thus he was as pure and bright,

And in his natural spirit gay,
With tears for nought but others' ills;
And then they flow'd like mountain rills,
Unless he could assuage the woe
Which he abhorr'd to view below.

The other was as pure of mind,
But form'd to combat with his kind;
Strong in his frame, and of a mood
Which 'gainst the world in war had stood,
And perish'd in the foremost rank
  With joy:—but not in chains to pine:
His spirit wither'd with their clank,
  I saw it silently decline—
  And so perchance in sooth did mine:
But yet I forced it on to cheer
Those relics of a home so dear.
He was a hunter of the hills,
  Had follow'd there the deer and wolf;
  To him this dungeon was a gulf,
And fetter'd feet the worst of ills.

  Lake Leman lies by Chillon's walls:
A thousand feet in depth below
Its massy waters meet and flow;
Thus much the fathom-line was sent
From Chillon's snow-white battlement
  Which round about the wave inthrals:
A double dungeon wall and wave
Have made—and like a living grave.
Below the surface of the lake
The dark vault lies wherein we lay,
We heard it ripple night and day;
  Sounding o'er our heads it knock'd;
And I have felt the winter's spray
Wash through the bars when winds were high
And wanton in the happy sky;
  And then the very rock hath rock'd,
  And I have felt it shake, unshock'd

Because I could have smiled to see
The death that would have set me free.

I said my nearer brother pined,
I said his mighty heart declined,
He loathed and put away his food;
It was not that 'twas coarse and rude,
For we were used to hunter's fare,
And for the like had little care.
The milk drawn from the mountain goat
Was changed for water from the moat,
Our bread was such as captives' tears
Have moistened many a thousand years,
Since man first pent his fellow men
Like brutes within an iron den;
But what were these to us or him?
These wasted not his heart or limb;
My brother's soul was of that mould
Which in a palace had grown cold,
Had his free breathing been denied
The range of the steep mountain's side.
But why delay the truth?—he died.
I saw, and could not hold his head,
Nor reach his dying hand—nor dead,—
Though hard I strove, but strove in vain
To rend and gnash my bonds in twain.
He died,—and they unlock'd his chain,
And scoop'd for him a shallow grave
Even from the cold earth of our cave.
I begg'd them, as a boon, to lay
His corse in dust whereon the day
Might shine—it was a foolish thought,
But then within my brain it wrought,
That even in death his freeborn breast
In such a dungeon could not rest.
I might have spared my idle prayer;
They coldly laugh'd—and laid him there:
The flat and turfless earth above
The being we so much did love;

His empty chain above it leant,
Such murder's fitting monument!

But he, the favourite and the flower,
Most cherish'd since his natal hour,
His mother's image in fair face,
The infant love of all his race,
His martyr'd father's dearest thought,
My latest care for whom I sought
To hoard my life, that his might be
Less wretched now, and one day free;
He, too, who yet had held untired
A spirit natural or inspired—
He, too, was struck, and day by day
Was wither'd on the stalk away.
Oh, God! it is a fearful thing
To see the human soul take wing
In any shape, in any mood:—
I've seen it rushing forth in blood,
I've seen it on the breaking ocean
Strive with a swoln convulsive motion,
I've seen the sick and ghastly bed
Of Sin delirious with its dread:
But these were horrors—this was woe
Unmix'd with such—but sure and slow.
He faded, and so calm and meek,
So softly worn, so sweetly weak,
So tearless, yet so tender—kind,
And grieved for those he left behind;
With all the while a cheek whose bloom
Was as a mockery of the tomb,
Whose tints as gently sunk away
As a departing rainbow's ray;
An eye of most transparent light,
That almost made the dungeon bright;
And not a word of murmur, not
A groan o'er his untimely lot,—
A little talk of better days,
A little hope my own to raise,
For I was sunk in silence—lost

In this last loss, of all the most;
And then the sighs he would suppress
Of fainting nature's feebleness,
More slowly drawn, grew less and less.
I listen'd, but I could not hear—
I call'd, for I was wild with fear;
I knew 't was hopeless, but my dread
Would not be thus admonishèd.
I call'd, and thought I heard a sound—
I burst my chain with one strong bound,
And rush'd to him:—I found him not,
I only stirr'd in this black spot,
I only lived, *I* only drew
The accursèd breath of dungeon-dew;
The last—the sole—the dearest link
Between me and the eternal brink,
Which bound me to my failing race,
Was broken in this fatal place.
One on the earth, and one beneath—
My brothers—both had ceased to breathe:
I took that hand which lay so still,
Alas! my own was full as chill;
I had not strength to stir, or strive,
But felt that I was still alive—
A frantic feeling, when we know
That what we love shall ne'er be so.
  I know not why
  I could not die,
I had no earthly hope—but faith,
And that forbade a selfish death.

What next befell me then and there
  I know not well—I never knew;
First came the loss of light, and air,
  And then of darkness too:
I had no thought, no feeling—none—
Among the stones, I stood a stone,
And was, scarce conscious what I wist,
As shrubless crags within the mist;
For all was blank, and bleak, and gray;

It was not night—it was not day;
It was not even the dungeon-light,
So hateful to my heavy sight,
But vacancy absorbing space,
And fixedness—without a place;
There were no stars, no earth, no time,
No check, no change, no good, no crime,
But silence, and a stirless breath
Which neither was of life nor death;
A sea of stagnant idleness,
Blind, boundless, mute, and motionless!

A light broke in upon my brain,—
  It was the carol of a bird;
It ceased, and then it came again,
  The sweetest song ear ever heard,
And mine was thankful till my eyes
Ran over with the glad surprise,
And they that moment could not see
I was the mate of misery.
But then by dull degrees came back
My senses to their wonted track;
I saw the dungeon walls and floor
Close slowly round me as before,
I saw the glimmer of the sun
Creeping as it before had done,
But through the crevice where it came
That bird was perched, as fond and tame,
  And tamer than upon the tree;
A lovely bird, with azure wings,
And song that said a thousand things,
  And seemed to say them all for me!
I never saw its like before,
I ne'er shall see its likeness more;
It seemed like me to want a mate,
But was not half so desolate,
And it was come to love me when
None lived to love me so again,
And cheering from my dungeon's brink,
Had brought me back to feel and think.

I know not if it late were free,
Or broke its cage to perch on mine,
But knowing well captivity,
Sweet bird! I could not wish for thine!
Or if it were, in wingèd guise,
A visitant from Paradise;
For—Heaven forgive that thought! the while
Which made me both to weep and smile—
I sometimes deem'd that it might be
My brother's soul come down to me;
But then at last away it flew,
And then 'twas mortal well I knew,
For he would never thus have flown,
And left me twice so doubly lone,
Lone—as the corse within its shroud,
Lone—as a solitary cloud,
A single cloud on a sunny day,
While all the rest of heaven is clear,
A frown upon the atmosphere
That hath no business to appear
When skies are blue and earth is gay.

A kind of change came in my fate,
My keepers grew compassionate;
I know not what had made them so,
They were inured to sights of woe,
But so it was:—my broken chain
With links unfasten'd did remain,
And it was liberty to stride
Along my cell from side to side,
And up and down, and then athwart,
And tread it over every part;
And round the pillars one by one,
Returning where my walk begun,
Avoiding only, as I trod,
My brothers' graves without a sod;
For if I thought with heedless tread
My steps profaned their lowly bed,
My breath came gaspingly and thick,
And my crush'd heart fell blind and sick.

I made a footing in the wall,
  It was not therefrom to escape,
For I had buried one and all
  Who loved me in a human shape;
And the whole earth would henceforth be
A wider prison unto me:
No child, no sire, no kin had I,
No partner in my misery;
I thought of this, and I was glad,
For thought of them had made me mad;
But I was curious to ascend
To my barr'd windows, and to bend
Once more, upon the mountains high,
The quiet of a loving eye.
I saw them—and they were the same.
They were not changed like me in frame;
I saw their thousand years of snow
On high—their wide long lake below,
And the blue Rhone in fullest flow;
I heard the torrents leap and gush
O'er channell'd rock and broken bush;
I saw the white-wall'd distant town,
And whiter sails go skimming down;
And then there was a little isle,
Which in my very face did smile,
  The only one in view;
A small green isle, it seem'd no more,
Scarce broader than my dungeon floor,
But in it there were three tall trees,
And o'er it blew the mountain breeze,
And by it there were waters flowing,
And on it there were young flowers growing
  Of gentle breath and hue.
The fish swam by the castle wall,
And they seem'd joyous each and all;
The eagle rode the rising blast,
Methought he never flew so fast
As then to me he seem'd to fly;
And then new tears came in my eye,
And I felt troubled and would fain

I had not left my recent chain.
And when I did descend again,
The darkness of my dim abode
Fell on me as a heavy load;
It was as is a new-dug grave,
Closing o'er one we sought to save;
And yet my glance, too much opprest,
Had almost need of such a rest.

It might be months, or years, or days—
I kept no count, I took no note,
I had no hope my eyes to raise,
And clear them of their dreary mote.
At last men came to set me free;
I ask'd not why, and reck'd not where,
It was at length the same to me,
Fetter'd or fetterless to be,
I learn'd to love despair.
And thus when they appear'd at last,
And all my bonds aside were cast,
These heavy walls to me had grown
A hermitage—and all my own!
And half I felt as they were come
To tear me from a second home:
With spiders I had friendship made,
And watch'd them in their sullen trade,
Had seen the mice by moonlight play,
And why should I feel less than they?
We were all inmates of one place,
And I, the monarch of each race,
Had power to kill—yet, strange to tell!
In quiet we had learn'd to dwell—
My very chains and I grew friends,
So much a long communion tends
To make us what we are:—even I
Regain'd my freedom with a sigh.

480 On the Castle of Chillon

Eternal Spirit of the chainless Mind!
Brightest in dungeons, Liberty, thou art,—
For there thy habitation is the heart—
The heart which love of Thee alone can bind;

And when thy sons to fetters are consign'd,
To fetters, and the damp vault's dayless gloom,
Their country conquers with their martyrdom,
And Freedom's fame finds wings on every wind.

Chillon! thy prison is a holy place
And thy sad floor an altar, for 'twas trod,
Until his very steps have left a trace

Worn as if thy cold pavement were a sod,
By Bonnivard! May none those marks efface!
For they appeal from tyranny to God.

481 Song of Saul Before His Last Battle

Warriors and chiefs! should the shaft or the sword
Pierce me in leading the host of the Lord,
Heed not the corse, though a king's in your path:
Bury your steel in the bosoms of Gath!

Thou who art bearing my buckler and bow,
Should the soldiers of Saul look away from the foe,
Stretch me that moment in blood at thy feet!
Mine be the doom which they dared not to meet.

Farewell to others, but never we part,
Heir to my royalty, son of my heart!
Bright is the diadem, boundless the sway,
Or kingly the death, which awaits us to-day!

482

The Isles of Greece

The isles of Greece! the isles of Greece!
  Where burning Sappho loved and sung,
Where grew the arts of war and peace,
  Where Delos rose, and Phœbus sprung!
Eternal summer gilds them yet,
But all, except their sun, is set.

The Scian and the Teian muse,
  The hero's harp, the lover's lute,
Have found the fame your shores refuse:
  Their place of birth alone is mute
To sounds which echo further west
Than your sires' 'Islands of the Blest.'

The mountains look on Marathon—
  And Marathon looks on the sea;
And musing there an hour alone,
  I dream'd that Greece might still be free;
For standing on the Persians' grave,
I could not deem myself a slave.

A king sate on the rocky brow
  Which looks o'er sea-born Salamis;
And ships, by thousands, lay below,
  And men in nations;—all were his!
He counted them at break of day—
And when the sun set, where were they?

And where are they? and where art thou,
  My country? On thy voiceless shore
The heroic lay is tuneless now—
  The heroic bosom beats no more!
And must thy lyre, so long divine,
Degenerate into hands like mine?

'Tis something in the dearth of fame,
Though link'd among a fetter'd race,
To feel at least a patriot's shame,
Even as I sing, suffuse my face;
For what is left the poet here?
For Greeks a blush—for Greece a tear.

Must *we* but weep o'er days more blest?
Must *we* but blush?—Our fathers bled.
Earth! render back from out thy breast
A remnant of our Spartan dead!
Of the three hundred grant but three,
To make a new Thermopylæ!

What, silent still? and silent all?
Ah! no;—the voices of the dead
Sound like a distant torrent's fall,
And answer, 'Let one living head,
But one, arise,—we come, we come!'
'Tis but the living who are dumb.

In vain—in vain: strike other chords;
Fill high the cup with Samian wine!
Leave battles to the Turkish hordes,
And shed the blood of Scio's vine!
Hark! rising to the ignoble call—
How answers each bold Bacchanal!

You have the Pyrrhic dance as yet;
Where is the Pyrrhic phalanx gone?
Of two such lessons, why forget
The nobler and the manlier one?
You have the letters Cadmus gave—
Think ye he meant them for a slave?

Fill high the bowl with Samian wine!
We will not think of themes like these!
It made Anacreon's song divine:
He served—but served Polycrates—
A tyrant; but our masters then
Were still, at least, our countrymen.

The tyrant of the Chersonese
  Was freedom's best and bravest friend;
That tyrant was Miltiades!
  O that the present hour would lend
Another despot of the kind!
Such chains as his were sure to bind.

Fill high the bowl with Samian wine!
  On Suli's rock, and Parga's shore,
Exists the remnant of a line
  Such as the Doric mothers bore;
And there, perhaps, some seed is sown,
The Heracleidan blood might own.

Trust not for freedom to the Franks—
  They have a king who buys and sells;
In native swords and native ranks
  The only hope of courage dwells:
But Turkish force and Latin fraud
Would break your shield, however broad.

Fill high the bowl with Samian wine!
  Our virgins dance beneath the shade—
I see their glorious black eyes shine;
  But gazing on each glowing maid,
My own the burning tear-drop laves,
To think such breasts must suckle slaves.

Place me on Sunium's marbled steep,
  Where nothing, save the waves and I,
May hear our mutual murmurs sweep;
  There, swan-like, let me sing and die:
A land of slaves shall ne'er be mine—
Dash down yon cup of Samian wine!

483

On This Day I Complete My Thirty-Sixth Year

'Tis time this heart should be unmoved,
  Since others it hath ceased to move:
Yet, though I cannot be beloved,
    Still let me love!

My days are in the yellow leaf;
  The flowers and fruits of love are gone;
The worm, the canker, and the grief
    Are mine alone!

The fire that on my bosom preys
  Is lone as some volcanic isle;
No torch is kindled at its blaze—
    A funeral pile.

The hope, the fear, the jealous care,
  The exalted portion of the pain
And power of love, I cannot share,
    But wear the chain.

But 'tis not *thus*—and 'tis not *here*—
  Such thoughts should shake my soul, nor *now*,
Where glory decks the hero's bier,
    Or binds his brow.

The sword, the banner, and the field,
  Glory and Greece, around me see!
The Spartan, borne upon his shield,
    Was not more free.

Awake! (not Greece—she *is* awake!)
  Awake, my spirit! Think through *whom*
Thy life-blood tracks its parent lake,
    And then strike home!

Tread those reviving passions down,
Unworthy manhood!—unto thee
Indifferent should the smile or frown
Of beauty be.

If thou regret'st thy youth, *why live?*
The land of honourable death
Is here:—up to the field, and give
Away thy breath!

Seek out—less often sought than found—
A soldier's grave, for thee the best;
Then look around, and choose thy ground,
And take thy rest.

AT MISSOLONGHI, *January* 22, 1824.

THOMAS MOORE

[*1779-1852*]

484

THE LIGHT OF OTHER DAYS

OFT in the stilly night
Ere slumber's chain has bound me,
Fond Memory brings the light
Of other days around me:
The smiles, the tears
Of boyhood's years,
The words of love then spoken;
The eyes that shone,
Now dimm'd and gone,
The cheerful hearts now broken!
Thus in the stilly night
Ere slumber's chain has bound me,
Sad Memory brings the light
Of other days around me.

When I remember all
The friends so link'd together
I've seen around me fall
Like leaves in wintry weather,

I feel like one
Who treads alone
Some banquet-hall deserted,
Whose lights are fled
Whose garlands dead,
And all but he departed!
Thus in the stilly night
Ere slumber's chain has bound me,
Sad Memory brings the light
Of other days around me.

485

Pro Patria Mori

When he who adores thee has left but the name
Of his fault and his sorrows behind,
O! say wilt thou weep, when they darken the fame
Of a life that for thee was resign'd!
Yes, weep, and however my foes may condemn,
Thy tears shall efface their decree;
For, Heaven can witness, though guilty to them,
I have been but too faithful to thee.

With thee were the dreams of my earliest love;
Every thought of my reason was thine:
In my last humble prayer to the Spirit above
Thy name shall be mingled with mine!
O! blest are the lovers and friends who shall live
The days of thy glory to see;
But the next dearest blessing that Heaven can give
Is the pride of thus dying for thee.

486

The Meeting of the Waters

There is not in the wide world a valley so sweet
As that vale in whose bosom the bright waters meet;
Oh! the last rays of feeling and life must depart,
Ere the bloom of that valley shall fade from my heart.

Yet it was not that nature had shed o'er the scene
Her purest of crystal and brightest of green;
'Twas not her soft magic of streamlet or hill,
Oh! no—it was something more exquisite still.

'Twas that friends, the beloved of my bosom, were near,
Who made every dear scene of enchantment more dear,
And who felt how the best charms of nature improve,
When we see them reflected from looks that we love.

Sweet vale of Avoca! how calm could I rest
In thy bosom of shade, with the friends I love best,
Where the storms that we feel in this cold world should
cease,
And our hearts, like thy waters, be mingled in peace.

487 THE LAST ROSE OF SUMMER

'TIS the last rose of summer
Left blooming alone;
All her lovely companions
Are faded and gone;
No flower of her kindred,
No rosebud is nigh,
To reflect back her blushes,
To give sigh for sigh.

I'll not leave thee, thou lone one!
To pine on the stem;
Since the lovely are sleeping,
Go, sleep thou with them.
Thus kindly I scatter
Thy leaves o'er the bed,
Where thy mates of the garden
Lie scentless and dead.

So soon may I follow,
When friendships decay,
And from Love's shining circle
The gems drop away.

When true hearts lie withered
  And fond ones are flown,
Oh! who would inhabit
  This bleak world alone?

488 The Harp that Once Through Tara's Halls

The harp that once through Tara's halls
  The soul of music shed,
Now hangs as mute on Tara's walls
  As if that soul were fled.
So sleeps the pride of former days,
  So glory's thrill is o'er,
And hearts, that once beat high for praise,
  Now feel that pulse no more.

No more to chiefs and ladies bright
  The harp of Tara swells:
The chord alone, that breaks at night,
  Its tale of ruin tells.
Thus Freedom now so seldom wakes,
  The only throb she gives,
Is when some heart indignant breaks,
  To show that still she lives.

489 A Canadian Boat-Song

Faintly as tolls the evening chime
Our voices keep tune and our oars keep time.
Soon as the woods on shore look dim,
We'll sing at St. Anne's our parting hymn.
Row, brothers, row, the stream runs fast,
The Rapids are near and the daylight's past!

Why should we yet our sail unfurl?
There is not a breath the blue wave to curl;
But, when the wind blows off the shore,
Oh! sweetly we'll rest our weary oar.
Blow, breezes, blow, the stream runs fast,
The Rapids are near and the daylight's past!

Utawa's tide! this trembling moon
Shall see us float over thy surges soon.
Saint of this green isle! hear our prayers,
Oh, grant us cool heavens and favouring airs.
Blow, breezes, blow, the stream runs fast,
The Rapids are near and the daylight's past!

490

The Journey Onwards

As slow our ship her foamy track
  Against the wind was cleaving,
Her trembling pennant still look'd back
  To that dear isle 'twas leaving.
So loth we part from all we love,
  From all the links that bind us;
So turn our hearts, as on we rove,
  To those we've left behind us!

When, round the bowl, of vanish'd years
  We talk with joyous seeming—
With smiles that might as well be tears,
  So faint, so sad their beaming;
While memory brings us back again
  Each early tie that twined us,
O, sweet's the cup that circles then
  To those we've left behind us!

And when, in other climes, we meet
  Some isle or vale enchanting,
Where all looks flowery, wild and sweet,
  And nought but love is wanting;
We think how great had been our bliss
  If Heaven had but assign'd us
To live and die in scenes like this,
  With some we've left behind us!

As travellers oft look back at eve
  When eastward darkly going,
To gaze upon that light they leave
  Still faint behind them glowing,—

So, when the close of pleasure's day
  To gloom hath near consign'd us,
We turn to catch one fading ray
  Of joy that's left behind us.

491 The Young May Moon

The young May moon is beaming, love,
The glow-worm's lamp is gleaming, love;
    How sweet to rove
    Through Morna's grove,
When the drowsy world is dreaming, love!
Then awake!—the heavens look bright, my dear,
'Tis never too late for delight, my dear;
    And the best of all ways
    To lengthen our days
Is to steal a few hours from the night, my dear!

Now all the world is sleeping, love,
But the Sage, his star-watch keeping, love,
    And I, whose star
    More glorious far
Is the eye from that casement peeping, love.
Then awake!—till rise of sun, my dear,
The Sage's glass we'll shun, my dear,
    Or in watching the flight
    Of bodies of light
He might happen to take thee for one, my dear!

492 Echoes

How sweet the answer Echo makes
To Music at night
When, roused by lute or horn, she wakes,
And far away o'er lawns and lakes
Goes answering light!

Yet Love hath echoes truer far
And far more sweet
Than e'er, beneath the moonlight's star,
Of horn or lute or soft guitar
The songs repeat.

'Tis when the sigh,—in youth sincere
And only then,
The sigh that's breathed for one to hear—
Is by that one, that only Dear
Breathed back again.

493 At the Mid Hour of Night

At the mid hour of night, when stars are weeping, I fly
To the lone vale we loved, when life shone warm in thine eye;
And I think oft, if spirits can steal from the regions of air
To revisit past scenes of delight, thou wilt come to me there
And tell me our love is remember'd, even in the sky!

Then I sing the wild song it once was rapture to hear
When our voices, commingling, breathed like one on the ear;
And as Echo far off through the vale my sad orison rolls,
I think, O my Love! 'tis thy voice, from the Kingdom of
Souls
Faintly answering still the notes that once were so dear.

CHARLES WOLFE

[1791-1823]

494 The Burial of Sir John Moore at Corunna

Not a drum was heard, not a funeral note,
As his corse to the rampart we hurried;
Not a soldier discharged his farewell shot
O'er the grave where our hero was buried.

We buried him darkly at dead of night,
The sods with our bayonets turning;
By the struggling moonbeam's misty light
And the lantern dimly burning.

No useless coffin enclosed his breast,
Not in sheet or in shroud we wound him;
But he lay like a warrior taking his rest,
With his martial cloak around him.

Few and short were the prayers we said,
And we spoke not a word of sorrow;
But we steadfastly gazed on the face that was dead,
And we bitterly thought of the morrow.

We thought, as we hollow'd his narrow bed
And smoothed down his lonely pillow,
That the foe and the stranger would tread o'er his head,
And we far away on the billow!

Lightly they'll talk of the spirit that's gone
And o'er his cold ashes upbraid him,—
But little he'll reck, if they let him sleep on
In the grave where a Briton has laid him.

But half of our heavy task was done
When the clock struck the hour for retiring:
And we heard the distant and random gun
That the foe was sullenly firing.

Slowly and sadly we laid him down,
From the field of his fame fresh and gory;
We carved not a line, and we raised not a stone,
But we left him alone with his glory.

PERCY BYSSHE SHELLEY

[*1792-1822*]

495

Hymn of Pan

From the forests and highlands
We come, we come;
From the river-girt islands,
Where loud waves are dumb,
Listening to my sweet pipings.
The wind in the reeds and the rushes,
The bees on the bells of thyme,
The birds on the myrtle bushes,
The cicale above in the lime,
And the lizards below in the grass,
Were as silent as ever old Tmolus was,
Listening to my sweet pipings.

Liquid Peneus was flowing,
And all dark Tempe lay
In Pelion's shadow, outgrowing
The light of the dying day,
Speeded by my sweet pipings.
The Sileni and Sylvans and Fauns,
And the Nymphs of the woods and waves,
To the edge of the moist river-lawns,
And the brink of the dewy caves,
And all that did then attend and follow,
Were silent with love, as you now, Apollo,
With envy of my sweet pipings.

I sang of the dancing stars,
I sang of the dædal earth,
And of heaven, and the giant wars,
And love, and death, and birth.
And then I changed my pipings—
Singing how down the vale of Mænalus
I pursued a maiden, and clasp'd a reed:
Gods and men, we are all deluded thus;

It breaks in our bosom, and then we bleed.
All wept—as I think both ye now would,
If envy or age had not frozen your blood—
At the sorrow of my sweet pipings.

496

Hellas

The world's great age begins anew,
The golden years return,
The earth doth like a snake renew
Her winter weeds outworn:
Heaven smiles, and faiths and empires gleam
Like wrecks of a dissolving dream.

A brighter Hellas rears its mountains
From waves serener far;
A new Peneus rolls his fountains
Against the morning star;
Where fairer Tempes bloom, there sleep
Young Cyclads on a sunnier deep.

A loftier Argo cleaves the main,
Fraught with a later prize;
Another Orpheus sings again,
And loves, and weeps, and dies;
A new Ulysses leaves once more
Calypso for his native shore.

O write no more the tale of Troy,
If earth Death's scroll must be—
Nor mix with Laian rage the joy
Which dawns upon the free,
Although a subtler Sphinx renew
Riddles of death Thebes never knew.

Another Athens shall arise,
And to remoter time
Bequeath, like sunset to the skies,
The splendour of its prime;

And leave, if naught so bright may live,
All earth can take or Heaven can give.

Saturn and Love their long repose
  Shall burst, more bright and good
Than all who fell, than One who rose,
  Than many unsubdued:
Not gold, not blood, their altar dowers,
But votive tears and symbol flowers.

O cease! must hate and death return?
  Cease! must men kill and die?
Cease! drain not to its dregs the urn
  Of bitter prophecy!
The world is weary of the past—
O might it die or rest at last!

497

Invocation

Rarely, rarely comest thou,
  Spirit of Delight!
Wherefore hast thou left me now
  Many a day and night?
Many a weary night and day
'Tis since thou art fled away.

How shall ever one like me
  Win thee back again?
With the joyous and the free
  Thou wilt scoff at pain.
Spirit false! thou hast forgot
All but those who need thee not.

As a lizard with the shade
  Of a trembling leaf,
Thou with sorrow art dismay'd;
  Even the sighs of grief
Reproach thee, that thou art not near,
And reproach thou wilt not hear.

Let me set my mournful ditty
  To a merry measure;—
Thou wilt never come for pity,
  Thou wilt come for pleasure;—
Pity thou wilt cut away
Those cruel wings, and thou wilt stay.

I love all that thou lovest,
  Spirit of Delight!
The fresh Earth in new leaves drest
  And the starry night;
Autumn evening, and the morn
When the golden mists are born.

I love snow and all the forms
  Of the radiant frost;
I love waves, and winds, and storms,
  Everything almost
Which is Nature's, and may be
Untainted by man's misery.

I love tranquil solitude,
  And such society
As is quiet, wise, and good;
  Between thee and me
What diff'rence? but thou dost possess
The things I seek, nor love them less.

I love Love—though he has wings,
  And like light can flee,
But above all other things,
  Spirit, I love thee—
Thou art love and life! O come!
Make once more my heart thy home!

498 Stanzas Written in Dejection Near Naples

The sun is warm, the sky is clear,
The waves are dancing fast and bright,
Blue isles and snowy mountains wear
The purple noon's transparent light:

The breath of the moist earth is light
Around its unexpanded buds;
Like many a voice of one delight—
The winds', the birds', the ocean-floods'—
The City's voice itself is soft like Solitude's.

I see the Deep's untrampled floor
With green and purple sea-weeds strown;
I see the waves upon the shore
Like light dissolved in star-showers thrown:
I sit upon the sands alone;
The lightning of the noon-tide ocean
Is flashing round me, and a tone
Arises from its measured motion—
How sweet! did any heart now share in my emotion.

Alas! I have nor hope nor health,
Nor peace within nor calm around,
Nor that Content, surpassing wealth,
The sage in meditation found,
And walk'd with inward glory crown'd—
Nor fame, nor power, nor love, nor leisure;
Others I see whom these surround—
Smiling they live, and call life pleasure;
To me that cup has been dealt in another measure.

Yet now despair itself is mild
Even as the winds and waters are;
I could lie down like a tired child,
And weep away the life of care
Which I have borne, and yet must bear,
Till death like sleep might steal on me,
And I might feel in the warm air
My cheek grow cold, and hear the sea
Breathe o'er my dying brain its last monotony.

499 I Fear Thy Kisses

I FEAR thy kisses, gentle maiden;
Thou needest not fear mine;

My spirit is too deeply laden
Ever to burthen thine.

I fear thy mien, thy tones, thy motion;
Thou needest not fear mine;
Innocent is the heart's devotion
With which I worship thine.

500

Lines to an Indian Air

I arise from dreams of Thee
In the first sweet sleep of night,
When the winds are breathing low
And the stars are shining bright:
I arise from dreams of thee,
And a spirit in my feet
Hath led me—who knows how?
To thy chamber-window, Sweet!

The wandering airs they faint
On the dark, the silent stream—
The champak odours fail
Like sweet thoughts in a dream;
The nightingale's complaint
It dies upon her heart,
As I must die on thine
O belovéd as thou art!

O lift me from the grass!
I die, I faint, I fail!
Let thy love in kisses rain
On my lips and eyelids pale.
My cheek is cold and white, alas!
My heart beats loud and fast;
O! press it close to thine again
Where it will break at last.

501

To a Skylark

Hail to thee, blithe Spirit!
Bird thou never wert,
That from heaven, or near it,
Pourest thy full heart
In profuse strains of unpremeditated art

Higher still and higher
From the earth thou springest
Like a cloud of fire;
The blue deep thou wingest,
And singing still dost soar, and soaring ever singest.

In the golden lightning
Of the sunken sun
O'er which clouds are brightening,
Thou dost float and run,
Like an unbodied joy whose race is just begun.

The pale purple even
Melts around thy flight;
Like a star of heaven
In the broad daylight
Thou art unseen, but yet I hear thy shrill delight:

Keen as are the arrows
Of that silver sphere,
Whose intense lamp narrows
In the white dawn clear
Until we hardly see, we feel that it is there.

All the earth and air
With thy voice is loud,
As, when night is bare,
From one lonely cloud
The moon rains out her beams, and heaven is overflow'd.

What thou art we know not;
What is most like thee?
From rainbow clouds there flow not
Drops so bright to see
As from thy presence showers a rain of melody.

Like a poet hidden
In the light of thought,
Singing hymns unbidden,
Till the world is wrought
To sympathy with hopes and fears it heeded not:

Like a high-born maiden
In a palace tower,
Soothing her love-laden
Soul in secret hour
With music sweet as love, which overflows her bower:

Like a glow-worm golden
In a dell of dew,
Scattering unbeholden
Its aerial hue
Among the flowers and grass, which screen it from the view:

Like a rose embower'd
In its own green leaves,
By warm winds deflower'd,
Till the scent it gives
Makes faint with too much sweet these heavy-winged thieves.

Sound of vernal showers
On the twinkling grass,
Rain-awaken'd flowers,
All that ever was
Joyous, and clear, and fresh, thy music doth surpass.

Teach us, sprite or bird,
What sweet thoughts are thine:

I have never heard
Praise of love or wine
That panted forth a flood of rapture so divine.

Chorus hymeneal
Or triumphal chaunt
Match'd with thine, would be all
But an empty vaunt—
A thing wherein we feel there is some hidden want.

What objects are the fountains
Of thy happy strain?
What fields, or waves, or mountains?
What shapes of sky or plain?
What love of thine own kind? what ignorance of pain?

With thy clear keen joyance
Languor cannot be:
Shadow of annoyance
Never came near thee:
Thou lovest; but ne'er knew love's sad satiety.

Waking or asleep
Thou of death must deem
Things more true and deep
Than we mortals dream,
Or how could thy notes flow in such a crystal stream?

We look before and after,
And pine for what is not:
Our sincerest laughter
With some pain is fraught;
Our sweetest songs are those that tell of saddest thought.

Yet if we could scorn
Hate, and pride, and fear;
If we were things born
Not to shed a tear,
I know not how thy joy we ever should come near.

Better than all measures
  Of delightful sound,
Better than all treasures
  That in books are found,
Thy skill to poet were, thou scorner of the ground!

Teach me half the gladness
  That thy brain must know,
Such harmonious madness
  From my lips would flow
The world should listen then, as I am listening now!

502

Love's Philosophy

The fountains mingle with the river
And the rivers with the ocean,
The winds of heaven mix for ever
With a sweet emotion;
Nothing in the world is single,
All things by a law divine
In one another's being mingle—
Why not I with thine?

See the mountains kiss high heaven
And the waves clasp one another;
No sister-flower would be forgiven
If it disdain'd its brother:
And the sunlight clasps the earth,
And the moonbeams kiss the sea—
What are all these kissings worth,
If thou kiss not me?

503

To the Night

Swiftly walk over the western wave,
  Spirit of Night!
Out of the misty eastern cave
Where, all the long and lone daylight,

Thou wovest dreams of joy and fear
Which make thee terrible and dear,—
Swift be thy flight!

Wrap thy form in a mantle gray
Star-inwrought!
Blind with thine hair the eyes of day,
Kiss her until she be wearied out:
Then wander o'er city and sea and land,
Touching all with thine opiate wand—
Come, long-sought!

When I arose and saw the dawn,
I sigh'd for thee;
When light rode high, and the dew was gone,
And noon lay heavy on flower and tree,
And the weary Day turn'd to his rest
Lingering like an unloved guest,
I sigh'd for thee.

Thy brother Death came, and cried
Wouldst thou me?
Thy sweet child Sleep, the filmy-eyed,
Murmur'd like a noon-tide bee
Shall I nestle near thy side?
Wouldst thou me?—And I replied
No, not thee!

Death will come when thou art dead,
Soon, too soon—
Sleep will come when thou art fled;
Of neither would I ask the boon
I ask of thee, belovéd Night—
Swift be thine approaching flight,
Come soon, soon!

504

Ode to the West Wind

O wild West Wind, thou breath of Autumn's being,
Thou, from whose unseen presence the leaves dead
Are driven, like ghosts from an enchanter fleeing,
Yellow, and black, and pale, and hectic red,
Pestilence-stricken multitudes: O thou
Who chariotest to their dark wintry bed
The wingéd seeds, where they lie cold and low,
Each like a corpse within its grave, until
Thine azure sister of the spring shall blow
Her clarion o'er the dreaming earth, and fill
(Driving sweet buds like flocks to feed in air)
With living hues and odours plain and hill:
Wild Spirit, which art moving everywhere;
Destroyer and Preserver; Hear, O hear!

Thou on whose stream, 'mid the steep sky's commotion,
Loose clouds like earth's decaying leaves are shed,
Shook from the tangled boughs of Heaven and Ocean,
Angels of rain and lightning; there are spread
On the blue surface of thine airy surge,
Like the bright hair uplifted from the head
Of some fierce Maenad, ev'n from the dim verge
Of the horizon to the zenith's height—
The locks of the approaching storm. Thou dirge
Of the dying year, to which this closing night
Will be the dome of a vast sepulchre,
Vaulted with all thy congregated might,
Of vapours, from whose solid atmosphere
Black rain, and fire, and hail, will burst: O hear!

Thou who didst waken from his summer-dreams
The blue Mediterranean, where he lay
Lull'd by the coil of his crystalline streams,
Beside a pumice isle in Baiae's bay,
And saw in sleep old palaces and towers
Quivering within the wave's intenser day,
All overgrown with azure moss and flowers

So sweet, the sense faints picturing them! Thou
For whose path the Atlantic's level powers
Cleave themselves into chasms, while far below
The sea-blooms and the oozy woods which wear
The sapless foliage of the ocean, know
Thy voice, and suddenly grow gray with fear
And tremble and despoil themselves: O hear!

If I were a dead leaf thou mightest bear;
If I were a swift cloud to fly with thee;
A wave to pant beneath thy power, and share
The impulse of thy strength, only less free
Than Thou, O uncontrollable! If even
I were as in my boyhood, and could be
The comrade of thy wanderings over heaven,
As then, when to outstrip thy skyey speed
Scarce seem'd a vision, I would ne'er have striven
As thus with thee in prayer in my sore need.
O lift me as a wave, a leaf, a cloud!
I fall upon the thorns of life! I bleed!
A heavy weight of hours has chain'd and bow'd
One too like thee: tameless, and swift, and proud.

Make me thy lyre, ev'n as the forest is:
What if my leaves are falling like its own!
The tumult of thy mighty harmonies
Will take from both a deep autumnal tone,
Sweet though in sadness. Be thou, Spirit fierce,
My spirit! be thou me, impetuous one!
Drive my dead thoughts over the universe
Like wither'd leaves, to quicken a new birth;
And, by the incantation of this verse,
Scatter, as from an unextinguish'd hearth
Ashes and sparks, my words among mankind!
Be through my lips to unawaken'd earth
The trumpet of a prophecy! O Wind,
If Winter comes, can Spring be far behind?

505 Written Among the Euganean Hills, North Italy

Many a green isle needs must be
In the deep wide sea of misery,
Or the mariner, worn and wan,
Never thus could voyage on
Day and night, and night and day,
Drifting on his dreary way,
With the solid darkness black
Closing round his vessel's track;
Whilst above, the sunless sky
Big with clouds, hangs heavily,
And behind the tempest fleet
Hurries on with lightning feet,
Riving sail, and cord, and plank,
Till the ship has almost drank
Death from the o'er-brimming deep;
And sinks down, down, like that sleep
When the dreamer seems to be
Weltering through eternity;
And the dim low line before
Of a dark and distant shore
Still recedes, as ever still
Longing with divided will,
But no power to seek or shun,
He is ever drifted on
O'er the unreposing wave,
To the haven of the grave.
What, if there no friends will greet;
What, if there no heart will meet
His with love's impatient beat;
Wander whereso'er he may,
Can he dream before that day
To find refuge from distress
In friendship's smile, in love's caress?
Then 'twill wreak him little woe
Whether such there be or no:
Senseless is the breast, and cold,

Which relenting love would fold;
Bloodless are the veins and chill
Which the pulse of pain did fill;
Every little living nerve
That from bitter words did swerve
Round the tortured lips and brow,
Are like sapless leaflets now
Frozen upon December's bough.

On the beach of a northern sea
Which tempests shake eternally,
As once the wretch there lay to sleep,
Lies a solitary heap,
One white skull and seven dry bones,
On the margin of the stones,
Where a few gray rushes stand,
Boundaries of the sea and land:
Nor is heard one voice of wail
But the sea-mews, as they sail
O'er the billows of the gale;
Or the whirlwind up and down
Howling, like a slaughtered town,
When a king in glory rides
Through the pomp of fratricides:
Those unburied bones around
There is many a mournful sound;
There is no lament for him,
Like a sunless vapour, dim,
Who once clothed with life and thought
What now moves nor murmurs not.

Ay, many flowering islands lie
In the waters of wide Agony:
To such a one this morn was led
My bark, by soft winds piloted.
—'Mid the mountains Euganean
I stood listening to the paean
With which the legion'd rooks did hail
The Sun's uprise majestical:

Gathering round with wings all hoar,
Through the dewy mist they soar
Like gray shades, till the eastern heaven
Bursts, and then,—as clouds of even
Fleck'd with fire and azure, lie
In the unfathomable sky,—
So their plumes of purple grain
Starr'd with drops of golden rain
Gleam above the sunlight woods,
As in silent multitudes
On the morning's fitful gale
Through the broken mist they sail;
And the vapours cloven and gleaming
Follow down the dark steep streaming,
Till all is bright, and clear, and still
Round the solitary hill.

Beneath is spread like a green sea
The waveless plain of Lombardy,
Bounded by the vaporous air,
Islanded by cities fair;
Underneath day's azure eyes,
Ocean's nursling, Venice lies, —
A peopled labyrinth of walls,
Amphrite's destined halls,
Which her hoary sire now paves
With his blue and beaming waves.
Lo! the sun upsprings behind,
Broad, red, radiant, half-reclined
On the level quivering line
Of the waters crystalline;
And before that chasm of light,
As within a furnace bright,
Column, tower, and dome, and spire,
Shine like obelisks of fire,
Pointing with inconstant motion
From the altar of dark ocean
To the sapphire-tinted skies;
As the flames of sacrifice
From the marble shrines did rise

As to pierce the dome of gold
Where Apollo spoke of old.

Sun-girt City! thou hast been
Ocean's child, and then his queen;
Now is come a darker day,
And thou soon must be his prey,
If the power that raised thee here
Hallow so thy watery bier.
A less drear ruin then than now
With thy conquest-branded brow
Stooping to the slave of slaves
From thy throne among the waves,
Wilt thou be,—when the sea-mew
Flies, as once before it flew,
O'er thine isles depopulate,
And all is in its ancient state,
Save where many a palace-gate
With green sea-flowers overgrown
Like a rock of ocean's own,
Topples o'er the abandon'd sea
As the tides change sullenly.
The fisher on his watery way
Wandering at the close of day,
Will spread his sail and seize his oar
Till he pass the gloomy shore,
Lest thy dead should, from their sleep,
Bursting o'er the starlight deep,
Lead a rapid masque of death
O'er the waters of his path.

Noon descends around me now:
'Tis the noon of autumn's glow,
When a soft and purple mist
Like a vaporous amethyst,
Or an air-dissolvéd star
Mingling light and fragrance, far
From the curved horizon's bound
To the point of heaven's profound,

Fills the overflowing sky;
And the plains that silent lie
Underneath; the leaves unsodden
Where the infant frost has trodden
With his morning-wingéd feet
Whose bright print is gleaming yet;
And the red and golden vines
Piercing with their trellised lines
The rough, dark-skirted wilderness;
The dun and bladed grass no less,
Pointing from this hoary tower
In the windless air; the flower
Glimmering at my feet; the line
Of the olive-sandall'd Apennine
In the south dimly islanded;
And the Alps, whose snows are spread
High between the clouds and sun;
And of living things each one;
And my spirit, which so long
Darken'd this swift stream of song,—
Interpenetrated lie
By the glory of the sky;
Be it love, light, harmony,
Odour, or the soul of all
Which from heaven like dew doth fall,
Or the mind which feels this verse,
Peopling the lone universe.

Noon descends, and after noon
Autumn's evening meets me soon,
Leading the infantine moon
And that one star, which to her
Almost seems to minister
Half the crimson light she brings
From the sunset's radiant springs:
And the soft dreams of the morn
(Which like wingéd winds had borne
To that silent isle, which lies
'Mid remember'd agonies,

The frail bark of this lone being),
Pass, to other sufferers fleeing,
And its ancient pilot, Pain,
Sits beside the helm again.

Other flowering isles must be
In the sea of life and agony:
Other spirits float and flee
O'er that gulf: ev'n now, perhaps,
On some rock the wild wave wraps,
With folding wings they waiting sit
For my bark, to pilot it
To some calm and blooming cove,
Where for me, and those I love,
May a windless bower be built,
Far from passion, pain, and guilt,
In a dell 'mid lawny hills
Which the wild sea-murmur fills,
And soft sunshine, and the sound
Of old forests echoing round,
And the light and smell divine
Of all flowers that breathe and shine.
—We may live so happy there,
That the spirits of the air
Envying us, may even entice
To our healing paradise
The polluting multitude;
But their rage would be subdued
By that clime divine and calm,
And the winds whose wings rain balm
On the uplifted soul, and leaves
Under which the bright sea heaves;
While each breathless interval
In their whisperings musical
The inspired soul supplies
With its own deep melodies;
And the Love which heals all strife
Circling, like the breath of life,
All things in that sweet abode
With its own mild brotherhood.

They, not it, would change; and soon
Every sprite beneath the moon
Would repent its envy vain,
And the Earth grow young again!

506 Hymn to the Spirit of Nature

Life of Life! Thy lips enkindle
With their love the breath between them;
And thy smiles before they dwindle
Make the cold air fire; then screen them
In those locks, where whoso gazes
Faints, entangled in their mazes.

Child of Light! Thy limbs are burning
Through the veil which seems to hide them,
As the radiant lines of morning
Through thin clouds, ere they divide them;
And this atmosphere divinest
Shrouds thee whereso'er thou shinest.

Fair are others: none beholds Thee;
But thy voice sounds low and tender
Like the fairest, for it folds thee
From the sight, that liquid splendour;
And all feel, yet see thee never,—
As I feel now, lost for ever!

Lamp of Earth! where'er thou movest
Its dim shapes are clad with brightness,
And the souls of whom thou lovest
Walk upon the winds with lightness
Till they fail, as I am failing,
Dizzy, lost, yet unbewailing!

507 A Lament

O World! O Life! O Time!
On whose last steps I climb,
Trembling at that where I had stood before;
When will return the glory of your prime?
No more—O never more!

Out of the day and night
A joy has taken flight:
Fresh spring, and summer, and winter hoar
Move my faint heart with grief, but with delight
No more—O never more!

508 A Dream of the Unknown

I dream'd that as I wander'd by the way
Bare Winter suddenly was changed to Spring,
And gentle odours led my steps astray,
Mix'd with a sound of waters murmuring
Along a shelving bank of turf, which lay
Under a copse, and hardly dared to fling
Its green arms round the bosom of the stream,
But kiss'd it and then fled, as Thou mightest in dream.

There grew pied wind-flowers and violets,
Daisies, those pearl'd Arcturi of the earth,
The constellated flower that never sets;
Faint oxlips; tender blue-bells, at whose birth
The sod scarce heaved; and that tall flower that wets
Its mother's face with heaven-collected tears,
When the low wind, its playmate's voice, it hears.

And in the warm hedge grew lush eglantine,
Green cow-bind and the moonlight-colour'd May,
And cherry-blossoms, and white cups, whose wine
Was the bright dew yet drain'd not by the day;
And wild roses, and ivy serpentine
With its dark buds and leaves, wandering astray;
And flowers azure, black, and streak'd with gold,
Fairer than any waken'd eyes behold.

And nearer to the river's trembling edge
There grew broad flag-flowers, purple prank't with
white,
And starry river-buds among the sedge,
And floating water-lilies, broad and bright,

Which lit the oak that overhung the hedge
  With moonlight beams of their own watery light;
And bulrushes, and reeds of such deep green
As soothed the dazzled eye with sober sheen.

Methought that of these visionary flowers
  I made a nosegay, bound in such a way
That the same hues, which in their natural bowers
  Were mingled or opposed, the like array
Kept these imprison'd children of the Hours
  Within my hand,—and then, elate and gay,
I hasten'd to the spot whence I had come
That I might there present it—O! to Whom?

509

The Invitation

Best and Brightest, come away,
Fairer far than this fair day,
Which, like thee, to those in sorrow
Comes to bid a sweet good-morrow
To the rough year just awake
In its cradle on the brake.
The brightest hour of unborn Spring
Through the winter wandering,
Found, it seems, the halcyon morn
To hoar February born;
Bending from Heaven, in azure mirth,
It kiss'd the forehead of the earth,
And smiled upon the silent sea,
And bade the frozen streams be free,
And waked to music all their fountains,
And breathed upon the frozen mountains,
And like a prophetess of May
Strew'd flowers upon the barren way,
Making the wintry world appear
Like one on whom thou smilest, Dear.

  Away, away, from men and towns,
To the wild wood and the downs—

To the silent wilderness
Where the soul need not repress
Its music, lest it should not find
An echo in another's mind,
While the touch of Nature's art
Harmonizes heart to heart.

Radiant Sister of the Day
Awake! arise! and come away!
To the wild woods and the plains,
To the pools where winter rains
Image all their roof of leaves,
Where the pine its garland weaves
Of sapless green, and ivy dun,
Round stems that never kiss the sun,
Where the lawns and pastures be
And the sandhills of the sea,
Where the melting hoar-frost wets
The daisy-star that never sets,
And wind-flowers and violets
Which yet join not scent to hue
Crown the pale year weak and new;
When the night is left behind
In the deep east, dim and blind,
And the blue noon is over us,
And the multitudinous
Billows murmur at our feet,
Where the earth and ocean meet,
And all things seem only one
In the universal Sun.

510

The Recollection

Now the last day of many days
All beautiful and bright as thou,
The loveliest and the last, is dead:
Rise, Memory, and write its praise!

Up, do thy wonted work! come, trace
The epitaph of glory fled,
For now the earth has changed its face,
A frown is on the Heaven's brow.

We wander'd to the Pine Forest
  That skirts the Ocean's foam;
The lightest wind was in its nest,
  The tempest in its home.
The whispering waves were half asleep,
  The clouds were gone to play,
And on the bosom of the deep
  The smile of Heaven lay;
It seem'd as if the hour were one
  Sent from beyond the skies
Which scatter'd from above the sun
  A light of Paradise!

We paused amid the pines that stood
  The giants of the waste,
Tortured by storms to shape as rude
  As serpents interlaced,—
And soothed by every azure breath
  That under heaven is blown
To harmonies and hues beneath,
  As tender as its own:
Now all the tree-tops lay asleep,
  Like green waves on the sea,
As still as in the silent deep
  The ocean-woods may be.

How calm it was!—the silence there
  But such a chain was bound,
That even the busy woodpecker
  Made stiller by her sound
The inviolable quietness;
  The breath of peace we drew
With its soft motion made not less
  The calm that round us grew.

There seem'd, from the remotest seat
  Of the wide mountain waste
To the soft flower beneath our feet
  A magic circle traced,
A spirit interfused around,
  A thrilling silent life;
To momentary peace it bound
  Our mortal nature's strife;—
And still I felt the centre of
  The magic circle there
Was one fair Form that fill'd with love
  The lifeless atmosphere.

We paused beside the pools that lie
  Under the forest bough;
Each seem'd as 'twere a little sky
  Gulf'd in a world below;
A firmament of purple light
  Which in the dark earth lay,
More boundless than the depth of night
  And purer than the day—
In which the lovely forests grew
  As in the upper air,
More perfect both in shape and hue
  Than any spreading there.
There lay the glade and neighbouring lawn,
  And through the dark-green wood
The white sun twinkling like the dawn
  Out of a speckled cloud.
Sweet views which in our world above
  Can never well be seen
Were imaged by the water's love
  Of that fair forest green:
And all was interfused beneath
  With an Elysian glow,
An atmosphere without a breath,
  A softer day below.
Like one beloved, the scene had lent
  To the dark water's breast

Its every leaf and lineament
With more than truth exprest;
Until an envious wind crept by,
Like an unwelcome thought
Which from the mind's too faithful eye
Blots one dear image out.
—Though Thou art ever fair and kind,
The forests ever green,
Less oft is peace in Shelley's mind
Than calm in waters seen!

511

To the Moon

Art thou pale for weariness
Of climbing heaven, and gazing on the earth,
Wandering companionless
Among the stars that have a different birth,—
And ever-changing, like a joyless eye
That finds no object worth its constancy?

512

A Widow Bird

A widow bird sate mourning for her Love
Upon a wintry bough;
The frozen wind crept on above
The freezing stream below.

There was no leaf upon the forest bare,
No flower upon the ground,
And little motion in the air
Except the mill-wheel's sound.

513

To a Lady, with a Guitar

Ariel to Miranda:—Take
This slave of music, for the sake
Of him, who is the slave of thee;
And teach it all the harmony
In which thou canst, and only thou,

Make the delighted spirit glow,
Till joy denies itself again
And, too intense, is turn'd to pain.
For by permission and command
Of thine own Prince Ferdinand,
Poor Ariel sends this silent token
Of more than ever can be spoken;
Your guardian spirit, Ariel, who
From life to life must still pursue
Your happiness, for thus alone
Can Ariel ever find his own;
From Prospero's enchanted cell,
As the mighty verses tell,
To the throne of Naples he
Lit you o'er the trackless sea,
Flitting on, your prow before,
Like a living meteor.
When you die, the silent Moon
In her interlunar swoon
Is not sadder in her cell
Than deserted Ariel;
When you live again on earth,
Like an unseen Star of birth
Ariel guides you o'er the sea
Of life from your nativity:
Many changes have been run
Since Ferdinand and you begun
Your course of love, and Ariel still
Has track'd your steps and served your will.
Now in humbler, happier lot,
This is all remember'd not;
And now, alas! the poor sprite is
Imprison'd for some fault of his
In a body like a grave—
From you he only dares to crave
For his service and his sorrow
A smile to-day, a song to-morrow.

The artist who this idol wrought
To echo all harmonious thought,

Fell'd a tree, while on the steep
The woods were in their winter sleep,
Rock'd in that repose divine
On the wind-swept Apennine;
And dreaming, some of autumn past,
And some of spring approaching fast,
And some of April buds and showers,
And some of songs in July bowers,
And all of love: And so this tree,—
Oh that such our death may be!—
Died in sleep, and felt no pain,
To live in happier form again:
From which, beneath Heaven's fairest star,
The artist wrought this loved Guitar;
And taught it justly to reply
To all who question skilfully
In language gentle as thine own;
Whispering in enamour'd tone
Sweet oracles of woods and dells,
And summer winds in sylvan cells;
—For it had learnt all harmonies
Of the plains and of the skies,
Of the forests and the mountains,
And the many-voicéd fountains;
The clearest echoes of the hills,
The softest notes of falling rills,
The melodies of birds and bees,
The murmuring of summer seas,
And pattering rain, and breathing dew
And airs of evening; and it knew
That seldom-heard mysterious sound
Which, driven on its diurnal round,
As it floats through boundless day,
Our world enkindles on its way:
—All this it knows, but will not tell
To those who cannot question well
The spirit that inhabits it;
It talks according to the wit
Of its companions; and no more
Is heard than has been felt before

By those who tempt it to betray
These secrets of an elder day.
But, sweetly as its answers will
Flatter hands of perfect skill,
It keeps its highest holiest tone
For our beloved Friend alone.

514 One Word is Too Often Profaned

One word is too often profaned
  For me to profane it,
One feeling too falsely disdain'd
  For thee to disdain it.
One hope is too like despair
  For prudence to smother,
And Pity from thee more dear
  Than that from another.

I can give not what men call love;
  But wilt thou accept not
The worship the heart lifts above
  And the Heavens reject not:
The desire of the moth for the star,
  Of the night for the morrow,
The devotion to something afar
  From the sphere of our sorrow?

515 Ozymandias of Egypt

I met a traveller from an antique land
Who said: Two vast and trunkless legs of stone
Stand in the desert. Near them on the sand
Half sunk, a shatter'd visage lies, whose frown
And wrinkled lip and sneer of cold command
Tell that its sculptor well those passions read
Which yet survive, stamp'd on these lifeless things,
The hand that mock'd them and the heart that fed;
And on the pedestal these words appear:

'My name is Ozymandias, king of kings:
Look on my works, ye Mighty, and despair!'
Nothing beside remains. Round the decay
Of that colossal wreck, boundless and bare,
The lone and level sands stretch far away.

516 The Flight of Love

When the lamp is shatter'd
The light in the dust lies dead—
When the cloud is scatter'd,
The rainbow's glory is shed.
When the lute is broken,
Sweet tones are remember'd not;
When the lips have spoken,
Loved accents are soon forgot.

As music and splendour
Survive not the lamp and the lute,
The heart's echoes render
No song when the spirit is mute—
No song but sad dirges,
Like the wind through a ruin'd cell,
Or the mournful surges
That ring the dead seaman's knell.

When hearts have once mingled,
Love first leaves the well-built nest;
The weak one is singled
To endure what it once possesst.
O Love! who bewailest
The frailty of all things here,
Why choose you the frailest
For your cradle, your home, and your bier?

Its passions will rock thee
As the storms rock the ravens on high;
Bright reason will mock thee
Like the sun from a wintry sky.
From thy nest every rafter
Will rot, and thine eagle home

Leave thee naked to laughter,
When leaves fall and cold winds come.

517

The Cloud

I bring fresh showers for the thirsting flowers,
From the seas and the streams;
I bear light shade for the leaves when laid
In their noonday dreams.
From my wings are shaken the dews that waken
The sweet buds every one,
When rocked to rest on their mother's breast,
As she dances about the sun.
I wield the flail of the lashing hail,
And whiten the green plains under,
And then again I dissolve it in rain,
And laugh as I pass in thunder.

I sift the snow on the mountains below,
And their great pines groan aghast;
And all the night 'tis my pillow white,
While I sleep in the arms of the blast.
Sublime on the towers of my skiey bowers,
Lightning my pilot sits,
In a cavern under is fretted the thunder,
It struggles and howls at fits;
Over earth and ocean, with gentle motion,
This pilot is guiding me,
Lured by the love of the genii that move
In the depths of the purple sea;
Over the rills, and the crags, and the hills,
Over the lakes and the plains,
Wherever he dream, under mountain or stream
The Spirit he loves remains;
And I all the while bask in heaven's blue smile,
Whilst he is dissolving in rains.

The sanguine sunrise, with his meteor eyes,
And his burning plumes outspread,
Leaps on the back of my sailing rack,
When the morning star shines dead,

As on the jag of a mountain crag,
    Which an earthquake rocks and swings,
An eagle alit one moment may sit
    In the light of its golden wings. [beneath,
And when sunset may breathe from the lit sea
    Its ardours of rest and of love,
And the crimson pall of eve may fall
    From the depth of heaven above,
With wings folded I rest, on mine airy nest,
    As still as a brooding dove.

That orbèd maiden with white fire laden,
    Whom mortals call the moon,
Glides glimmering o'er my fleece-like floor,
    By the midnight breezes strewn;
And wherever the beat of her unseen feet,
    Which only the angels hear,
May have broken the woof of my tent's thin roof,
    The stars peep behind her and peer;
And I laugh to see them whirl and flee,
    Like a swarm of golden bees,
When I widen the rent in my wind-built tent,
    Till the calm rivers, lakes, and seas,
Like strips of the sky fallen through me on high,
    Are each paved with the moon and these.

I bind the sun's throne with a burning zone,
    And the moon's with a girdle of pearl;
The volcanoes are dim, and the stars reel and swim,
    When the whirlwinds my banner unfurl.
From cape to cape, with a bridge-like shape,
    Over a torrent sea,
Sunbeam-proof, I hang like a roof,
    The mountains its columns be.
The triumphal arch through which I march
    With hurricane, fire, and snow, [chair,
When the powers of the air are chained to my
    Is the million-coloured bow;
The sphere-fire above its soft colours wove,
    While the moist earth was laughing below.

I am the daughter of the earth and water,
And the nursling of the sky;
I pass through the pores of the ocean and shores;
I change, but I cannot die.
For after the rain when with never a stain,
The pavilion of heaven is bare,
And the winds and sunbeams with their convex gleams,
Build up the blue dome of air,
I silently laugh at my own cenotaph,
And out of the caverns of rain, [tomb,
Like a child from the womb, like a ghost from the
I arise and unbuild it again.

518 Stanzas—April, 1814

Away! the moor is dark beneath the moon,
Rapid clouds have drank the last pale beam of even:
Away! the gathering winds will call the darkness soon,
And profoundest midnight shroud the serene lights of heaven.

Pause not! The time is past! Every voice cries, Away!
Tempt not with one last tear thy friend's ungentle mood:
Thy lover's eye, so glazed and cold, dares not entreat thy stay:
Duty and dereliction guide thee back to solitude.

Away, away! to thy sad and silent home;
Pour bitter tears on its desolated hearth;
Watch the dim shades as like ghosts they go and come,
And complicate strange webs of melancholy mirth.

The leaves of wasted autumn woods shall float around thine head:
The blooms of dewy spring shall gleam beneath thy feet:
But thy soul or this world must fade in the frost that binds the dead,
Ere midnight's frown and morning's smile, ere thou and peace may meet.

The cloud shadows of midnight possess their own repose,
For the weary winds are silent, or the moon is in the deep:
Some respite to its turbulence unresting ocean knows;
Whatever moves, or toils, or grieves, hath its appointed sleep.

Thou in the grave shalt rest—yet till the phantoms flee
Which that house and heath and garden made dear to thee erewhile,
Thy remembrance, and repentance, and deep musings are not free
From the music of two voices and the light of one sweet smile.

519 Music, When Soft Voices Die

Music, when soft voices die,
Vibrates in the memory—
Odours, when sweet violets sicken,
Live within the sense they quicken.

Rose leaves, when the rose is dead,
Are heap'd for the beloved's bed;
And so thy thoughts, when Thou art gone,
Love itself shall slumber on.

520 The Poet's Dream

On a Poet's lips I slept
Dreaming like a love-adept
In the sound his breathing kept;
Nor seeks nor finds he mortal blisses,
But feeds on the aërial kisses
Of shapes that haunt Thought's wildernesses.
He will watch from dawn to gloom
The lake-reflected sun illume
The yellow bees in the ivy-bloom,

Nor heed nor see what things they be—
But from these create he can
Forms more real than living Man,
Nurslings of Immortality!

521

The World's Wanderers

Tell me, thou Star, whose wings of light
Speed thee in thy fiery flight,
In what cavern of the night
Will thy pinions close now?

Tell me, Moon, thou pale and gray
Pilgrim of heaven's homeless way,
In what depth of night or day
Seekest thou repose now?

Weary Mind, who wanderest
Like the world's rejected guest,
Hast thou still some secret nest
On the tree or billow?

522

Adonais

An Elegy on the Death of John Keats

I weep for Adonais—he is dead!
O, weep for Adonais! though our tears
Thaw not the frost which binds so dear a head!
And thou, sad Hour, selected from all years
To mourn our loss, rouse thy obscure compeers,
And teach them thine own sorrow! Say: 'With me
Died Adonais; till the Future dares
Forget the Past, his fate and fame shall be
An echo and a light unto eternity!'

Where wert thou, mighty Mother, when he lay,
When thy Son lay, pierced by the shaft which flies
In darkness? where was lorn Urania
When Adonais died? With veilèd eyes,

'Mid listening Echoes, in her Paradise
She sate, while one, with soft enamoured breath,
Rekindled all the fading melodies
With which, like flowers that mock the corse beneath,
He had adorned and hid the coming bulk of death.

Oh weep for Adonais—he is dead!
Wake, melancholy Mother, wake and weep!
Yet wherefore? Quench within their burning bed
Thy fiery tears, and let thy loud heart keep,
Like his, a mute and uncomplaining sleep;
For he is gone, where all things wise and fair
Descend;—oh, dream not that the amorous Deep
Will yet restore him to the vital air;
Death feeds on his mute voice, and laughs at our despair.

Most musical of mourners, weep again!
Lament anew, Urania!—He died,
Who was the Sire of an immortal strain,
Blind, old, and lonely, when his country's pride,
The priest, the slave, and the liberticide,
Trampled and mocked with many a loathèd rite
Of lust and blood; he went, unterrified,
Into the gulf of death; but his clear Sprite
Yet reigns o'er earth; the third among the sons of light.

Most musical of mourners, weep anew!
Not all to that bright station dared to climb;
And happier they their happiness who knew,
Whose tapers yet burn through that night of time
In which suns perished; others more sublime,
Struck by the envious wrath of man or god,
Have sunk, extinct in their refulgent prime;
And some yet live, treading the thorny road,
Which leads, through toil and hate, to Fame's serene abode.

But now, thy youngest, dearest one has perished,
The nursling of thy widowhood, who grew,
Like a pale flower by some sad maiden cherished,
And fed with true-love tears, instead of dew;

Most musical of mourners, weep anew!
Thy extreme hope, the loveliest and last,
The bloom, whose petals nipt before they blew
Died on the promise of the fruit, is waste;
The broken lily lies—the storm is over-past.

To that high Capital, where kingly Death
Keeps his pale court in beauty and decay,
He came; and bought, with price of purest breath,
A grave among the eternal.—Come away!
Haste, while the vault of blue Italian day
Is yet his fitting charnel-roof! while still
He lies, as if in dewy sleep he lay;
Awake him not! surely he takes his fill
Of deep and liquid rest, forgetful of all ill.

He will awake no more, oh, never more!—
Within the twilight chamber spreads apace,
The shadow of white Death, and at the door
Invisible Corruption waits to trace
His extreme way to her dim dwelling-place;
The eternal Hunger sits, but pity and awe
Soothe her pale rage, nor dares she to deface
So fair a prey, till darkness, and the law
Of change shall o'er his sleep the mortal curtain draw.

Oh weep for Adonais!—The quick Dreams,
The passion-wingèd Ministers of thought,
Who were his flocks, whom near the living streams
Of his young spirit he fed, and whom he taught
The love which was its music, wander not,—
Wander no more, from kindling brain to brain,
But droop there, whence they sprung; and mourn
their lot
Round the cold heart, where, after their sweet pain,
They ne'er will gather strength, or find a home again.

And one with trembling hands clasps his cold head,
And fans him with her moonlight wings, and cries;
'Our love, our hope, our sorrow, is not dead;
See, on the silken fringe of his faint eyes,

Like dew upon a sleeping flower, there lies
A tear some Dream has loosened from his brain.'
Lost Angel of a ruined Paradise!
She knew not 'twas her own; as with no stain
She faded, like a cloud which had outwept its rain.

One from a lucid urn of starry dew
Washed his light limbs as if embalming them;
Another clipt her profuse locks, and threw
The wreath upon him, like an anadem,
Which frozen tears instead of pearls begem;
Another in her wilful grief would break
Her bow and wingèd reeds, as if to stem
A greater loss with one which was more weak;
And dull the barbèd fire against his frozen cheek.

Another Splendour on his mouth alit,
That mouth, whence it was wont to draw the breath
Which gave it strength to pierce the guarded wit,
And pass into the panting heart beneath
With lightning and with music: the damp death
Quenched its caress upon his icy lips;
And, as a dying meteor stains a wreath
Of moonlight vapour, which the cold night clips,
It flushed through his pale limbs, and passed to its eclipse.

And others came . . . Desires and Adorations,
Wingèd Persuasions and veiled Destinies,
Splendours and Glooms, and glimmering Incarnations
Of hopes and fears, and twilight Phantasies;
And Sorrow, with her family of Sighs,
And Pleasure, blind with tears, led by the gleam
Of her own dying smile instead of eyes,
Came in slow pomp;—the moving pomp might seem
Like pageantry of mist on an autumnal stream.

All he had loved, and moulded into thought,
From shape, and hue, and odour, and sweet sound,
Lamented Adonais. Morning sought
Her eastern watch-tower, and her hair unbound,

Wet with the tears which should adorn the ground,
Dimmed the aërial eyes that kindle day;
Afar the melancholy thunder moaned,
Pale Ocean in unquiet slumber lay,
And the wild winds flew round, sobbing in their dismay.

Lost Echo sits amid the voiceless mountains,
And feeds her grief with his remembered lay,
And will no more reply to winds or fountains,
Or amorous birds perched on the young green spray,
Or herdsman's horn, or bell at closing day;
Since she can mimic not his lips, more dear
Than those for whose disdain she pined away
Into a shadow of all sounds:—a drear
Murmur, between their songs, is all the woodmen hear.

Grief made the young Spring wild, and she threw down
Her kindling buds, as if she Autumn were,
Or they dead leaves; since her delight is flown
For whom should she have waked the sullen year?
To Phoebus was not Hyacinth so dear
Nor to himself Narcissus, as to both
Thou, Adonais: wan they stand and sere
Amid the faint companions of their youth,
With dew all turned to tears; odour, to sighing ruth.

Thy spirit's sister, the lorn nightingale,
Mourns not her mate with such melodious pain;
Not so the eagle, who like thee could scale
Heaven, and could nourish in the sun's domain
Her mighty youth with morning, doth complain,
Soaring and screaming round her empty nest,
As Albion wails for thee; the curse of Cain
Light on his head who pierced thy innocent breast,
And scared the angel soul that was its earthly guest!

Ah, woe is me! Winter is come and gone,
But grief returns with the revolving year;
The airs and streams renew their joyous tone:
The ants, the bees, the swallows re-appear;

Fresh leaves and flowers deck the dead Seasons' bier;
The amorous birds now pair in every brake,
And build their mossy homes in field and brere;
And the green lizard, and the golden snake,
Like unimprisoned flames, out of their trance awake.

Through wood and stream and field and hill and Ocean
A quickening life from the Earth's heart has burst
As it has ever done, with change and motion,
From the great morning of the world when first
God dawned on Chaos; in its stream immersed
The lamps of Heaven flash with a softer light;
All baser things pant with life's sacred thirst;
Diffuse themselves; and spend in love's delight,
The beauty and the joy of their renewèd might.

The leprous corpse touched by this spirit tender
Exhales itself in flowers of gentle breath;
Like incarnations of the stars, when splendour
Is changed to fragrance, they illumine death
And mock the merry worm that wakes beneath;
Nought we know, dies. Shall that alone which knows
Be as a sword consumed before the sheath
By sightless lightning?—the intense atom glows
A moment, then is quenched in a most cold repose.

Alas! that all we loved of him should be
But for our grief, as if it had not been,
And grief itself be mortal! Woe is me!
Whence are we, and why are we? of what scene
The actors or spectators? Great and mean
Meet massed in death, who lends what life must borrow.
As long as skies are blue, and fields are green,
Evening must usher night, night urge the morrow,
Month follow month with woe, and year wake year to
sorrow.

He will awake no more, oh, never more!
'Wake thou,' cried Misery, 'childless Mother, rise
Out of thy sleep, and slake, in thy heart's core,
A wound more fierce than his, with tears and sighs.'

And all the Dreams that watched Urania's eyes,
And all the Echoes whom their sister's song
Had held in holy silence, cried: 'Arise!'
Swift as a Thought by the snake Memory stung,
From her ambrosial rest the fading Splendour sprung.

She rose like an autumnal Night, that springs
Out of the East, and follows wild and drear
The golden Day, which, on eternal wings,
Even as a ghost abandoning a bier,
Had left the Earth a corpse. Sorrow and fear
So struck, so roused, so rapt Urania;
So saddened round her like an atmosphere
Of stormy mist; so swept her on her way
Even to the mournful place where Adonais lay.

Out of her secret Paradise she sped,
Through camps and cities rough with stone, and steel,
And human hearts, which to her airy tread
Yielding not, wounded the invisible
Palms of her tender feet where'er they fell:
And barbèd tongues, and thoughts more sharp than they
Rent the soft Form they never could repel,
Whose sacred blood, like the young tears of May,
Paved with eternal flowers that undeserving way.

In the death-chamber for a moment Death,
Shamed by the presence of that living Might,
Blushed to annihilation, and the breath
Revisited those lips, and Life's pale light
Flashed through those limbs, so late her dear delight.
'Leave me not wild and drear and comfortless,
As silent lightning leaves the starless night!
Leave me not!' cried Urania: her distress
Roused Death: Death rose and smiled, and met her vain
caress.

'Stay yet awhile! speak to me once again;
Kiss me, so long but as a kiss may live;
And in my heartless breast and burning brain
That word, that kiss, shall all thoughts else survive,

With food of saddest memory kept alive,
Now thou art dead, as dead, as if it were a part
Of thee, my Adonais! I would give
All that I am to be as thou now art!
But I am chained to Time, and cannot thence depart!

'O gentle child, beautiful as thou wert,
Why didst thou leave the trodden paths of men
Too soon, and with weak hands though mighty heart
Dare the unpastured dragon in his den?
Defenceless as thou wert, oh where was then
Wisdom the mirrored shield, or scorn the spear?
Or hadst thou waited the full cycle, when
Thy spirit should have filled its crescent sphere,
The monsters of life's waste had fled from thee like deer.

'The herded wolves, bold only to pursue;
The obscene ravens, clamorous o'er the dead;
The vultures to the conqueror's banner true
Who feed where Desolation first has fed,
And whose wings rain contagion;—how they fled,
When, like Apollo, from his golden bow,
The Pythian of the age one arrow sped
And smiled!—The spoilers tempt no second blow,
They fawn on the proud feet that spurn them lying low.

'The sun comes forth, and many reptiles spawn;
He sets, and each ephemeral insect then
Is gathered into death without a dawn,
And the immortal stars awake again;
So is it in the world of living men:
A godlike mind soars forth, in its delight
Making earth bare and veiling heaven, and when
It sinks, the swarms that dimmed or shared its light
Leave to its kindred lamps the spirit's awful night.'

Thus ceased she: and the mountain shepherds came,
Their garlands sere, their magic mantles rent;
The Pilgrim of Eternity, whose fame
Over his living head like Heaven is bent,

An early but enduring monument,
Came, veiling all the lightnings of his song
In sorrow; from her wilds Ierne sent
The sweetest lyrist of her saddest wrong,
And Love taught Grief to fall like music from his tongue.

Midst others of less note, came one frail Form,
A phantom among men; companionless
As the last cloud of an expiring storm
Whose thunder is its knell; he, as I guess,
Had gazed on Nature's naked loveliness,
Actæon-like, and now he fled astray
With feeble steps o'er the world's wilderness,
And his own thoughts, along that rugged way,
Pursued, like raging hounds, their father and their prey.

A pardlike Spirit beautiful and swift—
Love in desolation masked;—a Power
Girt round with weakness; —it can scarce uplift
The weight of the superincumbent hour;
It is a dying lamp, a falling shower,
A breaking billow;—even whilst we speak
Is it not broken? On the withering flower
The killing sun smiles brightly: on a cheek
The life can burn in blood, even while the heart may break.

His head was bound with pansies overblown,
And faded violets, white, and pied, and blue;
And a light spear topped with a cypress cone,
Round whose rude shaft dark ivy tresses grew
Yet dripping with the forest's noonday dew,
Vibrated, as the ever-beating heart
Shook the weak hand that grasped it; of that crew
He came the last, neglected and apart;
A herd-abandoned deer struck by the hunter's dart.

All stood aloof, and at his partial moan
Smiled through their tears; well knew that gentle band
Who in another's fate now wept his own;
As in the accents of an unknown land,

He sung new sorrow; sad Urania scanned
The Stranger's mien, and murmured: 'Who art thou?'
He answered not, but with a sudden hand
Made bare his branded and ensanguined brow,
Which was like Cain's or Christ's—oh, that it should be so!

What softer voice is hushed over the dead?
Athwart what brow is that dark mantle thrown?
What form leans sadly o'er the white death-bed,
In mockery of monumental stone,
The heavy heart heaving without a moan?
If it be He, who, gentlest of the wise,
Taught, soothed, loved, honoured the departed one;
Let me not vex, with inharmonious sighs
The silence of that heart's accepted sacrifice.

Our Adonais has drunk poison—Oh!
What deaf and viperous murderer could crown
Life's early cup with such a draught of woe?
The nameless worm would now itself disown:
It felt, yet could escape, the magic tone
Whose prelude held all envy, hate, and wrong,
But what was howling in one breast alone,
Silent with expectation of the song,
Whose master's hand is cold, whose silver lyre unstrung.

Live thou, whose infamy is not thy fame!
Live! fear no heavier chastisement from me,
Thou noteless blot on a remembered name!
But be thyself, and know thyself to be!
And ever at thy season be thou free
To spill the venom when thy fangs o'erflow:
Remorse and Self-contempt shall cling to thee;
Hot Shame shall burn upon thy secret brow,
And like a beaten hound tremble thou shalt—as now.

Nor let us weep that our delight is fled
Far from these carrion kites that scream below;
He wakes or sleeps with the enduring dead;
Thou canst not soar where he is sitting now.—

Dust to the dust! but the pure spirit shall flow
Back to the burning fountain whence it came,
A portion of the Eternal, which must glow
Through time and change, unquenchably the same,
Whilst thy cold embers choke the sordid hearth of shame.

Peace, peace! he is not dead, he doth not sleep—
He hath awakened from the dream of life—
'Tis we, who lost in stormy visions, keep
With phantoms an unprofitable strife,
And in mad trance, strike with our spirit's knife
Invulnerable nothings.—*We* decay
Like corpses in a charnel; fear and grief
Convulse us and consume us day by day,
And cold hopes swarm like worms within our living clay.

He has outsoared the shadow of our night;
Envy and calumny and hate and pain,
And that unrest which men miscall delight,
Can touch him not and torture not again;
From the contagion of the world's slow stain
He is secure, and now can never mourn
A heart grown cold, a head grown gray in vain;
Nor, when the spirit's self has ceased to burn,
With sparkless ashes load an unlamented urn.

He lives, he wakes—'tis Death is dead, not he;
Mourn not for Adonais.—Thou young Dawn,
Turn all thy dew to splendour, for from thee
The spirit thou lamentest is not gone;
Ye caverns and ye forests, cease to moan!
Cease, ye faint flowers and fountains, and thou Air
Which like a mourning veil thy scarf hadst thrown
O'er the abandoned Earth, now leave it bare
Even to the joyous stars which smile on its despair!

He is made one with Nature: there is heard
His voice in all her music, from the moan
Of thunder, to the song of night's sweet bird;
He is a presence to be felt and known

In darkness and in light, from herb and stone,
Spreading itself where'er that Power may move
Which has withdrawn his being to its own;
Which wields the world with never wearied love,
Sustains it from beneath, and kindles it above.

He is a portion of the loveliness
Which once he made more lovely: he doth bear
His part, while the one Spirit's plastic stress
Sweeps through the dull dense world, compelling there
All new successions to the forms they wear;
Torturing th' unwilling dross that checks its flight
To its own likeness, as each mass may bear;
And bursting in its beauty and its might
From trees and beasts and men into the Heaven's light.

The splendours of the firmament of time
May be eclipsed, but are extinguished not;
Like stars to their appointed height they climb
And death is a low mist which cannot blot
The brightness it may veil. When lofty thought
Lifts a young heart above its mortal lair,
And love and life contend in it, for what
Shall be its earthly doom, the dead live there
And move like winds of light on dark and stormy air.

The inheritors of unfulfilled renown
Rose from their thrones, built beyond mortal thought,
Far in the Unapparent. Chatterton
Rose pale,—his solemn agony had not
Yet faded from him; Sidney, as he fought
And as he fell and as he lived and loved
Sublimely mild, a Spirit without spot,
Arose; and Lucan, by his death approved:
Oblivion as they rose shrank like a thing reproved.

And many more, whose names on Earth are dark,
But whose transmitted effluence cannot die
So long as fire outlives the parent spark,
Rose, robed in dazzling immortality.

'Thou art become as one of us,' they cry,
'It was for thee yon kingless sphere has long
Swung blind in unascended majesty,
Silent alone amid an Heaven of Song.
Assume thy wingèd throne, thou Vesper of our throng!'

Who mourns for Adonais? Oh, come forth,
Fond wretch! and know thyself and him aright.
Clasp with thy panting soul the pendulous Earth;
As from a centre, dart thy spirit's light
Beyond all worlds, until its spacious might
Satiate the void circumference: then shrink
Even to a point within our day and night;
And keep thy heart light lest it make thee sink
When hope has kindled hope, and lured thee to the brink.

Or go to Rome, which is the sepulchre
Oh, not of him, but of our joy: 'tis nought
That ages, empires, and religions there
Lie buried in the ravage they have wrought;
For such as he can lend,—they borrow not
Glory from those who made the world their prey;
And he is gathered to the kings of thought
Who waged contention with their time's decay,
And of the past are all that cannot pass away.

Go thou to Rome,—at once the Paradise,
The grave, the city, and the wilderness;
And where its wrecks like shattered mountains rise,
And flowering weeds, and fragrant copses dress
The bones of Desolation's nakedness,
Pass, till the Spirit of the spot shall lead
Thy footsteps to a slope of green access
Where, like an infant's smile, over the dead
A light of laughing flowers along the grass is spread.

And gray walls moulder round, on which dull Time
Feeds, like slow fire upon a hoary brand;
And one keen pyramid with wedge sublime,
Pavilioning the dust of him who planned

This refuge for his memory, doth stand
Like flame transformed to marble; and beneath,
A field is spread, on which a newer band
Have pitched in Heaven's smile their camp of death,
Welcoming him we lose with scarce extinguished breath.

Here pause: these graves are all too young as yet
To have outgrown the sorrow which consigned
Its charge to each; and if the seal is set,
Here, on one fountain of a mourning mind,
Break it not thou! too surely shalt thou find
Thine own well full, if thou returnest home,
Of tears and gall. From the world's bitter wind
Seek shelter in the shadow of the tomb.
What Adonais is, why fear we to become?

The One remains, the many change and pass;
Heaven's light forever shines, Earth's shadows fly;
Life, like a dome of many-coloured glass,
Stains the white radiance of Eternity,
Until Death tramples it to fragments.—Die,
If thou wouldst be with that which thou dost seek!
Follow where all is fled!—Rome's azure sky,
Flowers, ruins, statues, music, words are weak
The glory they transfuse with fitting truth to speak.

Why linger, why turn back, why shrink, my Heart?
Thy hopes are gone before: from all things here
They have departed: thou shouldst now depart!
A light is passed from the revolving year,
And man, and woman; and what still is dear
Attracts to crush, repels to make thee wither.
The soft sky smiles,—the low wind whispers near;
'Tis Adonais calls! oh, hasten thither,
No more let Life divide what Death can join together.

That Light whose smile kindles the Universe,
That Beauty in which all things work and move,
That Benediction which the eclipsing Curse
Of birth can quench not, that sustaining Love

Which through the web of being blindly wove
By man and beast and earth and air and sea,
Burns bright or dim, as each are mirrors of
The fire for which all thirst; now beams on me,
Consuming the last clouds of cold mortality.

The breath whose might I have invoked in song
Descends on me; my spirit's bark is driven,
Far from the shore, far from the trembling throng
Whose sails were never to the tempest given;
The massy earth and spherèd skies are riven!
I am borne darkly, fearfully, afar;
Whilst, burning through the inmost veil of Heaven,
The soul of Adonais, like a star,
Beacons from the abode where the Eternal are.

JAMES HENRY LEIGH HUNT

[*1784-1859*]

523 Jenny Kiss'd Me

Jenny kiss'd me when we met,
Jumping from the chair she sat in;
Time, you thief, who love to get
Sweets into your list, put that in!
Say I'm weary, say I'm sad,
Say that health and wealth have miss'd me,
Say I'm growing old, but add,
Jenny kiss'd me.

524 Abou Ben Adhem

Abou Ben Adhem (may his tribe increase)
Awoke one night from a deep dream of peace,
And saw—within the moonlight in his room,
Making it rich and like a lily in bloom—
An angel, writing in a book of gold.
Exceeding peace had made Ben Adhem bold,

And to the presence in the room he said,
'What writest thou?'—The vision raised its head,
And, with a look made of all sweet accord,
Answered, 'The names of those who love the Lord.'
'And is mine one?' said Abou. 'Nay, not so,'
Replied the angel. Abou spoke more low,
But cheerly still, and said, 'I pray thee, then,
Write me as one that loves his fellow men.'

The angel wrote and vanished. The next night
It came again with a great wakening light,
And showed the names whom love of God had blessed,
And lo! Ben Adhem's name led all the rest.

JOHN KEATS

[1795-1821]

525

The Realm of Fancy

Ever let the Fancy roam!
Pleasure never is at home:
At a touch sweet Pleasure melteth,
Like to bubbles when rain pelteth;
Then let wingéd Fancy wander
Through the thought still spread beyond her:
Open wide the mind's cage-door,
She'll dart forth, and cloudward soar.
O sweet Fancy! let her loose;
Summer's joys are spoilt by use,
And the enjoying of the Spring
Fades as does its blossoming:
Autumn's red-lipp'd fruitage too,
Blushing through the mist and dew,
Cloys with tasting: What do then?
Sit thee by the ingle, when
The sear faggot blazes bright,
Spirit of a winter's night;
When the soundless earth is muffled,
And the cakéd snow is shuffled

From the ploughboy's heavy shoon;
When the Night doth meet the Noon
In a dark conspiracy
To banish Even from her sky.
—Sit thee there, and send abroad,
With a mind self-overaw'd
Fancy, high-commission'd:—send her!
She has vassals to attend her;
She will bring, in spite of frost,
Beauties that the earth hath lost;
She will bring thee, all together,
All delights of summer weather;
All the buds and bells of May
From dewy sward or thorny spray;
All the heapéd Autumn's wealth,
With a still, mysterious stealth:
She will mix these pleasures up
Like three fit wines in a cup,
And thou shalt quaff it:—thou shalt hear
Distant harvest-carols clear;
Rustle of the reapéd corn;
Sweet birds antheming the morn:
And, in the same moment—hark!
'Tis the early April lark,
Or the rooks, with busy caw,
Foraging for sticks and straw.
Thou shalt, at one glance, behold
The daisy and the marigold;
White-plumed lilies, and the first
Hedge-grown primrose that hath burst;
Shaded hyacinth, alway
Sapphire queen of the mid-May;
And every leaf, and every flower
Pearléd with the self-same shower.
Thou shalt see the field-mouse peep
Meagre from its celléd sleep;
And the snake all winter-thin
Cast on sunny bank its skin;
Freckled nest-eggs thou shalt see
Hatching in the hawthorn-tree,

When the hen-bird's wing doth rest
Quiet on her mossy nest;
Then the hurry and alarm
When the bee-hive casts its swarm;
Acorns ripe down-pattering,
While the autumn breezes sing.

Oh, sweet Fancy! let her loose;
Everything is spoilt by use:
Where's the cheek that doth not fade,
Too much gazed at? Where's the maid
Whose lip mature is ever new?
Where's the eye, however blue,
Doth not weary? Where's the face
One would meet in every place?
Where's the voice, however soft,
One would hear so very oft?
At a touch sweet Pleasure melteth
Like to bubbles when rain pelteth.
Let then wingéd Fancy find
Thee a mistress to thy mind:
Dulcet-eyed as Ceres' daughter,
Ere the God of Torment taught her
How to frown and how to chide;
With a waist and with a side
White as Hebe's, when her zone
Slipt its golden clasp, and down
Fell her kirtle to her feet,
While she held the goblet sweet,
And Jove grew languid.—Break the mesh
Of the Fancy's silken leash;
Quickly break her prison-string,
And such joys as these she'll bring:
—Let the wingéd Fancy roam!
Pleasure never is at home.

526

Ode on the Poets

Bards of Passion and of Mirth
Ye have left your souls on earth!

Have ye souls in heaven too,
Double-lived in regions new?
—Yes, and those of heaven commune
With the spheres of sun and moon;
With the noise of fountains wonderous
And the parle of voices thunderous;
With the whisper of heaven's trees
And one another, in soft ease
Seated on Elysian lawns
Browsed by none but Dian's fawns;
Underneath large blue-bells tented,
Where the daisies are rose-scented,
And the rose herself has got
Perfume which on earth is not;
Where the nightingale doth sing
Not a senseless, trancéd thing,
But divine melodious truth;
Philosophic numbers smooth;
Tales and golden histories
Of heaven and its mysteries.

Thus ye live on high, and then
On the earth ye live again;
And the souls ye left behind you
Teach us, here, the way to find you,
Where your other souls are joying,
Never slumber'd, never cloying.
Here, your earth-born souls still speak
To mortals, of their little week;
Of their sorrows and delights;
Of their passions and their spites;
Of their glory and their shame;
What doth strengthen and what maim:—
Thus ye teach us, every day,
Wisdom, though fled far away.

Bards of Passion and of Mirth
Ye have left your souls on earth!
Ye have souls in heaven too,
Double-lived in regions new!

527

The Mermaid Tavern

Souls of Poets dead and gone,
What Elysium have ye known,
Happy field or mossy cavern,
Choicer than the Mermaid Tavern?
Have ye tippled drink more fine
Than mine host's Canary wine?
Or are fruits of Paradise
Sweeter than those dainty pies
Of Venison? O generous food!
Drest as though bold Robin Hood
Would, with his Maid Marian,
Sup and bowse from horn and can.

I have heard that on a day
Mine host's sign-board flew away
Nobody knew whither, till
An astrologer's old quill
To a sheepskin gave the story—
Said he saw you in your glory
Underneath a new-old Sign
Sipping beverage divine,
And pledging with contented smack
The Mermaid in the Zodiac!

Souls of Poets dead and gone,
What Elysium have ye known—
Happy field or mossy cavern—
Choicer than the Mermaid Tavern?

528

Happy Insensibility

In a drear-nighted December,
Too happy, happy Tree,
Thy branches ne'er remember
Their green felicity:
The north cannot undo them

With a sleety whistle through them,
Nor frozen thawings glue them
From budding at the prime.

In a drear-nighted December,
Too happy, happy Brook,
Thy bubblings ne'er remember
Apollo's summer look;
But with a sweet forgetting
They stay their crystal fretting,
Never, never petting
About the frozen time.

Ah would 'twere so with many
A gentle girl and boy!
But were there ever any
Writhed not at passéd joy?
To know the change and feel it,
When there is none to heal it
Nor numbéd sense to steal it—
Was never said in rhyme.

529 Ode to a Nightingale

My heart aches, and a drowsy numbness pains
My sense, as though of hemlock I had drunk,
Or emptied some dull opiate to the drains
One minute past, and Lethe-wards had sunk:
'Tis not through envy of thy happy lot,
But being too happy in thy happiness,—
That thou, light-wingéd Dryad of the trees,
In some melodious plot
Of beechen green, and shadows numberless,
Singest of summer in full-throated ease.

O, for a draught of vintage, that hath been
Cool'd a long age in the deep-delvéd earth,
Tasting of Flora and the country green,
Dance, and Provençal song, and sun-burnt mirth!

O for a beaker full of the warm South,
  Full of the true, the blushful Hippocrene,
    With beaded bubbles winking at the brim,
        And purple-stainéd mouth;
That I might drink, and leave the world unseen,
  And with thee fade away into the forest dim:

Fade far away, dissolve, and quite forget
  What thou among the leaves hast never known,
The weariness, the fever, and the fret
  Here, where men sit and hear each other groan;
Where palsy shakes a few, sad, last gray hairs,
  Where youth grows pale, and spectre-thin, and dies;
    Where but to think is to be full of sorrow
        And leaden-eyed despairs;
  Where Beauty cannot keep her lustrous eyes,
    Or new Love pine at them beyond to-morrow.

Away! away! for I will fly to thee,
  Not charioted by Bacchus and his pards,
But on the viewless wings of Poesy,
  Though the dull brain perplexes and retards:
Already with thee! tender is the night,
  And haply the Queen-Moon is on her throne,
    Cluster'd around by all her starry Fays;
        But here there is no light
  Save what from heaven is with the breezes blown
    Through verdurous glooms and winding mossy ways.

I cannot see what flowers are at my feet,
  Nor what soft incense hangs upon the boughs,
But, in embalméd darkness, guess each sweet
  Wherewith the seasonable month endows
The grass, the thicket, and the fruit-tree wild;
  White hawthorn, and the pastoral eglantine;
    Fast fading violets cover'd up in leaves;
        And mid-May's eldest child,
  The coming musk-rose, full of dewy wine,
    The murmurous haunt of flies on summer eves.

Darkling I listen; and for many a time
 I have been half in love with easeful Death,
Call'd him soft names in many a muséd rhyme,
 To take into the air my quiet breath;
Now more than ever seems it rich to die,
 To cease upon the midnight with no pain,
  While thou art pouring forth thy soul abroad
   In such an ecstasy!
 Still wouldst thou sing, and I have ears in vain—
  To thy high requiem become a sod.

Thou wast not born for death, immortal Bird!
 No hungry generations tread thee down;
The voice I hear this passing night was heard
 In ancient days by emperor and clown:
Perhaps the self-same song that found a path
 Through the sad heart of Ruth, when, sick for home,
  She stood in tears amid the alien corn;
   The same that oft-times hath
 Charm'd magic casements, opening on the foam
  Of perilous seas, in faery lands forlorn.

Forlorn! the very word is like a bell
 To toll me back from thee to my sole self!
Adieu! the fancy cannot cheat so well
 As she is famed to do, deceiving elf.
Adieu! adieu! thy plaintive anthem fades
 Past the near meadows, over the still stream,
  Up the hill-side; and now 'tis buried deep
   In the next valley-glades:
 Was it a vision, or a waking dream?
  Fled is that music:—do I wake or sleep?

530 Ode on a Grecian Urn

Thou still unravish'd bride of quietness,
 Thou foster-child of Silence and slow Time,
Sylvan historian, who canst thus express
 A flowery tale more sweetly than our rhyme:
What leaf-fringed legend haunts about thy shape

Of deities or mortals, or of both,
In Tempe or the dales of Arcady?
What men or gods are these? What maidens loth?
What mad pursuit? ? What struggle to escape?
What pipes and timbrels? What wild ecstasy?

Heard melodies are sweet, but those unheard
Are sweeter; therefore, ye soft pipes, play on;
Not to the sensual ear, but, more endear'd,
Pipe to the spirit ditties of no tone:
Fair youth, beneath the trees, thou canst not leave
Thy song, nor ever can those trees be bare;
Bold Lover, never, never canst thou kiss,
Though winning near the goal—yet, do not grieve;
She cannot fade, though thou hast not thy bliss,
For ever wilt thou love, and she be fair!

Ah, happy, happy boughs! that cannot shed
Your leaves, nor ever bid the Spring adieu;
And, happy melodist, unwearièd,
For ever piping songs for ever new;
More happy love! more happy, happy love!
For ever warm and still to be enjoy'd,
For ever panting and for ever young;
All breathing human passion far above,
That leaves a heart high-sorrowful and cloy'd,
A burning forehead, and a parching tongue.

Who are these coming to the sacrifice?
To what green altar, O mysterious priest,
Lead'st thou that heifer lowing at the skies,
And all her silken flanks with garlands drest?
What little town by river or sea-shore,
Or mountain-built with peaceful citadel,
Is emptied of its folk, this pious morn?
And, little town, thy streets for evermore
Will silent be; and not a soul, to tell
Why thou art desolate, can e'er return.

O Attic shape! fair attitude! with brede
  Of marble men and maidens overwrought,
With forest branches and the trodden weed;
  Thou, silent form! dost tease us out of thought
As doth eternity. Cold Pastoral!
  When old age shall this generation waste,
    Thou shalt remain, in midst of other woe
  Than ours, a friend to man, to whom thou say'st,
'Beauty is truth, truth beauty,—that is all
    Ye know on earth, and all ye need to know.'

531 **Ode to Autumn**

SEASON of mists and mellow fruitfulness,
Close bosom-friend of the maturing sun;
Conspiring with him how to load and bless
With fruit the vines that round the thatch-eaves run;
To bend with apples the moss'd cottage-trees,
And fill all fruit with ripeness to the core;
To swell the gourd, and plump the hazel shells
With a sweet kernel; to set budding more,
And still more, later flowers for the bees,
Until they think warm days will never cease;
For Summer has o'erbrimm'd their clammy cells.

Who hath not seen Thee oft amid thy store?
Sometimes whoever seeks abroad may find
Thee sitting careless on a granary floor,
Thy hair soft-lifted by the winnowing wind;
Or on a half-reap'd furrow sound asleep,
Drowsed with the fume of poppies, while thy hook
Spares the next swath and all its twinéd flowers:
And sometimes like a gleaner thou dost keep
Steady thy laden head across a brook;
Or by a cider-press, with patient look,
Thou watchest the last oozings, hours by hours.

Where are the songs of Spring? Ay, where are they?
Think not of them, thou hast thy music too,
While barréd clouds bloom the soft-dying day

And touch the stubble-plains with rosy hue;
Then in a wailful choir the small gnats mourn
Among the river-sallows, borne aloft
Or sinking as the light wind lives or dies;
And full-grown lambs loud bleat from hilly bourn;
Hedge-crickets sing, and now with treble soft
The redbreast whistles from a garden-croft;
And gathering swallows twitter in the skies.

532 Ode to Psyche

O goddess! hear these tuneless numbers, wrung
By sweet enforcement and remembrance dear,
And pardon that thy secrets should be sung
Even into thine own soft-conchèd ear:
Surely I dream'd to-day, or did I see
The wingèd Psyche with awaken'd eyes?
I wander'd in a forest thoughtlessly,
And, on the sudden, fainting with surprise,
Saw two fair creatures, couchèd side by side
In deepest grass, beneath the whisp'ring roof
Of leaves and trembled blossoms, where there ran
A brooklet, scarce espied:
'Mid hush'd, cool-rooted flowers fragrant-eyed,
Blue, silver-white, and budded Tyrian,
They lay calm-breathing on the bedded grass;
Their arms embracèd, and their pinions too;
Their lips touch'd not, but had not bade adieu,
As if disjoinèd by soft-handed slumber,
And ready still past kisses to outnumber
At tender eye-dawn of aurorean love:
The wingèd boy I knew;
But who wast thou, O happy, happy dove?
His Psyche true!

O latest-born and loveliest vision far
Of all Olympus' faded hierarchy!
Fairer than Phœbe's sapphire-region'd star,
Or Vesper, amorous glow-worm of the sky;

Fairer than these, though temple thou hast none,
Nor altar heap'd with flowers;
Nor Virgin-choir to make delicious moan
Upon the midnight hours;
No voice, no lute, no pipe, no incense sweet
From chain-swung censer teeming;
No shrine, no grove, no oracle, no heat
Of pale-mouth'd prophet dreaming.

O brightest! though too late for antique vows,
Too, too late for the fond believing lyre,
When holy were the haunted forest boughs,
Holy the air, the water, and the fire;
Yet even in these days so far retired
From happy pieties, thy lucent fans,
Fluttering among the faint Olympians,
I see, and sing, by my own eyes inspired.
So let me be thy choir, and make a moan
Upon the midnight hours;
Thy voice, thy lute, thy pipe, thy incense sweet
From swingèd censer teeming:
Thy shrine, thy grove, thy oracle, thy heat
Of pale-mouth'd prophet dreaming.

Yes, I will be thy priest, and build a fane
In some untrodden region of my mind,
Where branchèd thoughts, new grown with pleasant pain,
Instead of pines shall murmur in the wind:
Far, far around shall those dark-cluster'd trees
Fledge the wild-ridgèd mountains steep by steep;
And there by zephyrs, streams, and birds, and bees,
The moss-lain Dryads shall be lull'd to sleep;
And in the midst of this wide quietness
A rosy sanctuary will I dress
With the wreath'd trellis of a working brain,
With buds, and bells, and stars without a name,
With all the gardener Fancy e'er could feign,
Who, breeding flowers, will never breed the same;

And there shall be for thee all soft delight
That shadowy thought can win,
A bright torch, and a casement ope at night,
To let the warm Love in!

533 Ode on Melancholy

No, no! go not to Lethe, neither twist
Wolf's-bane, tight-rooted, for its poisonous wine;
Nor suffer thy pale forehead to be kist
By nightshade, ruby grape of Proserpine;
Make not your rosary of yew-berries,
Nor let the beetle, nor the death-moth be
Your mournful Psyche, nor the downy owl
A partner in your sorrow's mysteries;
For shade to shade will come too drowsily,
And drown the wakeful anguish of the soul.

But when the melancholy fit shall fall
Sudden from heaven like a weeping cloud,
That fosters the droop-headed flowers all,
And hides the green hill in an April shroud;
Then glut thy sorrow on a morning rose,
Or on the rainbow of the salt sand-wave,
Or on the wealth of globèd peonies;
Or if thy mistress some rich anger shows,
Emprison her soft hand, and let her rave,
And feed deep, deep upon her peerless eyes.

She dwells with Beauty—Beauty that must die;
And Joy, whose hand is ever at his lips
Bidding adieu; and aching Pleasure nigh,
Turning to poison while the bee-mouth sips:
Ay, in the very temple of Delight
Veil'd Melancholy has her sovran shrine,
Though seen of none save him whose strenuous tongue
Can burst Joy's grape against his palate fine;
His soul shall taste the sadness of her might,
And be among her cloudy trophies hung.

534 The Eve of St. Agnes

St. Agnes' Eve!—Ah, bitter chill it was!
The owl, for all his feathers, was a-cold;
The hare limp'd trembling through the frozen grass,
And silent was the flock in woolly fold:
Numb were the Beadsman's fingers, while he told
His rosary, and while his frosted breath,
Like pious incense from a censer old,
Seem'd taking flight for heaven, without a death,
Past the sweet Virgin's picture, while his prayer he saith.

His prayer he saith, this patient, holy man;
Then takes his lamp, and riseth from his knees,
And back returneth, meagre, barefoot, wan,
Along the chapel aisle by slow degrees:
The sculptur'd dead, on each side, seem to freeze,
Emprison'd in black, purgatorial rails:
Knights, ladies, praying in dumb orat'ries,
He passeth by; and his weak spirit fails
To think how they may ache in icy hoods and mails.

Northward he turneth through a little door,
And scarce three steps, ere Music's golden tongue
Flatter'd to tears this aged man and poor;
But no—already had his deathbell rung;
The joys of all his life were said and sung:
His was harsh penance on St. Agnes' Eve:
Another way he went, and soon among
Rough ashes sat he for his soul's reprieve,
And all night kept awake, for sinners' sake to grieve.

That ancient Beadsman heard the prelude soft;
And so it chanc'd, for many a door was wide,
From hurry to and fro. Soon, up aloft,
The silver, snarling trumpets 'gan to chide:
The level chambers, ready with their pride,
Were glowing to receive a thousand guests:

The carved angels, ever eager-eyed,
Star'd where upon their heads the cornice rests,
With hair blown back, and wings put cross-wise on their breasts.

At length burst in the argent revelry,
With plume, tiara, and all rich array,
Numerous as shadows haunting fairily
The brain, new stuff'd, in youth, with triumphs gay
Of old romance. These let us wish away,
And turn, sole-thoughted, to one Lady there,
Whose heart had brooded, all that wintry day,
On love, and wing'd St. Agnes' saintly care,
As she had heard old dames full many times declare.

They told her how, upon St. Agnes' Eve,
Young virgins might have visions of delight,
And soft adorings from their loves receive
Upon the honey'd middle of the night
If ceremonies due they did aright;
As, supperless to bed they must retire,
And couch supine their beauties, lily white;
Nor look behind, nor sideways, but require
Of Heaven with upward eyes for all that they desire.

Full of this whim was thoughtful Madeline;
The music, yearning like a God in pain,
She scarcely heard: her maiden eyes divine,
Fix'd on the floor, saw many a sweeping train
Pass by—she heeded not at all: in vain
Came many a tiptoe, amorous cavalier,
And back retir'd; not cool'd by high disdain,
But she saw not: her heart was otherwhere:
She sigh'd for Agnes' dreams, the sweetest of the year.

She danc'd along with vague, regardless eyes,
Anxious her lips, her breathing quick and short:
The hallow'd hour was near at hand: she sighs
Amid the timbrels, and the throng'd resort
Of whisperers in anger, or in sport;

'Mid looks of love, defiance, hate and scorn,
Hoodwink'd with faery fancy; all amort,
Save to St. Agnes and her lambs unshorn,
And all the bliss to be before to-morrow morn.

So, purposing each moment to retire,
She linger'd still. Meantime, across the moors,
Had come young Porphyro, with heart on fire
For Madeline. Beside the portal doors,
Buttress'd from moonlight, stands he, and implores
All saints to give him sight of Madeline,
But for one moment in the tedious hours,
That he might gaze and worship all unseen;
Perchance speak, kneel, touch, kiss—in sooth such things have been.

He ventures in: let no buzz'd whisper tell:
All eyes be muffled, or a hundred swords
Will storm his heart, Love's fev'rous citadel;
For him, those chambers held barbarian hordes,
Hyena foemen, and hot-blooded lords,
Whose very dogs would execrations howl
Against his lineage: not one breast affords
Him any mercy, in that mansion foul,
Save one old beldame, weak in body and in soul.

Ah, happy chance! the aged creature came,
Shuffling along with ivory-headed wand,
To where he stood, hid from the torch's flame,
Behind a broad hall-pillar, far beyond
The sound of merriment and chorus bland:
He startled her; but soon she knew his face,
And grasp'd his fingers in her palsied hand,
Saying, 'Mercy, Porphyro! hie thee from this place;
They are all here to-night, the whole blood-thirsty race!

'Get hence! get hence! there's dwarfish Hildebrand;
He had a fever late and in the fit
He cursed thee and thine, both house and land:
Then there's that old Lord Maurice, not a whit

More tame for his grey hairs—Alas me! flit!
Flit like a ghost away.'—' Ah, Gossip dear,
We're safe enough; here in this armchair sit,
And tell me how '—' Good Saints! not here, not here;
Follow me, child, or else these stones will be thy bier.'

He follow'd through a lowly arched way,
Brushing the cobwebs with his lofty plume;
And as she mutter'd ' Well-a—well-a-day!
He found him in a little moonlight room,
Pale, lattic'd, chill, and silent as a tomb.
' Now tell me where is Madeline,' said he,
' O tell me, Angela, by the holy loom
Which none but secret sisterhood may see,
When they St. Agnes' wool are weaving piously.'

' St. Agnes! Ah! it is St. Agnes' Eve—
Yet men will murder upon holy days:
Thou must hold water in a witch's sieve,
And be liege-lord of all the Elves and Fays,
To venture so: it fills me with amaze
To see thee, Porphyro!—St. Agnes' Eve!
God's help! my lady fair the conjurer plays
This very night: good angels here deceive!
But let me laugh awhile, I've mickle time to grieve.'

Feebly she laugheth in the languid moon,
While Porphyro upon her face doth look,
Like puzzled urchin on an aged crone
Who keepeth clos'd a wond'rous riddle-book,
As spectacled she sits in chimney nook.
But soon his eyes grew brilliant, when she told
His lady's purpose; and he scarce could brook
Tears, at the thought of those enchantments cold,
And Madeline asleep in lap of legends old.

Sudden a thought came like a full-blown rose,
Flushing his brow, and in his pained heart
Made purple riot: then doth he propose
A stratagem, that makes the beldame start:

'A cruel man, and impious thou art:
Sweet lady, let her pray, and sleep, and dream
Alone with her good angels, far apart
From wicked men like thee. Go, go!—I deem
Thou canst not surely be the same that thou didst seem.'

'I will not harm her, by all saints I swear,'
Quoth Porphyro: 'O may I ne'er find grace
When my weak voice shall whisper its last prayer,
If one of her soft ringlets I displace,
Or look with ruffian passion in her face:
Good Angela, believe me by these tears;
Or I will, even in a moment's space,
Awake, with horrid shout, my foemen's ears,
And beard them, though they be more fang'd than wolves
and bears.'

'Ah! why wilt thou affright a feeble soul?
A poor, weak, palsy-stricken churchyard thing,
Whose passing-bell may ere the midnight toll;
Whose prayers for thee, each morn and evening,
Were never miss'd.' Thus plaining, doth she bring
A gentler speech from burning Porphyro;
So woful, and of such deep sorrowing,
That Angela gives promise she will do
Whatever he shall wish, betide her weal or woe.

Which was, to lead him, in close secrecy,
Even to Madeline's chamber, and there hide
Him in a closet, of such privacy
That he might see her beauty unespied,
And win perhaps that night a peerless bride,
While legion'd faeries pac'd the coverlet,
And pale enchantment held her sleepy-eyed.
Never on such a night have lovers met,
Since Merlin paid his Demon all the monstrous debt.

'It shall be as thou wishest,' said the Dame:
'All cates and dainties shall be stored there
Quickly on this feast-night: by the tambour frame

Her own lute thou wilt see: no time to spare,
For I am slow and feeble, and scarce dare
On such a catering trust my dizzy head.
Wait here, my child, with patience; kneel in prayer
The while: Ah! thou must needs the lady wed,
Or may I never leave my grave among the dead.'

So saying, she hobbled off with busy fear.
The lover's endless minutes slowly pass'd;
The dame return'd, and whisper'd in his ear
To follow her; with agèd eyes aghast
From fright of dim espial. Safe at last,
Through many a dusky gallery, they gain
The maiden's chamber, silken, hush'd, and chaste;
Where Porphyro took covert, pleas'd amain.
His poor guide hurried back with agues in her brain.

Her falt'ring hand upon the balustrade
Old Angela was feeling for the stair,
When Madeline, St. Agnes' charmèd maid,
Rose, like a mission'd spirit, unaware:
With silver taper's light, and pious care,
She turn'd, and down the agèd gossip led
To a safe level matting. Now prepare,
Young Porphyro, for gazing on that bed;
She comes, she comes again, like ring-dove fray'd and fled.

Out went the taper as she hurried in;
Its little smoke, in pallid moonshine, died;
She clos'd the door, she panted, all akin
To spirits of the air, and visions wide:
No uttered syllable, or, woe betide!
But to her heart, her heart was voluble,
Paining with eloquence her balmy side;
As though a tongueless nightingale should swell
Her throat in vain, and die, heart-stifled, in her dell.

A casement high and triple-arch'd there was,
All garlanded with carven imag'ries
Of fruits, and flowers, and bunches of knot-grass,

And diamonded with panes of quaint device,
Unnumerable of stains and splendid dyes.
As are the tiger-moth's deep-damask'd wings;
And in the midst, 'mong thousand heraldries,
And twilight saints, and dim emblazonings,
A shielded scutcheon blush'd with blood of queens and kings.

Full on this casement shone the wintry moon,
And threw warm gules on Madeline's fair breast,
As down she knelt for heaven's grace and boon;
Rose-bloom fell on her hands, together prest,
And on her silver cross soft amethyst,
And on her hair a glory, like a saint:
She seem'd a splendid angel, newly drest,
Save wings, for heaven: Porphyro grew faint:
She knelt, so pure a thing, so free from mortal taint.

Anon his heart revives: her vespers done,
Of all its wreathèd pearls her hair she frees;
Unclasps her warmed jewels one by one;
Loosens her fragrant bodice; by degrees
Her rich attire creeps rustling to her knees;
Half-hidden, like a mermaid in seaweed,
Pensive awhile she dreams awake, and sees
In fancy, fair St. Agnes in her bed,
But dares not look behind, or all the charm is fled.

Soon, trembling in her soft and chilly nest,
In sort of wakeful swoon, perplex'd she lay,
Until the poppied warmth of sleep oppress'd
Her soothèd limbs, and soul fatigued away;
Flown, like a thought, until the morrow-day;
Blissfully haven'd both from joy and pain;
Clasp'd like a missal where swart Paynims pray;
Blinded alike from sunshine and from rain,
As though a rose should shut, and be a bud again.

Stol'n to this paradise, and so entranced,
Porphyro gazed upon her empty dress,
And listen'd to her breathing, if it chanced

To wake into a slumberous tenderness;
Which when he heard, that minute did he bless,
And breath'd himself: then from the closet crept,
Noiseless as fear in a wide wilderness,
And over the hush'd carpet, silent, stepped,
And 'tween the curtains peep'd, where, lo!—how fast she slept.

Then by the bed-side, where the faded moon
Made a dim, silver twilight, soft he set
A table, and, half-anguish'd, threw thereon
A cloth of woven crimson, gold, and jet:—
O for some drowsy Morphean amulet!
The boisterous, midnight, festive clarion,
The kettle-drum, and far-heard clarionet,
Affray his ears, though but in dying tone:—
The hall door shuts again, and all the noise is gone.

And still she slept an azure-lidded sleep,
In blanched linen, smooth, and lavender'd,
While he from forth the closet brought a heap
Of candied apple, quince, and plum, and gourd:
With jellies soother than the creamy curd,
And lucent syrops, tinct with cinnamon;
Manna and dates, in argosy transferr'd
From Fez; and spiced dainties, every one,
From silken Samarcand to cedar'd Lebanon.

These delicates he heap'd with glowing hand
On golden dishes and in baskets bright
Of wreathèd silver: sumptuous they stand
In the retired quiet of the night,
Filling the chilly room with perfume light.—
'And now, my love, my seraph fair, awake!
Thou art my heaven, and I thine eremite:
Open thine eyes, for meek St. Agnes' sake,
Or I shall drowse beside thee, so my soul doth ache.'

Thus whispering, his warm, unnerved arm
Sank in her pillow. Shaded was her dream
By the dusk curtains:—'twas a midnight charm

Impossible to melt as icèd stream:
The lustrous salvers in the moonlight gleam:
Broad golden fringe upon the carpet lies:
It seem'd he never, never could redeem
From such a steadfast spell his lady's eyes;
She mus'd awhile, entoil'd in woofed phantasies.

Awakening up, he took her hollow lute,—
Tumultuous,—and, in chords that tenderest be,
He play'd an ancient ditty, long since mute,
In Provence call'd, 'La belle dame sans mercy:'
Close to her ear touching the melody;—
Wherewith disturb'd, she utter'd a soft moan:
He ceased—she panted quick—and suddenly
Her blue affrighted eyes wide open shone:
Upon his knees he sank, as smooth-sculptured stone.

Her eyes were open, but she still beheld,
Now wide awake, the vision of her sleep:
There was a painful change, that nigh expell'd
The blisses of her dream so pure and deep
At which fair Madeline began to weep,
And moan forth witless words with many a sigh;
While still her gaze on Porphyro would keep;
Who knelt, with joined hands and piteous eye,
Fearing to move or speak, she look'd so dreamingly.

'Ah, Porphyro!' said she, 'but even now
Thy voice was at sweet tremble in mine ear,
Made tuneable with every sweetest vow;
And those sad eyes were spiritual and clear:
How chang'd thou art! how pallid, chill, and drear!
Give me that voice again, my Porphyro,
Those looks immortal, those complainings dear!
Oh leave me not in this eternal woe,
For if thou diest, my Love, I know not where to go.'

Beyond a mortal man impassion'd far
At these voluptuous accents, he arose,
Ethereal, flush'd, and like a throbbing star

Seen mid the sapphire heaven's deep repose;
Into her dream he melted, as the rose
Blendeth its odour with the violet,—
Solution sweet: meantime the frost-wind blows
Like Love's alarum pattering the sharp sleet
Against the window-panes; St. Agnes' moon hath set.

'Tis dark: quick pattereth the flaw-blown sleet:
'This is no dream, my bride, my Madeline!'
'Tis dark: the icèd gusts still rave and beat:
'No dream, alas! alas! and woe is mine!
Porphyro will leave me here to fade and pine.—
Cruel! what traitor could thee hither bring?
I curse not, for my heart is lost in thine,
Though thou forsakest a deceived thing:—
A dove forlorn and lost with sick unprunèd wing!'

'My Madeline! sweet dreamer! lovely bride!
Say, may I be for aye thy vassal blest?
Thy beauty's shield, heart-shap'd and vermeil dyed?
Ah, silver shrine, here will I take my rest
After so many hours of toil and quest,
A famish'd pilgrim,—saved by miracle.
Though I have found, I will not rob thy nest
Saving of thy sweet self; if thou think'st well
To trust, fair Madeline, to no rude infidel.

'Hark! 'tis an elfin-storm from faery land,
Of haggard seeming, but a boon indeed:
Arise—arise! the morning is at hand;—
The bloated wassaillers will never heed:—
Let us away, my love, with happy speed;
There are no ears to hear, or eyes to see,—
Drown'd all in Rhenish and the sleepy mead:
Awake! arise! my love, and fearless be,
For o'er the southern moors I have a home for thee.'

She hurried at his words, beset with fears,
For there were sleeping dragons all around,
At glaring watch, perhaps, with ready spears—

Down the wide stairs a darkling way they found.—
In all the house was heard no human sound.
A chain-droop'd lamp was flickering by each door;
The arras, rich with horseman, hawk, and hound,
Flutter'd in the besieging wind's uproar
And the long carpets rose along the gusty floor.

They glide, like phantoms, into the wide hall;
Like phantoms, to the iron porch, they glide;
Where lay the Porter, in uneasy sprawl,
With a huge empty flagon by his side:
The wakeful bloodhound rose, and shook his hide,
But his sagacious eye an inmate owns:
By one, and one, the bolts full easy slide:—
The chains lie silent on the footworn stones;—
The key turns, and the door upon its hinges groans.

And they are gone: aye, ages long ago
These lovers fled away into the storm.
That night the Baron dreamt of many a woe,
And all his warrior-guests, with shade and form
Of witch, and demon, and large coffin-worm,
Were long be-nightmar'd. Angela the old
Died palsy-twitch'd, with meagre face deform;
The Beadsman, after thousand aves told,
For aye unsought for slept among his ashes cold.

535 La Belle Dame Sans Merci

'O what can ail thee, knight-at-arms,
Alone and palely loitering?
The sedge has wither'd from the lake,
And no birds sing.

'O what can ail thee, knight-at-arms!
So haggard and so woe-begone?
The squirrel's granary is full,
And the harvest's done.

'I see a lily on thy brow
  With anguish moist and fever-dew,
And on thy cheeks a fading rose
  Fast withereth too.

'I met a lady in the meads,
  Full beautiful—a faery's child,
Her hair was long, her foot was light,
  And her eyes were wild.

'I made a garland for her head,
  And bracelets too, and fragrant zone;
She look'd at me as she did love,
  And made sweet moan.

'I set her on my pacing steed
  And nothing else saw all day long,
For sidelong would she bend, and sing
  A fairy's song.

'She found me roots of relish sweet,
  And honey wild and manna-dew,
And sure in language strange she said
  "I love thee true."

'She took me to her elfin grot,
  And there she wept and sigh'd full sore,
And there I shut her wild wild eyes
  With kisses four.

'And there she lulléd me asleep,
  And there I dream'd—Ah! woe betide!
The latest dream I ever dream'd
  On the cold hill's side.

'I saw pale kings and princes too,
  Pale warriors, death-pale were they all,
They cried—"La belle Dame sans Merci
  Hath thee in thrall!"

'I saw their starved lips in the gloam
  With horrid warning gapéd wide,
And I awoke and found me here
  On the cold hill's side.

'And this is why I sojourn here
  Alone and palely loitering,
Though the sedge is wither'd from the lake,
  And no birds sing.'

536

On the Grasshopper and Cricket

The poetry of earth is never dead;
When all the birds are faint with the hot sun,
And hide in cooling trees, a voice will run
From hedge to hedge about the new-mown mead;
That is the grasshopper's—he takes the lead
In summer luxury,—he has never done
With his delights, for when tired out with fun
He rests at ease beneath some pleasant weed.
The poetry of earth is ceasing never:
On a lone winter evening, when the frost
Has wrought a silence, from the stove there shrills
The cricket's song, in warmth increasing ever,
And seems to one in drowsiness half lost,
The grasshopper's among some grassy hills.

537

On First Looking into Chapman's Homer

Much have I travell'd in the realms of gold
And many goodly states and kingdoms seen;
Round many western islands have I been
Which bards in fealty to Apollo hold.

Oft of one wide expanse had I been told
That deep-brow'd Homer ruled as his demesne:
Yet did I never breathe its pure serene
Till I heard Chapman speak out loud and bold:

—Then felt I like some watcher of the skies
When a new planet swims into his ken;
Or like stout Cortez—when with eagle eyes

He stared at the Pacific—and all his men
Look'd at each other with a wild surmise—
Silent, upon a peak in Darien.

538 To Sleep

O soft embalmer of the still midnight!
  Shutting with careful fingers and benign
Our gloom-pleased eyes, embower'd from the light,
  Enshaded in forgetfulness divine;
O soothest Sleep! if so it please thee, close,
  In midst of this thine hymn, my willing eyes,
Or wait the amen, ere thy poppy throws
  Around my bed its lulling charities;
  Then save me, or the passèd day will shine
Upon my pillow, breeding many woes;
Save me from curious conscience, that still lords
  Its strength for darkness, burrowing like a mole;
Turn the key deftly in the oilèd wards,
  And seal the hushèd casket of my soul.

539 The Human Seasons

Four Seasons fill the measure of the year;
There are four seasons in the mind of Man:
He has his lusty Spring, when fancy clear
Takes in all beauty with an easy span:

He has his Summer, when luxuriously
Spring's honey'd cud of youthful thought he loves
To ruminate, and by such dreaming high
Is nearest unto heaven: quiet coves

His soul has in its Autumn, when his wings
He furleth close; contented so to look
On mists in idleness—to let fair things
Pass by unheeded as a threshold brook:—

He has his Winter too of pale misfeature,
Or else he would forego his mortal nature.

540 Great Spirits Now on Earth Are Sojourning

Great spirits now on earth are sojourning;
He of the cloud, the cataract, the lake,
Who on Helvellyn's summit, wide awake,
Catches his freshness from Archangel's wing;
He of the rose, the violet, the spring,
The social smile, the chain for Freedom's sake:
And lo!—whose steadfastness would never take
A meaner sound than Raphael's whispering.
And other spirits there are standing apart
Upon the forehead of the age to come;
These, these will give the world another heart
And other pulses. Hear ye not the hum
Of mighty workings in the human mart?
Listen awhile, ye nations, and be dumb.

541 The Terror of Death

When I have fears that I may cease to be
Before my pen has glean'd my teeming brain,
Before high-pilèd books, in charact'ry
Hold like rich garners the full-ripen'd grain;

When I behold, upon the night's starr'd face,
Huge cloudy symbols of a high romance,
And think that I may never live to trace
Their shadows, with the magic hand of chance;

And when I feel, fair Creature of an hour!
That I shall never look upon thee more,
Never have relish in the fairy power
Of unreflecting love—then on the shore
Of the wide world I stand alone, and think
Till Love and Fame to nothingness do sink.

542

Last Sonnet

Bright Star! would I were steadfast as thou art:—
Not in lone splendour hung aloft the night,
And watching, with eternal lids apart,
Like Nature's patient sleepless Eremite,

The moving waters at their priestlike task
Of pure ablution round earth's human shores,
Or gazing on the new soft fallen mask
Of snow upon the mountains and the moors:—

No—yet still steadfast, still unchangeable,
Pillow'd upon my fair Love's ripening breast
To feel for ever its soft fall and swell,
Awake for ever in a sweet unrest;

Still, still to hear her tender-taken breath,
And so live ever,—or else swoon to death.

WALTER SAVAGE LANDOR

[1775-1864]

543

Rose Aylmer

Ah, what avails the sceptred race!
  Ah, what the form divine!
What every virtue, every grace!
  Rose Aylmer, all were thine.

Rose Aylmer, whom these wakeful eyes
  May weep, but never see,
A night of memories and sighs
  I consecrate to thee.

544

Twenty Years Hence

Twenty years hence my eyes may grow,
If not quite dim, yet rather so;
Yet yours from others they shall know,
Twenty years hence.

Twenty years hence, though it may hap
That I be call'd to take a nap
In a cool cell where thunder-clap
Was never heard,

There breathe but o'er my arch of grass
A not too sadly sigh'd 'Alas!'
And I shall catch, ere you can pass,
That wingèd word.

545

Proud Word You Never Spoke

Proud word you never spoke, but you will speak
Four not exempt from pride some future day.
Resting on one white hand a warm wet cheek,
Over my open volume you will say,
'This man loved *me*'—then rise and trip away.

546

Absence

Here, ever since you went abroad,
If there be change, no change I see:
I only walk our wonted road,
The road is only walk'd by me.

Yes; I forgot; a change there is—
Was it of *that* you bade me tell?
I catch at times, at times I miss
The sight, the tone, I know so well.

547

Dirce

Stand close around, ye Stygian set,
  With Dirce in one boat convey'd!
Or Charon, seeing, may forget
  That he is old and she a shade.

548

Corinna to Tanagra, from Athens

Tanagra! think not I forget
  Thy beautifully storied streets;
Be sure my memory bathes yet
  In clear Thermodon, and yet greets
The blithe and liberal shepherd-boy,
Whose sunny bosom swells with joy
When we accept his matted rushes
Upheav'd with sylvan fruit; away he bounds, and
  blushes.

A gift I promise: one I see
  Which thou with transport wilt receive,
The only proper gift for thee,
  Of which no mortal shall bereave
In later times thy mouldering walls,
Until the last old turret falls;
A crown, a crown from Athens won,
A crown no God can wear, beside Latona's son.

There may be cities who refuse
  To their own child the honours due,
And look ungently on the Muse;
  But ever shall those cities rue
The dry, unyielding, niggard breast,
Offering no nourishment, no rest,
To that young head which soon shall rise
Disdainfully, in might and glory, to the skies.

Sweetly where cavern'd Dirce flows
 Do white-arm'd maidens chant my lay,
Flapping the while with laurel-rose
 The honey-gathering tribes away;
And sweetly, sweetly Attic tongues
Lisp your Corinna's early songs;
To her with feet more graceful come
The verses that have dwelt in kindred breasts at home.

O let thy children lean aslant
 Against the tender mother's knee,
And gaze into her face, and want
 To know what magic there can be
In words that urge some eyes to dance,
While others as in holy trance
Look up to heaven: be such my praise!
Why linger? I must haste, or lose the Delphic bays.

549 Mother, I Cannot Mind My Wheel

Mother, I cannot mind my wheel;
 My fingers ache, my lips are dry:
Oh! if you felt the pain I feel!
 But oh, who ever felt as I?
No longer could I doubt him true—
 All other men may use deceit;
He always said my eyes were blue,
 And often swore my lips were sweet.

550 Well I Remember

Well I remember how you smiled
 To see me write your name upon
The soft sea-sand—'*O! what a child!*
 You think you're writing upon stone!'

I have since written what no tide
 Shall ever wash away, what men
Unborn shall read o'er ocean wide
 And find Ianthe's name again.

551

No, My Own Love

No, my own love of other years!
  No, it must never be.
Much rests with you that yet endears,
  Alas! but what with me?

Could those bright years o'er me revolve
  So gay, o'er you so fair,
The pearl of life we would dissolve,
  And each the cup might share.

You show that truth can ne'er decay,
  Whatever fate befalls;
I, that the myrtle and the bay
  Shoot fresh on ruined walls.

552

Robert Browning

There is delight in singing, though none hear
Beside the singer; and there is delight
In praising, though the praiser sit alone
And see the praised far off him, far above.
Shakespeare is not our poet, but the world's,
Therefore on him no speech! and brief for thee,
Browning! Since Chaucer was alive and hale,
No man hath walked along our roads with step
So active, so inquiring eye, or tongue
So varied in discourse. But warmer climes
Give brighter plumage, stronger wing: the breeze
Of Alpine heights thou playest with, borne on
Beyond Sorrento and Amalfi, where
The Siren waits thee, singing song for song.

553

The Death of Artemidora

'Artemidora! Gods invisible,
While thou art lying faint along the couch,
Have tied the sandal to thy veinèd feet
And stand beside thee, ready to convey

Thy weary steps where other rivers flow.
Refreshing shades will waft thy weariness
Away, and voices like thine own come nigh
And nearer, and solicit an embrace.'
  Artemidora sigh'd, and would have pressed
The hand now pressing hers, but was too weak.
Iris stood over her dark hair unseen
While thus Elpenor spake. He looked into
Eyes that had given light and life erewhile
To those above them, but now dim with tears
And wakefulness. Again he spake of joy
Eternal. At that word, that sad word, *joy,*
Faithful and fond her bosom heav'd once more:
Her head fell back; and now a loud deep sob
Swell'd thro' the darken'd chamber; 'twas not hers.

554

IPHIGENEIA

IPHIGENEIA, when she heard her doom
At Aulis, and when all beside the king
Had gone away, took his right hand, and said,
"O father, I am young and very happy.
I do not think the pious Calchas heard
Distinctly what the Goddess spake. Old-age
Obscures the senses. If my nurse, who knew
My voice so well, sometimes misunderstood
While I was resting on her knee both arms
And hitting it to make her mind my words,
And looking in her face, and she in mine,
Might he not also hear one word amiss,
Spoken from so far off, even from Olympus?"
The father placed his cheek upon her head,
And tears dropped down it, but the king of men
Replied not. Then the maiden spake once more.
"O father! sayst thou nothing? Hear'st thou not
Me whom thou ever hast, until this hour,
Listened to fondly, and awakened me
To hear my voice among the voice of birds,
When it was inarticulate as theirs,

And the down deadened it within the nest?"
He moved her gently from him, silent still,
And this, and this alone, brought tears from her,
Although she saw fate nearer: then with sighs,
"I thought to have laid down my hair before
Benignant Artemis, and not have dimmed
Her polished altar with my virgin blood;
I thought to have selected the white flowers
To please the nymphs, and to have asked of each
By name, and with no sorrowful regret,
Whether, since both my parents willed the change,
I might at Hymen's feet bend my clipt brow;
And (after those who mind us girls the most)
Adore our own Athena, that she would
Regard me mildly with her azure eyes.
But, father! to see you no more, and see
Your love, O father! go ere I am gone"—
Gently he moved her off, and drew her back,
Bending his lofty head far over hers,
And the dark depths of nature heaved and burst.
He turned away; not far, but silent still.
She now first shuddered; for in him so nigh,
So long a silence seemed the approach of death,
And like it. Once again she raised her voice.
"O father! if the ships are now detained,
And all your vows move not the Gods above,
When the knife strikes me there will be one prayer
The less to them: and purer can there be
Any, or more fervent than the daughter's prayer
For her dear father's safety and success?"
A groan that shook him shook not his resolve.
An aged man now entered, and without
One word, stept slowly on, and took the wrist
Of the pale maiden. She looked up, and saw
The fillet of the priest and calm cold eyes.
Then turned she where her parent stood, and cried
"O father! grieve no more: the ships can sail."

555

'Do You Remember Me?'

'Do you remember me? or are you proud?'
Lightly advancing thro' her star-trimm'd crowd,
Ianthe said, and looked into my eyes.
'A *yes*, a *yes*, to both: for Memory
Where you but once have been must ever be,
And at your voice Pride from his throne must rise.'

556

For an Epitaph at Fiesole

Lo! where the four mimosas blend their shade
In calm repose at last is Landor laid,
For ere he slept he saw them planted here
By her his soul had ever held most dear,
And he had lived enough when he had dried her tear.

557

On Lucretia Borgia's Hair

Borgia, thou once wert almost too august
And high for adoration; now thou'rt dust;
All that remains of thee these plaits unfold,
Calm hair, meandering in pellucid gold.

558

On His Seventy-Fifth Birthday

I strove with none; for none was worth my strife,
Nature I loved, and next to Nature, Art;
I warmed both hands before the fire of life,
It sinks, and I am ready to depart.

559

To My Ninth Decade

To my ninth decade I have totter'd on,
And no soft arm bends now my steps to steady;
She, who once led me where she would, is gone,
So when he calls me, Death shall find me ready.

560 DEATH STANDS ABOVE ME

DEATH stands above me, whispering low
  I know not what into my ear;
Of his strange language all I know
  Is, there is not a word of fear.

561 ON LIVING TOO LONG

Is it not better at an early hour
  In its calm cell to rest the weary head,
While birds are singing and while blooms the bower,
  Than sit the fire out and go starv'd to bed?

THOMAS HOOD

[*1798-1845*]

562 FAIR INES

O SAW ye not fair Ines?
  She's gone into the West,
To dazzle when the sun is down,
  And rob the world of rest:
She took our daylight with her,
  The smiles that we love best,
With morning blushes on her cheek,
  And pearls upon her breast.

O turn again, fair Ines,
  Before the fall of night,
For fear the Moon should shine alone,
  And stars unrivall'd bright;
And blessèd will the lover be
  That walks beneath their light,
And breathes the love against thy cheek
  I dare not even write!

Would I had been, fair Ines,
  That gallant cavalier,
Who rode so gaily by thy side,
  And whisper'd thee so near!
Were there no bonny dames at home,
  Or no true lovers here,
That he should cross the seas to win
  The dearest of the dear?

I saw thee, lovely Ines,
  Descend along the shore,
With bands of noble gentlemen,
  And banners waved before;
And gentle youth and maidens gay,
  And snowy plumes they wore:
It would have been a beauteous dream,—
  If it had been no more!

Alas, alas! fair Ines,
  She went away with song,
With Music waiting on her steps,
  And shoutings of the throng;
But some were sad, and felt no mirth,
  But only Music's wrong,
In sounds that sang Farewell, farewell,
  To her you've loved so long.

Farewell, farewell, fair Ines!
  That vessel never bore
So fair a lady on its deck,
  Nor danced so light before,—
Alas for pleasure on the sea,
  And sorrow on the shore!
The smile that bless'd one lover's heart
  Has broken many more!

563

The Bridge of Sighs

One more Unfortunate
Weary of breath
Rashly importunate,
Gone to her death!

Take her up tenderly,
Lift her with care;
Fashion'd so slenderly,
Young, and so fair!

Look at her garments
Clinging like cerements;
Whilst the wave constantly
Drips from her clothing;
Take her up instantly,
Loving, not loathing.

Touch her not scornfully;
Think of her mournfully,
Gently and humanly;
Not of the stains of her—
All that remains of her
Now is pure womanly.

Make no deep scrutiny
Into her mutiny
Rash and undutiful:
Past all dishonour,
Death has left on her
Only the beautiful.

Still, for all slips of hers,
One of Eve's family—
Wipe those poor lips of hers
Oozing so clammily.

Loop up her tresses
Escaped from the comb,
Her fair auburn tresses;
Whilst wonderment guesses
Where was her home?

Who was her father?
Who was her mother?
Had she a sister?
Had she a brother?
Or was there a dearer one
Still, and a nearer one
Yet, than all other?

Alas! for the rarity
Of Christian charity
Under the sun!
O! it was pitiful!
Near a whole city full,
Home she had none.

Sisterly, brotherly,
Fatherly, motherly
Feelings had changed:
Love, by harsh evidence,
Thrown from its eminence;
Even God's providence
Seeming estranged.

Where the lamps quiver
So far in the river,
With many a light
From window and casement,
From garret to basement,
She stood, with amazement,
Houseless by night.

The bleak wind of March
Made her tremble and shiver;
But not the dark arch,
Or the black flowing river:

Mad from life's history,
Glad to death's mystery
Swift to be hurl'd—
Any where, any where
Out of the world!

In she plunged boldly,
No matter how coldly
The rough river ran,
Over the brink of it,—
Picture it, think of it,
Dissolute Man!
Lave in it, drink of it,
Then, if you can!

Take her up tenderly,
Lift her with care;
Fashion'd so slenderly,
Young, and so fair!

Ere her limbs frigidly
Stiffen too rigidly,
Decently, kindly,
Smooth and compose them;
And her eyes, close them,
Staring so blindly!

Dreadfully staring
Thro' muddy impurity,
As when with the daring
Last look of despairing
Fix'd on futurity.

Perishing gloomily,
Spurr'd by contumely,
Cold inhumanity,
Burning insanity,
Into her rest.
—Cross her hands humbly
As if praying dumbly,
Over her breast!

Owning her weakness,
Her evil behaviour,
And leaving, with meekness,
Her sins to her Saviour.

564

The Death Bed

We watch'd her breathing thro' the night,
Her breathing soft and low,
As in her breast the wave of life
Kept heaving to and fro.

But when the morn came dim and sad
And chill with early showers,
Her quiet eyelids closed—she had
Another morn than ours.

565

Past and Present

I remember, I remember
The house where I was born,
The little window where the sun
Came peeping in at morn;
He never came a wink too soon
Nor brought too long a day;
But now, I often wish the night
Had borne my breath away.

I remember, I remember
The roses, red and white,
The violets, and the lily-cups—
Those flowers made of light!
The lilacs where the robin built,
And where my brother set
The laburnum on his birthday,—
The tree is living yet!

I remember, I remember
Where I was used to swing,
And thought the air must rush as fresh
To swallows on the wing;
My spirit flew in feathers then
That is so heavy now,
And summer pools could hardly cool
The fever on my brow.

I remember, I remember
The fir-trees dark and high;
I used to think their slender tops
Were close against the sky:
It was a childish ignorance,
But now 'tis little joy
To know I'm farther off from Heaven
Than when I was a boy.

SIR AUBREY DE VERE

[1788-1846]

566

Glengariff

I

Gazing from each low bulwark of this bridge,
How wonderful the contrast! Dark as night,
Here, amid cliffs and woods, with headlong might
The black stream whirls, through ferns and drooping sedge,
'Neath twisted roots moss-brown, and weedy ledge,
Gushing;—aloft, from yonder birch-clad height
Leaps into air a cataract, snow-white;
Falling to gulfs obscure. The mountain ridge,
Like a grey Warder, guardian of the scene,
Above the cloven gorge gloomily towers:
O'er the dim woods a gathering tempest lours;
Save where athwart the moist leaves' lucid green
A sunbeam, glancing through disparted showers,
Sparkles along the rill with diamond sheen!

II

A sun-burst on the Bay! Turn and behold!
The restless waves, resplendent in their glory,
Sweep glittering past yon purpled promontory,
Bright as Apollo's breastplate. Bathed in gold,
Yon bastioned islet gleams. Thin mists are rolled,
Translucent, through each glen. A mantle hoary
Veils those peaked hills shapely as e'er in story
Delphic, or Alpine, or Vesuvian old,
Minstrels have sung. From rock and headland proud
The wild wood spreads its arms around the bay:
The manifold mountain cones, now dark, now bright,
Now seen, now lost, alternate from rich light
To spectral shade; and each dissolving cloud
Reveals new mountains while it floats away.

HARTLEY COLERIDGE

[*1796-1849*]

567

She Is Not Fair

She is not fair to outward view
As many maidens be;
Her loveliness I never knew
Until she smiled on me.
O then I saw her eye was bright,
A well of love, a spring of light.

But now her looks are coy and cold,
To mine they ne'er reply,
And yet I cease not to behold
The love-light in her eye:
Her very frowns are fairer far
Than smiles of other maidens are.

JOSEPH BLANCO WHITE

[*1775-1841*]

568

To Night

Mysterious Night! when our first parent knew
Thee from report divine, and heard thy name,
Did he not tremble for this lovely frame,
This glorious canopy of light and blue?
Yet 'neath a curtain of translucent dew,
Bathed in the rays of the great setting flame,
Hesperus with the host of heaven came,
And lo! Creation widened in man's view.

Who could have thought such darkness lay concealed
Within thy beams, O sun! or who could find,
Whilst fly and leaf and insect stood revealed,
That to such countless orbs thou mad'st us blind!
Why do we then shun death with anxious strife?
If Light can thus deceive, wherefore not Life?

GEORGE DARLEY

[*1795-1846*]

569

The Loveliness of Love

It is not Beauty I demand,
  A crystal brow, the moon's despair,
Nor the snow's daughter, a white hand,
  Nor mermaid's yellow pride of hair:

Tell me not of your starry eyes,
  Your lips that seem on roses fed,
Your breasts, where Cupid tumbling lies
  Nor sleeps for kissing of his bed:—

A bloomy pair of vermeil cheeks
  Like Hebe's in her ruddiest hours,
A breath that softer music speaks
  Than summer winds a-wooing flowers,

These are but gauds; nay, what are lips:
  Coral beneath the ocean-stream,
Whose brink when your adventurer slips
  Full oft he perisheth on them.

And what are cheeks but ensigns oft
  That wave hot youth to fields of blood?
Did Helen's breast, though ne'er so soft,
  Do Greece or Ilium any good?

Eyes can with baleful ardour burn;
  Poison can breathe, than erst perfumed;
There's many a white hand holds an urn
  With lovers' hearts to dust consumed.

For crystal brows there's nought within;
  They are but empty cells for pride;
He who the Syren's hair would win
  Is mostly strangled in the tide.

Give me, instead of Beauty's bust,
  A tender heart, a loyal mind
Which with temptation I would trust,
  Yet never link'd with error find,—

One in whose gentle bosom I
  Could pour my secret heart of woes,
Like the case-burthen'd honey-fly
  That hides his murmurs in the rose—

My earthly Comforter! whose love
  So indefeasible might be
That, when my spirit wonn'd above
  Hers could not stay, for sympathy.

THOMAS BABINGTON MACAULAY, LORD MACAULAY

[*1800-1859*]

570 The Armada

Attend, all ye who list to hear our noble England's praise;
I tell of the thrice famous deeds she wrought in ancient days,
When that great fleet invincible against her bore in vain
The richest spoils of Mexico, the stoutest hearts of Spain:
It was about the lovely close of a warm summer day,
There came a gallant merchant-ship full sail to Plymouth Bay;
Her crew had seen Castile's black fleet beyond Aurigny's isle,
At earliest twilight, on the waves lie heaving many a mile.
At sunrise she escaped their van, by God's especial grace,
And the tall *Pinta,* till the noon, had held her close in chase.
Forthwith a guard at every gun was placed along the wall;
The beacon blazed upon the roof of Edgecumbe's lofty hall;
Many a light fishing-bark put out to pry along the coast,
And with loose rein and bloody spur rode inland many a post.
With his white hair, unbonneted, the stout old sheriff comes;
Behind him march the halberdiers; before him sound the drums;
His yeomen round the market cross make clear an ample space;
For there behoves him to set up the standard of Her Grace.
And haughtily the trumpets peal, and gaily dance the bells,
As slow upon the labouring wind the royal blazon swells.
Look how the Lion of the sea lifts up his ancient crown,
And underneath his deadly paw treads the gay lilies down.
So stalked he when he turned to flight, on that famed Picard field,
Bohemia's plume, and Genoa's bow, and Caesar's eagle shield.
So glared he when at Agincourt in wrath he turned to bay,

And crushed and torn beneath his claws the princely hunters lay.
Ho! strike the flagstaff deep, sir Knight: ho! scatter flowers, fair maids:
Ho! gunners, fire a loud salute: ho! gallants, draw your blades:
Thou sun, shine on her joyously; ye breezes, waft her wide;
Our glorious *semper eadem,* the banner of our pride.
The freshening breeze of eve unfurled that banner's massy fold;
The parting gleam of sunshine kissed that haughty scroll of gold:
Night sank upon the dusky beach, and on the purple sea,
Such night in England ne'er had been, nor e'er again shall be.
From Eddystone to Berwick bounds, from Lynn to Milford Bay,
That time of slumber was as bright and busy as the day;
For swift to east and swift to west the ghastly war-flame spread,
High on St. Michael's Mount it shone: it shone on Beachy Head.
Far on the deep the Spaniard saw, along each southern shire,
Cape beyond cape, in endless range, those twinkling points of fire.
The fisher left his skiff to rock on Tamar's glittering waves:
The rugged miners poured to war from Mendip's sunless caves:
O'er Longleat's towers, o'er Cranbourne's oaks, the fiery herald flew
And roused the shepherds of Stonehenge, the rangers of Beaulieu.
Right sharp and quick the bells all night rang out from Bristol town,
And ere the day three hundred horse had met on Clifton down;
The sentinel on Whitehall gate looked forth into the night,
And saw o'erhanging Richmond Hill that streak of blood-red light.

Then bugle's note and cannon's roar the death-like silence
broke,
And with one start, and with one cry, the royal city woke.
At once on all her stately gates arose the answering fires;
At once the wild alarum clashed from all her reeling spires;
From all the batteries of the Tower pealed loud the voice
of fear;
And all the thousand masts of Thames sent back a louder
cheer:
And from the farthest wards was heard the rush of hurrying
feet,
And the broad streams of pikes and flags rushed down each
roaring street;
And broader still became the blaze, and louder still the din,
As fast from every village round the horse came spurring in;
And eastward straight from wild Blackheath the warlike
errand went,
And roused in many an ancient hall the gallant squires of
Kent.
Southward from Surrey's pleasant hills flew those bright
couriers forth;
High on bleak Hampstead's swarthy moor they started for
the north;
And on, and on, without a pause, untired they bounded
still:
All night from tower to tower they sprang; they sprang from
hill to hill:
Till the proud Peak unfurled the flag o'er Darwin's rocky
dales
Till like volcanoes flared to heaven the stormy hills of
Wales,
Till twelve fair counties saw the blaze on Malvern's lonely
height,
Till streamed in crimson on the wind the Wrekin's crest of
light,
Till broad and fierce the star came forth on Ely's stately
fane,
And tower and hamlet rose in arms o'er all the boundless
plain;
Till Belvoir's lordly terraces the sign to Lincoln sent,

And Lincoln sped the message on o'er the wide vale of Trent;
Till Skiddaw saw the fire that burned on Gaunt's embattled pile,
And the red glare on Skiddaw roused the burghers of Carlisle.

571

A Jacobite's Epitaph

To my true king I offered, free from stain,
Courage and faith; vain faith, and courage vain.
For him I threw lands, honours, wealth, away,
And one dear hope, that was more prized than they.
For him I languished in a foreign clime,
Grey-haired with sorrow in my manhood's prime;
Heard on Lavernia Scargill's whispering trees,
And pined by Arno for my lovelier Tees;
Beheld each night my home in fevered sleep,
Each morning started from the dream to weep;
Till God, who saw me tried too sorely, gave
The resting-place I asked, an early grave.
O thou, whom chance leads to this nameless stone,
From that proud country which was once mine own,
By those white cliffs I never more must see,
By that dear language which I spake like thee,
Forget all feuds, and shed one English tear
O'er English dust. A broken heart lies here.

SIR WILLIAM EDMONDSTOUNE AYTOUN

[1813-1865]

572

The Refusal of Charon

Why look the distant mountains
So gloomy and so drear?
Are rain-clouds passing o'er them,
Or is the tempest near?

No shadow of the tempest
  Is there, nor wind nor rain—
'Tis Charon that is passing by,
  With all his gloomy train.

The young men march before him,
  In all their strength and pride;
The tender little infants,
  They totter by his side;
The old men walk behind him,
  And earnestly they pray—
Both old and young imploring him
  To grant some brief delay.

'O Charon! halt, we pray thee,
  Beside some little town,
Or near some sparkling fountain,
  Where the waters wimple down!
The old will drink and be refreshed,
  The young the disc will fling,
And the tender little children
  Pluck flowers beside the spring.'

'I will not stay my journey,
  Nor halt by any town,
Near any sparkling fountain,
  Where the waters wimple down:
The mothers coming to the well
  Would know the babes they bore,
The wives would clasp their husbands,
  Nor could I part them more.'

HUGH MILLER

[*1802-1856*]

573

The Babie

Nae shoon to hide her tiny taes,
  Nae stockings on her feet;
Her supple ankles white as snow
  Of early blossoms sweet.

Her simple dress of sprinkled pink,
  Her double, dimpled chin;
Her pucker'd lip and bonny mou',
  With nae ane tooth between.

Her een sae like her mither's een,
  Twa gentle, liquid things;
Her face is like an angel's face—
  We're glad she has nae wings.

HELEN SELINA, LADY DUFFERIN

[*1807-1867*]

574 LAMENT OF THE IRISH EMIGRANT

I'M sittin' on the stile, Mary,
  Where we sat side by side
On a bright May mornin' long ago,
  When first you were my bride;
The corn was springin' fresh and green,
  And the lark sang loud and high—
And the red was on your lip, Mary,
  And the love-light in your eye.

The place is little changed, Mary,
  The day is bright as then,
The lark's loud song is in my ear,
  And the corn is green again;
But I miss the soft clasp of your hand,
  And your breath warm on my cheek,
And I still keep list'ning for the words
  You never more will speak.

'Tis but a step down yonder lane,
  And the little church stands near,
The church where we were wed, Mary,
  I see the spire from here.

But the graveyard lies between, Mary,
And my step might break your rest—
For I've laid you, darling! down to sleep,
With your baby on your breast.

I'm very lonely now, Mary,
For the poor make no new friends,
But, O, they love the better still,
The few our Father sends!
And you were all *I* had, Mary,
My blessin' and my pride:
There's nothin' left to care for now,
Since my poor Mary died.

Yours was the good, brave heart, Mary,
That still kept hoping on,
When the trust in God had left my soul,
And my arm's young strength was gone:
There was comfort ever on your lip,
And the kind look on your brow—
I bless you, Mary, for that same,
Though you cannot hear me now.

I thank you for the patient smile
When your heart was fit to break,
When the hunger pain was gnawin' there,
And you hid it, for my sake!
I bless you for the pleasant word,
When your heart was sad and sore—
O, I'm thankful you are gone, Mary,
Where grief can't reach you more!

I'm biddin' you a long farewell,
My Mary—kind and true!
But I'll not forget you, darling!
In the land I'm goin' to;
They say there's bread and work for all,
And the sun shines always there—
But I'll not forget old Ireland,
Were it fifty times as fair!

And often in those grand old woods
  I'll sit, and shut my eyes,
And my heart will travel back again
  To the place where Mary lies;
And I'll think I see the little stile
  Where we sat side by side:
And the springin' corn, and the bright May morn,
  When first you were my bride.

CHARLES TENNYSON TURNER

[1808-1879]

575

Letty's Globe

When Letty had scarce pass'd her third glad year,
  And her young artless words began to flow,
One day we gave the child a colour'd sphere
  Of the wide earth, that she might mark and know,
By tint and outline, all its sea and land.
  She patted all the world; old empires peep'd
Between her baby fingers; her soft hand
  Was welcome at all frontiers. How she leap'd,
  And laugh'd and prattled in her world-wide bliss;
But when we turn'd her sweet unlearnèd eye
On our own isle, she raised a joyous cry—
'Oh! yes, I see it, Letty's home is there!'
  And while she hid all England with a kiss,
Bright over Europe fell her golden hair.

SIR SAMUEL FERGUSON

[1810-1886]

576

The Fair Hills of Ireland

From the Irish

A plenteous place is Ireland for hospitable cheer,
    Uileacan dubh O!
Where the wholesome fruit is bursting from the yellow
  barley ear;
    Uileacan dubh O!

There is honey in the trees where her misty vales expand,
And her forest paths in summer are by falling waters fann'd,
There is dew at high noontide there, and springs i' the
    yellow sand,
        On the fair hills of holy Ireland.

Curl'd he is and ringleted, and plaited to the knee—
        Uileacan dubh O!
Each captain who comes sailing across the Irish Sea;
        Uileacan dubh O!
And I will make my journey, if life and health but stand,
Unto that pleasant country, that fresh and fragrant strand,
And leave your boasted braveries, your wealth and high
    command,
        For the fair hills of holy Ireland.

Large and profitable are the stacks upon the ground,
        Uileacan dubh O!
The butter and the cream do wondrously abound;
        Uileacan dubh O!
The cresses on the water and the sorrels are at hand,
And the cuckoo's calling daily his note of music bland,
And the bold thrush sings so bravely his song i' the forests
    grand,
        On the fair hills of holy Ireland.

ELIZABETH BARRETT BROWNING

[*1806-1861*]

577

A Musical Instrument

What was he doing, the great god Pan,
  Down in the reeds by the river?
Spreading ruin and scattering ban,
Splashing and paddling with hoofs of a goat,
And breaking the golden lilies afloat
  With the dragon-fly on the river.

He tore out a reed, the great god Pan,
From the deep cool bed of the river;
The limpid water turbidly ran,
And the broken lilies a-dying lay,
And the dragon-fly had fled away,
Ere he brought it out of the river.

High on the shore sat the great god Pan,
While turbidly flow'd the river;
And hack'd and hew'd as a great god can
With his hard bleak steel at the patient reed,
Till there was not a sign of the leaf indeed
To prove it fresh from the river.

He cut it short, did the great god Pan
(How tall it stood in the river!),
Then drew the pith, like the heart of a man,
Steadily from the outside ring,
And notch'd the poor dry empty thing
In holes, as he sat by the river.

'This is the way,' laugh'd the great god Pan
(Laugh'd while he sat by the river),
'The only way, since gods began
To make sweet music, they could succeed.'
Then dropping his mouth to a hole in the reed,
He blew in power by the river.

Sweet, sweet, sweet, O Pan!
Piercing sweet by the river!
Blinding sweet, O great god Pan!
The sun on the hill forgot to die,
And the lilies revived, and the dragon-fly
Came back to dream on the river.

Yet half a beast is the great god Pan,
To laugh as he sits by the river,
Making a poet out of a man:
The true gods sigh for the cost and pain—
For the reed which grows nevermore again
As a reed with the reeds of the river.

Sonnets from the Portuguese

578 I

I THOUGHT once how Theocritus had sung
Of the sweet years, the dear and wished-for years,
Who each one in a gracious hand appears
To bear a gift for mortals, old or young:
And, as I mused it in its antique tongue,
I saw, in gradual vision through my tears,
The sweet, sad years, the melancholy years,
Those of my own life, who by turns had flung
A shadow across me. Straightway I was 'ware,
So weeping, how a mystic Shape did move
Behind me, and drew me backward by the hair;
And a voice said in mastery, while I strove,—
"Guess now who holds thee?"—"Death," I said. But, there,
The silver answer rang,—"Not Death, but Love."

579 II

BUT only three in all God's universe
Have heard this word thou hast said,—Himself, beside
Thee speaking, and me listening! and replied
One of us . . . *that* was God, . . . and laid the curse
So darkly on my eyelids, as to amerce
My sight from seeing thee,—that if I had died,
The deathweights, placed there, would have signified
Less absolute exclusion. "Nay" is worse
From God than from all others, O my friend!
Men could not part us with their worldly jars,
Nor the seas change us, nor the tempests bend;
Our hands would touch for all the mountain-bars:
And, heaven being rolled between us at the end,
We should but vow the faster for the stars.

580 III

UNLIKE are we, unlike, O princely Heart!
Unlike our uses and our destinies.
Our ministering two angels look surprise

On one another, as they strike athwart
Their wings in passing. Thou, bethink thee, art
A guest for queens to social pageantries,
With gages from a hundred brighter eyes
Than tears even can make mine, to play thy part
Of chief musician. What hast *thou* to do
With looking from the lattice-lights at me,
A poor, tired, wandering singer, singing through
The dark, and leaning up a cypress tree?
The chrism is on thine head,—on mine, the dew,—
And Death must dig the level where these agree.

581 IV

THOU hast thy calling to some palace-floor,
Most gracious singer of high poems! where
The dancers will break footing, from the care
Of watching up thy pregnant lips for more.
And dost thou lift this house's latch too poor
For hand of thine? and canst thou think and bear
To let thy music drop here unaware
In folds of golden fulness at my door?
Look up and see the casement broken in,
The bats and owlets builders in the roof!
My cricket chirps against thy mandolin.
Hush, call no echo up in further proof
Of desolation! there's a voice within
That weeps . . . as thou must sing . . . alone, aloof.

582 V

I LIFT my heavy heart up solemnly,
As once Electra her sepulchral urn,
And looking in thine eyes, I overturn
The ashes at thy feet. Behold and see
What a great heap of grief lay hid in me,
And how the red wild sparkles dimly burn
Through the ashen grayness. If thy foot in scorn
Could tread them out to darkness utterly,
It might be well perhaps. But if instead

Thou wait beside me for the wind to blow
The gray dust up, . . . those laurels on thine head,
O my Belovèd, will not shield thee so,
That none of all the fires shall scorch and shred
The hair beneath. Stand farther off then! go.

583 VI

Go from me. Yet I feel that I shall stand
Henceforward in thy shadow. Nevermore
Alone upon the threshold of my door
Of individual life, I shall command
The uses of my soul, nor lift my hand
Serenely in the sunshine as before,
Without the sense of that which I forbore—
Thy touch upon the palm. The widest land
Doom takes to part us, leaves thy heart in mine
With pulses that beat double. What I do
And what I dream include thee, as the wine
Must taste of its own grapes. And when I sue
God for myself, He hears that name of thine,
And sees within my eyes the tears of two.

584 VII

THE face of all the world is changed, I think,
Since first I heard the footsteps of thy soul
Move still, oh, still, beside me, as they stole
Betwixt me and the dreadful outer brink
Of obvious death, where I, who thought to sink,
Was caught up into love, and taught the whole
Of life in a new rhythm. The cup of dole
God gave for baptism, I am fain to drink,
And praise its sweetness, Sweet, with thee anear.
The names of country, heaven, are changed away
For where thou art or shalt be, there or here;
And this . . . this lute and song . . . loved yesterday,
(The singing angels know) are cnly dear
Because thy name moves right in what they say.

585 VIII

WHAT can I give thee back, O liberal
And princely giver, who hast brought the gold
And purple of thine heart, unstained, untold,
And laid them on the outside of the wall
For such as I to take or leave withal,
In unexpected largesse? am I cold,
Ungrateful, that for these most manifold
High gifts, I render nothing back at all?
Not so; not cold,—but very poor instead.
Ask God who knows. For frequent tears have run
The colors from my life, and left so dead
And pale a stuff, it were not fitly done
To give the same as pillow to thy head.
Go farther! let it serve to trample on.

586 IX

CAN it be right to give what I can give?
To let thee sit beneath the fall of tears
As salt as mine, and hear the sighing years
Re-sighing on my lips renunciative
Through those infrequent smiles which fail to live
For all thy adjurations? O my fears,
That this can scarce be right! We are not peers,
So to be lovers; and I own, and grieve,
That givers of such gifts as mine are, must
Be counted with the ungenerous. Out, alas!
I will not soil thy purple with my dust,
Nor breathe my poison on thy Venice-glass,
Nor give thee any love—which were unjust.
Beloved, I only love thee! let it pass.

587 X

YET, love, mere love, is beautiful indeed
And worthy of acceptation. Fire is bright,
Let temple burn, or flax; an equal light
Leaps in the flame from cedar-plank or weed:
And love is fire. And when I say at need

I love thee . . . mark! . . . *I love thee*—in thy sight
I stand transfigured, glorified aright,
With conscience of the new rays that proceed
Out of my face toward thine. There's nothing low
In love, when love the lowest: meanest creatures
Who love God, God accepts while loving so.
And what I *feel,* across the inferior features
Of what I *am,* doth flash itself, and show
How that great work of Love enhances Nature's.

588 XI

AND therefore if to love can be desert,
I am not all unworthy. Cheeks as pale
As these you see, and trembling knees that fail
To bear the burden of a heavy heart,—
This weary minstrel-life that once was girt
To climb Aornus, and can scarce avail
To pipe now 'gainst the valley nightingale
A melancholy music,—why advert
To these things? O Belovèd, it is plain
I am not of thy worth nor for thy place!
And yet, because I love thee, I obtain
From that same love this vindicating grace,
To live on still in love, and yet in vain,—
To bless thee, yet renounce thee to thy face.

589 XII

INDEED this very love which is my boast,
And which, when rising up from breast to brow,
Doth crown me with a ruby large enow
To draw men's eyes and prove the inner cost,—
This love even, all my worth, to the uttermost,
I should not love withal, unless that thou
Hadst set me an example, shown me how,
When first thine earnest eyes with mine were crossed,
And love called love. And thus, I cannot speak
Of love even, as a good thing of my own:

Thy soul hath snatched up mine all faint and weak,
And placed it by thee on a golden throne,—
And that I love (O soul, we must be meek!)
Is by thee only, whom I love alone.

590 XIII

And wilt thou have me fashion into speech
The love I bear thee, finding words enough,
And hold the torch out, while the winds are rough,
Between our faces, to cast light on each?—
I drop it at thy feet. I cannot teach
My hand to hold my spirit so far off
From myself—me—that I should bring thee proof
In words, of love hid in me out of reach.
Nay, let the silence of my womanhood
Commend my woman-love to thy belief,—
Seeing that I stand unwon, however wooed,
And rend the garment of my life, in brief,
By a most dauntless, voiceless fortitude,
Lest one touch of this heart convey its grief.

591 XIV

If thou must love me, let it be for nought
Except for love's sake only. Do not say
"I love her for her smile—her look—her way
Of speaking gently,—for a trick of thought
That falls in well with mine, and certes brought
A sense of pleasant ease on such a day"—
For these things in themselves, Belovèd, may
Be changed, or change for thee,—and love, so wrought,
May be unwrought so. Neither love me for
Thine own dear pity's wiping my cheeks dry,—
A creature might forget to weep, who bore
Thy comfort long, and lose thy love thereby!
But love me for love's sake, that evermore
Thou mayst love on, through love's eternity.

592 XV

Accuse me not, beseech thee, that I wear
Too calm and sad a face in front of thine;
For we two look two ways, and cannot shine
With the same sunlight on our brow and hair.
On me thou lookest with no doubting care,
As on a bee shut in a crystalline;
Since sorrow hath shut me safe in love's divine,
And to spread wing and fly in the outer air
Were most impossible failure, if I strove
To fail so. But I look on thee—on thee—
Beholding, besides love, the end of love,
Hearing oblivion beyond memory;
As one who sits and gazes from above,
Over the rivers to the bitter sea.

593 XVI

And yet, because thou overcomest so,
Because thou art more noble and like a king,
Thou canst prevail against my fears and fling
Thy purple round me, till my heart shall grow
Too close against thine heart henceforth to know
How it shook when alone. Why, conquering
May prove as lordly and complete a thing
In lifting upward, as in crushing low!
And as a vanquished soldier yields his sword
To one who lifts him from the bloody earth,
Even so, Belovèd, I at last record,
Here ends my strife. If *thou* invite me forth,
I rise above abasement at the word.
Make thy love larger to enlarge my worth.

594 XVII

My poet, thou canst touch on all the notes
God set between His After and Before,
And strike up and strike off the general roar
Of the rushing worlds a melody that floats
In a serene air purely. Antidotes
Of medicated music, answering for

Mankind's forlornest uses, thou canst pour
From thence into their ears. God's will devotes
Thine to such ends, and mine to wait on thine.
How, Dearest, wilt thou have me for most use?
A hope, to sing by gladly? or a fine
Sad memory, with thy songs to interfuse?
A shade, in which to sing—of palm or pine?
A grave, on which to rest from singing? Choose.

595 XVIII

I NEVER gave a lock of hair away
To a man, Dearest, except this to thee,
Which now upon my fingers thoughtfully,
I ring out to the full brown length and say
"Take it." My day of youth went yesterday:
My hair no longer bounds to my foot's glee,
Nor plant I it from rose or myrtle-tree,
As girls do, any more; it only may
Now shade on two pale cheeks the mark of tears,
Taught drooping from the head that hangs aside
Through sorrow's trick. I thought the funeral-shears
Would take this first, but love is justified,—
Take it thou, finding pure, from all those years,
The kiss my mother left here when she died.

596 XIX

THE soul's Rialto hath its merchandise;
I barter curl for curl upon that mart,
And from my poet's forehead to my heart
Receive this lock which outweighs argosies,—
As purply black, as erst to Pindar's eyes
The dim purpureal tresses gloomed athwart
The nine white Muse-brows. For this counterpart,
The bay-crown's shade, Belovèd, I surmise,
Still lingers on thy curl, it is so black!
Thus, with a fillet of smooth-kissing breath,
I tie the shadows safe from gliding back,
And lay the gift where nothing hindereth;

Here on my heart, as on thy brow, to lack
No natural heat till mine grows cold in death.

597 XX

Belovèd, my Belovèd, when I think
That thou wast in the world a year ago,
What time I sat alone here in the snow
And saw no footprint, heard the silence sink
No moment at thy voice, but, link by link,
Went counting all my chains as if that so
They never could fall off at any blow
Struck by thy possible hand,—why, thus I drink
Of life's great cup of wonder! Wonderful,
Never to feel thee thrill the day or night
With personal act or speech,—nor ever cull
Some prescience of thee with the blossoms white
Thou sawest growing! Atheists are as dull,
Who cannot guess God's presence out of sight.

598 XXI

Say over again, and yet once over again,
That thou dost love me. Though the word repeated
Should seem "a cuckoo-song," as thou dost treat it,
Remember, never to the hill or plain,
Valley and wood, without her cuckoo-strain
Comes the fresh Spring in all her green completed.
Belovèd, I, amid the darkness greeted
By a doubtful spirit-voice, in that doubt's pain
Cry, "Speak once more—thou lovest!" Who can fear
Too many stars, though each in heaven shall roll,
Too many flowers, though each shall crown the year?
Say thou dost love me, love me, love me—toll
The silver iterance!—only minding, Dear,
To love me also in silence with thy soul.

599 XXII

When our two souls stand up erect and strong,
Face to face, silent, drawing nigh and nigher,

Until the lengthening wings break into fire
At either curvèd point,—what bitter wrong
Can the earth do to us, that we should not long
Be here contented? Think. In mounting higher,
The angels would press on us and aspire
To drop some golden orb of perfect song
Into our deep, dear silence. Let us stay
Rather on earth, Belovèd,—where the unfit
Contrarious moods of men recoil away
And isolate pure spirits, and permit
A place to stand and love in for a day,
With darkness and the death-hour rounding it.

600 XXIII

Is it indeed so? If I lay here dead,
Wouldst thou miss any life in losing mine?
And would the sun for thee more coldly shine
Because of grave-damps falling round my head?
I marvelled, my Belovèd, when I read
Thy thought so in the letter. I am thine—
But . . . *so* much to thee? Can I pour thy wine
While my hands tremble? Then my soul, instead
Of dreams of death, resumes life's lower range.
Then, love me, Love! look on me—breathe on me!
As brighter ladies do not count it strange,
For love, to give up acres and degree,
I yield the grave for thy sake, and exchange
My near sweet view of Heaven, for earth with thee!

601 XXIV

Let the world's sharpness, like a clasping knife,
Shut in upon itself and do no harm
In this close hand of Love, now soft and warm,
And let us hear no sound of human strife
After the click of the shutting. Life to life—
I lean upon thee, Dear, without alarm,
And feel as safe as guarded by a charm
Against the stab of worldlings, who if rife

Are weak to injure. Very whitely still
The lilies of our lives may reassure
Their blossoms from their roots, accessible
Alone to heavenly dews that drop not fewer,
Growing straight, out of man's reach, on the hill.
God only, who made us rich, can make us poor.

602 XXV

A HEAVY heart, Belovèd, have I borne
From year to year until I saw thy face,
And sorrow after sorrow took the place
Of all those natural joys as lightly worn
As the stringed pearls, each lifted in its turn
By a beating heart at dance-time. Hopes apace
Were changed to long despairs, till God's own grace
Could scarcely lift above the world forlorn
My heavy heart. Then *thou* didst bid me bring
And let it drop adown thy calmly great
Deep being! Fast it sinketh, as a thing
Which its own nature doth precipitate,
While thine doth close above it, mediating
Betwixt the stars and the unaccomplished fate.

603 XXVI

I LIVED with visions for my company
Instead of men and women, years ago,
And found them gentle mates, nor thought to know
A sweeter music than they played to me.
But soon their trailing purple was not free
Of this world's dust, their lutes did silent grow,
And I myself grew faint and blind below
Their vanishing eyes. Then THOU didst come—to be,
Belovèd, what they seemed. Their shining fronts,
Their songs, their splendors (better, yet the same,
As river-water hallowed into fonts),
Met in thee, and from out thee overcame
My soul with satisfaction of all wants:
Because God's gifts put man's best dreams to shame.

604 XXVII

My own Belovèd, who hast lifted me
From this drear flat of earth where I was thrown,
And, in betwixt the languid ringlets, blown
A life-breath, till the forehead hopefully
Shines out again, as all the angels see,
Before thy saving kiss! My own, my own,
Who camest to me when the world was gone,
And I who looked for only God, found *thee!*
I find thee; I am safe, and strong, and glad.
As one who stands in dewless asphodel
Looks backward on the tedious time he had
In the upper life,—so I, with bosom-swell,
Make witness, here, between the good and bad,
That Love, as strong as Death, retrieves as well.

605 XXVIII

My letters! all dead paper, mute and white!
And yet they seem alive and quivering
Against my tremulous hands which loose the string
And let them drop down on my knee to-night.
This said,—he wished to have me in his sight
Once, as a friend: this fixed a day in spring
To come and touch my hand . . . a simple thing,
Yet I wept for it!—this, . . . the paper's light . . .
Said, *Dear, I love thee;* and I sank and quailed
As if God's future thundered on my past.
This said, *I am thine*—and so its ink has paled
With lying at my heart that beat too fast.
And this . . . O Love, thy words have ill availed
If, what this said, I dared repeat at last!

606 XXIX

I think of thee!—my thoughts do twine and bud
About thee, as wild vines, about a tree,
Put out broad leaves, and soon there's nought to see
Except the straggling green which hides the wood.

Yet, O my palm-tree, be it understood
I will not have my thoughts instead of thee
Who art dearer, better! Rather, instantly
Renew thy presence; as a strong tree should,
Rustle thy boughs and set thy trunk all bare,
And let these bands of greenery which insphere thee
Drop heavily down,—burst, shattered, everywhere!
Because, in this deep joy to see and hear thee
And breathe within thy shadow a new air,
I do not think of thee—I am too near thee.

607 XXX

I SEE thine image through my tears to-night,
And yet to-day I saw thee smiling. How
Refer the cause?—Beloved, is it thou
Or I, who makes me sad? The acolyte
Amid the chanted joy and thankful rite
May so fall flat, with pale insensate brow,
On the altar-stair. I hear thy voice and vow,
Perplexed, uncertain, since thou art out of sight,
As he, in his swooning ears, the choir's Amen.
Beloved, dost thou love? or did I see all
The glory as I dreamed, and fainted when
Too vehement light dilated my ideal,
For my soul's eyes? Will that light come again,
As now these tears come—falling hot and real?

608 XXXI

THOU comest! all is said without a word.
I sit beneath thy looks as children do
In the noon-sun, with souls that tremble through
Their happy eyelids from an unaverred
Yet prodigal inward joy. Behold, I erred
In that last doubt! and yet I cannot rue
The sin most, but the occasion—that we two
Should for a moment stand unministered
By a mutual presence. Ah, keep near and close,
Thou dovelike help! and, when my fears would rise,
With thy broad heart serenely interpose:

Brood down with thy divine sufficiencies
These thoughts which tremble when bereft of those,
Like callow birds left desert to the skies.

609 XXXII

The first time that the sun rose on thine oath
To love me, I looked forward to the moon
To slacken all those bonds which seemed too soon
And quickly tied to make a lasting troth.
Quick-loving hearts, I thought, may quickly loathe;
And, looking on myself, I seemed not one
For such man's love;—more like an out-of-tune
Worn viol, a good singer would be wroth
To spoil his song with, and which, snatched in haste,
Is laid down at the first ill-sounding note.
I did not wrong myself so, but I placed
A wrong on *thee*. For perfect strains may float
'Neath master-hands, from instruments defaced,—
And great souls, at one stroke, may do and doat.

610 XXXIII

Yes, call me by my pet-name! let me hear
The name I used to run at, when a child,
From innocent play, and leave the cowslips piled,
To glance up in some face that proved me dear
With the look of its eyes. I miss the clear
Fond voices which, being drawn and reconciled
Into the music of Heaven's undefiled,
Call me no longer. Silence on the bier,
While I call God—call God!—So let thy mouth
Be heir to those who are now exanimate.
Gather the north flowers to complete the south,
And catch the early love up in the late.
Yes, call me by that name,—and I, in truth,
With the same heart, will answer and not wait.

611 XXXIV

With the same heart, I said, I'll answer thee
As those, when thou shalt call me by my name—

Lo, the vain promise! is the same, the same,
Perplexed and ruffled by life's strategy?
When called before, I told how hastily
I dropped my flowers or brake off from a game,
To run and answer with the smile that came
At play last moment, and went on with me
Through my obedience. When I answer now,
I drop a grave thought, break from solitude;
Yet still my heart goes to thee—ponder how—
Not as to a single good, but all my good!
Lay thy hand on it, best one, and allow
That no child's foot could run fast as this blood.

612 XXXV

If I leave all for thee, wilt thou exchange
And be all to me? Shall I never miss
Home-talk and blessing and the common kiss
That comes to each in turn, nor count it strange,
When I look up, to drop on a new range
Of walls and floors, another home than this?
Nay, wilt thou fill that place by me which is
Filled by dead eyes too tender to know change?
That's hardest. If to conquer love, has tried,
To conquer grief, tries more, as all things prove;
For grief indeed is love and grief beside.
Alas, I have grieved so I am hard to love.
Yet love me—wilt thou? Open thine heart wide,
And fold within the wet wings of thy dove.

613 XXXVI

When we met first and loved, I did not build
Upon the event with marble. Could it mean
To last, a love set pendulous between
Sorrow and sorrow? Nay, I rather thrilled,
Distrusting every light that seemed to gild
The onward path, and feared to overlean
A finger even. And, though I have grown serene
And strong since then, I think that God has willed
A still renewable fear . . . O love, O troth . . .

Lest these enclaspèd hands should never hold,
This mutual kiss drop down between us both
As an unowned thing, once the lips being cold.
And Love, be false! if *he,* to keep one oath,
Must lose one joy, by his life's star foretold.

614 XXXVII

PARDON, oh, pardon, that my soul should make,
Of all that strong divineness which I know
For thine and thee, an image only so
Formed of the sand, and fit to shift and break.
It is that distant years which did not take
Thy sovranty, recoiling with a blow,
Have forced my swimming brain to undergo
Their doubt and dread, and blindly to forsake
Thy purity of likeness and distort
Thy worthiest love to a worthless counterfeit:
As if a shipwrecked Pagan, safe in port,
His guardian sea-god to commemorate,
Should set a sculptured porpoise, gills a-snort
And vibrant tail, within the temple-gate.

615 XXXVIII

FIRST time he kissed me, he but only kissed
The fingers of this hand wherewith I write;
And ever since, it grew more clean and white,
Slow to world-greetings, quick with its "Oh, list,"
When the angels speak. A ring of amethyst
I could not wear here, plainer to my sight,
Than that first kiss. The second passed in height
The first, and sought the forehead, and half missed,
Half falling on the hair. O beyond meed!
That was the chrism of love, which love's own crown,
With sanctifying sweetness, did precede.
The third upon my lips was folded down
In perfect, purple state; since when, indeed,
I have been proud and said, "My love, my own."

616 XXXIX

Because thou hast the power and own'st the grace
To look through and behind this mask of me
(Against which years have beat thus blanchingly
With their rains), and behold my soul's true face,
The dim and weary witness of life's race,—
Because thou hast the faith and love to see,
Through that same soul's distracting lethargy,
The patient angel waiting for a place
In the new Heavens,—because nor sin nor woe,
Nor God's infliction, nor death's neighborhood,
Nor all which others viewing, turn to go,
Nor all which makes me tired of all, self-viewed,—
Nothing repels thee, . . . Dearest, teach me so
To pour out gratitude, as thou dost, good!

617 XL

Oh, yes! they love through all this world of ours!
I will not gainsay love, called love forsooth.
I have heard love talked in my early youth,
And since, not so long back but that the flowers
Then gathered, smell still. Mussulmans and Giaours
Throw kerchiefs at a smile, and have no ruth
For any weeping. Polypheme's white tooth
Slips on the nut if, after frequent showers,
The shell is over-smooth,—and not so much
Will turn the thing called love, aside to hate,
Or else to oblivion. But thou art not such
A lover, my Belovèd! thou canst wait
Through sorrow and sickness, to bring souls to touch,
And think it soon when others cry "Too late."

618 XLI

I thank all who have loved me in their hearts,
With thanks and love from mine. Deep thanks to all
Who paused a little near the prison-wall
To hear my music in its louder parts
Ere they went onward, each one to the mart's

Or temple's occupation, beyond call.
But thou, who, in my voice's sink and fall
When the sob took it, thy divinest Art's
Own instrument didst drop down at thy foot
To hearken what I said between my tears, . . .
Instruct me how to thank thee! Oh, to shoot
My soul's full meaning into future years,
That *they* should lend it utterance, and salute
Love that endures, from Life that disappears!

619 XLII

"*My future will not copy fair my past*"—
I wrote that once; and thinking at my side
My ministering life-angel justified
The word by his appealing look upcast
To the white throne of God, I turned at last,
And there, instead, saw thee, not unallied
To angels in thy soul! Then I, long tried
By natural ills, received the comfort fast,
While budding, at thy sight, my pilgrim's staff
Gave out green leaves with morning dews impearled.
I seek no copy now of life's first half:
Leave here the pages with long musing curled,
And write me new my future's epigraph,
New angel mine, unhoped for in the world!

620 XLIII

How do I love thee? Let me count the ways.
I love thee to the depth and breadth and height
My soul can reach, when feeling out of sight
For the ends of Being and ideal Grace.
I love thee to the level of everyday's
Most quiet need, by sun and candle-light.
I love thee freely, as men strive for Right;
I love thee purely, as they turn from Praise.
I love thee with the passion put to use
In my old griefs, and with my childhood's faith.
I love thee with a love I seemed to lose

With my lost saints,—I love thee with the breath,
Smiles, tears, of all my life!—and, if God choose,
I shall but love thee better after death.

621 XLIV

Belovèd, thou hast brought me many flowers
Plucked in the garden, all the summer through
And winter, and it seemed as if they grew
In this close room, nor missed the sun and showers.
So, in the like name of that love of ours,
Take back these thoughts which here unfolded too,
And which on warm and cold days I withdrew
From my heart's ground. Indeed, those beds and bowers
Be overgrown with bitter weeds and rue,
And wait thy weeding; yet here's eglantine,
Here's ivy!—take them, as I used to do
Thy flowers, and keep them where they shall not pine.
Instruct thine eyes to keep their colors true,
And tell thy soul their roots are left in mine.

622 The Sleep

He giveth his beloved sleep—Ps. cxxvii. 2.

Of all the thoughts of God that are
Borne inward unto souls afar,
Along the Psalmist's music deep,
Now tell me if that any is,
For gift or grace, surpassing this—
'He giveth His belovèd sleep'?

What would we give to our beloved?
The hero's heart to be unmoved,
The poet's star-tuned harp, to sweep,
The patriot's voice, to teach and rouse,
The monarch's crown, to light the brows?—
He giveth His belovèd, sleep.

What do we give to our beloved?
A little faith all undisproved,

A little dust to overweep,
And bitter memories to make
The whole earth blasted for our sake.
He giveth His belovèd, sleep.

'Sleep soft, beloved!' we sometimes say,
But have no tune to charm away
Sad dreams that through the eye-lids creep.
But never doleful dream again
Shall break the happy slumber when
He giveth His belovèd, sleep.

O earth, so full of dreary noises!
O men, with wailing in your voices!
O delvèd gold, the wailers heap!
O strife, O curse, that o'er it fall!
God strikes a silence through you all,
He giveth His belovèd, sleep.

His dews drop mutely on the hill;
His cloud above it saileth still,
Though on its slope men sow and reap.
More softly than the dew is shed,
Or cloud is floated overhead,
He giveth His belovèd, sleep.

Aye, men may wonder while they scan
A living, thinking, feeling man
Confirmed in such a rest to keep;
But angels say, and through the word
I think their happy smile is *heard*—
'He giveth His belovèd, sleep.'

For me, my heart that erst did go
Most like a tired child at a show,
That sees through tears the mummers leap,
Would now its wearied vision close,
Would child-like on His love repose,
Who giveth His belovèd, sleep.

And, friends, dear friends,—when it shall be
That this low breath is gone from me,
And round my bier ye come to weep,
Let One, most loving of you all,
Say, 'Not a tear must o'er her fall;
He giveth His belovèd, sleep.'

EDWARD FITZGERALD

[*1809-1883*]

657 RUBÁIYÁT OF OMAR KHAYYAM OF NAISHÁPŪR

Second Edition

I

WAKE! For the Sun behind yon Eastern height
Has chased the Session of the Stars from Night;
And to the field of Heav'n ascending, strikes
The Sultán's Turret with a Shaft of Light.

II

Before the phantom of False morning died,
Methought a Voice within the Tavern cried,
"When all the Temple is prepared within,
Why lags the drowsy Worshipper outside?"

III

And, as the Cock crew, those who stood before
The Tavern shouted—"Open then the Door!
You know how little while we have to stay,
And, once departed, may return no more."

IV

Now the New Year reviving old Desires,
The thoughtful Soul to Solitude retires,

Where the WHITE HAND OF MOSES on the Bough
Puts out, and Jesus from the Ground suspires.

V

Iram indeed is gone with all his Rose,
And Jamshýd's Sev'n-ring'd Cup where no one knows;
But still a Ruby gushes from the Vine,
And many a Garden by the Water blows.

VI

And David's lips are lockt; but in divine
High-piping Péhlevi, with "Wine! Wine! Wine!
Red Wine!"—the Nightingale cries to the Rose
That sallow cheek of hers to incarnadine.

VII

Come, fill the Cup, and in the fire of Spring
Your Winter-garment of Repentance fling:
The Bird of Time has but a little way
To flutter—and the Bird is on the Wing.

VIII

Whether at Naishápúr or Babylon,
Whether the Cup with sweet or bitter run,
The Wine of Life keeps oozing drop by drop,
The Leaves of Life keep falling one by one.

IX

Morning a thousand Roses brings, you say;
Yes, but where leaves the Rose of Yesterday?
And this first Summer month that brings the Rose
Shall take Jamshýd and Kaikobád away.

X

Well, let it take them! What have we to do
With Kaikobád the Great, or Kaikhosrú?
  Let Rustum cry "To Battle!" as he likes,
Or Hátim Tai 'To supper!"—heed not you.

XI

With me along the strip of Herbage strown
That just divides the desert from the sown,
  Where name of Slave and Sultán is forgot—
And Peace to Máhmúd on his golden Throne!

XII

Here with a little Bread beneath the Bough,
A Flask of Wine, a Book of Verse—and Thou
  Beside me singing in the Wilderness—
Oh, Wilderness were Paradise enow!

XIII

Some for the Glories of This World; and some
Sigh for the Prophet's Paradise to come;
  Ah, take the Cash, and let the Promise go,
Nor heed the music of a distant Drum!

XIV

Were it not Folly, Spider-like to spin
The Thread of present Life away to win—
  What? for ourselves, who know not if we shall
Breathe out the very Breath we now breathe in!

XV

Look to the blowing Rose about us—"Lo,
Laughing," she says, "into the world I blow,
  At once the silken tassel of my Purse
Tear, and its Treasure on the Garden throw."

XVI

For those who husbanded the Golden grain,
And those who flung it to the winds like Rain,
  Alike to no such aureate Earth are turn'd
As, buried once, Men want dug up again.

XVII

The Worldly Hope men set their Hearts upon
Turns Ashes—or it prospers; and anon,
  Like Snow upon the Desert's dusty Face,
Lighting a little hour or two—was gone.

XVIII

Think, in this batter'd Caravanserai
Whose Portals are alternate Night and Day,
  How Sultán after Sultán with his Pomp
Abode his destined Hour, and went his way.

XIX

They say the Lion and the Lizard keep
The Courts where Jamshýd gloried and drank deep:
  And Bahrám, that great Hunter—the Wild Ass
Stamps o'er his Head, but cannot break his Sleep.

XX

The Palace that to Heav'n his pillars threw,
And Kings the forehead on his threshold drew—
  I saw the solitary Ringdove there,
And "Coo, coo, coo," she cried; and "Coo, coo, coo."

XXI

Ah, my Belovéd, fill the Cup that clears
TO-DAY of past Regret and Future Fears:
  To-morrow!—Why, To-morrow I may be
Myself with Yesterday's Sev'n thousand Years.

XXII

For some we loved, the loveliest and the best
That from his Vintage rolling Time has prest,
  Have drunk their Cup a Round or two before,
And one by one crept silently to rest.

XXIII

And we, that now make merry in the Room
They left, and Summer dresses in new bloom,
  Ourselves must we beneath the Couch of Earth
Descend—ourselves to make a Couch—for whom?

XXIV

I sometimes think that never blows so red
The Rose as where some buried Cæsar bled;
  That every Hyacinth the Garden wears
Dropt in her Lap from some once lovely Head.

XXV

And this delightful Herb whose living Green
Fledges the River's Lip on which we lean—
  Ah, lean upon it lightly! for who knows
From what once lovely Lip it springs unseen!

XXVI

Ah, make the most of what we yet may spend,
Before we too into the Dust descend;
  Dust into Dust, and under Dust to lie
Sans Wine, sans Song, sans Singer, and—sans End!

XXVII

Alike for those who for TO-DAY prepare,
And those that after some TO-MORROW stare,
  A Muezzín from the Tower of Darkness cries,
"Fools! your Reward is neither Here nor There!"

XXVIII

Another Voice, when I am sleeping, cries,
"The Flower should open with the Morning skies."
And a retreating Whisper, as I wake—
"The Flower that once has blown for ever dies."

XXIX

Why, all the Saints and Sages who discuss'd
Of the Two Worlds so learnedly are thrust
Like foolish Prophets forth; their Words to Scorn
Are scatter'd, and their Mouths are stopt with Dust.

XXX

Myself when young did eagerly frequent
Doctor and Saint, and heard great argument
About it and about: but evermore
Came out by the same door as in I went.

XXXI

With them the seed of Wisdom did I sow,
And with my own hand wrought to make it grow;
And this was all the Harvest that I reap'd—
"I came like Water, and like Wind I go."

XXXII

Into this Universe, and *Why* not knowing
Nor *Whence,* like Water willy-nilly flowing;
And out of it, as Wind along the Waste,
I know not *Whither,* willy-nilly blowing.

XXXIII

What, without asking, hither hurried *Whence?*
And, without asking, *Whither* hurried hence!
Ah, contrite Heav'n endowed us with the Vine
To drug the memory of that insolence!

XXXIV

Up from Earth's Centre through the Seventh Gate
I rose, and on the Throne of Saturn sate;
  And many Knots unravel'd by the Road;
But not the Master-knot of Human Fate.

XXXV

There was the Door to which I found no Key:
There was the Veil through which I could not see:
  Some little talk awhile of Me and Thee
There was—and then no more of Thee and Me.

XXXVI

Earth could not answer; nor the Seas that mourn
In flowing Purple, of their Lord forlorn;
  Nor Heaven, with those eternal Signs reveal'd
And hidden by the sleeve of Night and Morn.

XXXVII

Then of the Thee in Me who works behind
The Veil of Universe I cried to find
  A Lamp to guide me through the Darkness; and
Something then said—"An Understanding blind."

XXXVIII

Then to the Lip of this poor earthen Urn
I lean'd, the secret Well of Life to learn:
  And Lip to Lip it murmur'd—"While you live,
Drink!—for, once dead, you never shall return."

XXXIX

I think the Vessel, that with fugitive
Articulation answer'd, once did live,
  And drink; and that impassive Lip I kiss'd,
How many Kisses might it take—and give!

XL

For I remember stopping by the way
To watch a Potter thumping his wet Clay:
And with its all-obliterated Tongue
It murmur'd—"Gently, Brother, gently, pray!"

XLI

For has not such a Story from of Old
Down Man's successive generations roll'd
Of such a clod of saturated Earth
Cast by the Maker into Human mould?

XLII

And not a drop that from our Cups we throw
On the parcht herbage, but may steal below
To quench the fire of Anguish in some Eye
There hidden—far beneath, and long ago.

XLIII

As then the Tulip for her wonted sup
Of Heavenly Vintage lifts her chalice up,
Do you, twin offspring of the soil, till Heav'n
To Earth invert you like an empty Cup.

XLIV

Do you, within your little hour of Grace,
The waving Cypress in your Arms enlace,
Before the Mother back into her arms
Fold, and dissolve you in a last embrace.

XLV

And if the Cup you drink, the Lip you press,
End in what All begins and ends in—Yes;
Imagine then you *are* what heretofore
You *were*—hereafter you shall not be less.

XLVI

So when at last the Angel of the Drink
Of Darkness finds you by the river-brink,
And, proffering his Cup, invites your Soul
Forth to your Lips to quaff it—do not shrink.

XLVII

And fear not lest Existence closing *your*
Account, should lose, or know the type no more;
The Eternal Sákì from that Bowl has pour'd
Millions of Bubbles like us, and will pour.

XLVIII

When You and I behind the Veil are past,
Oh, but the long long while the World shall last,
Which of our Coming and Departure heeds
As much as Ocean of a pebble-cast.

XLIX

One Moment in Annihilation's Waste,
One Moment, of the Well of Life to taste—
The Stars are setting, and the Caravan
Draws to the Dawn of Nothing—Oh make haste.

L

Would you that spangle of Existence spend
About THE SECRET—quick about it, Friend!
A Hair, they say, divides the False and True—
And upon what, prithee, does Life depend?

LI

A Hair, they say, divides the False and True;
Yes; and a single Alif were the clue—
Could you but find it—to the Treasure-house,
And peradventure to THE MASTER too;

LII

Whose secret Presence, through Creation's veins
Running, Quicksilver-like eludes your pains;
Taking all shapes from Máh to Máhi; and
They change and perish all—but He remains;

LIII

A moment guess'd—then back behind the Fold
Immerst of Darkness round the Drama roll'd
Which, for the Pastime of Eternity,
He does Himself contrive, enact, behold.

LIV

But if in vain, down on the stubborn floor
Of Earth, and up to Heav'n's unopening Door,
You gaze TO-DAY, while You are You—how then
TO-MORROW, You when shall be You no more?

LV

Oh, plagued no more with Human or Divine,
To-morrow's tangle to itself resign,
And lose your fingers in the tresses of
The Cypress-slender Minister of Wine.

LVI

Waste not your Hour, nor in the vain pursuit
Of This and That endeavour and dispute;
Better be merry with the fruitful Grape
Than sadden after none, or bitter, Fruit.

LVII

You know, my Friends, how bravely in my House
For a new Marriage I did make Carouse;
Divorced old barren Reason from my Bed,
And took the Daughter of the Vine to Spouse.

LVIII

For "Is" and "Is-not" though with Rule and Line
And "Up-and-down" by Logic I define,
  Of all that one should care to fathom, I
Was never deep in anything but—Wine.

LIX

Ah, but my Computations, People say,
Have squared the Year to human compass, eh?
  If so, by striking from the Calendar
Unborn To-morrow, and dead Yesterday.

LX

And lately, by the Tavern Door agape,
Came shining through the Dusk an Angel Shape
  Bearing a Vessel on his Shoulder; and
He bid me taste of it; and 'twas—the Grape!

LXI

The Grape that can with Logic absolute
The Two-and-Seventy jarring Sects confute:
  The sovereign Alchemist that in a trice
Life's leaden metal into Gold transmute:

LXII

The mighty Mahmúd, Allah-breathing Lord,
That all the misbelieving and black Horde
  Of Fears and Sorrows that infest the Soul
Scatters before him with his whirlwind Sword.

LXIII

Why, be this Juice the growth of God, who dare
Blaspheme the twisted tendril as a Snare?
  A Blessing, we should use it, should we not?
And if a Curse—why, then, Who set it there?

LXIV

I must abjure the Balm of Life, I must,
Scared by some After-reckoning ta'en on trust,
Or lured with Hope of some Diviner Drink,
When the frail Cup is crumbled into Dust!

LXV

If but the Vine and Love-abjuring Band
Are in the Prophet's Paradise to stand,
Alack, I doubt the Prophet's Paradise
Were empty as the hollow of one's Hand.

LXVI

Oh threats of Hell and Hopes of Paradise!
One thing at least is certain—*This* Life flies;
One thing is certain and the rest is Lies;
The Flower that once is blown for ever dies.

LXVII

Strange, is it not? that of the myriads who
Before us pass'd the door of Darkness through,
Not one returns to tell us of the Road,
Which to discover we must travel too.

LXVIII

The Revelations of Devout and Learn'd
Who rose before us, and as Prophets burn'd,
Are all but Stories, which, awoke from Sleep
They told their fellows, and to Sleep return'd.

LXIX

Why, if the Soul can fling the Dust aside,
And naked on the Air of Heaven ride,
Is't not a Shame—is't not a Shame for him
So long in this Clay Suburb to abide?

LXX

But that is but a Tent wherein may rest
A Sultán to the realm of Death addrest;
The Sultán rises, and the dark Ferrásh
Strikes, and prepares it for another Guest.

LXXI

I sent my Soul through the Invisible,
Some letter of that After-life to spell:
And after many days my Soul return'd,
And said, "Behold, Myself am Heav'n and Hell:"

LXXII

Heav'n but the Vision of fulfill'd Desire,
And Hell the Shadow of a Soul on fire,
Cast on the Darkness into which Ourselves,
So late emerged from, shall so soon expire.

LXXIII

We are no other than a moving row
Of visionary Shapes that come and go
Round with this Sun-illumin'd Lantern held
In Midnight by the Master of the Show;

LXXIV

Impotent Pieces of the Game He plays
Upon this Chequer-board of Nights and Days;
Hither and thither moves, and checks, and slays,
And one by one back in the Closet lays.

LXXV

The Ball no question makes of Ayes and Noes,
But Right or Left as strikes the Player goes;
And He that toss'd you down into the Field,
He knows about it all—HE knows—*HE* knows!

LXXVI

The Moving Finger writes; and, having writ,
Moves on: nor all your Piety nor Wit
Shall lure it back to cancel half a Line,
Nor all your Tears wash out a Word of it.

LXXVII

For let Philosopher and Doctor preach
Of what they will, and what they will not—each
Is but one Link in an eternal Chain
That none can slip, nor break, nor over-reach.

LXXVIII

And that inverted Bowl we call The Sky,
Whereunder crawling coop'd we live and die,
Lift not your hands to *It* for help—for It
As impotently rolls as you or I.

LXXIX

With Earth's first Clay They did the Last Man knead,
And there of the Last Harvest sow'd the Seed:
And the first Morning of Creation wrote
What the Last Dawn of Reckoning shall read.

LXXX

YESTERDAY *This* Day's Madness did prepare;
TO-MORROW'S Silence, Triumph, or Despair:
Drink! for you know not whence you came, nor why:
Drink! for you know not why you go, nor where.

LXXXI

I tell you this—When, started from the Goal,
Over the flaming shoulders of the Foal
Of Heav'n Parwín and Mushtari they flung,
In my predestined Plot of Dust and Soul

LXXXII

The Vine had struck a fibre: which about
If clings my being—let the Dervish flout;
Of my Base metal may be filed a Key,
That shall unlock the Door he howls without.

LXXXIII

And this I know: whether the one True Light
Kindle to Love, or Wrath-consume me quite,
One Flash of It within the Tavern caught
Better than in the Temple lost outright.

LXXXIV

What! out of senseless Nothing to provoke
A conscious Something to resent the yoke
Of unpermitted Pleasure, under pain
Of Everlasting Penalties, if broke!

LXXXV

What! from his helpless Creature be repaid
Pure Gold for what he lent us dross-allay'd
Sue for a Debt we never did contract,
And cannot answer—Oh the sorry trade!

LXXXVI

Nay, but, for terror of his wrathful Face,
I swear I will not call Injustice Grace;
Not one Good Fellow of the Tavern but
Would kick so poor a Coward from the place.

LXXXVII

Oh Thou, who didst with pitfall and with gin
Beset the Road I was to wander in,
Thou wilt not with Predestined Evil round
Enmesh, and then impute my Fall to Sin!

LXXXVIII

Oh, Thou, who Man of baser Earth didst make,
And ev'n with Paradise devise the Snake:
  For all the Sin the Face of wretched Man
Is black with—Man's Forgiveness give—and take!

* * * *

LXXXIX

As under cover of departing Day
Slunk hunger-stricken Ramazán away,
  Once more within the Potter's house alone
I stood, surrounded by the Shapes of clay.

XC

And once again there gather'd a scarce heard
Whisper among them; as it were, the stirr'd
  Ashes of some all but extinguisht Tongue,
Which mine ear kindled into living Word.

XCI

Said one among them—"Surely not in vain
My substance from the common Earth was ta'en
  That he who subtly wrought me into Shape
Should stamp me back to shapeless Earth again?"

XCII

Another said—"Why, ne'er a peevish Boy
Would break the Cup from which he drank in Joy;
  Shall He that of His own free Fancy made
The Vessel, in an after-rage destroy!"

XCIII

None answer'd this; but after silence spake
Some Vessel of a more ungainly Make;
  "They sneer at me for leaning all awry:
What! did the Hand then of the Potter shake?"

XCIV

Thus with the Dead as with the Living, *What?*
And *Why?* so ready, but the *Wherefor* not,
  One on a sudden peevishly exclaim'd,
"Which is the Potter, pray, and which the Pot?"

XCV

Said one—"Folks of a surly Master tell,
And daub his Visage with the Smoke of Hell;
  They talk of some sharp Trial of us—Pish!
He's a Good Fellow, and 'twill all be well."

XCVI

"Well," said another, "Whoso will, let try,
My Clay with long Oblivion is gone dry:
  But fill me with the old familiar Juice,
Methinks I might recover by and by."

XCVII

So while the Vessels one by one were speaking,
One spied the little Crescent all were seeking:
  And then they jogg'd each other, "Brother! Brother!
Now for the Porter's shoulder-knot a-creaking!"

*   *   *   *

XCVIII

Ah, with the Grape my fading Life provide,
And wash my Body whence the Life has died,
  And lay me, shrouded in the living Leaf,
By some not unfrequented Garden-side.

XCIX

Whither resorting from the vernal Heat
Shall Old Acquaintance Old Acquaintance greet,
  Under the Branch that leans above the Wall
To shed his Blossom over head and feet.

C

Then ev'n my buried Ashes such a snare
Of Vintage shall fling up into the Air
  As not a True-believer passing by
But shall be overtaken unaware.

CI

Indeed the Idols I have loved so long
Have done my credit in Men's eyes much wrong:
  Have drown'd my Glory in a shallow Cup
And sold my Reputation for a Song.

CII

Indeed, indeed, Repentance oft before
I swore—but was I sober when I swore?
  And then and then came Spring, and Rose-in-hand
My thread-bare Penitence apieces tore.

CIII

And much as Wine has play'd the Infidel,
And robb'd me of my Robe of Honour—Well,
  I often wonder what the Vintners buy
One half so precious as the ware they sell.

CIV

Yet Ah, that Spring should vanish with the Rose!
That Youth's sweet-scented manuscript should close!
  The Nightingale that in the branches sang,
Ah whence, and whither flown again, who knows!

CV

Would but the Desert of the Fountain yield
One glimpse—if dimly, yet indeed, reveal'd,
  Toward which the fainting Traveller might spring,
As springs the trampled herbage of the field!

CVI

Oh if the World were but to re-create,
That we might catch ere closed the Book of Fate,
  And make The Writer on a fairer leaf
Inscribe our names, or quite obliterate!

CVII

Better, oh better, cancel from the Scroll
Of Universe one luckless Human Soul,
  Than drop by drop enlarge the Flood that rolls
Hoarser with Anguish as the Ages roll.

CVIII

Ah Love! could you and I with Fate conspire
To grasp this sorry Scheme of Things entire,
  Would not we shatter it to bits—and then
Re-mould it nearer to the Heart's Desire!

CIX

But see! The rising Moon of Heav'n again
Looks for us, Sweet-heart, through the quivering Plane:
  How oft hereafter rising will she look
Among those leaves—for one of us in vain!

CX

And when Yourself with silver Foot shall pass
Among the Guests Star-scatter'd on the Grass,
  And in your joyous errand reach the spot
Where I made One—turn down an empty Glass!

TAMÁM